COMPUTER
BOOK SERIES
FROM IDG

Networking with NetWare For Dummies, 3rd Ed.

Cheat Sheet

W9-BIF-348

Helpful Keys to Take You around NetWare

Esc	Exit a program, discontinue a process, or return to the previous menu.
Ctrl+PgUp	Go to the beginning of a list.
Ctrl+PgDn	Go to the end of a list.
Yes	Confirm.
No	Cancel.
PgUp	Go to the top of the screen.
PgDn	Go to the bottom of the screen.
Up-arrow↑	Move up one line.
Down-arrow↓	Move down one line.
Backspace	Erase the character to the left of the cursor.
Ctrl+Alt+Delete	Reboot your workstation.
Ins	See a list of options.
Delete	Delete an option previously selected.
Home	Go to the beginning of the line.
End	Go to the end of the line.

Managing Your Network

DOWN	Take the file server "down" so that users cannot use it.
DSREPAIR	Repair the NDS database.
DSUTILS	Perform directory services operations from DOS.
EDIT	Edit NCF or ASCII files from the file server console.
EXIT	Return to DOS before shutting off the file server.
HELP	Display the help information for file server console commands.
INSTALL	Mirror or duplex drives, format your hard disk, load NetWare floppy disks, configure devices added to the file server, change or create volumes.
MIGRATE	Migrate NetWare v2.x or v3.x binderies to Novell Directory Services.
RCONSOLE	Look at the file server console without ever leaving your desk.
SERVER	Bring up your server.
VREPAIR	Fix problems with volumes.

Order from the Menu — No Substitutions Allowed

COLORPAL	Lets you change the colors of your soothing NetWare menus.
FILER	Shows you current directory information and displays the contents of the directory. Lets you choose and change directories, and view information about volumes, attributes, and effective rights. Lets you copy files, move files, and set file attributes.
SALVAGE	Helps out when you have erased a file on a NetWare server that you really didn't want to erase.
SESSION	Moves from directory to directory.
SYSCON	Shows you (a user) all the information about yourself, which groups you are in, and your effective rights. It's the NetWare control center in NetWare 3.x.

Moving Around the File Server Console

Two simple keystroke combinations get you around:

| Ctrl+Esc | Brings up the list of active programs. |
| Alt+Esc | Cycles from session to session. |

The Rule of the First Letter

NetWare uses the first-letter rule to help you get around its menu utilities: If you enter the first letter of the selection you want, NetWare takes you to the selection.

...For Dummies: #1 Computer Book Series for Beginners

COMPUTER BOOK SERIES FROM IDG

Networking with NetWare® For Dummies®, 3rd Ed.

Cheat Sheet

Getting Your Bearings: File and Directory Utilities

ATTACH	Connects to other file servers after you have logged in. In NetWare 4.x, ATTACH is replaced by the LOGIN servername /NS command.
CD	Moves you around the directory structure.
CX	Replaces the CD command.
FLAG	Displays and lets you change file or directory attributes.
MAP	Lets you assign network drives to different directories and subdirectories.
NCOPY	Copies files across the network.
NDIR	Shows you the size of files, when they last were changed, when they were created, their attributes, and who owns the file.
NETUSER	Lets you print, send messages to other users, move around on the network, change your password, and change your context.
NLIST	Lets you see objects (such as users, groups, and printers), search for objects, and find out whatever you need to know about them.
PURGE	Permanently erases files that you have erased before.
RENDIR	Renames directories.
RIGHTS	Gives other users access to the things you own such as files, directories, and volumes.
SEND	Sends a message.
SETPASS	Changes your password.

NetWare Menu Hot Keys

F1	See Help screens.
F3	Edit an entry.
F5	Mark an entry to delete items.
F6	Mark selections.
F7	Cancel changes you have made.
F8	Unmark marked selections.
F9	Change modes.
Alt-F10	Exit from a menu utility.

Utilities You Don't Want to Forget

MONITOR	Diagnostic and monitoring utility.
NDS Manager	Manage the Directory tree.
NetWare Administrator	NetWare 4.x's all-purpose management utility.
NetWare Application Launcher (NAL)	Run applications from the desktop.
NMENU	Create menus for users.
SYSCON	NetWare v3.x's all-purpose management utility.

...For Dummies: #1 Computer Book Series for Beginners

®

References for the Rest of Us!®

COMPUTER BOOK SERIES FROM IDG

Are you intimidated and confused by computers? Do you find that traditional manuals are overloaded with technical details you'll never use? Do your friends and family always call you to fix simple problems on their PCs? Then the *...For Dummies*® computer book series from IDG Books Worldwide is for you.

...For Dummies books are written for those frustrated computer users who know they aren't really dumb but find that PC hardware, software, and indeed the unique vocabulary of computing make them feel helpless. *...For Dummies* books use a lighthearted approach, a down-to-earth style, and even cartoons and humorous icons to diffuse computer novices' fears and build their confidence. Lighthearted but not lightweight, these books are a perfect survival guide for anyone forced to use a computer.

> *"I like my copy so much I told friends; now they bought copies."*
>
> **Irene C., Orwell, Ohio**

> *"Quick, concise, nontechnical, and humorous."*
>
> **Jay A., Elburn, Illinois**

> *"Thanks, I needed this book. Now I can sleep at night."*
>
> **Robin F., British Columbia, Canada**

Already, hundreds of thousands of satisfied readers agree. They have made *...For Dummies* books the #1 introductory level computer book series and have written asking for more. So, if you're looking for the most fun and easy way to learn about computers, look to *...For Dummies* books to give you a helping hand.

™

IDG BOOKS
WORLDWIDE

NETWORKING
WITH
NETWARE®
FOR DUMMIES®

3RD EDITION

by Ed Tittel,
Deni Connor,
& Earl Follis

IDG
BOOKS
WORLDWIDE

IDG Books Worldwide, Inc.
An International Data Group Company

Foster City, CA ♦ Chicago, IL ♦ Indianapolis, IN ♦ Southlake, TX

Networking with NetWare® For Dummies®, 3rd Edition

Published by
IDG Books Worldwide, Inc.
An International Data Group Company
919 E. Hillsdale Blvd.
Suite 400
Foster City, CA 94404
www.idgbooks.com (IDG Books Worldwide Web Site)
http://www.dummies.com (Dummies Press Web Site)

Library of Congress Catalog Card No.: 96-77269

ISBN: 0-7645-0002-3

Printed in the United States of America

10 9 8 7 6 5 4 3 2 1

3E/RT/RR/ZW/IN

Distributed in the United States by IDG Books Worldwide, Inc.

Distributed by Macmillan Canada for Canada; by Contemporanea de Ediciones for Venezuela; by Distribuidora Cuspide for Argentina; by CITEC for Brazil; by Ediciones ZETA S.C.R. Ltda. for Peru; by Editorial Limusa SA for Mexico; by Transworld Publishers Limited in the United Kingdom and Europe; by Academic Bookshop for Egypt; by Levant Distributors S.A.R.L. for Lebanon; by Al Jassim for Saudi Arabia; by Simron Pty. Ltd. for South Africa; by Pustak Mahal for India; by The Computer Bookshop for India; by Toppan Company Ltd. for Japan; by Addison Wesley Publishing Company for Korea; by Longman Singapore Publishers Ltd. for Singapore, Malaysia, Thailand, and Indonesia; by Unalis Corporation for Taiwan; by WS Computer Publishing Company, Inc. for the Philippines; by WoodsLane Pty. Ltd. for Australia; by WoodsLane Enterprises Ltd. for New Zealand. Authorized Sales Agent: Anthony Rudkin Associates for the Middle East and North Africa.

For general information on IDG Books Worldwide's books in the U.S., please call our Consumer Customer Service department at 800-762-2974. For reseller information, including discounts and premium sales, please call our Reseller Customer Service department at 800-434-3422.

For information on where to purchase IDG Books Worldwide's books outside the U.S., please contact our International Sales department at 415-655-3172 or fax 415-655-3295.

For information on foreign language translations, please contact our Foreign & Subsidiary Rights department at 415-655-3021 or fax 415-655-3281.

For sales inquiries and special prices for bulk quantities, please contact our Sales department at 415-655-3200 or write to the address above.

For information on using IDG Books Worldwide's books in the classroom or for ordering examination copies, please contact our Educational Sales department at 800-434-2086 or fax 817-251-8174.

For press review copies, author interviews, or other publicity information, please contact our Public Relations department at 415-655-3000 or fax 415-655-3299.

For authorization to photocopy items for corporate, personal, or educational use, please contact Copyright Clearance Center, 222 Rosewood Drive, Danvers, MA 01923, or fax 508-750-4470.

is a trademark under exclusive license to IDG Books Worldwide, Inc., from International Data Group, Inc.

About the Authors

Ed Tittel

Ed is the author of numerous books about computing and a regular contributor to the computer trade press. He's the co-author of three other ...*For Dummies* books, including *Windows NT Networking For Dummies* (co-authored with Earl Follis and Mary Madden), *HTML For Dummies,* 2nd Edition, and *MORE HTML For Dummies* (both HTML books were co-written with Stephen N. James). For IDG Books, he's also co-authored two books on CGI programming, including *Foundations of WWW Programming with HTML and CGI* and *Web Programming Secrets,* as well as books on Java and VRML.

In a previous life, Ed was Director of Technical Marketing for Novell, Inc., where he was responsible for the technical content of Novell's trade shows and developer conferences. Today, he works as a full-time freelance writer and consultant, with a focus on networking and Internet technologies. He's also a member of the NetWorld + Interop Program Committee and a consultant to SoftBank for their Interop.Com tradeshow.

Ed is a principal at LANWrights, Inc., a networking consultancy based in Austin, Texas. You can reach Ed at etittel@lanw.com or through his Web site at http://www.lanw.com.

Deni Connor

Deni is a long-time computer-industry journalist who has specialized in networking since the beginning of time. She is the editor-in-chief for *NetWare Solutions,* an independent magazine for Novell system managers, published by New Media Productions in Austin, Texas.

In addition to the many hundreds of articles Deni has written for magazines, she has been a regular contributor to the trade press, including *InfoWorld, Datamation, PC Today, PC Novice,* and other publications.

You can reach Deni on CompuServe at 75146,2545.

Earl Follis

Earl is an independent network consultant and principal of Zora Consulting, Inc., in Austin, Texas. He serves as a network advisor to corporate clientele in the central Texas area. He is also a developer of network-related training materials and teaches networking classes for a national training firm. He has over fifteen years experience in the computer industry, with the last six years devoted to network consulting and teaching. Earl is a co-author (with Ed Tittel and Mary Madden) of *Windows NT Networking For Dummies,* and he occasionally writes articles for network-related publications.

Earl and family live at Mauve Acres in the sprawling metropolis of Pflugerville, just outside Austin, Texas. He is a gentleman sheep farmer (though the sheep are a little nervous) and avid private pilot. In his very sparse spare time, he is the keyboard, harmonica, accordion, and spoons player in the local rock band favorite known as *Bleu Chunks.* Okay, he doesn't really play the spoons.

You can contact Earl via e-mail at efollis@io.com.

ABOUT IDG BOOKS WORLDWIDE

Welcome to the world of IDG Books Worldwide.

IDG Books Worldwide, Inc., is a subsidiary of International Data Group, the world's largest publisher of computer-related information and the leading global provider of information services on information technology. IDG was founded more than 25 years ago and now employs more than 8,500 people worldwide. IDG publishes more than 275 computer publications in over 75 countries (see listing below). More than 60 million people read one or more IDG publications each month.

Launched in 1990, IDG Books Worldwide is today the #1 publisher of best-selling computer books in the United States. We are proud to have received eight awards from the Computer Press Association in recognition of editorial excellence and three from *Computer Currents'* First Annual Readers' Choice Awards. Our best-selling *...For Dummies*® series has more than 30 million copies in print with translations in 30 languages. IDG Books Worldwide, through a joint venture with IDG's Hi-Tech Beijing, became the first U.S. publisher to publish a computer book in the People's Republic of China. In record time, IDG Books Worldwide has become the first choice for millions of readers around the world who want to learn how to better manage their businesses.

Our mission is simple: Every one of our books is designed to bring extra value and skill-building instructions to the reader. Our books are written by experts who understand and care about our readers. The knowledge base of our editorial staff comes from years of experience in publishing, education, and journalism — experience we use to produce books for the '90s. In short, we care about books, so we attract the best people. We devote special attention to details such as audience, interior design, use of icons, and illustrations. And because we use an efficient process of authoring, editing, and desktop publishing our books electronically, we can spend more time ensuring superior content and spend less time on the technicalities of making books.

You can count on our commitment to deliver high-quality books at competitive prices on topics you want to read about. At IDG Books Worldwide, we continue in the IDG tradition of delivering quality for more than 25 years. You'll find no better book on a subject than one from IDG Books Worldwide.

John J. Kilcullen

John Kilcullen
President and CEO
IDG Books Worldwide, Inc.

Eighth Annual Computer Press Awards ≥1992

WINNER
Ninth Annual Computer Press Awards ≥1993

WINNER
Tenth Annual Computer Press Awards ≥1994

Eleventh Annual Computer Press Awards ≥1995

Publisher's Acknowledgments

We're proud of this book; please send us your comments about it by using the Reader Response Card at the back of the book or by e-mailing us at feedback/dummies@idgbooks.com. Some of the people who helped bring this book to market include the following:

Acquisitions, Development, and Editorial

Associate Project Editor: Leah P. Cameron

Assistant Acquisitions Editor: Gareth Hancock

Product Development Manager: Mary Bednarek

Copy Editors: Tina Sims, Suzanne Packer

Technical Reviewer: James A. Huggans

Editorial Manager: Mary C. Corder

Editorial Assistants: Constance Carlisle, Chris H. Collins, Michael D. Sullivan

Production

Project Coordinator: Debbie Stailey

Layout and Graphics: E. Shawn Aylsworth, Brett Black, Cameron Booker, Linda M. Boyer, Elizabeth Cárdenas-Nelson, Dominique DeFelice, Maridee V. Ennis, Angela F. Hunckler, Todd Klemme, Anna Rohrer, Brent Savage, Michael Sullivan

Proofreaders: Kathleen Prata, Rachel Garvey, Dwight Ramsey, Robert Springer, Karen York

Indexer: Sherry Massey

General and Administrative

IDG Books Worldwide, Inc.: John Kilcullen, President & CEO; Steven Berkowitz, COO & Publisher

Dummies, Inc.: Milissa Koloski, Executive Vice President & Publisher

Dummies Technology Press & Dummies Editorial: Diane Graves Steele, Vice President and Associate Publisher; Judith A. Taylor, Brand Manager

Dummies Trade Press: Kathleen A. Welton, Vice President & Publisher; Stacy S. Collins, Brand Manager

IDG Books Production for Dummies Press: Beth Jenkins, Production Director; Cindy L. Phipps, Supervisor of Project Coordination; Kathie S. Schutte, Supervisor of Page Layout; Shelley Lea, Supervisor of Graphics and Design; Debbie J. Gates, Production Systems Specialist; Tony Augsburger, Reprint Coordinator; Leslie Popplewell, Media Archive Coordinator

Dummies Packaging & Book Design: Patti Sandez, Packaging Assistant; Kavish+Kavish, Cover Design

◆

The publisher would like to give special thanks to Patrick J. McGovern, without whom this book would not have been possible.

◆

Authors' Acknowledgments

As always, there are more people to thank than we possibly have room for. That's why we'll begin by thanking everybody who helped that we don't mention by name. Actually, we couldn't have done it without you, even if your name isn't featured here. Thanks!!

Ed Tittel

I can't believe we're doing a 3rd Edition already! Let me begin by thanking the many people who bought this book and made it possible for us to do the revisions to keep it up to date. Then, there's my family: Suzy, Austin, Chelsea, and Dusty — you were there for me when it counted. Thanks! Second, a talented crew of other people helped me over a variety of humps, large and small, technical and informational. Let me specifically thank Kirk Fallbacker, Mary Madden, Michael Stewart, and Lenley Hensarling. You guys are the greatest! Third, there's a whole crowd of other folks whose information has helped me over the years, especially the NetWire Sys*Ops. Thanks also to the developers at Novell, who continue to improve on a complex and powerful product that has been the source of much joy and frustration to us.

Deni Connor

My thanks to Terry Ahnstedt, who not only provided lots of assistance for this book, moral and otherwise, but who also put up with the LAN outgrowing our office and snaking its way across the hallway into the living room and terminating in the dining room. My thanks and considerable respect also go to Mark Anderson, Ed Liebing, and Dave Kearns, who agreed with me that a book of this nature was worth working on, and who taught me almost everything I know about LANs. And of course, there are two people, and only two people, who made this all possible — my parents.

Earl Follis

Thanks to the most important person in my life, my lovely wife and partner, Kaye. Thanks, Babe, for sticking by me through thick and thin. Thanks also to Matt, Haley, and Karly for being the best kids a guy could ever love. Thanks to Mom and Dad for teaching me that hard work and a good Thesaurus can be a man's best friend. Thanks to the wonderful folks at Waterside Productions and IDG Publishing for their considerable efforts on my behalf. Thanks also to David Parma and Terry Middleton for allowing me the time to work on this towering monument to "Big Red." And, as usual, many more thanks go to Ed Tittel for the opportunity to contribute to another rewarding (and time-consuming) writing project.

We especially want to acknowledge the work of Jim Huggans, our superb technical reviewer whose attention to detail is much appreciated. We'd also like to thank Susan Price, sole proprietoress of Susan Price and Associates, who did the killer graphics for the book. Last, we want to thank the editorial staff at IDG books, especially Leah Cameron, our project editor; Tina Sims and Suzanne Packer, our copy editors; Gareth Hancock, the man who made it all happen; and the other editorial folks, including Mary Corder and Mary Bednarek.

Please feel free to contact any of us, care of IDG Books Worldwide, Inc., 919 East Hillsdale Blvd, Suite 400, Foster City, CA 94404. If you like CompuServe, Ed's ID is 76376,606, Deni's ID is 75730,2465, and Earl's is 71022,47. If you're on the Internet, you can reach Ed at etittel@lanw.com, Earl at efollis@io.com, and for Deni use 75730.2465@compuserve.com. Please, drop us a line sometime!

Cartoons at a Glance

By Rich Tennant • Fax: 508-546-7747 • E-mail: the5wave@tiac.net

"Careful, Sundance, this one's been locked up and forced to troubleshoot network problems ALLL week and he's itching for a fight".

page 213

"Just as I suspected. We've got shorts in the wiring".

page 327

"Well network communication isn't perfect. Some departments still seem to get more information than others".

page 7

"You know that network OS has quite a sense of humor".

page 359

"Nobody knows how it happened! We were running peripherals into the network about the same time Sally was braiding her corn-rows, and, well, just don't turn anything on!"

page 101

Contents at a Glance

Table of Contents

Introduction

●●

*W*elcome to *Networking with NetWare For Dummies,* 3rd Edition the book that helps anybody who may be unfamiliar with Novell NetWare or with networks in general — even someone who may already be PC-literate — find his or her way into and around this mysterious world. Networks are the coming thing, if they're not here already, and we all will have to use them one day, sooner or later.

Even though a few experienced individuals out there may already be familiar with NetWare and networks, an awful lot more of us are not just unfamiliar, but downright scared, of networking technology. To those who may be worried about the prospect of facing new and daunting technologies, we say, "Never fear." Using a network is not beyond anyone's intelligence or abilities — but the trick is mostly a matter of putting things in terms that mere mortals can understand.

This book talks about using NetWare and networks in everyday — and often irreverent — terms. Nothing is too wonderful to be made fun of, nor nothing too mysterious to be put into basic English. This book focuses on you and your needs. In this book, you encounter everything you need to know about NetWare and networking to be able to find your way around without having to know lots of arcane jargon and without having a Ph.D. in computer science. Plus, we want you to enjoy yourself — if networking really is the now thing, getting the most out of your network is important. We sincerely want to help!

About This Book

This book is designed so that you can pick it up at any point and begin reading — like a reference. Each one of the first 22 chapters covers a specific topic about networking or NetWare — networking basics, the various flavors of NetWare, setting up and using networked drives and printers, running networked applications (such as a Web server), and the like. Each chapter is broken up into self-sufficient collections of information, all related to the major theme of the chapter. The chapter on LAN technology, for example, contains collections of information like this:

- ✔ The concept of a network service and why it's important
- ✔ How independent computers can share network services as peers, called peer-to-peer networking

- ✔ The rules of etiquette involved in sharing things with fellow users on a network, or how to be a good network client

- ✔ Learning how to find and use network services because asking for them isn't the same as getting them!

- ✔ The concept of a network server, along with a discussion of what servers are for and how they get used

- ✔ How to avoid overkill when you work with a network, or which tools are available and which ones make sense to use and when

You don't have to memorize things from this book. Each section is designed to supply the information you need and to make it easy to use. On some occasions, you may want to work directly from the text to make sure that you get things right, but we do our best to warn you when that's happening. In most cases, you can go straight from the book and get right down to work.

How to Use This Book

This book works like a reference. Start with the topic you want to learn more about; look it up in the table of contents or in the index to get started. The table of contents supplies chapter and section titles and page numbers. The index supplies topics and page numbers. Turn to the index entry you select to find the related information you need. You can use the table of contents to identify areas of interest or broad topics; the index works best to pinpoint single concepts, individual topics, or particular NetWare capabilities, tools, or commands.

After you have found what you're looking for, you can quickly close the book and go through the task you have set for yourself — without having to grapple with anything else. Of course, if you want to find out additional information about your selected topic, or about something entirely different, you can check many of the cross-references used throughout this book or just continue reading from wherever you get started. We think that reading Part I, "Introducing Local-Area Networks (LANs)," is a good idea if you've never worked on a network; otherwise, just dig in!

If you really want to learn all the nitty-gritty details about networks and NetWare, you need more information than you can find in this book. In addition to making yourself familiar with the voluminous manuals or online information that Novell typically furnishes with its products, we recommend that you look into the training classes on NetWare that are available, and that you consult the networking section of your local bookstore. Better yet, try a university bookstore or one that specializes in technical subjects. Some great tutorials and classes exist, as well as books and magazine articles that can expand your understanding. We cannot recommend anything offhand because nobody's offered us a kickback here!

What You're Not to Read

Computers swim in boatloads of technical information, much of it gibberish to the uninitiated. To better protect you from the uglier details, we have enclosed the most technical stuff in sidebars that are clearly marked as technical information. In most cases, you really don't have to read it. Sometimes, it's just a more detailed or complicated explanation of things we've already told you — it's aimed at those of you who have to know why or why not, or how a left-handed frammistat really works. Reading that information may teach you something substantial about networking or NetWare, but that's not our real goal here: We want you to be able to get on with your life and work, without having to get bogged down in too many details.

Foolish Assumptions

We're going to go out on a limb and make some potentially foolish assumptions about you, our gentle reader. You have a computer and a network — and probably some NetWare, or you are at least thinking about getting some — and you need to use it to *do* something. You know what you need to do, and you may even be able to do it, if somebody can just show you how (hopefully somebody more knowledgeable than yourself). Our goal in this book is to decrease your need for such a person, but we don't recommend telling him or her that out loud — at least not any time soon!

Conventions Used in This Book

When you need to key in something, the text you need to type appears as follows:

```
TYPE THIS LINE
```

Or, if the text you need to type, like **TYPE THIS LINE**, is in the middle of an explanatory sentence, it appears in monospaced font.

In either case, you're expected to type **TYPE THIS LINE** at the keyboard and then to press the Enter key. Because typing stuff can get confusing, we always try to describe what it is you're typing and why you need to type it.

When we describe a message or other information that you should see on your screen, we present it as follows:

```
This is an on-screen message
```

Because using the resources of the Internet and hooking up your business network as an intranet are hot topics, you see some network addresses (like those used on the Internet, or in intranets) scattered around the text. We show you those addresses on a separate line, as follows:

```
http://www.internic.net/
```

Or if in a paragraph, the address looks like this: `http://www.internic.net/`.

This book occasionally suggests that you consult the NetWare manuals or online help system for additional information. In most cases, though, you can find everything you need to know about a particular topic right here — except for some of the extremely bizarre and little-used details that abound in NetWare, and information about applications that run with or on top of NetWare. If there's a topic we don't cover for those reasons, we suggest that you look for a book on that subject in the *...For Dummies* series, published by IDG Books Worldwide. We also provide information so that you can get help when you need it, even if you choose not to investigate other *...For Dummies* titles.

How This Book Is Organized

This book is broken into four major parts, each of which is divided into chapters. Every chapter covers a major topic and is divided into sections, which discuss particular issues or concerns about the topic. That's how things in this book are organized, but how you read it is your choice. Pick a topic, a chapter, a section — whatever strikes your fancy or fits your needs — and start reading. Any related information is cross-referenced in the text, to help guide you through the entire book.

Following are the parts and what they contain:

Part I: Introducing Local-Area Networks (LANs)

This part contains networking basics, including fundamentals of technology, operation, usage, and etiquette. If you're not familiar with networks, this section comes in really handy. If you're already an old hand, it's optional. Look here for discussions about a great deal of networking terminology, such as client, server, NIC, topology, and much more.

Part II: Organizing and Managing Your NetWare Network

This part covers Novell's client-server network operating systems, known to one and all as NetWare, ranging from early versions to the more powerful and capable versions available today. Part II starts with a road map to help you figure out which version you have and what to do with it. This part then talks about rules for running NetWare, the NetWare file system, network security, directory services, printing, and lots more. In this part, you can find much of the real meat of the book, especially for those of you who already have NetWare and who want to become more familiar with it right away.

We devote the bulk of our attention to NetWare 4.11, the latest version, with only passing references to previous versions. Unlike previous editions of this book, we've eliminated most references to NetWare 2.*x* versions, NetWare Lite, and Personal NetWare, since all these products are pretty much obsolete.

Part III: Maintaining, Protecting, and Growing Your NetWare Network

This section concentrates on presenting the network-related activities and the NetWare-related components that you use on a regular basis. You find out the importance of backing up your data, understanding the mysteries of system configuration, and doing some troubleshooting. Part III offers useful techniques for working with NetWare's system utilities, tools, and services. And of course, we take a look at IntranetWare, the exciting bundle of NetWare products and services that helps you jump into the intranet arena.

Part IV: The Part of Tens

This part serves in the grand tradition of the ...*For Dummies* books — namely, it provides lists of information (which we hope is mostly review), plus tips and suggestions, all organized into short and convenient chapters. This supplemental information is supposed to be helpful and is supplied at no additional charge.

Icons Used in This Book

The icons used in this book point you to important (and not-so-important) topics discussed in this book.

This icon lets you know that you're about to get swamped in technical details. We include this information because we love it, not because we think that you absolutely have to master it in order to use networking or NetWare. If you're aspiring to apprentice nerd status, you probably want to read it; if you're already a nerd, you can write us letters about stuff we left out or other information we should put in.

This icon usually signals that helpful advice is at hand, or provides some insight that we hope will make networking or NetWare more interesting or easier to use. For example, when you are adding a new piece of equipment to your computer, make sure that you unplug it before cracking open the case!

Oh gosh, we're getting older — we can't recall what this icon means. Maybe you should check one out and see whether it's worth your time!

This one means what it says — that you need to be careful with the information it covers. Nine times out of ten, it's warning you not to do something that can have particularly nasty or painful consequences, as in "Have you ever played *Bet Your Job?*"

This icon refers you to another area in the book that more fully describes the topic being discussed.

These icons label the two major versions of NetWare still in use today: NetWare 3.*x* (3.11 and 3.12 mostly; we hope very little 3.0 and 3.1); and NetWare 4.*x* (4.01, 4.02, 4.1, and 4.11). If you haven't yet upgraded to 4.11, we strongly recommend that you do so. NetWare 4.11 bundles many things that used to cost extra and includes new capabilities missing in older versions of NetWare.

Where to Go from Here

With this book at hand, you're ready to go out and wrestle with networking, and be ready to take on even the most advanced version of NetWare. Find a subject, turn to its page, and you'll be ready to rock 'n' roll! Also, feel free to mark up this book, fill in the blanks, dog-ear the pages, and do anything that might make a serious librarian queasy. The important things are to make good use of this book and to enjoy yourself doing it!

Part I
Introducing Local-Area Networks (LANs)

"Well network communication isn't perfect. Some departments <u>still</u> seem to get more information than others".

In this part . . .

You can use this part to get acquainted with the basics of local-area networks, or LANs. We present the raw essentials here: important concepts like how computers communicate with each other, why their communication is a good idea, and what makes it all happen. We also deal, of course, with such vital topics as proper network etiquette, the hardware and software that make up a LAN, and networking terms that no one has ever bothered to explain (but everyone assumes that you already know). We even perform the dance of the seven veils as we reinterpret a standard, but ho-hum, model for the way networking really works.

We present each chapter's material in small, easy-to-understand sections. And if information is really technical (mostly worth skipping, in other words), we clearly mark it or isolate it in a sidebar.

Chapter 1

A Network Is Just Like Tin Cans and String — Only Better!

● ●

In This Chapter

▶ Looking at a network

▶ Making a network work

▶ Talking trash: what computers say to each other

▶ Playing network trivia: the state of the art

▶ Touring a typical network

▶ Traveling on the network: how programs work

▶ Sharing resources on a network

▶ Networking applications

● ●

*I*f you have ever built a tin-can-and-string telephone, you know more about networking than you think you do. If you haven't, we can't help you to recover your lost childhood, but we can make some basic points about networking anyway. If you're feeling nostalgic or adventurous, you can even try to build a tin-can-and-string telephone today. Go ahead — go for it. We dare you.

From an electronic perspective, a networked PC has a lot in common with a telephone handset or a household intercom system. If you extend the tin-can-and-string metaphor, a network requires the ability to listen or to talk over a connection between at least two machines. Although computerized networks may seem more mysterious than this basic idea, sooner or later, all networks boil down to providing a communication link. When computer networks aren't working, they boil down to even less than that.

Now that we've demystified some of the magic of networking PCs (or so we hope), you can relax and enjoy this chapter, which provides a gentle introduction to networking. You can find out some basic ideas about networking in this chapter, which is a primer for the rest of the book.

Primitive communications or nostalgia trip?

The way the tin-can-and-string telephone works is that two cans are attached by a string. One kid yells into the open end of one tin can, and the other kid holds the open end of his tin can around his ear and strains to hear what the other kid bellows. The two secrets to building a good tin-can-and-string telephone are as follows:

1. Make the knots at the end of the string big enough to plug the small holes that the string gets threaded through.

2. Stretch the string taut between the yeller (the sender) and the yellee (the receiver).

The key ingredients are that someone talks while the other person listens, and that the string between the cans is capable of transmitting the sound. In addition to being much more reliable than the tin-can telephone, an electronic network is much more efficient and much more precise. No yelling is required, although it does seem to help sometimes, especially when things get weird.

What Is a Network?

What is this networking stuff about, anyway? Why is everyone so excited about it? What is a network interface? Why do I have to worry about which kind of network I'm using? All these topics are important to networking, and you want to understand the pieces and parts to be better equipped to deal with connecting your computer to a network.

A *network* is a collection of at least two computers that are linked together so that they can communicate with each other. Most networks are based around some kind of cable — typically, copper wire of some sort — that links computers together through a connection that permits the computer to talk (and listen) to the wire. More than just hardware is involved in this communication. Cables and connections are essential to networking, but without computer software to use these hardware elements, they're purely decorative.

A really simple-minded view of networking has these three fundamental requirements:

✔ **Connections:** Include the physical pieces of gear needed to hook up a computer to the network and the wires or other materials — known as the networking *medium* — used to carry messages from one computer to another, or among multiple computers. Because the gear that hooks up a computer to a network acts as an intermediary between the computer and the network, that gear is called the *network interface* (for PCs, attaching to the network requires an add-in board called a *network interface card,* or *NIC*). Without physical connections, computers are isolated from the network and have no means to communicate with it.

✔ **Communications:** Establish the rules for how computers talk to each other or what things mean. Because one computer can — and often does — run radically different software than another one does, this requirement states that computers must speak a "shared language" to communicate successfully with each other. Without shared communications, computers can't exchange information with each other, and they remain isolated.

✔ **Services:** Define the things computers can talk about with each other. Put differently, services are the things that computers can *do* for each other, including sending or receiving files, sending or receiving messages, looking up and managing information, and talking to printers. Without services, computers cannot understand requests from, or formulate replies to, other computers. Again, without the capability to *do* things for each other, computers still remain isolated.

What Makes a Network Work?

The three fundamentals of networking — connections, communications, and services — must come together in order for a network to function. But what really makes a network work?

Networking prehistory (you can skip this background material)

Networks were invented back when computers were really big — most computers then filled very large, specially ventilated rooms that housed only computers. Computers were also really expensive — most of them cost more than a thousand times the average worker's annual salary. Because computers were such scarce and fabulously costly beasts, they weren't expected to be widely available or easy to access. People communicated with the main computer, called a *mainframe,* from *dumb terminals.* These terminals act just like they sound — they don't have any brains, and without the mainframe to round them up and get them working, nothing gets done.

Even though the scope, cost, and size of networking have changed radically since those pioneering days, the key concept of sharing remains one of the best justifications for networking. Networking makes it possible to share things that may still be scarce or expensive. Those scarce and expensive devices aren't computers anymore — the brains for computers have become so cheap that most people can afford at least one computer on their desks. The cost of the peripheral devices attached to the network — the plotters, modems, and printers — is what adds up. You may say "Whoa there, a single printer doesn't cost much," but when you begin to calculate the cost of putting a printer on every desk, the cost adds up quickly. So for sharing and cost control, networking is still the preferred method of bringing together people and resources.

First, the connections have to work so that any computer can talk or listen to the wire (or other medium) that provides the highway over which electrical signals called *data* can move between computers. Without a connection, nothing happens. Think of a network as a telephone at the phone store, sitting on a shelf. The telephone is perfectly capable of working after you hook it up to the phone system; without a connection, however, it cannot do anything. If it did ring, who would answer it?

Second, the communications have to work so that, when one computer talks (sends a message), the others can listen to what that computer is saying and, hopefully, even understand what it's saying. Without communications, nothing meaningful happens. The phone system analogy is illustrative here. Put yourself in a place where you don't understand the local language, and no one speaks yours either. You can try to talk to other telephone users, including the operator, but because you don't understand what anyone is saying (and the operator doesn't understand you), you can't have any kind of productive conversation.

Third, the computers have to be able to work together so that one can ask for things that the other can deliver, and vice versa. Without a shared set of services, neither computer can do anything for the other. Without a shared set of services, nothing can happen. This situation is like trying to buy tires at a flower shop, or flowers at a tire store. Even though everyone knows what flowers and tires are, what you want isn't what they have.

Networking depends on being able to talk (having a working connection), being able to understand what other speakers are saying (sharing communications), and having something useful to say or do as a consequence of speaking (sharing services). Networking probably sounds simple, and it should. But making sure that all those components are doing what they're supposed to can be a difficult experience.

In short, all these different components must work properly in order for a network to be usable. As you become familiar with networks, you realize that no one really notices when things are working okay; as soon as something goes wrong, however, everyone notices that things aren't working.

When Computers Talk to Each Other, What Do They Say?

When you look at what computers do to communicate with each other, the analogy to a telephone conversation breaks down somewhat. The basic principles are still there, however — unless you're talking to a teenager, and then all bets are off. Breaking down a typical conversation, as shown in Table 1-1, shows some striking similarities between the ways humans talk to humans and computers talk to computers.

Table 1-1	How Humans and Computers Converse
Human Conversation	*Computer Conversation*
Hello, this is Bob.	Computer states name and address of sender.
Is Mary there?	Computer states name and address of receiver.
Can I speak to her, please?	Computer asks for and sets up connection and establishes access to receiver.
Mary, do you want to buy some insurance?	Computer requests or offers services.
Mary, I can offer you a whole-life plan for only $100 a year.	Computer makes specific request or provides specific service.
Thanks for your time.	Computer closes service.
Good-bye.	Computer breaks connection.

On the surface, human and computer conversations aren't all that different — the basic pieces of each exchange are pretty much equivalent. When you look at the actual contents of the pieces, of course, you quickly realize that humans communicate with sounds that have specific but very flexible meanings and that computers communicate with electronic bit patterns (for now, ignore the way they're shipped over the medium) that have specific and highly inflexible interpretations. Remember that the important thing still has to do with those two cans and the piece of string: For every message, you have a yeller, a yellee, the tin-can connections, and the media used to communicate.

The answer to the question about what computers say is that they spend a small amount of time establishing a connection so that they can talk, the bulk of their time exchanging information about a specific service or request, and a small amount of time breaking the connection so that others can use the network. This process sidesteps the nitty-gritty details but captures the stages of communications.

The devil is in the details!

Most of what computers do when they communicate is pass very specific electronic messages between themselves. Looking at communications from a gross level helps you to understand the basics of what's going on, although most people never know — and don't care — about exactly what's happening. This statement is as true for the networking guru as it is for the average person. Most concerns about networking, no matter how technical, relate to getting things working and letting the details take care of themselves.

What's Normal? A Look at Network Industry Trends

The preceding section looked at how networks work and what computers say to each other when they're communicating. This section looks at a typical network. Because of the range of networks out in the world, the incredible variation in network sizes, and the wide differences among the users who participate, looking at a typical network is an exercise in abstraction. In other words, the information about what's typical is based on industry statistics (and you know what statistics are worth).

Estimates indicate that a NetWare server of one kind or another is in use on some 70 percent of these networks. This figure fits Novell's claims, made in 1996, that it sold more than 300,000 copies of NetWare in the first quarter of that year. This figure also fits the company's claims that between 90 and 120 million individuals (a number that's growing almost too fast to keep up with) use some kind of NetWare regularly.

If the numbers don't lie — or at least don't misrepresent the truth too much — most networks now are fairly small and simple. The trend, however, is toward ever-increasing size and complexity. The number of individual networks per company, including all sizes of businesses, is up from a modest 0.78 in 1988 to a more aggressive 2.02 in 1996, and it continues to grow. When you consider that

Three kinds of data: lies, damned lies, and statistics

The networking world is an interesting place to find yourself, and an increasingly common place, too. Because you're reading this book, the industry trend statistics that we report probably pretty well describe your network, or you may be networking on an even smaller scale. If you're not in with the trend, taking a look at the networking in your immediate vicinity may still fit this industry model. As you find out later, large, aggregated networks usually break down into collections of small, individual networks. When it comes to understanding what's going on, your own, immediate neighborhood is always the most important one to know well.

Even though lots of networks are in use — by most industry estimates, between 7 and 10 million networks worldwide, with more than 55 percent of them in the United States alone — the number of users per individual network averages a modest 15. This estimate puts the total number of network users worldwide between 100 and 150 million individuals. The basic point is that lots of networks are out there, with many users taking advantage of their capabilities.

95 percent of all businesses fall on the "small" end of the continuum, this figure makes for some pretty large and complicated networks in the remaining 5 percent. This 5 percent has most of the networks in daily use, but it means that small business is where you may expect to see the biggest growth as we push into the 21st century.

This list describes the picture that emerges from the numbers:

- ✔ The average network handles a small number of users, that is, 15 or fewer.
- ✔ The average network uses a small amount of dedicated networking equipment, including one server, one or two printers, and a small amount of other gear to get things working.
- ✔ Most networks are too small to justify hiring dedicated networking specialists, which means that average folks — like you — end up being responsible for running them.

Networks travel in threes

If you investigate networking software, you run up against three terms: *host/terminal*, *client/ server*, and *peer-to-peer*. All three terms identify types of network communications.

- ✔ **Host/terminal networks** are those networks of yesteryear that you reach from a Wayback Machine — in a host/terminal network, computers without processors, or dumb terminals, communicate with a large computer that has a brain. This computer, called a host, parcels out parts of its intelligence to workers at their terminals. The terminal is only capable of displaying information and responding to host calls to action. Sounds dumb, huh? It is, but when the cost of a mainframe can break the budget of a small Third World nation, it's kind of smart, too. Lots of people still work on host/terminal networks!

- ✔ **Client/server networks** are made up of a few or bunches of intelligent machines. One of these machines is equipped with massive stores of data and runs software that allows it to serve other machines in a dedicated fashion — it's called a *server*. The machines that the server provides services to are called *clients*. You've heard of client/server networks, or *server-based networks* as they're sometimes called, if you're using NetWare. The Microsoft Windows NT Server and Banyan's VINES are also client/ server networks.

- ✔ **Peer-to-peer networks** are where true equality in networking takes place. In the peer-to-peer environment, all machines are equal: They can act as servers, or clients, or both. No dedicated machine controls operations as it does in client-server networks; everyone is expected to be a good networker and to share information willingly with others. If you're using the built-in networking available from Windows NT Workstation, Windows 95, or Windows for Workgroups, you already know what peer-to-peer networking is.

A Tour of the Facilities

If you take a tour of a statistically average network, you generally find several classes of equipment and a variety of different kinds of software in use. If you make an inventory of these pieces and parts as you take the tour, you can use the inventory to try to figure out what's out there, what the pieces and parts are for, and what they do. Ready or not, let's do it.

First stop: Your desktop

Part of the great beauty of networking comes from taking the perspective that you can extend what you do at your desk — and we hope, for your sake, that you can best describe your activities as *productive work* — by merely adding a network. From that point of view, adding networking to your bag of tricks gets you to resources and other things that otherwise may be unavailable to you or at least much less affordable. Taking this view doesn't require taking a giant leap of faith — just stretching the boundaries of your desktop.

For convenience, call the computer you work at every day your *desktop* computer or, simply, your *workstation*. It's where you do the bulk of your work and, we hope, also some play. A key goal of networking is to take all the desktop computers (whether they run DOS, Windows 3.*x*, Windows 95, Windows NT, OS/2, UNIX, or Macintosh OS) in use in an organization and hook them together so that they can communicate with each other and share resources. These shared resources can include large disk drives, expensive laser or color printers, access to a CD-ROM or the Internet, or whatever else users may need to do their jobs.

In a networked environment, a normal user-to-desktop ratio is close to one-to-one, and a normal computer-to-user ratio is almost as close. Put another way, every user has access to, if not exclusive possession of, a workstation attached to the network. Because workstations are typically the source of requests for resources and services, calling a workstation a *client on the network* or, simply, a *client* is reasonable. The name *workstation* focuses on the computer's role in supporting an individual, typically working at a desk; calling the computer a *client* focuses on its connection to the network. Whatever you call it, it's still the same thing — the machine that you sit in front of when you're working.

Next stop: Services come from servers

Without access to a shared set of services, or without a shared set of requests for information or service — and replies to match those requests — networking is a sterile exercise. Because networks aren't useful unless you can *do* something with them, access to services is a critical component of networking.

You use a server to get a resource or to get something done. When you want to access a networked printer, you can safely assume that a print server is lurking somewhere in the background to handle your print job. When you want to save or retrieve files from a networked drive, you can safely assume that a file server also is lurking somewhere in the background.

The same thing is true for most networked services, including such things as electronic mail, database management systems, and so on. For almost every service, a server can handle what's necessary in order to deliver that service. At least one network is taking orders for pizza — does that mean it has a dedicated pizza server? Sometimes one server may provide many services; at other times, a server may be dedicated to only a particular service.

So even though a service may not be handled exclusively by a single computer that provides only that capability — and this is seldom the case these days — you can think of the computers that provide services as *servers*. A server's job is to listen for requests for its particular services and to satisfy all the legal requests that it receives across the network. You spend a great deal of time considering this idea as you read other parts of this book.

Last stop: The ties that bind it all together (the glue)

In an era of Clintonomics, talking about the infrastructure became fashionable. This specific infrastructure is the system of roads, bridges, highways, and other avenues of transit that link our country into a working whole called the *highway system*. From a networking standpoint, the pieces of equipment that hook computers into a network, the wires or other media that make up the network, and the specialized pieces of hardware and software used to control a network make up its particular infrastructure.

By the same token, you can reasonably call this collection of connections, cables, interfaces, and other paraphernalia the *glue* because it ties computers together into a working network. But, just as highways are useless without cars and trucks moving across them, networks are useless without computers to send and receive traffic across their links and pathways.

At this level, you may begin to worry about which kind of wiring to use — or which kinds of wireless technologies, if applicable. You also may be concerned about the kind of networking you're doing, the software that does it, and the pieces that make it all fit together. Because networking is invisible when it works as it's supposed to, it's also one of the easiest components of the computing puzzle to overlook, even if it is the most common source of problems.

Figure 1-1 is a simple diagram of the typical network that we discuss in this chapter. Notice that client desktops outnumber servers and that the infrastructure must be everywhere in order to connect all the pieces and parts. Networking follows the rules of supply and demand — the more clients you have, the more servers you need, and (you hope) the more work gets done.

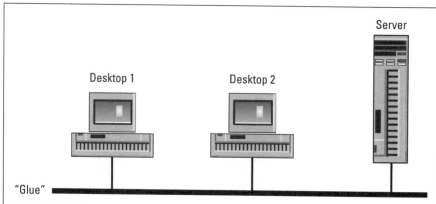

Figure 1-1:
A typical
network
with
desktops,
servers, and
glue.

How Programs Use the Network

The critical ingredients for using a network include the necessary hardware to make a physical connection, at least one other computer on the network to communicate with, and a shared set of services that represent what the network can do for you. With all these requirements, what actually has to happen so that your computer can use the network? The answer is that your computer must know how to ask for services from the network and must know precisely what to request.

Asking for services doesn't mean asking for favors

Knowing how to ask for network services means being able to tell the difference between what's local to and immediately available from your own computer and what's available from the network. Determining this difference is the key to handling networks properly, and it depends on some specialized software to handle this job.

Sometimes, you can use a program that keeps track of what you own and control on your own machine versus what's available across the network to discriminate between local requests and network requests. Because this piece of software takes requests for service and redirects any request that cannot be delivered by your own computer to a service provider (also known as a server) on the network, it's called — surprisingly enough — a *requester* or, sometimes, a *redirector.* Using a requester is a pretty common way to handle network access from a desktop.

A local computer's main control program usually is called its *operating system* because it's the program that lets the computer operate and run the programs you're really interested in using to get things done. This control program sometimes gets a special augmentation or uses a modified version to incorporate "network intelligence" with an understanding of what's happening locally on the desktop.

This augmentation is sometimes called a *network requester* or, simply, a *requester.* The requester handles all service requests and passes along things that aren't local to the network.

The server uses a special operating system called a *network operating system* that adds to the functions of its operating system and provides sharing functions. In the NetWare environment, all these clients — DOS (with or without Microsoft Windows 3.*x*), Windows 95, Windows NT, OS/2, UNIX, or the Macintosh operating system — can request services from a NetWare server.

Networking is becoming a common built-in feature of computer operating systems. Rather than bolt on a requester or a shell to add networking intelligence, these operating system programs already understand networking and include it as a member of the set of functions they provide. As networking becomes more commonplace, network support seems to be gaining a foothold in computer operating systems. Including networking support in their core functions is one of the ways that AppleShare, UNIX, Windows for Workgroups, Windows 95, and Windows NT Workstation provide networking capability.

A tech tip for tech types

You hear the word *requester, redirector,* and *shell program* thrown around interchangeably. That's because Novell and Microsoft changed their minds. What originally was a tidy little program called the redirector changed to the requester when Microsoft changed DOS to include network access. To make things more complicated, this program is also called the NetWare shell by NetWare users — it sits there between the workstation operating system and the network and shells out DOS requests to the local machine and network requests to the network. Only real byte-heads need to know the difference, but if you want to impress those around you, it helps to use the correct technical terms. Most newer versions of Windows use a built-in network requester, but plenty of workstations still use the old reliable NetWare shell (`netx.com`).

Whatever the network operating system, or the kind of network access it needs, the point is that a set of network services gets defined and a way to talk and listen to the network becomes available. Now you want to figure out how to use this capability.

What's on the services menu?

For a computer to use network services, it must know how to ask for them, but knowing what to ask for is equally important. In most cases, your applications supply the knowledge about which network services are available, either through information supplied by the requester or by intelligence built right into so-called networked applications. Electronic-mail and remote-control software are good examples of programs built to use networking capabilities directly.

Sometimes, all you need in order to add network know-how to your computer is to augment local applications or commands to make them network-aware: Extending directory listings or other DOS file-handling commands (DIR, TYPE, DELETE, and COPY, for example) to talk to networked drives is a classic illustration, as is extending other basic commands, such as printing and sharing data files.

Working through a specific command or a particular kind of program also means that you're working with a well-developed understanding of what you want the network to do. This understanding helps users interact with the network, and it also helps the people who write the programs that you use to do what you expect them to.

Whether you treat the network as a basic part of your desktop or look at it as an extension of your local world, you can interact well with the network only as long as you know exactly what you're trying to do. This statement may sound incredibly basic, but the crucial aspect of defining a common service is to work from a shared and explicit understanding of what that service is and what it does. Nothing less will do.

Whether this process happens is a function of the networking software and how it's set up. Even though all flavors of NetWare covered in this book can notify you when a print job is finished, they don't do so unless you set things up that way. (Don't worry — you can find much more information about this subject in Chapter 15.)

This discussion doesn't really capture all the nuances of how programs talk to the network, but it does capture the basics: knowing about a service, requesting that service, providing the information to handle the request (in this case, the file to be printed), and waiting for a reply (the optional notification that the file has printed successfully).

How networking works is . . . magic!

When a program is running — a spreadsheet, for example — and you want to print a copy to a networked printer, the sequence of actions works something like this:

1. Request print services from the spreadsheet.

2. Program formats the spreadsheet and then builds a print file for the printer.

3. The spreadsheet program sends the file to the printer.

4. The local networking software (whether it's a requester or built-in operating system extension) recognizes that the chosen printer isn't local and ships the print file to a print server somewhere else on the network. The network knows how to get to the print server and how to ship it the required print file.

5. The print file gets copied across the network to a holding tank for the chosen printer, where it gets in line behind any print files that may have arrived ahead of it and that have not yet been printed. When you say that you queue up, that's exactly what happens to print jobs, too.

6. The print file gets printed when its turn comes.

7. In this optional step, the user may get notified when the file has finished printing (so that you don't have to wait around the printer for your stuff to come out).

Every model and make of printer is a little different from all the other models and makes. To make the stuff coming from the printer look like what's on your screen — or to format it the way it's supposed to look, anyway — a spreadsheet program, for example, must translate the information that you're trying to print from its internal format to an external format aimed at the printer that you're printing to, or at least to a standard format, such as PostScript, that the printer understands. Sounds complicated, right? Well, it is. But that's what makes computing fun!

Sharing Resources Is Where It's At!

Sharing is the key to networking. After you master this idea, everything else about networking makes more sense. See the sidebar titled "How networking works is . . . magic!" in this chapter for an example of how network resources get used — by asking for them and by providing the right information so that services can be supplied. Because many users can send files to be printed on the printer in this example, it's also a classic illustration of how resources get shared.)

The secret to sharing is making sure that everyone gets a shot at what needs to be shared. Sharing access to a printer, for example, requires a "stand-in-line" mechanism so that print files can hang around until it's their turn to get printed; the stand-in-line mechanism also provides a dandy way of keeping track of who goes next.

This kind of waiting in line is called "first come, first served" because whoever gets in line first gets first crack at the printer. It's analogous to buying groceries — whoever is in line first gets checked out first. Other services may take a different approach to fulfilling requests, but they all must have some way to keep track of who has asked for what, and in what order, so that they can handle requests from multiple users in a reasonable way. Cutting in line is sometimes permitted, but isn't that what sharing's all about?

The most important job that a server performs is keeping track of the requests for service that it receives, controlling access to its resources, and delivering on valid requests as soon as it possibly can. The mechanisms that make that delivery possible also make sharing possible. Ain't it grand? Next, please. . . .

Chapter 2

Linking Up Your Network, or Lost in the Wires

. . . .

In This Chapter

▶ Making connections that work

▶ Identifying common cable types

▶ Wrestling with the wires to come out on top

▶ Cabling up: network wiring schemes

▶ Introducing the Big Four network access methods, plus one

. . . .

Chapter 1 describes networking as requiring three fundamental components: connections, communications, and services. This chapter looks deep within the connections that tie networks together to see how they behave.

Connections are the wires or other media that move electronic signals from computer to computer, along with the interfaces that hook up the computers to the media.

Because wires on networks behave much like pipes do for plumbing, this chapter looks at the pipes that move data around. We hope that you will be better able to understand how things work, and why they sometimes don't work, on your real networks if we follow the metaphorical pipes around to see where they go and what they do.

The Tangled Web: Making Connections Work

Without a working connection, information can't get from one machine to another. A working connection is the most fundamental requirement for networking, and a faulty connection is the most common source of problems and failures.

Many people can sum up their secret to success in the business world in one word: connections. In the networking world, too, the right connections can result in success; loose connections, however, cause most networking problems.

Take the example of Alice in accounting. She — and her desk chair — ricochet around her office like a crazed projectile as she answers the ceaseless stream of questions from upper management about payables and receivables. She's always racing from one set of files to another, compiling the meaningless statistics that keep the fat cats happy. So what if she runs over the cables that stick out of the back of her PC every now and then. They still look okay, don't they? Don't they?

How the cables *look* isn't what really matters. What matters is how they conduct electricity (or light waves, or whatever) when the network is running. And, as for who cares about the condition or integrity of her network cables, the answer may very well be "everyone." For several kinds of networks, failure of one cable means failure of the whole network. A well-run network fades into the background, but a broken network throbs worse than a finger slammed in a car door. If you don't believe us, break your network on purpose and see what happens.

As contrived as the scenario with Alice may seem, it doesn't even come close to capturing all the wacky ways that loose connections can come back to bite you — or at least your network. The truth-is-stranger-than-fiction department of wiring problems includes notable quotes like these:

- "I needed something to tie up a package."
- "What do you mean, I can't unhook my computer from these wires whenever I want to?"
- "Oh, I borrowed that cable to hook up my VCR."
- "I didn't even know we had a network!"
- "The electrician" (or the plumber, the A/C guy, or whoever) said that these wires weren't important and, anyway, they were in his way."

We hope that you're beginning to get the idea. If not, here it is again — no wires (or no medium) means no network. Break the wires (or damage the medium) and you break the network. Got it?

Common Cable Types

Before we can get into much detail about how you can arrange wires and how networks can use them, we have to tell you a little about what kinds of wires that networks typically use.

Look, Ma — no wires!

Just to make things more confusing, you can omit wiring entirely when you build a network or connect pieces of a network. This concept is called — surprise! — *wireless networking*. Wireless networking typically uses some kind of broadcast frequency that ranges from infrared for short-range or special-purpose connections to radio frequencies for spread-spectrum devices all the way up to microwaves for high-speed LAN-to-LAN links.

Today, cellular telephone modems and battery-powered laptop computers supply the foundations for so-called virtual networks, in which everyone can move around and yet remain connected to each other. Wireless networking is still too expensive to be a reasonable choice for everybody, but it's definitely an emerging trend. When wireless networking does become affordable for everyone, you'll never be able to get away from the office! We can hardly wait. You probably can't either.

Networks typically use three basic kinds of cable these days:

- ✔ Twisted-pair
- ✔ Coaxial cable
- ✔ Fiber-optic cable

Twisted-pair wiring

Twisted-pair wiring lives up to its name, as depicted in Figure 2-1. Twisted-pair's greatest strength is also its greatest weakness because TP, as it's called, is also similar to the type of cabling that telephone systems use. This means that TP is everywhere. The easy access to telephone cables also means that the temptation is nearly irresistible to use telephone wiring for LANs as well as for telephones. Although recycling unused telephone wiring has the appeal of saving money — believe it or not, the biggest single expense item for most new networks is cabling costs — and works perfectly well for today's voice-grade phone lines, it doesn't always work that well for networks.

The secret lies in the twisting of the pairs

Some telephone cable is also called *silver satin*, because of its silvery, smooth outer covering. Don't be deceived by thinking that silver satin will work on your network, however. Although it's sometimes called twisted-pair, nothing is twisted about silver satin, including the twisting of the pairs. If stroll through Radio Shack and then down the aisles at your local cabling superstore, you find that real TP wire is actually cheaper than silver satin, especially in the quantities that you need to cable up your network.

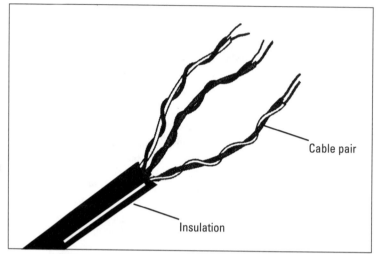

Cable pair

Insulation

Figure 2-1:
Twisted-pair
wiring
revealed.

If you do get wrapped up in silver satin for some reason beyond your control, remember that it may work just fine for two, three, or even four nodes. As your network grows, though, problems creep in that have to do with the twisting of the pairs (or lack thereof, as the case is with silver satin wire).

Recycling is a wonderful idea, and saving money resonates with preserving the bottom line. Nevertheless, you would be wise to have someone test your TP wiring system before blithely assuming that it will do the job for your LAN. Rebuilding a network is much more expensive than building one right in the first place. So if you're thinking about reusing already installed TP wiring for your LAN, make sure that you avail yourself of the services of a cable-testing technician who can tell you whether recycling TP wiring is a wise move or a pipe dream.

TP comes in two flavors: shielded and unshielded, sometimes abbreviated as STP for *shielded twisted-pair* and UTP for *unshielded twisted-pair*. The difference between the two, of course, is that one has a foil or wire braid wrapped around the individual wires that are twisted around each other in pairs, and the other does not.

What's worse than no network at all? A network that doesn't — or cannot ever — work is much worse than no network. Take heed of our advice to test your already installed TP wiring before trying to build a network around it. An ounce of testing is worth a pound of later expense. Testing your wiring may also be worth your job.

For better or worse, TP is the wiring system of choice for bringing network connections to people's desktops. Recent advances in networking technology make TP safe and usable, if the wiring is up to snuff. Compared to TP wiring, older wiring can be a real pain.

For every spot, always a spec

There are as many specifications for cabling as there are types of cable. For most networks, you can use twisted-pair cabling of Category 3, 4, or 5. For the really fast networks, those that run at 100 Mbps (megabits per second), be sure that you have Category 5 cable. To leave yourself room to grow into faster technologies, therefore, we strongly recommend that any new TP cable you install be Category 5.

The upside of TP is that the wiring and its connectors are cheap, it's easy to install if new cable is needed, and you can use existing telephone equipment for networking as well as for telephone needs. If you work for a company that's big enough to care about these things, you probably already use TP.

One downside of TP is that it requires specialized hardware, called *hubs,* to connect more than two computers, which adds costs to the construction of a network. Hubs do have an upside, though — they generally provide better cable monitoring and management than schemes that don't use hubs, and many hubs can even reconfigure themselves to block out failing cables or connections as soon as they're detected.

Another TP negative is that it can handle only short distances between the hub and the desks it must reach and is more susceptible than other media to interference from motors, radios, and electrical sources. The actual distance that TP can handle varies with the type of cable that you use, but a good rule of thumb for maximum TP reach is 100 feet from hub to desktop, and that ain't as the crow flies — it's as the cable runs.

Coaxial cable

Coaxial cable consists of a two-element cable: a center conductor, which can be solid or stranded, that is wrapped by an insulator, and an outer conductor, typically a wire braid, which wraps around the center conductor and is covered by still more insulation. Cable TV also uses coaxial cable, or *coax* as it prefers to be known. Even if you don't think that you know what coaxial cable is, you probably can relate to cable TV. If not, check out Figure 2-2 — it shows all the different parts.

We know one network manager, who knew less about networking than you do now and used cable TV media to wire part of the network. When data started colliding with refrains from 4 Non Blondes, everyone knew something was wrong. Networks use RG-58 or RG-62 media. (RG is the US Military's designation for coaxial cable; RG-58 is used for 10Base2 Ethernet, and RG-62 is used for ARCnet.) In coaxial cable, just as in twisted pair, the importance is in the numbering.

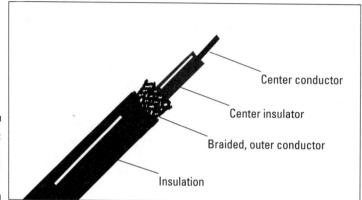

Figure 2-2:
Inside a
coaxial
cable.

Coaxial cable can handle many signals across a broad range of frequencies. Look at it this way: Each TV channel eats a fair amount of spectrum, and a single coax cable can carry as many as 200 channels and more these days. So it's no sweat to use coax for networking, either.

The downside of coaxial cable is that it's thick and relatively stiff, especially in comparison to TP. It also requires expensive, specialized connectors and well-trained, knowledgeable installers to handle it. If you have ever tried to make your own cables to run between your TV and VCR, you may begin to relate to one of our wire stories earlier in this chapter. Even though coax is much stronger than TP, coax is also much more difficult to repair if it does break.

The upside of coaxial is that it's moderately resistant to electrical and magnetic interference, which can be a problem in some office buildings. You can also use coax to build networks that span much larger areas than TP can cover. Again, the maximum length per cable varies with the kind of cable in use, but it ranges from 500 to 1,500 feet. Many network designs use both TP and coax, with TP used on a per-floor basis to run wires to individual desktops and with coax used to wire together multiple floors. Who says that you can't have the best of both worlds?

Another advantage of coaxial cable is that you often already have it in your walls from computing prehistory, when SNA- (Systems Network Architecture-) based equipment ruled the deck. You can reuse this cable, called RG-62 coax, for ARCnet networks. But because ARCnet's pretty much passé these days (so are terminal-based networks, come to think of it), this recycling opportunity has lost some of its cachet.

You might consider using coax for very small networks because you can buy prefabricated cables of varying lengths. You can hook up your network quickly and easily and can change things around equally easily when you must. We're writing this book on a LAN that's been cabled together with something called Thin Ethernet (a.k.a. 10Base2). Its biggest attraction is that you can go to the electronics store and buy everything that you need to cable up a small network (including each computer's network interface card) for about $80 per workstation.

Fiber-optic cable

Unlike its twisted-pair and coax cousins, *fiber-optic cable* isn't metallic. Figure 2-3 shows that the anatomy of fiber-optic cable closely resembles that of coax. Take our word for it, though: Only the drawings look similar, not the cables.

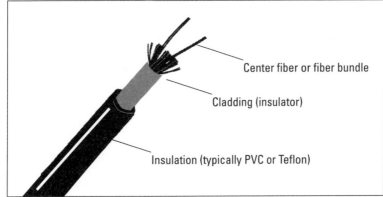

Center fiber or fiber bundle

Cladding (insulator)

Insulation (typically PVC or Teflon)

Figure 2-3:
Fiber optic
cable's
innards.

Fiber-optic is much more flexible than typical coaxial, but you still must handle it carefully — its core is made of glass. Fiber-optic cable runs can also be pretty long, ranging from $1/2$ mile to 20 miles per cable, depending on which kind of cable and network is in use. In fact, if you run cable between networks in different buildings, fiber-optic cable is the only way to go.

On the plus side, fiber-optic cable is immune to environmental interference, short of a black hole wandering nearby. If a black hole *does* happen by your neighborhood, we'd bet anything that problems with your fiber-optic cable will be very low on your priority list anyway. Fiber's biggest advantage is the amount of information that it can carry, called the *bandwidth*. Fiber-optic can handle thousands of times more data than twisted-pair or coax.

On the downside, fiber is more expensive than coax or twisted-pair. Even though the cable costs aren't that different, installation costs for fiber are much higher. The costs are higher because each end of a fiber must be polished to achieve maximum light transmission, and a human technician, working on one cable at a time, still does the best polishing.

Because of the sensitivity and precision necessary to achieve the best results, experienced fiber-optic installers are scarce, and their labor charges come at a premium. Installation costs are the main reason that fiber still costs twice as much as copper — or more. The interface costs also are still high, at about the same ratio as installation costs. If you add up all the costs and aren't prepared to amortize it over the long run, fiber isn't worth it.

Never, never, never hire a cable installer who cannot provide multiple references for fiber-optic installations. Always check those references, too. What the installer says isn't what counts — what paid-up customers think is what makes the difference. Don't spend your money to be someone's guinea pig. The cost can be more than you would ever want to know — or spend!

Cabling for Do-It-Yourselfers

If you're going to mess around with wiring, either to extend an existing LAN or to build an entirely new one, you should attend to the following things as you go about your business:

- ✔ Observe local, state, and federal building codes. If you plan to run cable, some of it will probably be in the ceiling. If that area is used also for A/C ventilation (it's called plenum airspace or plenum air return), fire codes require you to use nontoxic, nonflammable cables — Teflon-coated cable — in these areas. The Teflon-coated cable costs more, but it doesn't release toxic fumes, as plain plastic coatings will, if the place ever catches on fire. Plus, using the Teflon cable is the law!

- ✔ The make-versus-build argument is worth reviewing for coaxial UTP cable, but not for fiber. If you decide to build your own copper cables, buy the best cable and connectors that you can afford. Then buy a professional crimping tool, whether you can afford one or not. These tools rarely go for less than $100 a pop, and they require special insets, called dies, for each specific cable and connector diameter. Although a cheap crimping tool — and you can find them for as little as $20 — screws up your work every time, a good one brings home the bacon.

- ✔ When it comes to TP, buy the best cable you can get. Remember the categories — 5 is the best. Better quality means better conduction for TP of any kind and, because TP is marginal stuff to begin with, you'd be smart to hedge your bets and go with the best possible cable.

- ✔ If you have to lay cable in any amount, large or small, make sure that you check the building's electrical plans before getting started, especially if you are using TP cable. More than once, someone has botched a LAN installation by running cable right next to large motors or transformers (elevators usually have big samples of each genre, right near the shaft) that then interfere with network transmissions forever after. An ounce of planning is worth lots of expensive cure.

✔ If you plan to lay any cable yourself, be prepared for slow, dirty, backbreaking work. Check your budget again. If you have to be a do-it-yourselfer, spend at least enough money to get an experienced installer to review your installation plan and help you get started. Laying cable is best left to professionals, and experience is a dear teacher.

✔ Above all, plan ahead and stay upbeat when things get weird — and they always do. If you know what you need to do and are confident about what you can accomplish, you will know when to move ahead and when to ask for help. These are truly words to live by — and not just when you are installing cable. Good luck!

Now that you have looked at the wiring itself, the next step is to examine how wiring typically gets laid out.

It's Not a Wiring Layout, It's a Topology!

Mathematicians love to create fancy words for abstruse ideas and other mysterious stuff. The term to describe wiring layouts comes from their sick minds. Any arrangement of lines can be called a *topology*, and that's what network-savvy folks call the different kinds of networking schemes. A topology is simply the shape of the network. Like people, some topologies look like beanpoles, and others are round and gently curved. The *star* and *bus* discussed here are short for *star topology* and *bus topology*. Likewise, a *ring topology* refers to a wiring pattern laid out in a circular manner. Isn't that special?

Fiber, you light up my life!

Fiber-optic cables are built around conductive elements that move light, not electricity. For most fiber-optic cables, the conductive element is most likely a form of special glass fiber rather than copper or some other conductive metal. This property means, among other things, that you must be careful when you handle fiber-optic cable — a sharp bend or an overly tight stretch makes the glass fibers act the same way as any other overstressed piece of glass might. Mistreat it too much, and it breaks.

You can lay out network wiring in many ways. Figure 2-4 shows the two most common layouts — the star and the bus.

Just like flowers, topologies can cross-pollinate themselves. Take a star topology network and add it to a bus topology network; what you end up with is a distributed-star network, also known as a hybrid. Most networks can be shaped like hybrids, but some networks work better if you stick to the simple stuff. When in doubt, do as the cable masters do: build individual subnets as either stars or buses and use another single bus or star, called a *backbone,* to link them all together.

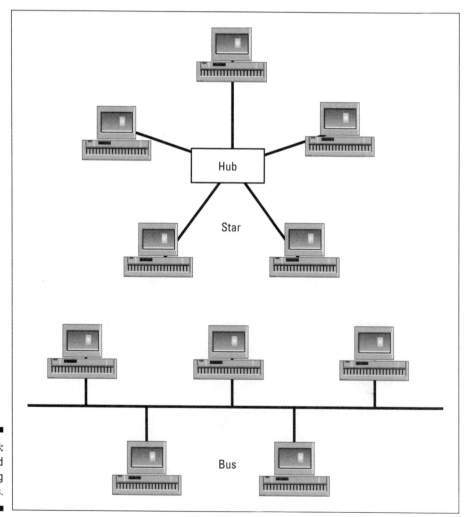

Figure 2-4:
The star and bus wiring layouts.

Stars get in your eyes

A star consists of separate wires that run from a central point (the hub, 'cause it's in the middle) to devices — typically, computers — on the other end of each wire. A bus consists of a single cable to which all the computers on a network, or a piece of a network, get attached. If you break a wire in a star, the break affects only the link that's broken; if you break a wire on a bus, it affects everything connected to it. Although wire breaks are more catastrophic on a bus than in a star, you won't care which kind of layout you have if your machine is the one that's affected by the break.

In a star topology, the hub at the center of the star acts as a relay for computers attached to its arms. The process works like this:

1. The sending computer sends a chunk of information — let's call it a message — across the wire to the destination computer.

2. The hub, positioned between computers, passes the message to the destination computer, if it's attached to the same hub, or to another hub if it's not.

3. The hub to which the destination computer is attached resends the message to the destination computer.

On a large network, the middle step may be repeated several times as the message jumps from the hub to which the sender is attached, across hubs between the sender's and receiver's hubs, until the message reaches the receiver's hub and then, finally, the destination computer.

You're either on the bus or off the bus!

On a bus topology, every computer on the wire sees every message that gets sent. If sender and receiver are on the same wire, messages get delivered very quickly. If sender and receiver are not on the same wire, called a *segment,* a special message-forward computer passes the message from the sender's wire to the receiver's wire.This message passing consists of copying the message as sent and then retransmitting it over another wire.

Just as you might have to forward a message through multiple hubs in a star topology, you can forward a message through multiple message-forwarding computers, called *bridges,* on a bus topology.

Running rings around the network

The ring is another type of topology. Because this structure is too prone to failure, real rings seldom get built. But networks do use the idea of a ring in conjunction with other topologies. That is, a ring can be combined with a bus or a star, or can take the form of a redundant ring with multiple cables and pathways. These combined wiring structures help to improve the odds that the network keeps running. This topology sounds strange, but mapping a ring onto a star or a bus is the way some network access methods work, including ARCnet (bus and star) and token ring (star).

It's Only Logical to Get Physical

Networking topologies can be physical or logical. The physical topology — the way the wiring runs — of token-ring is a star, but the logical topology — the way data passes from one computer to another — is a ring. ARCnet, too, may be a physical bus or star, but logically it's a bus. Not even Ethernet is exempt from this dichotomy between physical wiring layout and logical message-passing behavior. That is, when Ethernet is wired as a bus, it acts like a bus, but when it's wired as a star, it still acts like a bus. Confused? Don't be. As we said, connections aren't always physical — sometimes they're logical. An Ethernet star topology that acts like a bus demonstrates that the logical topology describes the way the network behaves.

Some buses and rings are attractive because they keep track of who gets to send a message by circulating an electronic permission form around and around the network. The *token,* as this permission form is called, keeps every workstation from trying to send a message at the same time and can greatly improve network availability for everyone. The idea is that you must wait until the token comes around to your computer before your computer can send a message. Everyone then must wait about the same amount of time to send a message. Thus, tokens permit the full use of networks before the networks start slowing down.

By the Same Token

Networks use sets of rules to communicate with each other. Some use tokens to control the communications; others rely on a free-for-all effect, in which any computer can send data at any time, and the luckiest computer gets its data through. Actually, network communication is not that simple.

Networks that send tokens are called *token-passing networks* — they use rules called *protocols*, in this case the token-passing protocol, to regulate access to the media. Networks that let multiple computers send data whenever they need to communicate (subject to a set of access rules) are called *Carrier Sense, Multiple Access /Collision Detection (CSMA/CD)*. These networks use the CSMA/

CD protocol. In these networks, computers that want to use the network must first listen to the media to see if electrical signals, representing data, are present. If the computer doesn't hear anything, it goes ahead and sends its data. Just like two people separated across the floor of a big warehouse trying to talk to each other, someone may not hear that the someone else has also started talking at about the same time. When this happens on a CSMA/CD network, data collides, and all computers hear the collision. In that case, both parties that tried to talk, back off, wait a random amount of time, and then try again (as long as the network isn't already busy). For more about this fascinating subject, see our sidebar, "Think of Ethernet as bumper cars for networks," in this chapter.

The kinds of networks — like token ring, Ethernet, and ARCnet — that we talk about in this chapter, are different implementations of token-passing (token ring and ARCnet) and CSMA/CD (Ethernet) protocols. These names for types of networks are also called *access methods* — because they describe how networked computers access the media. People often confuse topologies with access methods, but now that you're straight, you can proceed into the details of the access methods.

Brand X Basics: The Kinds of Networks

Although literally hundreds of different kinds of networks are available, the kinds of networks fit into five different categories. You can distinguish them from one another by answering the following questions:

- What kind of access method, protocol, and topology does the network use?
- How does the network work?
- What are the network's technical pros and cons?
- What kinds of media does the network support?
- How business-friendly (concerning cost, availability, reliability, and so on) is this network?

This chapter discusses these basic concerns about networks and compares and contrasts the mystery network candidates. Then we make some admittedly biased recommendations.

Introducing the Contestants

When you start talking about kinds of networks, you refer to the name for and type of access method around which the network hardware is built.

Distinguishing between a network topology and an access method is an important key to understanding networks.

The *topology* identifies a network's wiring scheme. Topology describes how communications move around and among the computers and the other devices that send and receive information across a network.

The *access method* identifies how the network behaves. Access method describes the network's electrical characteristics, the type of signaling it uses, what the connectors look like, how the interfaces work, how big a message can travel across the media, and everything else necessary to build a working environment.

Topology deals with network layout; access method deals with how the network operates. Put another way, a topology describes a wiring layout, and an access method is what you buy to make it work.

For the purposes of this book, four different access methods exist (but that's a gross oversimplification, as you see in a minute):

- Ethernet
- Token ring
- Fiber Distributed Data Interface (FDDI)
- ARCnet
- Other

Acronym-o-phobes beware!

Acronyms provide a useful form of shorthand. Referring to something by its initials, such as FDDI rather than Fiber Distributed Data Interface, is a way of life in the computing industry in general and in the networking industry in particular. If the idea of swimming in a bowl of alphabet soup makes you queasy, maybe networking isn't the right thing for you.

We're trying to make the point that we introduce and use networking acronyms throughout this book. This use of networking acronyms is not deliberate torture — it's just the way the networking world operates. We tried to beat them and failed, so we have joined them. We try to make joining up as simple and painless a process for you as we possibly can. Hang in there!

If you get lost or forget what something means, we do our best to make sure that all the acronyms that we use in this book appear in the glossary at the back of the book. Think of it as reading a novel by Dostoyevsky, where you have to make a list of all the characters' names to keep track of the cast.

Counted 'em yet? Five, not four! The first four access methods are the important ones, but there's enough left over in the "other" category to make it worth mentioning as a networking grab bag.

Entertaining Ethernet

As network access methods go, Ethernet has been around longer than most — since the mid-to-late 1970s. Ethernet was the brainchild of Xerox's Palo Alto Research Center (PARC) and adopted by Digital, Intel, and Xerox — which is why the old-fashioned, 15-pin D connectors for thick-wire Ethernet are still called DIX connectors. Ethernet has long since passed into commodity status. Today Ethernet is the most well-known, widely used, and readily available networking technology.

Description

Ethernet uses the Carrier Sense, Multiple Access/ Collision Detection protocol. The sidebar titled "Think of Ethernet as bumper cars for networks" in this chapter explains what this stuff means, in as close to everyday English as the subject allows.

Think of Ethernet as bumper cars for networks

The acronym that describes Ethernet is CSMA/CD, which stands for *Carrier Sense, Multiple Access/Collision Detection*. For those who are unfamiliar with this terminology, echoes are the auditory equivalent of a collision, and a collision means that you must repeat everything we have just said. The following list provides a definition for each term in this acronym:

✔ **Carrier sense:** Everyone attached to the network is always listening to the wire, and no one's allowed to send while someone else is already sending. When a message is moving across the wire, an electrical signal called a carrier is used, so listening to the wire lets you know when the wire is busy because you can *sense* that signal.

✔ **Multiple access:** All those attached to the network can send a message whenever they want, as long as no carrier is being sensed. Because this statement means that multiple senders can begin at roughly the same time — when they think things are quiet — this Ethernet feature is called *multiple access.*

✔ **Collision detection:** If two or more senders begin sending at roughly the same time, sooner or later their messages run into each other on the wire, which is called a *collision.* Collisions are easy to recognize because they always produce a garbage signal that bears no resemblance to a valid message. Ethernet hardware includes circuitry to recognize this garbage quickly. As a result, senders must stop sending immediately and wait a random amount of time before listening to the wire (in case it's already busy) and trying to send again.

The easiest way to think about how Ethernet works is "Listen before sending, listen while sending, quit if garbage happens, and if it does, try again later."

Strengths and weaknesses

Ethernet has many strengths: It's robust and reliable and comes in a broad and affordable range of flavors. Its weaknesses are collisions and more difficult troubleshooting. For emerging high-volume applications such as real-time video or multimedia — you have those on your desktop, right? — Ethernet's speed of 10 Mbps is on the slow end.

For high-volume applications — lots of volume typically means lots of use — or for networks that are heavily trafficked by more familiar applications, Ethernet does not perform well. In fact, Ethernet's CSMA/CD access method means that its real ceiling is between 56 percent and 60 percent of total bandwidth (or 5.6 to 6.0 Mbps), because that range is the level of use where collisions start making Ethernet slow down significantly.

That doesn't mean that hope isn't on the horizon though. Two 100 Mbps Ethernets, called 100BASE-VG and 100BASE-T, are sold for those of you with higher bandwidth needs. Likewise, special switching hubs exist for Ethernet that can let it run faster than its more customary 10 Mbps ceiling. These switching hubs create and manage multiple 10 Mbps connections as they're used (which is why this approach is called *fast switched Ethernet* or *fast switching*).

Three-plus flavors are available

Ethernet comes in all the basic flavors you want, which means that it can run over all the major cabling types and works in both bus and star topologies.

The major cabling types are twisted-pair, coaxial cable (thin and thick), and fiber-optic cable. Ethernet devices to mix and match these cable types are readily available, which means that you can use Ethernet to build networks of just about any size or for even the most hostile environments. For more details, check out the section titled "Common Cable Types" earlier in this chapter.

The business side

In spite of its age, Ethernet remains the most widespread and popular networking technology. Twisted-pair leads the pack for new Ethernet cabling choices, but lots of coax is still in use out there. Fiber-based Ethernet is typically limited to connecting campus environments, where long distances and electrical-interference issues are greatest. However, fiber-based Ethernet is often used in elevator shafts to connect multiple floors in a single building. (Remember what we said about elevators shafting your networks?)

The main reasons for Ethernet's continuing use are the following:

- **Affordability:** Cabling is cheap, and interfaces range from less than $80 for desktops to less than $300 for servers. Ethernet isn't the cheapest of all available network access methods, but it's close.

- **Many choices:** Ethernet supports all cabling types, it offers lots of gear for building hybrid cabling setups, and many manufacturers offer Ethernet-based hardware. If you have a specialized need for networking gear, chances are that an Ethernet variant is on someone's drawing board, if it's not on a retailer's shelves.

- **Experience:** Because Ethernet has been around for so long, Ethernet-savvy people are easy to find. Many training courses, books, and other resources are available to help you or your colleagues become more knowledgeable.

- **Continuing innovation:** At 10 Mbps, Ethernet isn't the fastest networking technology — not by a long shot. But some vendors do make special high-speed network switches for Ethernet, and several 100 Mbps varieties mentioned earlier in this chapter are also available. That speed should help Ethernet survive the climb to the next level of networking, where far-out things such as real-time video and multimedia are everyday network needs.

Let's talk token ring

Token ring hasn't been around as long as Ethernet or ARCnet, at least not in commercial form, but it has gained a substantial foothold in the marketplace. Token ring, based on technology that IBM refined and originally marketed, is more commonly found in places where IBM is entrenched rather than in other kinds of computing environments. You see, when personal computers started taking desktop space away from the dumb terminals that connect to IBM mainframes, IBM took action. It developed token ring as a method to tie errant PCs to the mainframe computers.

Description

Token ring, which uses a *token-passing* protocol, is a collection of individual point-to-point links that happen to form a circulating pattern. *Point-to-point* means that one device is hooked to another; for token-ring, point-to-point typically describes a computer attached to a hub, which itself may be attached to other hubs or computers.

Type cast

Token ring cable uses both categories and types. You hear about Type 1 cable — that's the thick shielded twisted-pair cable originally employed for 4 Mbps token ring. Type 3, which corresponds to Category 3 wire, also exists, but Type 3 often refers to Category 3, 4, or 5. If you are using 4 Mbps token ring, Category 3 wire is fine; however, if 16 Mbps token ring is more your idea of fun, then Category 5 wire is the way to go. Once again: we strongly recommend Category 5 wiring for all new installations: it's the only form of TP that can be reused for higher-speed networking later on (like fast Ethernet or fast token-ring).

The nice things about token ring are that it's fair to everyone who participates and that it guarantees that traffic can't overwhelm it. Token ring is fair because it constantly passes an electronic permission slip, called a *token,* around the network. Any computer that wants to send a message must wait until it has possession of the token to do so. The token doesn't get released until the message has been delivered (or until it's obvious that it cannot be delivered). Everyone gets a regular shot at using the token, so token-ring is equally fair to all computers on the network.

The easiest way to think about how token ring works can be stated as "Wait for a token; when the token comes by, if you want to send a message, tack it on to the token; when the token comes around again, strip off your message, and send the token on."

Strengths and weaknesses

Token ring's strengths are its fairness and its guaranteed-delivery capabilities. What these strengths boil down to, operationally speaking, is that token ring works predictably and reliably, even when it's loaded to the max. Token ring is available in two speeds. The lower (and older) version runs at 4 Mbps, 40 percent of the purported speed of Ethernet but really runs only slightly slower because of Ethernet's incapability to use its full capacity. The higher (and newer) version, 16 Mbps token ring, runs at 160 percent of Ethernet's purported speed, but it really runs much faster because it can use multiple tokens simultaneously and because it can use 100 percent of its total bandwidth. Waiting in the wings is full-duplex token ring, which works in a similar fashion to switched Ethernet. For those who need higher speeds, IBM is considering a 100 Mbps variant.

So if token ring is so great, why does anyone buy anything else? Token ring's weaknesses have more to do with inflexibility and expense than with technical reasons. Its main downside is its requirement for expensive hub-like devices, called *multistation access units* (MAUs), and its requirements to run double-stranded cable from computer to hub (one for the outbound trip and the other for the return trip). These requirements add to the expense and reduce the maximum distance between computer and hub. Token ring is also more complicated and, depending on the media type you use, requires fancier connectors than Ethernet or ARCnet.

Three-plus flavors are available

Even though token ring implementations for TP and fiber are all available, TP is by far the most common implementation, and it's the most likely medium for tying desktops to hubs. Fiber is the cable of choice for spanning longer distances and daisy-chaining MAUs together. Only limited amounts of shielded twisted-pair get used for token-ring networking these days. Because of individual cable-length limitations and maximum ring-size limitations, cabling a token ring network takes more planning and number-crunching than does cabling ARCnet or Ethernet.

The business side

From a cost-benefit perspective, the upside factors of reliability, fairness, and guaranteed performance of token ring do not offset its higher costs. Token ring now costs between 75 percent and 150 percent more than Ethernet without necessarily conveying significant performance or reliability advantages. Although one school of network thought proclaims, "Token ring: Don't do it," and another says "We're token-passing bigots. What's Ethernet?" we're not about to go out on either limb. If someone is giving token ring away at a price that's too good to pass up, or if that's what you're told to use, go ahead and use it. It won't kill you, and it works just fine. It's just not the technology of choice for starter networks.

Fabulous FDDI

As network access methods go, FDDI is about as fast as you can get and still order it through the mail. The Fiber Distributed Data Interface was designed in the mid-1980s — at least 10 years after the options already covered in this chapter — to provide a high-speed, fiber-based, token-passing network. A successor, named FDDI II, has already been designed that adds support for video, image, and voice data to conventional network traffic. You don't have to worry about this distinction, though. Both versions are lumped together and are just called FDDI.

One of the authors of this book pronounces FDDI using the letters — "eff dee dee eye"; another pronounces it "fiddy" — which rhymes with "giddy" or "Liddy" (as in G. Gordon, of Watergate fame). We don't care how you pronounce it, but to be safe, use the letters for clarity in writing. (Can you guess which author wrote this tip?)

Description

FDDI was originally designed to tie together multiple networks, as a kind of superhighway for network data. The FDDI data rate is a speedy 100 Mbps, which ranges from 40 times faster than ARCnet to 8.5 times faster than fast token ring. Figure 2-5 covers all these numbers for you, in a way we think is easy to understand. The figure is also a pretty good indicator of how all the access methods discussed here stack up against each other.

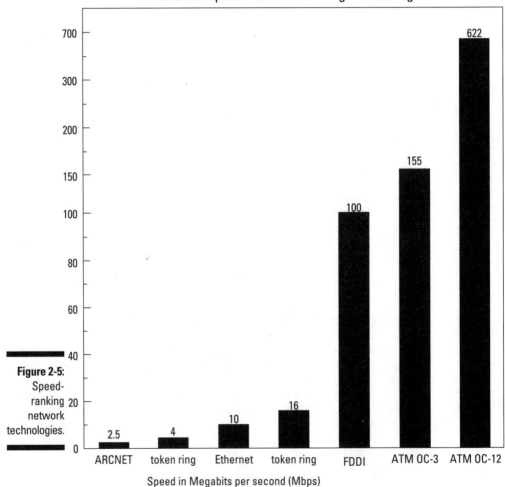

Figure 2-5: Speed-ranking network technologies.

Relative Speeds for Networking Technologies

Speed in Megabits per second (Mbps)

One of FDDI's best uses today is as a networking backbone. Just as your backbone ties the rest of your body together and carries all the important neural information throughout your body, a network backbone provides a special-purpose, high-speed link for tying lots of networks together. All FDDI networks aren't backbones, though, nor is every backbone an FDDI network. FDDI and backbones go together quite well because functioning as a backbone is one of the things FDDI was made to do.

FDDI uses the token-passing protocol. FDDI cabling uses a real ring topology, but it consists of two rings — one transmits messages clockwise; the other, counterclockwise. If either ring breaks, the other ring automatically functions as a backup. If both rings get cut at the same place — look out for the guy with a backhoe! — the two rings automatically splice together to form a ring of about twice the length that is still capable of functioning.

Although FDDI functions well as a network that services other networks, it is also available for use as a LAN access method to hook computers together for high-speed connections. FDDI is far more typical as a backbone technology today, but its LAN applications keep growing. We expect that FDDI to the desktop will become more prevalent over time, however, as applications get more demanding and the technology gets cheaper.

Strengths and weaknesses

Certainly, FDDI's biggest advantage is speed — and lots of it. But you may find more to like about FDDI. It supports rings as much as 200 kilometers in circumference (that's *124 miles*, or thereabouts, for you nonmetric types). FDDI also supports as many as 500 active devices on a single cable segment, which also is considerably more than any of the other access methods we discuss. Speed, distance, and coverage — what more could anyone want?

On the downside, FDDI requires fiber-optic cable for runs of any length. Even though a *CDDI* (*C* stands for copper, but otherwise it's the same as FDDI) does exist, CDDI doesn't support cable runs of longer than 75 feet and isn't widely available yet.

Cost is another negative. FDDI uses fiber, resulting in expensive installation, and higher-cost cables, and FDDI adapters range from a low of $800 to a high of $2,000 per computer. As the technology gets cheaper, FDDI looks better and better.

The business side

For widespread use, FDDI is still a little ahead of the business curve. Not many operations are willing to bite the bullet to the tune of running fiber everywhere and spending upward of a grand per networked desktop. Plenty of companies are working toward FDDI, though, and several of them deploy FDDI backbones.

Arguing ARCnet

Datapoint Corp., of San Antonio, Texas, originated ARCnet, which stands for Attached Resource Computer NETwork. ARCnet is in use in more than 6 million computers worldwide, but that number is not as large as it could have been. Whereas both groups that fomented Ethernet and token ring pushed for their technologies to become engineering standards (and lost control over those technologies in the process), Datapoint tried to maintain exclusive control over ARCnet to take better financial advantage of it.

The irony is that, by letting go, the other companies benefited far more than did Datapoint, which elected to hold on to its own technology. If Datapoint had not played its technology cards a little too closely to its vest, the complexion of the computer industry might be radically different today. As the situation now stands, we no longer recommend using ARCnet for new network installations, unless you have compelling reasons why nothing else will do.

Description

ARCnet is called a *token-bus technology*. In this technology, the wires act like a bus — everything gets broadcast to everyone at more or less the same time — but a token-passing protocol circulates the electronic permission slip that controls when a computer is permitted to transmit information.

Just as token ring implementations typically map a ring topology onto a star configuration, ARCnet typically maps itself onto a star. ARCnet also supports coax buses, TP daisy chains (in which each machine hooks to each of its neighbors on a separate cable), and a variety of other configurations. From a cabling standpoint, ARCnet is the most forgiving and flexible of all the networking access methods covered in this section. But those benefits also make ARCnet incredibly slow by modern networking standards.

Strengths and weaknesses

ARCnet's upsides are cost, flexibility, and ease of use. Of all the major commercially available access methods, ARCnet is the cheapest. You find Ethernet interfaces in the range from less than $80 to more than $400, and you find equivalent ARCnet interfaces ranging from less than $40 to $250. ARCnet's easy-to-purchase prefabricated cables and other components let you put together a home-baked, hybrid network that will still be robust and reliable. You can also easily mix and match components and cable types without planning all the details in advance. Finally, ARCnet offers the longest cable-length restrictions — from 300 to 2,000 feet per segment — of the three access methods we've talked about so far, and an equally capacious 20,000 feet (which you can double and redouble at the cost of slowing things down) for total network span.

The primary downside is a function of the technology's age: a speed limit of 2.5 Mbps, only one-fourth of Ethernet's official rating and roughly one-half to one-seventh of token ring's rating. ARCnet still works very well for basic business applications, such as word processing and spreadsheet use; it bogs down, however, for the more demanding applications that loom on today's business horizons — multimedia, real-time video, and whatever else the futurists dream up as the next big thing.

Three-plus flavors are available

As with Ethernet and token ring, ARCnet is available for TP, coax, and fiber-optic cable, with plenty of hubs that link together any two or all three of these wiring types. ARCnet's flexibility and electrically forgiving nature make it ideal for small networks or for networks that have to keep moving around a lot.

The business side

From a business perspective, ARCnet is every bit as much a commodity as Ethernet. Despite its bandwidth limitations, ARCnet is just as fair as token ring, and it also guarantees delivery. ARCnet is the cheapest of all the access methods discussed in this section, but it's only marginally less expensive than Ethernet. Because ARCnet appears stuck in its current design — Datapoint tried to promote a design for a 20-Mbps version called ARCnet-Plus, but it never went anywhere — it doesn't have much room to grow into the twenty-first century.

Here's how you should approach ARCnet:

✔ If you already have ARCnet, keep using it. You can even add more ARCnet, but add it judiciously.

✔ If you have to go absolutely bottom dollar, ARCnet is as low as you can go without pulling out the tin cans and string. Before you take this option, shop around for used Ethernet or token ring gear; we think used versions of either are better than new ARCnet in today's day and age.

✔ If you're not forced to go with ARCnet, choose Ethernet or token ring (or something even faster). ARCnet is not the right place to start anymore.

What else is there?

If you have to ask, you're probably wondering why this book doesn't mention your networking access method. We're sorry to bear sad tidings, but if you're not using one of the four access methods already covered — Ethernet, token-ring, ARCnet, or FDDI — networking may be harder for you than for most folks. Sorry.

The sad thing is that literally hundreds of other kinds of networks are out there. If *A* is for AppleTalk, and *W* is for wireless, networks starting with all the letters of the alphabet in between probably exist, too.

Using exotic networking access methods can be a problem for NetWare, too. If you're involved with an exotic network access method, find out whether NetWare works with it before you spend any money on the software (we explain how to locate such information in Appendix C). The good news is that NetWare runs over the widest range of available networking technologies of any network operating system. The bad news is that you will have to do some research to find out whether your stuff is supported or not. The worst news is that you will have to work harder to do basic stuff that the more commercial methods take for granted, and you may have to forgo more exotic options, such as LAN-attached printers.

One exception to the "if it's exotic, it must be difficult" rule that we just mentioned is an emerging star in the area of high-speed networking. Known as *ATM,* short for *Asynchronous Transfer Mode,* this technology is growing rapidly at the high end of the networking market. ATM is particularly well suited for demanding applications and high-volume traffic. The long-distance phone companies — who define what *high-volume traffic* really means — already use ATM implementations that run at 155 (OC-3) and 622 (OC-12) Mbps, but current ATM specifications include speeds of 1.2 (OC-24) and 2.4 (OC-48) Gbps (gigabits per second) as well. Hardly anybody's using those extreme speeds — yet.

ATM is a fast switching technology that requires hub-like switching devices and network interfaces for each computer. Recently, several companies have started building LAN equipment based on ATM. Several options for using ATM with NetWare are already available, representing the highest end of the bandwidth spectrum in today's marketplace. Expect to spend at least $2,000 per workstation (including allocated switch and fiber-optic cable costs) to bring ATM to your LAN.

The best way to find out what's what is to get up on CompuServe or the Internet and ask the collective wisdom (about Novell's products) that's represented in those avenues of cyberspace: "Does my QuackNet work with NetWare?" (For instructions on using the Internet or CompuServe, see Appendix C.) Chances are that you can get the right answer within a day. If you don't have access to CompuServe or the Internet, ask around. With many millions of users worldwide, you shouldn't have to look far to find someone who can help you. Good luck!

The Polls Are In!

If you have to make a choice for a new network access method today, with no constraints, go for Ethernet. It's the only widely available technology whose 100 Mbps versions leave significant room for growth. Token ring is worth considering only for new networks if an IBM mainframe or minicomputer operating system is somewhere in the picture or if other considerations — such as company policy or deterministic requirements — dictate it.

Chapter 3

Message in a Bottle: Mastering the Art of Protocols

● ●

In This Chapter

▶ Finding out how protocols work

▶ Using protocols to let computers speak

▶ Moving messages

● ●

*C*hapter 1 describes networking as requiring three fundamental components: connections, communications, and services. Here, the book leaves behind the connections — the wires and interfaces — and invites you to climb inside the network to look at its communications. You also see how messages moving across the network are fielded by their senders and receivers. From the proper perspective, everything in life is a football game, right?

Communications are based on a shared set of rules about how to exchange information and about what things mean at the most rudimentary levels — such as what's the convention used to represent digital data, or what's a one and what's a zero? Communications also specify the formats of and meanings for network addresses and other necessary information. Communications don't tell you, however, about that football-shaped box on your desk, or why it's ticking. Maybe someone wants to tell you something.

Rather than play network football, though, and go out for the bomb, in this chapter you continue your look at the network plumbing. This time, instead of looking at the pipes and connections that tie the network together, you look at what's moving through the pipes — the messages that computers send to each other. This examination may help you better understand how computers communicate — and why they sometimes don't — on your real network.

How Do Computers Really Communicate with Each Other?

Chapter 1 compares a computer conversation to a human conversation. In that chapter, Table 1-1 illustrates that all kinds of communication, whether between humans or computers, have much in common. Although some similarities do exist, at even more than a superficial level, we all know that computers use ones and zeroes and that humans use words to communicate.

In addition to the things humans and computers have in common as communicators, many differences exist between the ways people talk to each other and the ways that computers talk to each other. Understanding the differences will help you to understand networking better, too.

Do what I mean, not what I say!

When they're communicating, human beings are always interpreting things and misunderstanding things. What one person says is not always what the other person hears. Humans can also rely on shared understandings and assumptions when they communicate, meaning they may know what's being talked about at any time. For example, a relatively empty phrase such as "How 'bout da Bears?" means something specific to a couple of Chicago Bears fans — the person asking the question doesn't have to go into much detail. That understanding is possible because humans are good communicators and because all of us have a common frame of reference to draw on at any time. This common frame of reference can help supply meaning when the total substance of a conversation is implied rather than explicitly stated.

Computers, on the other hand, can do only exactly what they're told to do — neither more nor less. For computers to communicate, for any information to be delivered, every little bit of information that sender and receiver exchange must be supplied, not implied. For computers to communicate, they must start out with complete agreement about the following issues (we use the first-person pronoun *I* to state questions from a particular computer's point of view):

- ✔ What's my address? How do I find it out? How do I find out other computers' addresses?
- ✔ How do I signal another computer that I'm ready to send a message? That I'm ready to receive a message? That I'm busy? That I can wait if it's busy?

Finding the answers to these questions is really just the tip of a large, cold, technological iceberg. You must completely map out and then implement the answers in software before computers can communicate with each other.

You must know and understand the answers to the questions that a computer might ask if the computers are to communicate. If in fact, the collection of these answers forms the basis of a set of rules about how computers can communicate, those computers can then use those rules to handle the networking part of their activity.

Rules . . . in a knife fight?

Building a complete set of communications rules is time-consuming, persnickety, and completely boring to most normal people. In the early days of the computer industry, individual companies or groups decided that they wanted to do something (such as networking), and they put a group of programmers to work building programs to do just that. Over time, this process led to many different ways of doing things (such as networking), none of which would work with anything the talented programmers over at some other companies were doing.

In the early days, incompatibilities like these were not a big deal (or so it seemed). As networking became more widespread, however, the people who bought computers from companies A and Z naturally began to say "Well, gee, if my company A computers can talk to each other, and my company Z computers can talk to each other, why can't the As talk to the Zs and vice versa?"

Why not, indeed?

Uncle Sam played an important role in bringing order to this emerging trend toward network chaos. He tried to get his computers — from companies A through Z — to talk to each other and learned that he had a compatibility problem — in spades! What emerged from this fracas was a consensus that a set of rules was absolutely necessary for networking. Even more important, the industry learned that networking was difficult, if not impossible, when everyone didn't share the same set of rules.

We would like this story to have a happy ending, one that went like this: "Today, there's only one set of networking rules, which everyone is using wisely and well." Too bad that that's not true. Even though the chaos has been reduced, plenty of confusion still exists, and vendors always try to get an edge by inventing more communication rules as they go.

Protocols Let Computers Speak the Languages of Love

Calling these protocols "sets of networking rules" is starting to get clumsy. They're usually called *networking protocols* or *networking standards,* or even *standard networking protocols.* You get the drift.

In diplomacy, protocol refers to the rules for behavior that let representatives from sovereign governments communicate with each other in a way calculated to keep things peaceful, or at least under control. The existence of protocol explains why diplomats refer to heated screaming matches as "frank and earnest discussions" or to insoluble disagreements as "exploratory dialogue." Double-talk aside, the word protocol captures very nicely the flavor of what these sets of rules do for networks, and that's why we use the word.

The key to a networking protocol is that any two computers that want to communicate must have in common an identical protocol — they're peers in any communication that takes place. The protocol defines the language, the structure, and the rules for communicating that the computers use to exchange information.

How suite it is!

Even though this book is about NetWare and focuses some of its attention on Novell protocols, we would do an injustice to you not to admit that these protocols are just one member of a large cast. Novell has become surprisingly catholic in its support for protocols and has finally included full-blown support for government standards (TCP/IP, or Transmission Control Protocol/Internet Protocol) in NetWare. At the same time, Novell continues to support its own proprietary protocols, known as IPX/SPX (Internetwork Packet eXchange/ Sequenced Packet eXchange) because they remain the most widely-used of any of the networking protocols. But since the Internet rides on the government standard TCP/IP protocols, and more and more in-house networks use these same protocols themselves (which is why they're sometimes called *intranets*), Novell can no longer relegate TCP/IP to second-class status. You're probably not surprised to learn, therefore, that NetWare supports all the most popular networking protocols in use today.

One last remark on protocols: They rarely, if ever, occur in the singular. Most networking protocols consist of a named collection of specific message formats and rules for interaction rather than a single set of formats and rules. For that reason, we also call protocols *protocol suites,* not because they like to lounge around on matched collections of furniture, but because they travel in packs.

Raising the standards

Any discussion of networking rules becomes interesting because both the vendors and the standards groups call their stuff a *standard.* Some vendors expel a lot of hot air talking about the difference between *de facto* and *de jure* standards. De facto means, "It ain't official, but a lot of people use it, so we can call it a standard if we want"; de jure means, "It's a standard because XYZ (a standards-setting group) has declared it to be so and has published this foot-high stack of documentation to prove it."

Part of the heat behind the discussion of what's standard and what's not is a control issue. Purists of all stripes — including academicians, researchers, techno-weenies, and others — flatly assert that only a standards-setting group can be "objective and fair." Purists also say that only they can appreciate the chore of selecting the very best rules that technology has to offer and putting those rules in their standard. The purists say they are making the world a better place for us to live.

The other source of the heat behind the discussion is the vendors who try to build products and get them out the door as fast as they can. Although the objectivity, fairness, and leading-edge character of many standards are not in dispute, setting standards involves groups of individuals who must agree on what's in those standards. And reaching agreement takes time. In the meantime, technology keeps evolving, and nothing goes stale faster than leading-edge technology. Vendors, in their desperation to keep up with the market and their customers' demands, struggle mightily to get their products out the door. "Of course we have to be in control of our technology," they say. "It's the only way we can keep up!"

Whether networking technologies are standards or not, or de facto or de jure, doesn't matter. The real action takes place in the markets. The funny thing about the vendor versus standards group debate is that vendors must be involved on both sides because they can't afford to miss any of the technology boats that sail from port. Some vendors are astute enough to publish their standards and to give customers and industry people sufficient documentation and input to keep things working and current with technology. Some standards bodies are bold enough to realize that a standard is a good thing only when it's implemented in large quantities. As a result, these standards bodies are giving vendors opportunities to deal with the real-world concerns of getting products to market. Both camps have winners, and those winning sets of rules are the ones that customers use the most.

A protocol's work is never done

Okay, fine. So now you know that your computer cannot talk to another computer without sharing a common protocol. Where does this protocol stuff come from? Put differently, who decides which protocols get used?

Protocols span the range of networking capability, all the way from software to hardware. The programs that run on your computer that let you access the network must use a protocol to interact with it. This protocol continues all the way down to the edge of the hardware, where the computer says "send this message" to talk to the network or "give me the message" when the hardware tells the computer that the computer has something to look at.

The answer to where the protocol stuff comes from is "a little from here and a little from there." For example, most protocols don't care which kind of network they're talking through. Protocols don't even notice, in most cases, if they're talking through an Ethernet or token ring network. The reason for the protocol's indifference to hardware is that part of the software that provides network capability comes from a piece of software called a *LAN driver,* and part of it comes from other sources.

You install the LAN driver on a computer to tell the computer exactly how to talk to the network interface in your machine. If you're lucky, you use a network machine such as a Macintosh. If not, you must locate and install a LAN driver for your network interface so that your computer can talk to the network interface, and so that the network interface can talk to the network. "Bigger fleas have littler fleas . . ." is what it all comes down to.

Some applications may know how to communicate directly with a network through a special kind of software interface. Applications with this kind of network savvy used to be pretty rare, but they're becoming more common as networks become more widespread. Other applications may use standard computer system access and end up talking through the network without necessarily being aware that the network is being accessed.

The key to accessing the network from applications, or from a computer's operating system, is a collection of software that implements the protocol suite being used. The operating system is a program, like DOS on a PC, that keeps the computer running and doing the jobs that you ask it to do.

The application vendor may supply all or part of the network access software, down to the LAN driver if an application is network-savvy. If the operating system is network-savvy, a system vendor may supply all or part of this software.

For NetWare, both Novell and Microsoft supply IPX/SPX software for all of the Windows clients; in addition, Novell supplies client software for OS/2, Macintosh, and other platforms. Likewise, the NetWare support for TCP/IP ensures that UNIX machines and other systems can gain ready access to NetWare. Of the desktops that NetWare supports, Windows for Workgroups, Windows 95, Windows NT, UNIX, OS/2, and Macintosh can use their own networking software. DOS, however, must use networking software that Novell supplies for those machines, along with NetWare. (DOS can also use networking software that Novell obtains from Microsoft or other sources.)

This networking software is where the protocol stuff comes from. For a picture of these possible software relationships, look at Figure 3-1. It shows that you need a software component, called a *shell* or *requester,* to communicate over the network. The figure also shows that additional software, called the LAN driver, that you need to use the network interface provides the link between programs and hardware.

Moving Messages, or the LAN Must Go Through!

So now you know that a protocol suite lets computers share a set of common rules for communications. You also know that these protocols handle the movement of information between the hardware on the computer that inter-faces to the network and the applications you run on your machine. The next question is, what happens between the applications and the hardware while the protocols do their thing?

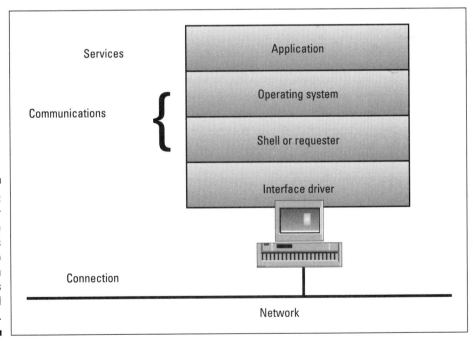

Figure 3-1:
Driver
software
bridges
the gap
between
applications
and
networks.

The Dance of the Seven Layers

Much of what happens between applications and hardware consists of taking messages, breaking them down, and stuffing them into envelopes as you move farther from the application and closer to the hardware. The transfer of information works the other way, too — moving from hardware to applications, where the protocols would unpack envelopes and stick individual pieces together to build a complete (and, we hope, meaningful) message.

A post office analogy works well here. You may think that the post office handles mail, but it really handles envelopes, packages, or whatever — things that have addresses on them with sufficient postage to pay their way. How does the post office deliver a letter? It goes something like this:

1. You address a letter and drop it at a mail pickup.

2. The mail carrier on whose route the pickup is located gets the letter.

3. The mail carrier delivers the mail to the local post office.

4. The mail sorters check the zip code and route the letter.

5. The letter gets shipped to the post office that services the destination on the address.

6. The mail sorters check the street address and route the letter to the mail carrier who covers that address.

7. The mail carrier delivers the letter to the address.

8. The recipient gets the letter.

The key ingredients for successful mail delivery are timely pickup, short transit time, and correct delivery. The factors that most influence transit time and delivery (other than the mind-numbing effects of a federal bureaucracy) are correct identification of and routing to the mailing address.

The crucial similarity between networking protocols and the postal service lies in recognizing addresses, routing messages from senders to receivers, and providing delivery. The main difference is that the postal service doesn't care what's in the envelopes or packages that you send (within reason) — as long as they meet size, weight, and materials restrictions. Networking protocols, on the other hand, spend most of their time dealing with envelopes of varying sizes and kinds.

Another example helps to explain this process. Imagine that you want to copy a file across the network from your computer to another computer somewhere across the wire. It's a sizable file, about 1 MB (megabyte). Because the file is the spreadsheet covering your sales forecast for the next quarter, you want it to get there quickly and correctly.

If you use the post office, you copy the file to a floppy and mail it to the recipient, but that takes at least a day. That's not fast enough. Over the network, the file arrives in less than a minute. While the file is moving from your machine across the network to the other machine, a lot goes on that you can't see.

Actually, size consideration — the biggest chunk of data that you're allowed to move across the network — is only one reason the envelope game gets played. Handling addresses is another reason. In the postal service example, the pickup post office cares only about the destination zip code, but the delivering mail carrier worries about the street address. In the same vein, one protocol may care only about the name of the computer that the file needs to be shipped to; at a lower level, however, the protocol must know not just that computer's address but also where to direct the chunks of data moving from sender to receiver so that the file can be reassembled on delivery.

When you send something from your computer, the protocol software spends most of its time taking things apart in order to deliver them accurately and efficiently. When you receive something, the computer spends its time stripping off packaging information and putting things back together. Notice that sender and receiver keep talking to each other along the way in order to monitor the accuracy and effectiveness of their communications and to determine if and when delivery is complete. Protocols also keep track of the quality and usability of network links.

Chapter 4

Who's Out There? Round Up the Usual Suspects!

. . . .

In This Chapter

▶ Identifying common NetWare protocols and fellow travelers

▶ Introducing IPX

▶ Toasting TCP/IP: Score one for the government

▶ Applying AppleTalk: Bringing Macs into the fold

▶ Mixing multiple stacks

▶ Recognizing and categorizing your protocols

. . . .

*I*n this chapter, you're still finding out about the way computers communicate over networks, but you also see how to recognize which kinds of communications you're dealing with. You also figure out which kinds of protocols go with which operating systems or with specific applications. By the time you finish, you're ready to figure out what you have been using all this time, or what you will be using soon.

For networking, a *network protocol* is a set of rules that govern the way computers can communicate with each other. For computers to communicate, they must have protocols in common.

Network protocols are usually organized into groups of capabilities that handle everything from sending and receiving messages from the network interface — talking to the hardware — to enabling applications to use the network to do their thing — talking to the software. Because protocols travel in packs, they're generically referred to as *protocol families* or *protocol suites*. This process of grouping network protocols involves stacking multiple layers of functionality, and software often goes with each layer. *Protocol stack,* therefore, is the logical name for the software that supports a particular network protocol and gets loaded on a computer. Each computer on the network loads all or part of this stack, and when computers communicate with each other, they become peers. In that situation, the computers use the same parts of the stack, called *peer protocols.*

In this chapter, you meet the most popular protocol stacks for the NetWare environment. We discuss how to tell the protocol stacks apart and what they're most commonly used for. In the process, you also find out a little more about how networks work and what kinds of built-in functionality help to keep things that way.

Just as diplomatic protocols help grease the wheels of diplomacy, network protocols help keep your networks running. If you get to know the players, you may even be able to help things along.

Welcome to the Rogues' Gallery

In dealing with the protocols that you commonly encounter in the NetWare environment, you must rattle off strange-sounding collections of letters (and sometimes even numbers) with aplomb. You also must know which acronyms belong together and, in some cases, how to understand how these pieces fit together.

In setting up and troubleshooting a NetWare network, you should understand the kinds of jobs that various protocols do and be able to make an educated guess about the kinds of problems each protocol is subject to. When things get weird, you have to be acquainted with this rogues' gallery of protocols so that you can recognize who the perpetrators may be.

Warning: Entering the acronym zone!

Most protocol families consist entirely of members whose names are made up of abbreviations. You will encounter more strange alphabetic combinations, and even a few odd-looking combinations of letters and numbers, than you ever suspected could exist.

Meet the basic NetWare protocols

Novell's basic protocols are called IPX, for Internetwork Packet eXchange; SPX, for Sequenced Packet eXchange; and NCP, for NetWare Core Protocol. Surprisingly, IPX, SPX, and NCP are the most widely used networking protocols in the world, with as many as 120 million regular users. This number also represents the size of NetWare's estimated user population, so a close identification exists between these protocols and NetWare itself, historically speaking. This section presents just an introduction, though. IPX is used with NetWare on DOS (with or without vanilla Windows), Macintosh, Windows NT 3.5, OS/2, and some versions of UNIX.

NetWare 4.11's introduction of parity between IPX/SPX and TCP/IP may dethrone IPX/SPX from its current place atop the NetWare protocol heap.

The government protocols

No, government protocols don't refer to a set of rules for doing business with foreign heads of state. They are the outgrowth of Department of Defense funding for networks, which began in the early 1970s to tie together government computers. These protocols are more commonly referred to as DoD (Department of Defense) protocols, because the DoD requires that all computers it purchases be capable of running the protocols, or as Internet protocols because you need them in order to use the Internet.

The real name of this government protocol suite is TCP/IP, which stands for two of its members, the Transmission Control Protocol and the Internet Protocol. Dr. Vinton Cerf, a founding father of the Internet, says that more than 1,000,000 networks are part of the Internet today and another 400,000 or more private networks use TCP/IP. Because of those usage figures, most people outside the Novell/NetWare camp consider TCP/IP to be *the* major player in the protocol game. TCP/IP has deep roots in the UNIX community, and it also often links different kinds of computers, including a plethora of free or inexpensive implementations for PCs and Macintoshes.

Other faces in the gallery

Lots of other protocols exist on networks all over the world, but you probably can find the ones discussed in this section on NetWare networks or in the operations that use NetWare:

- **AppleTalk:** The name of the set of protocols developed by Apple Computer, whose Macintosh was one of the first mass-market computers to offer built-in networking capabilities. In most cases, where there's a Mac, there's also AppleTalk.

- **ISO/OSI:** Not a cruel technician's idea of a nifty palindrome. It stands for the International Standards Organization's Open Systems Interconnect family of networking protocols. Although it was highly touted as the successor to TCP/IP and the next big networking thing, OSI has yet to live up to its promise. Few OSI protocols are in common use; most use occurs in Europe, where OSI protocols have gained a foothold.

  Because many governments, formerly including Uncle Sam, require systems to be OSI-compliant, a good bit of OSI is still used in industry, government, business, and academia. Like TCP/IP, ISO/OSI is available for a broad range of systems, from PCs to supercomputers. Most protocol stacks resemble OSI, and like any reference model, the OSI model lets techno-weenies know which layer someone else is talking about.

✔ **SNA:** Systems Network Architecture is IBM's basic protocol suite. Where you find a mainframe or an AS/400, you also typically find SNA. Because SNA was one of the pioneering protocols, companies that invested heavily in mainframe technology in the 1960s and 1970s typically also invested in building large-scale SNA networks.

Numerically, more SNA networks exist than any other kind, but because they are old, cumbersome, and expensive, the number is dropping. Those drawbacks also explain why IBM's newer operating systems, such as OS/2 and AIX, offer other protocols in addition to links to SNA. This topic is a special, esoteric networking one, and you don't see much more of it in this book.

✔ **NetBIOS:** NetBIOS, or Networked Basic Input-Output System, was designed by Sytek and IBM as a networked extension to PC BIOS. NetBIOS is a higher-level protocol that runs on top of many lower-level protocols, including IPX and TCP/IP, in addition to others. Even though NetBIOS is pretty old, programming with it is easy; consequently, many different networked applications on a broad range of computers and operating systems use NetBIOS. It has one big disadvantage, though. You can't get from network A to network B with NetBIOS. You have to use another protocol.

✔ **NetBEUI:** The NetBIOS Extended User Interface was designed by Microsoft to extend the functions of NetBIOS. You can call NetBIOS and NetBEUI a matched set. Microsoft and IBM use NetBIOS and NetBEUI with some of their networking products.

You may find NetWare networks that use NetBIOS, but not NetBEUI, or you may find hybrid networks that use both IPX and NetBEUI, along with NetBIOS. What networks use depends on what they install. Because NetBIOS is not explicitly part of NetWare, though, we don't deal with it in much more detail in this book.

The world is home to hundreds of protocol families, each with its own collection of acronyms and its own special outlook on the world. We hope that you don't have to get to know each of them intimately, but believe us — they're out there, along with a host of other, even more exotic ones we don't mention in this chapter.

Natively NetWare IPX/SPX

NetWare's roots began to grow in the late 1970s and early 1980s, when networking was still in its early childhood.

NetWare protocols are based on a set of protocols developed at Xerox, called the Xerox Networking System and abbreviated as XNS. Many XNS-derived protocols are in the world today, proving again that Xerox is great at delivering ideas that other people end up delivering as products.

Connection-handling helps classify protocols

IPX is a connectionless protocol, and SPX is connection-oriented. What does this mean? Why should you care?

Chapter 3, titled "Message in a Bottle: Mastering the Art of Protocols," established that the most important job of a lower-level protocol — and both IPX and SPX qualify — is to break up application information of an arbitrary size into digestible, same-size chunks for sending and to put those chunks back together into their original form when they are receiving. These chunks, called *packets,* form the basic message unit for information moving across a network. These chunks of data, which are further divided and stuffed in envelopes by the access method being used, are called *frames*. Look at it this way: Packets move up and down the protocol stack; frames dance across the wire.

Connectionless protocols work the same as mailing letters with the postal service: You drop off a letter and expect it to get delivered. You may or may not find out whether it doesn't get where it's supposed to go — unless it's a bill, in which case you typically don't care that much anyway. IPX provides no guarantee of delivery, and frames can arrive in any order, which may differ from the order in which they're sent.

Connection-oriented protocols use a *handshake* to start communications, and they more closely resemble a conversation. Connection-oriented protocols act more like the process of sending a registered letter, in which information about its delivery, such as who signed for it, is returned to the sender. SPX packets are sequenced so that they arrive in proper order. SPX is more reliable and not only notices when delivery fails but also can request redelivery or send error notices to applications when successful delivery is impossible. The sad truth, however, is that in NetWare, SPX is rarely used except by diagnostic programs, which need the additional error-checking SPX provides.

IPX and other connectionless protocols are considered lightweight. They're typically fast and don't require much overhead. SPX and other connection-oriented protocols (like TCP) offer higher reliability. They run more slowly than connectionless protocols do because they have to keep track of what has been sent and received. In addition, connection-oriented protocols also run slower because they handle more record keeping information built in to each packet that gets sent (such as keeping track of sequence numbers and deliveries).

The NetWare protocol family is called IPX, which is short for Internetwork Packet eXchange. It's also sometimes called IPX/SPX, where SPX stands for Sequenced Packet eXchange. These two protocols are the foundation on which the rest of NetWare's protocols are built.

IPX and SPX handle the basic job of moving packets around NetWare networks and are the workhorses of everyday networking. This list shows four other important NetWare protocols that you encounter on your NetWare networks:

✔ **NCP (NetWare Core Protocols):** These are the service protocols for NetWare. For virtually every service that NetWare can provide, an NCP is used to let users send requests for that service — to begin the process of delivering in response to their requests. The kinds of services provided by the NetWare NCPs range from file transfer to directory services lookups. NCP requests and responses start the communication process and are sealed inside IPX packets for transport across the media by the access method.

✔ **RIP (Routing Information Protocol):** This is a broadcast protocol (meaning that it is addressed to everyone who's listening on a network) that every IPX router on a network uses one time per minute to declare what it knows about how to get around on the network. (For NetWare 3.11 or higher-numbered versions, any server can be a router.)

Routers exchange RIP packets to keep the common knowledge of how a collection of individual networks — called an *internetwork* — is laid out. This information moves packets around, which is why the servers that do the moving are called *routers*.

✔ **NLSP (NetWare Link State Protocol):** This protocol can replace RIP and SAP in NetWare 3.x and 4.x. NLSP was designed to reduce the amount of unnecessary and costly communication over internetworks and wide-area networks; it gets rid of RIPs and SAPs so that network status and configuration are communicated more efficiently.

✔ **SAP (Service Advertisement Protocol):** This protocol advertises the services available on the network. Like RIP, SAP is a broadcast protocol. Each server sends out its collection of SAPs once per minute in versions of NetWare before 4.x. NetWare 4.x and higher-numbered versions use directory services to deliver and advertise services, so the only services that must be advertised in that environment are the directory services themselves (called DSAP, for Directory SAP).

IPX/SPX is Novell's property, which is why it's called *proprietary* technology. Even though it has undisputed control, Novell has been tolerant about sharing IPX/SPX technologies with other companies, such as Microsoft, which used IPX/SPX as its default protocols in Windows NT 3.5 and 3.51. This openness explains why Novell is still the number-one networking vendor. In the minds of some users, however, a stigma is still attached to proprietary technologies of any kind. For that reason, Novell lets NetWare 4.11 be configured to eschew IPX/SPX in favor of our next contestant, TCP/IP.

Score One for the Uncle: TCP/IP's a Winner!

Because TCP/IP has roots in the defense community, you probably expect a certain martial air of performance and reliability to characterize TCP/IP — and you are right!

TCP/IP originally was developed because of the government's penchant for buying at least one of everything known to man, including one of every kind of computer system imaginable. Because most early networking development done by vendors assumed that all the machines being networked used their hardware and software, a purely proprietary perspective on networking invariably left the government's hodgepodge out in the cold.

Also, these defense community computers were scattered all over the country, and beyond — some in such truly remote spots as Thule, Greenland, where no one goes unless one absolutely must! So from the ground up, TCP/IP was designed to link up different systems and to work as well over wide-area connections as over local-area ones. This design helps to explain TCP/IP's enduring appeal.

TCP/IP is in the hands of a governing body called the Internet Architecture Board (IAB). This consortium of government, academic, and research and development (R&D) types takes seriously their custodianship of the rules and regulations governing TCP/IP formats and interfaces. Because a not-for-profit group governs the IAB and does not belong to any particular company, TCP/IP is regarded as a standard (*de jure*) protocol suite.

TCP/IP includes a set of high-level, basic services, along with the protocols that move messages around the network. These services include a universal *terminal emulator* called Telnet. (A terminal emulator lets one computer pretend that it's a terminal attached to another computer over the network — in grand government tradition, the terminal emulator is capable of taking any smart computer and turning it into a dumb one). The services also include a file-transfer program named FTP (for *file-transfer protocol*), which can copy files between any two TCP/IP-equipped computers. These services also provide programs for remotely controlling other machines and for electronic mail between machines that want to talk to each other.

A set of military specifications governs the basic requirements for acceptable implementations of TCP/IP, and these specifications include requirements for Telnet and FTP support. These specifications have the advantage of letting users assume that basic services, as well as a common language for networked communication, will be available from TCP/IP-capable machines.

Two of the protocols in TCP/IP gave the protocol suite its name. TCP, which stands for Transmission Control Protocol, is a guaranteed-delivery, reliable protocol (much like SPX) that is widely used. IP, which stands for Internet Protocol, provides the basic packet structure used to move all messages in a TCP/IP environment.

Even though TCP/IP has been around since the late 1970s, it continues to grow and to be more widely deployed as a networking protocol. Despite its age, TCP/IP remains usable and effective thanks to continued innovations and an open-minded governing body. TCP/IP is probably the most widely used and best-known large-scale networking protocol in use today. Despite many prema-ture predictions of its demise among protocol pundits, TCP/IP is chugging happily along and promises to be around well into the twenty-first century.

Applying AppleTalk: Making the Mac Connection

Like IPX/SPX, AppleTalk is a proprietary protocol stack. The property of Apple Computer, AppleTalk is considered the most likely way to network Macintoshes. Even though IPX and TCP/IP implementations for the Mac are available, AppleTalk is the most frequently used Macintosh networking protocol simply because it's built in to the Macintosh environment and is incredibly easy to use. AppleTalk defines a model for plug-and-play networking that any implementa-tion would benefit from following. We wish that more protocols had tried as hard to be as easy as this one is.

AppleTalk has a lot going for it, especially in terms of ease of use. However, friendliness and performance tend to be at somewhat opposite poles of the spectrum. Novell's NetWare for Macintosh has consistently been the top-performing AppleTalk file server platform since 1989, when it was first intro-duced, despite being based on a PC platform.

But Wait — There's More!

We can go on discussing network protocols almost indefinitely, but by now you probably know that every protocol suite includes a cast of characters, each of which has its own special job in making networking happen. This chapter explains most of the common concerns, which include moving frames across the network (packet or datagram delivery), connectionless versus connection-oriented communications, address handling, network management, service advertisement, routing, and service protocols of all kinds.

A close look at any protocol suite typically displays some, if not all, of these capabilities. After you grasp the idea that frame delivery, routing services, address handling, and the rest are part of what supplying a workable network means, things should begin making at least a perverted kind of sense. Don't worry if the acronyms are unfamiliar or the terminology is strange; the main thing is to concentrate on learning how protocols help to connect programs and services to the network. If you know about those concepts, you know all that's important.

Hybrid Vigor: Mixing Protocols

In some situations, you may need to use more than one kind of network from a single computer. Although using more than one kind of network can require some contortions, depending on the network interface and drivers in use, it is typically very doable. The key is to understand whether the machine has to be capable of interacting with both networks at will or whether it's always one *or* the other, as opposed to one *and* the other.

IPX/SPX and TCP/IP, for example, can — and do — run successfully together on PCs every day. NetWare 4.11 includes drivers and installation tools to easily mix and match the two environments so that users can use both networks in a single DOS command. For example, you can transfer a file from a NetWare networked drive to a TCP/IP computer using the file-transfer protocol (FTP). With NetWare 4.11, you can even choose to use only TCP/IP for a completely functional connection.

Likewise, Macintoshes can run AppleTalk and TCP/IP quite easily, and UNIX can run as many protocol stacks as necessary to provide the right range of network services. This capability means that a UNIX machine's protocol collection can include TCP/IP, OSI, and IPX, or perhaps even more, for truly diverse networking environments.

The key to mixing protocols is to obtain LAN drivers that can switch between one protocol stack and another as necessary. Some drivers are not that flexible, and the computer to be restarted must switch from one stack to another on the same interface. You might even have to install two network interface cards on the same network to provide simultaneous support for two stacks. This problem is most acute for DOS and Windows because those environments cannot change their configurations on the fly. Most other operating systems and platforms, including Macintosh, OS/2, Windows NT, and UNIX, are designed to be more flexible and accommodating.

No matter which type of operating system or machine you use, one consequence of using multiple stacks is constant: The more protocols you use, the more resources they consume. Each stack has a certain memory requirement, and each one you add increases the overhead needed to run your system. Again, multiple stacks weigh heaviest on DOS and Windows, but working with multiple network protocols imposes greater overhead than working with only one, no matter which platform the network runs on.

ODI, dish me up some NDIS

To make LAN driver and protocol stack cooperation easier, Novell and Microsoft each developed their own specifications that dictate how vendors should write LAN drivers and protocols. Novell's spec is called the Open Datalink Interface (ODI) specification; Microsoft's is called the Network Driver Interface Specification (NDIS). They're both pretty much the same —

they let one LAN driver talk to several protocol stacks. Both sets of specifications are so well accepted, in fact, that an ODI client can operate on a network that calls for NDIS drivers, and vice versa. When you talk about NetWare, however, you hear ODI. If Windows NT, OS/2 LAN Server, or Banyan VINES has caught your fancy, you probably will use NDIS all the way.

Reading Between the Lines: How to Tell What's What

Although the details may differ from machine to machine, you can use a NetWare command to determine which protocols you're using and which version of NetWare you're running. When you enter the NetWare command, WHOAMI, your machine tells you (that is, displays on-screen) your account name (such as ETITTEL) and what version of NetWare the responding server is running (such as 4.11). The only way to figure out what protocols you're running is to observe the system dialog that occurs as you log into the NetWare server: This dialog should tell you everything you need to know.

What to Do with What You Learn

Whether you write down what the computer says on bootup or go digging for information on your machine, this information usually suffices to identify what's what to the knowledgeable. Your next step then is to find someone knowledgeable and ask for help.

Remember — if you don't know where to look for assistance, you can always call the people who sold you the machine or the vendor with whose operating system it runs. Network software information is generally so common that there are lots of ways to skin this particular cat. If you learn that what you have is not so hot or could be newer, these same people usually can steer you to a source for the latest and greatest drivers.

The network interface vendor can also be an invaluable source for information on the protocols and software versions you're using. The vendor is usually the owner, if not the author, of the drivers for its gear. Persistence pays off and should help you to make sure that your protocol stacks and drivers are the right vintage for your particular environment.

Chapter 5

NICs and Knocks: How to Understand Network Interface Cards

*T*his chapter helps you tackle the joys and sorrows of installing network interfaces. Previous chapters discuss the basics of connections, which is a topic we return to here. To get your network interface working, you may find it helpful to have a basic understanding of connections. If you need a quick refresher on the topic, turn to Chapter 2.

If you have an IBM PC or a PC clone, you probably want to read this chapter because we discuss how to install network interfaces for such machines. If you use a Macintosh or something else that's not a PC or a clone, you can skip this chapter with impunity.

NIC is an acronym for *n*etwork *i*nterface *c*ard. Most NICs plug into computers and provide the essential link between the wire (the medium of communication) and the computer (the sender and receiver of communications).

What's in a NIC?

A typical NIC, as its name suggests, is an add-in card configured to fit your computer. The role of a NIC in your PC is to work both sides of the network connection:

✔ The NIC's capability to plug in to the computer's bus lets the NIC talk to the central processing unit (CPU) and lets the CPU talk to it. This capability makes the connection between the computer and the NIC possible.

✔ The NIC's accommodation for a network connection to the network typically involves an external connector that lets you hook up the network medium. Hooking up with a cable of some kind makes the connection between the NIC and the network possible. Some NICs come with more than one connector, so if you change your network or your mind, you don't have to throw out the old to put in the new.

✔ The NIC's ability to talk on the network is defined by the network access method you choose. NICs exist for all types of network access methods, including Ethernet, token ring, FDDI, and ATM. Unlike connectors, adapters that have combinations of two or more access methods are not available.

Figure 5-1 shows a schematic diagram of a typical NIC and illustrates its bus connector and the media interface.

Bus connectors vary according to the kind of bus on your computer, and media connectors vary according to the networking access method and cabling type you use. Learning to recognize what networking access method and cabling type you have helps you to select the right kind of NIC for your machine and also helps you to get the NIC properly connected to your network.

Not all NICs come in the form of cards that plug inside your computer, though. For laptops, portables, and other machines that may not be built to accommodate standard internal interfaces, you may have to attach an external network interface instead. Even though these interfaces aren't cards, they do the same job as other, more conventional NICs and are often called NICs as well. In addition to such parallel port interfaces, PC Card adapters are available that you can install or uninstall at your networking whim.

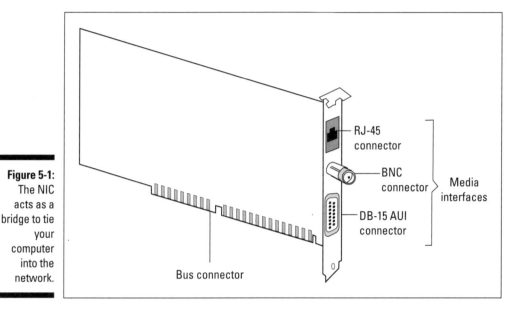

Figure 5-1:
The NIC acts as a bridge to tie your computer into the network.

RJ-45 connector

BNC connector

DB-15 AUI connector

Media interfaces

Bus connector

Figure 5-2 shows an external interface, called a *parallel-port connector,* that can attach to a computer's parallel port.

PC Card adapters (formerly called PCMCIA adapters) look something like fat credit cards — they slide in and out of your computer's pocketbook (PC Card slot, really) with ease.

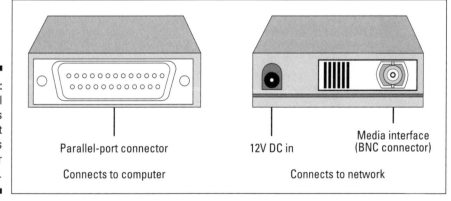

Figure 5-2:
An external interface is a NIC that attaches outside your computer.

Parallel-port connector

Connects to computer

12V DC in

Media interface (BNC connector)

Connects to network

Which Bus Do You Have to Catch — ISA, EISA, VLB, or Micro Channel?

If your computer is a PC, you have to match its NIC to the type of internal bus connections your machine needs. If your computer is not a PC, the only decision you have to make is whether to go with a NIC or an external interface. Either way, you don't have to grapple with the subtleties that would-be networked PCs have to master. If that's the case, feel free to skip the rest of this section.

The business end of a NIC that plugs in to the computer is called an *edge connector.* By looking at your computer's bus, you should recognize which kind of interfaces the bus can handle. Likewise, by looking at a NIC, you should be able to tell for which kind of bus the NIC was designed.

ISA and EISA are related

The term ISA, which stands for Industry Standard Architecture, describes the bus that most PCs have used since IBM introduced the PC AT (Advanced Technology) in 1985. ISA is still the most common PC bus, and it most likely is the one you use to plug in to your NIC.

EISA, or Extended ISA, is an attempt to extend the capabilities of the ISA bus. EISA is *backward-compatible* with ISA, which means that you can plug in ISA cards to an EISA bus and they work just fine. EISA cards use a different edge connector from ISA cards, even though they both can plug in to an EISA slot. Most EISA adapters give you higher performance than ISA adapters, but EISA never really caught on in the marketplace. If your server is an EISA machine, by all means buy EISA NICs to use with it; newer machines will probably feature PCI (Peripheral Component Interconnect) or VLB (VESA Local Bus, sometimes called Video Local Bus). If PCI or VLB is present on your server, buy interfaces for those bus types instead. (If both are available, pick PCI — its bandwidth is twice that of VLB's.)

The difference between ISA and EISA is based on the two changes made to ISA to extend its capabilities that created EISA:

✔ ISA uses a 16-bit *data path,* and EISA uses a 32-bit data path. To put it in English, an ISA interface can move only half as much data across the bus between the NIC and the CPU as an EISA interface.

Widening the bus has two benefits: It enables an EISA interface to move more data in the same amount of time and does a better job of matching modern CPUs, which are built for 32-bit data paths themselves. The PC AT CPU is an Intel 80286, which uses a 16-bit data path; if you have an 80386 or higher-numbered processor, it uses a 32-bit data path.

✔ EISA is capable of running much faster than ISA. ISA's bus speed is based around the clock speed of the original IBM PC AT, which was introduced at 4.77 MHz and later upped to 8 MHz. EISA, on the other hand, can run as fast as 33 MHz. EISA, therefore, not only moves more data than ISA but also moves it from four to seven times faster.

Under these circumstances, why would anyone use ISA? The answer is that speed and performance always have a price. In this case, EISA computers used to cost at least $200 more than their ISA cousins, and corresponding EISA interfaces cost around twice as much as their ISA counterparts. (It's easy, for example, to find $80 ISA Ethernet NICs, but $200 is about as low as you can go for an EISA Ethernet equivalent, if you can find one.) Since EISA's pretty much passé by now, replaced by faster and cheaper technologies, you probably can't buy an EISA computer, except on the used-equipment market.

Catch the local: VLB and PCI

In the past five years, two new buses, called *local bus technologies,* have joined the fleet. They rely on the addition of a special-purpose, high-speed bus to link a PC's CPU to a limited set of peripherals such as display cards (to drive your video display), disk controllers (to handle your disk drives), and network interface cards (to connect you to the network). Local bus technologies have been specifically built to increase speed (VLB is a 32-bit bus, and PCI is a 64-bit one) and to make the connection of vital computer subsystems as fast and efficient as possible.

VESA Local Bus (VLB) is the older of these two technologies. VLB is the brainchild of the Video Electronics Standards Association, in San Jose, California. Along with eight leading video board manufacturers, NEC Home Electronics founded VESA in 1988. The association's main goal was to standardize technical issues surrounding 800 x 600 resolution video displays, commonly known as Super VGA. VESA also issued a standard called *local bus,* a new, high-speed bus for the PC. Local bus is designed to move data between the CPU and peripherals a lot faster than the conventional AT bus, where up to three VLB slots can be placed on a computer's motherboard.

VLB runs at speeds up to 66 MHz; it is a 32-bit bus, with 64-bit capability for Pentium machines. A VLB slot uses one 32-bit Micro Channel slot placed adjacent to standard ISA, EISA, or Micro Channel slots, allowing vendors to design boards that use only the local bus or both buses at the same time. VLB also supports bus mastering, which relieves the CPU of the burden of running the bus. (The CPU is thus free to do other things, thereby speeding overall system performance.)

Music for Computers?

Micro Channel used to have the acronym MCA, until the Music Corporation of America (MCA) decided it didn't like IBM getting in the music industry. Since when do NetWare and music have anything to do with each other, except when things are really humming along? This is almost as silly as Steve Jobs having to get a dispensation from the Beatles for the name of his company.

Intel developed PCI to provide a high-speed data path between the CPU and up to ten peripherals (video, disk, network, and so on) — as opposed to only three peripherals for VLB. Like other expansion buses, the PCI bus coexists in the PC with ISA or EISA. With PCI, ISA and EISA boards still plug into an ISA or EISA slot, while high-speed PCI controllers plug into a PCI slot. The PCI bus runs up to 100 MHz and supports 32-bit and 64-bit data paths and bus mastering. Because of Intel's considerable clout, more vendors support PCI adapters than any other kind of expansion bus (including VLB and EISA). Because of this vendor support, we recommend that you consider adding PCI NICs to your servers and power users' machines, if PCI is a viable option.

Micro Channel: A better idea?

The Micro Channel Architecture, like ISA, is also the brainchild of IBM. Like the other expansion buses we discuss, Micro Channel is a 32-bit bus, with most of the same advantages: higher speed and a broader data path. If you have a MicroChannel computer, though, you have no choice but to buy Micro Channel NICs to go with it (it's a replacement bus, not an expansion bus). Micro Channel's main advantage is that, in most cases, you can plug in your NIC and Micro Channel handles its own configuration from there. You pay for this privilege, however.

What's the right bus for you?

We think that high-speed buses like EISA, PCI, and VLB are great, but they're overkill for many workstations (if you use a Micro Channel machine, you won't have many choices in the matter). Unless you're sure that the machine that needs a NIC will be a high-volume network consumer, don't bother installing an EISA, VLB, or PCI NIC, even if your machine can accommodate one. What constitutes high-volume? The following elements justify the use of such NICs:

Closing the gate after the livestock have run off

Around 1986, IBM realized that it had lost control over the PC marketplace by letting the whole world get access to the specifications for PCs and their buses, disk drives, and so on. This loss of control was a terrific boon to consumers because it resulted in rock-bottom prices. IBM's PC division felt that it was losing out, however, because it couldn't compete against all the garage-based, fly-by-night outfits that were walking off with the bulk of the PC business — and the bulk of people's money, too.

In an effort to regain control of the leading edge of the PC market, IBM introduced its Personal System 2 (PS/2) line. The company touted PS/2 as the next generation of PC computing and sold it heavily through its internal sales force and dealers. Even though PS/2s cost a bunch more than conventional PCs, IBM did well with this product family, especially within corporate America, which had long been used to doing business with IBM.

One significant advantage of the PS/2 family of computers was its inclusion of a hot, new 32-bit bus called the Micro Channel Architecture.

Unlike EISA, Micro Channel was completely different in size and connector design from the old PC AT bus. IBM's idea was that consumers should throw away their old PCs and buy these great new ones. And, while they were at it, they should throw away all their old interfaces and buy new ones for them, too!

Because IBM didn't invite vendors to participate in the PS/2 bonanza the way it did with the original PC family, vendors didn't come out in droves to support this new architecture. To this day, the PS/2 family and Micro Channel are not nearly as popular, or as widely supported, as ISA, VLB, PCI, and EISA. PS/2 and Micro Channel are also still at least 40 percent more expensive than their counterparts. Maybe the price is one reason that IBM is hurtin' these days! Be that as it may, however, Micro Channel is enjoying a bit of a comeback because a beefed-up version is used in IBM's RISC/6000 minicomputers, which are reasonably popular within the (huge) IBM customer base. So don't count Micro Channel all the way out.

- ✔ A network server
- ✔ A high-speed access method (faster than fast token ring, that is)
- ✔ A power user who runs CAD, 3D design, or other software that puts a heavy load on the network (big documents usually mean heavy traffic)
- ✔ A dead certainty that your machine will be the focus of lots of network traffic (using high-volume database applications or a computer-aided design package, for example)

If you're dealing with these high-volume factors, spending the extra money pays off in improved performance (or acceptable performance, anyway). If not, save your money.

Avoid Trouble: Get Off to a Good Start

Before you start mucking around inside your PC, you should do a few things to get ready. Because messing with the system is one of the few things that can kill a computer deader than a doornail, taking some preventive steps can keep you out of trouble. These preventive steps may also get you back to work more quickly.

Please recognize, too, that you may end up back where you started. Your NIC installation maneuvers can turn out in one of two ways. If you're lucky, your brand-spanking-new NIC will be safely ensconced in your PC, doing exactly what it's supposed to be doing. If you're not lucky, your NIC will be back in its original packaging, ready to be replaced with what you now know that you *really* need. If at first you don't succeed, you have no choice but to try again.

Unplugged: It's not just an MTV thing

Electricity is your friend, but you don't conduct it very well on a personal level. *Never, never, never* open a machine that's plugged in to a wall socket. This mistake can get you fried, or it can create all sorts of creative opportunities for you to fry your equipment. Neither alternative is a good one, so remember to unplug your computer before you open the case. The easiest way is to start by detaching the power cord from the case. While you're at it, unplugging all the other cables from the back of the computer is also a good idea.

Getting back to where you began

Assuming that nothing gets fried, what's the worst thing that can possibly happen if you install something new? You can turn on the computer — or try to — to a big, resounding nothing. Zero — zip — nada! If the situation is really bad, you may have to send the computer to the shop so that a real professional can fix it. Most commonly, if you take out the new stuff (and reverse any software changes you may have made to go along with it), you will be back where you started.

Software changes, you ask? These changes lead to a crucial preemptive step you should always take before getting down to your hardware: *Always* back up any system that you will be fiddling with, before you start fiddling. Backing up has two vital benefits. First, assuming that the worst case happens — a computer is DOA — you can install your backup on another, similarly configured machine and keep working until your original machine returns. Second, if the new installation doesn't work for any reason, you can use the backup to quickly restore the machine to the pristine state it enjoyed before you mucked with it. Backups take time, and the temptation is always to ignore this safety tip, but ignore it *at your peril.*

Figure out what you're dealing with

PCs can seem like minefields, or at least like strange, exotic beasts, when you are adding yet another interface to an already jam-packed machine. If you don't have an inventory of what's already installed and configuration information to go along with it, take the time to figure out what's in the PC before you start trying to change things. This step makes quick work of doing an installation and might head off configuration confusion before it has a chance to happen.

You can use any good diagnostic software program to scope out what's installed on your computer. For PCs running DOS or Windows, Symantec's Norton Utilities includes a great system diagnostics program. Quarterdeck's QEMM includes a terrific utility called Manifest, and numerous other shareware and freeware diagnostic programs are available. Likewise, Macintosh and UNIX users can find similar software, either commercial or shareware/freeware, for the same purpose. If you run such utilities, they can tell you useful things about your computer's configuration that can steer you toward the clear spots you need to install a NIC.

Use a tool, or your own research, to build a list of what's installed and the settings for each item. This step documents what's on the system and keeps you from trying to occupy settings that are already taken.

Be ready for trouble

Although we can't guarantee that things will get weird when you install a NIC, we do know that they sometimes do. This statement is especially true for machines that already have lots of adapters and stuff in them. One potential problem is a conflict in which two interfaces such as the network adapter and the video adapter can occupy only overlapping settings — which means that one of them has to go (which also rarely happens). Another problem may be not knowing what changes you need to make in order to get things to fit together.

Therefore, gather all the manuals about your system that you can find. Hunt down the manuals for your PC and for every interface installed in it. And, for good luck — or at least, good use — try to find a general-purpose PC book for all-around reference. We recommend *PCs For Dummies,* 4th Edition, by Dan Gookin (IDG Books Worldwide, Inc.) or *PC Secrets,* 2nd Edition, by Caroline M. Halliday (IDG Books Worldwide, Inc.).

Give yourself room to maneuver

Clear off some space for yourself to work even if this step takes more effort and extra time. Be sure to bring some small paper cups, clean ashtrays, or other small containers to put screws and connectors in. If you're really going to take things apart, label what goes where. This system eliminates guesswork and lets you get back to work rather than tear out your hair. Also, bring the right tools for the job. Most computer stores will happily sell you general purpose tool kits for $50 to $100 that contain everything you need when you install stuff in a computer. The tool kits come in handy little zip-up cases and should go with you whenever you open up a computer and fiddle with its innards.

Also before you do anything else, get your feet firmly on the ground. As you walk across carpets, you build up static electricity. That means you should never carry a network interface card except in the anti-static material that it came in, and before you ever put your hands in a machine or handle any computer hardware, ground yourself. Anti-static wristbands and heel-caps are available, but you can do nearly as well to dissipate static build-up by touching the chassis of the computer before doing anything else.

Know the lay of your LAN

If you are installing a NIC, you eventually want to connect it to your network. Part of the configuration drill is to know the names and addresses of the servers, users, and networks around you. Make sure that you read the installation requirements before you get started, and then run down any of the network-related details you will have to supply during the installation process. This step heads off the need to stop halfway through an installation procedure to research the information and lets you knock off the installation in one fell swoop.

All in all, investing in the ounce of prevention helps to avoid expensive, time-consuming chores.

It's All in the Cards: Beware the Golden Fingers

When you read the manuals that offshore manufacturers provide, you have unparalleled opportunities to encounter bizarre brands of written English. Although the technically correct term for the part of a NIC that plugs in to a bus slot is an *edge connector,* we like a Taiwanese company's description of that part: *golden fingers.* Even though golden fingers are really brass-colored and not truly golden, they're what plug into the bus and make NICs work.

Even if the fingers are brass and not gold, when you plug NIC into an empty bus slot, make sure that the NIC is firmly seated and fully connected. In other words, make sure that you hide the edge connector from view and that you correctly position the network interface on the side of the card in the cutout on the back of your PC case.

Be careful when you install the edge connector into the computer's bus socket. Don't jam it in, and rock it carefully if you must. Force can peel the golden fingers away from the edge of the adapter, and then nothing works, even though it should.

Normally, you also should screw the metal tab into place, by using the screw that attached the placeholder before you removed it to insert your NIC. To help you visualize what we're talking about, Figure 5-3 shows the placeholder with the screw hole.

Figure 5-3:
Placeholders
close off
empty slots,
keeping dust
and dirt out
of your
PC case.

You should remember two things about placeholders:

✔ Be careful when you're messing with the little screw that holds placeholders in place. Dropping one can lead to all kinds of crazy contortions to recover them. If you drop one, pick up the PC case and rock it gently back and forth — you can usually get the screw to show itself more readily that way. And, don't ever (repeat, *ever*) use a magnetized screwdriver to pick up the screw you've dropped, or your computer's data may become the screw-ee, and everyone knows what that makes you.

✔ Be sure to put the placeholder in a toolbox or spare-parts drawer so that you can find it again. If you ever have to remove the NIC (or any other interface), you want to be able to close the case again. Some cases use odd-size placeholders, so finding the right placeholder when you need it beats the pants off trying to scare one up. We put all our placeholders and extra screws in a coffee cup at work, so we always know where to find them.

Dealing with Doublespeak: How to Read a Manual

The first rule of installing NICs is to skip ahead in the installation manual until you find a picture of the NIC, with all the important stuff highlighted. With a well thought out manual, this step can save you the bother of reading the whole thing. Even for the more usual manuals — which often are boring and hard to follow — jumping ahead to the picture can help you to figure out what you really need to know more quickly than starting at the beginning does. Our suggestion: Go for the pictures!

The second rule in installing NICs is to understand exactly what you must do to make the installation work. If you have peered at the pictures and have puzzled through the text and still aren't sure what to do, call the NIC vendor's technical support hotline and ask someone to explain NIC installation to you. This step lets you check up on your drivers at the same time and can shortcut the learning process. The wonderful folks at tech support deal with confused people every day, and they can steer you clear of the pitfalls better than anyone else can. The help is worth a long-distance call.

NIC Configuration

Configuring an NIC requires making all the right hardware selections and choosing the right software settings, to make sure that the NIC can work in your PC. You must therefore deal with a number of different kinds of settings. You also must make sure that the right information gets supplied to the software drivers that make your NIC and PC work together in perfect harmony. Become familiar with all seven subsections in this section to understand what's involved in configuring an NIC.

NICcus interruptus: Setting interrupts

Because activity on the network can happen at any time, a NIC must be capable of signaling the CPU whenever a message arrives so that incoming data can be received. Likewise, the CPU has to talk to the NIC to tell it when to handle outgoing traffic.

The most common method for handling this type of activity is to reserve an *interrupt request line* for the NIC's exclusive use. PCs offer 16 interrupt request addresses, called IRQs, that are numbered 0 through 15. Interfaces use IRQs to signal activity. Each NIC requires that one of a particular restricted range of IRQs be selected for its use, and no two interfaces are typically allowed to share a common IRQ.

We hope that this discussion helps to explain why mapping out your existing configuration is a good idea. Your mission here, like it or not, is to find an unused IRQ that the NIC can accept. If none is available, you must reconfigure other stuff to free up an IRQ that the NIC can use (which is why we told you to get out *all* the manuals).

Setting IRQs generally requires setting *DIP switches* (DIP stands for *dual in*-line *package*) or moving *jumpers* to select the right IRQ number for the NIC to use. Some PCs may assist in the configuration process or use software-based configuration tools, especially if you work with EISA, Micro Channel, or Plug and Play systems.

DIPsy doodles

Figure 5-4 shows a typical DIP switch. Most DIP switches, which are really banks of individual switches, show you which way is On and which way is Off. If you can't tell and the manual doesn't help, don't delay — call the tech support department right away. The folks there know the answer and can save you unneeded guessing and experimentation.

Jumper jeepers!

Jumper blocks consist of two rows of adjacent pins that are connected with itty-bitty connectors called *jumpers* (see Figure 5-5). The pins typically are numbered, and sliding the jumper over both pins turns that jumper on. To turn off a

Figure 5-4:
DIP switches and jumper blocks often control a NIC's settings (more modern hardware handles all this information in software through the driver).

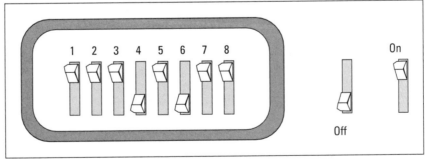

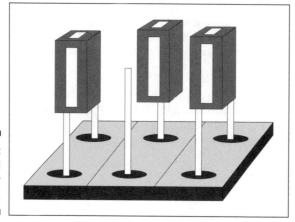

Figure 5-5:
A typical
jumper
block.

numbered pin set, remove the jumper from both pins and slide it over one of the two pins so that it sticks out from the pin block. Typically, when you set IRQs with jumpers, you see one jumper inserted for an entire block of pins, and the pin set you jump with it selects your chosen IRQ. In that case, make sure that the jumper covers both pins in the set. Otherwise, you have nothing selected, and the NIC probably won't work.

Doing defaults

Before you worry about DIP switches or jumpers, first check the manual to find out where the factory set the IRQ. If this particular IRQ, called the *default setting,* is not in use, you can stick with the default and not do anything. We like it when this happens.

The right port in a storm: The I/O port address

Each card in a system has its own unique I/O port address, where certain addresses are reserved for some interfaces, especially video cards. NICs aren't quite that picky and usually can get an I/O port address assigned from a reserved range of addresses. A DIP switch most likely handles this particular address on most NICs because a broad range of potential settings usually is available.

An I/O port gets set up to let the computer read from or write to memory that belongs to an interface. When an interrupt gets signaled, it tells the computer to read from the I/O port address, indicating incoming data. When the computer wants to send data, it signals the NIC to get ready to receive and writes to that address. The information written to or read from that address gets copied across the bus between the NIC and the computer's brain, or CPU.

Possible I/O port addresses for NICs commonly range from 2E0h to 380h. The most usual default port I/O address is 300h; 300h is a typical default for lots of interfaces, though, so you still have to do your configuration homework before you let your NIC use that address.

Computer addresses are often computed in base 16, also called *hexadecimal*. The lowercase *h* after the number tells you that it's hexadecimal, as shown in the following example:

```
2E0h = 2*16@sup#2 + 14*16 + 0 = 736 (decimal)
```

In hexadecimal, letters *A* through *F* stand for 10 through 15 because 10 hex equals 16 decimal, and six more digits are needed to get from 9 to 10 in hex.

Getting direct with memory: Setting the DMA

Some NICs use a technique called *direct memory access* (*DMA*) for moving information between the NIC and the CPU. This technique allows for fast copying of information from the computer's memory to the NIC, and vice versa. As equipment and computers have gotten faster, this technique is less necessary.

DMA works by matching up two areas of memory, one on the computer and the other on the NIC. Writing to the memory area on the computer automatically causes that data to get copied to the NIC, and vice versa. *Setting a DMA address* means to find an unoccupied DMA memory block to assign to your NIC. Again, your earlier research on what addresses are taken helps you to avoid conflicts. Just pick an unoccupied block, make the right NIC settings, and you're on your way. If conflict exists, you must figure out a way to resolve it. Remember to check your defaults here, too.

Running the NIC address bases: The MemBase setting

NICs contain their own RAM to provide working space for information coming on and off the network. This RAM is called *buffer space* because it provides room to store incoming and outgoing data. You must assign this buffer space an equivalent region in the PC's memory. For DOS and Windows, this buffer space usually is located in the high memory area between 640K and 1024K, which is reserved for such uses.

Just like the IRQs and DMA, this setting must be unique. You must watch out for potential address conflicts and steer around them. You usually use jumpers to set the *base memory address* (also known as MemBase) for your NIC. Common settings for network cards include C000h, D000h, and D800h.

In the Driver's Seat: Loading NIC Drivers

After the hardware is in place, you must deal with the software. If you have purchased your NIC recently — and it hasn't been sitting on a distributor's shelf somewhere since the last Ice Age — the drivers on the disk that comes with the NIC may actually be worth something.

If you're lucky, you can load the disk, run an installation program, maybe supply a few values here and there, and then you are ready to roll. If you're not lucky — and we rank this up there with the probability of winning small in the lottery — you must chase down new drivers and use them instead.

Our advice: Win or lose, always check to determine the latest and greatest drivers for your NICs before you begin the installation process. Ask for help in this order:

1. From the outfit that sold you the card.

2. From the vendor that built the card.

3. On CompuServe, GO MSFF and use either NDIS or ODI as keywords in the File Finder, or use the Search facility with the same keywords on the Novell Web site. For more information about CompuServe and the Internet — all good sources for LAN drivers — see Appendix C.

If the NIC vendor doesn't automate driver installation for you, you may have to manually edit configuration files, such as AUTOEXEC.BAT and CONFIG.SYS. If you're running Windows 3.*x*, you may also have to edit SYSTEM.INI to insert the correct .DRV (driver) reference. (If you're running Windows 95 or Windows NT, either system does a pretty good job of identifying cards and helping you install the right drivers, as long as the cards are supported for the particular operating system in question.) Again, when in doubt, get some help.

Cabling Up to the NIC

Okay, you installed the software and plugged in the hardware. All you have left to do is to cable the NIC to the network. For modular technologies such as twisted-pair Ethernet or token ring, you must plug in the modular connector on the LAN cable to the receptacle on the NIC. For other technologies, you hook up a T-connector or a transceiver cable from the LAN to your NIC. Whichever option you must use, make sure that your connection is tight and well seated and that the NIC has stayed put in its slot. Now you're ready to fire up the NIC and see what happens.

Looking for Trouble in All the Right Places

You've worked your way through the maze of potentially conflicting addresses, and you have set your NIC to steer clear of all the shoals. You installed the software, and everything should work, right? Well, sometimes it does (hooray!) and sometimes it doesn't (boo, hiss!). When things don't work, you find out in one of three ways:

1. **Your PC doesn't boot.** This problem is pretty obvious. If it happens, you'll know; when it does, you have to start undoing what you have just done. First, restore the system to the way it was before you started fiddling (you *do* have a backup, right?). If this step works, you know that the NIC is the problem. Time to get some help from one of the recommended sources. If the PC still doesn't work when you're back at square one, you have bigger problems. Time to call in a service tech.

2. **Your PC boots, but it doesn't load the drivers.** The most common causes of failure to load drivers are shown in this list:

   • **Loose connections.** Check to make sure that the wire is tight and properly seated on the NIC, and make sure that the wire is plugged in to something on the other end.

   • **Installation problems.** Make sure that the drivers are in the right directory and that the directory is referenced directly in your bootup files or defined in your DOS PATH. If the computer can't see the drivers, it can't use 'em.

   • **Conflict.** Maybe you missed something and have introduced a configuration conflict. Try all your other stuff; if something else also has quit working, it's a dead giveaway that you have a configuration conflict. Time to go back to square one and recheck all system settings. Something, somewhere, is fishy, so be extra careful.

   The good news here is that the problem is most likely a loose connection or a configuration boo-boo. If you don't have one of those two problems, you'll have to get serious and figure out what *is* causing the problem.

3. **You try to use the network and it doesn't respond.** This more subtle variant of the preceding problem usually has one or more of the same causes. An extra element of mystery exists here, though, because the problem can be a conflict with another application you have installed and

not a driver problem. Only by working through a careful process of elimination can you find your way to an answer. All we can say is good luck, think hard, and take lots of breaks. You *will* figure it out. If you have to, ask for help.

Ready to Rock n Roll?

After you have made it over the hump and can talk to the network, you're ready to get to work. Or, if you're learning the ropes as a network administrator, you have the pleasure of letting someone else get to work. Either way, you have the satisfaction of pushing the networking wave another workstation ahead.

Chapter 6
Any Good LAN Has a Pedigree

*A*fter you begin working around networks on a regular basis, you get the hang of how things work in general. By now, you've been exposed to most of the basic principles of networking, and you probably have a pretty good idea about how things are supposed to work, if not how they *do* work.

As you quickly realize, however, when you spend time around networks, what you *think* about them isn't nearly as important as what you *know* about them. You may have to wrestle with networks regularly because that's your job, or you may mess with networks so that you can get your real job done. Either way, a network map is the best way to help you keep track of what's out there on the network and to let you know where you may find things if you need to.

What's on a Network Map? Why Should You Bother?

What we recommend that you do requires more than just a map, which might simply indicate where items are located. A map that clearly marks where each item is situated is just a handy, visual way of organizing the following information:

✔ A list of all the computers on your network, with supporting documentation

✔ A list of all the networking equipment — including such things as routers, hubs, and servers — with supporting documentation

It's a map, and an inventory, and a database, and a . . .

By now, the idea should be clear: A network map is a way to track and organize detailed information about what's on your network. A network map is a combination inventory, configuration database, and catch-all for other useful bits of trivia. It should also tell you where your network cables are and, if it's a really good map, how long each cable section is and where to find cable ends. In short, this annotated map contains just about everything you should know about your network and just about everything anyone else needs to know about your network if anything ever happened to you.

✔ A list of all the printers and other specialized equipment on the network, with supporting documentation

✔ Lines to indicate where network cable runs and where junctions, taps, and other items are located

Formalizing Your Network Map

Because a network map is such an important and powerful tool, we think that you should go out and make one right away. Be prepared to spend some time at it because the map incorporates a great deal of information that's probably scattered all over the place.

Building this kind of map is a worthwhile investment, though, and pays for itself many times over if you take this assignment seriously. At worst, you probably will learn more than you ever want to know about your network; at best, you will get acquainted with your network and may even find some things that can benefit from some time and attention.

Where should you start?

If you obtain a set of architectural drawings or engineering plans for your building, you can take them to almost any architectural supply house and have copies made. The most common copying technology uses an ammonia-based reproduction system called a blueline. Large-size plans can be copied for less than $20 apiece. You can mark up copies and use them as your base map.

If you cannot locate plans, sketch out a room-by-room layout of your working area on rectangular grid paper (like an engineering pad). Mark where machines are located, with approximate locations for cable runs and so on. If a professional cabling outfit installed your cable, you probably can get a copy of its cabling plans, which should also work nicely as a master layout for your network map.

What should you record?

Anything that merits attention or costs money is worth recording on your map. You probably don't need to take it to a level of detail that includes each connector, nor is it necessary to know the exact length of every cable (approximate lengths to within a yard or so are okay). But you should indicate every major cable run, every computer, and every other piece of gear attached to the network.

You probably won't be able to write all this information directly on the map, but you should key this information to a machine or cable name and store the details on your computer in a file with the same name. Or, if you prefer a different scheme, pick one and use it religiously. Write up some brief notes that describe how your scheme works — again, the idea is that someone else can take over without necessarily being able to talk it over with you. Building a map and keying the rest of your network information to the map is the important thing.

Keeping Track: Building a Network Inventory

The information you gather to support your network map is nothing more than a detailed inventory of what's out there. Unfortunately, as you quickly realize, you have a large volume of information. One way to proceed is to build a file template (or to print hard copies of that template) that you fill out for each item. In this way, you make sure to collect consistent information. You can even enlist the aid of your coworkers to help you complete the inventory.

This list shows what your inventory should include:

For each computer on the network:

✔ The hardware configuration, including a list of all interfaces and their configuration settings, information about the RAM and drives that are installed, and the make and model of the keyboard, display, and so on.

Accounting departments typically take responsibility for keeping track of equipment, so you will want to check out your capital asset inventory (if you have one). This inventory should give you a place to get all the serial numbers and other identification for hardware on the network. If somebody doesn't already have this information, go ahead and collect it. It's valuable. If you can find out who sold you the equipment, write that down, too.

✔ The software configuration, including listings of configuration files, the operating system and version installed, and a list of programs and versions also installed on the machine.

✔ The network configuration, including the make and model of NIC and a list of driver files with names, version numbers, dates, and sizes (editing a DOS DIR or similar directory listing should do the trick nicely).

For other equipment (such as hubs, routers, and printers):

✔ Note the manufacturer, model, make, and serial number. If the equipment incorporates memory modules or disk drives, get the information about them, too. If the equipment uses software, get a rundown on it like the one you compile for computers. In fact, the computer template works well for other equipment, too.

For the cable plant, compile a listing of all the cable segments. Give each one a name or a number, and key its information to that identifier. You should record the type and make of cable, its length, and the locations of its ends and other significant connections.

✔ Make a list of all the vendors who have worked on your network, or its machines, with names and phone numbers. This list can be a source of information about what's what and a valuable resource for technical support. Over time, you will want to add the names and phone numbers of tech support individuals who prove to be knowledgeable and helpful.

This list describes a database of everything you need to know about your network. If you're database-savvy, you may even want to consider building an honest-to-gosh computer database to hold this information; if you're not, the file- or paper-based approaches already described should be fine. Whatever method you use, take that inventory and make it complete.

Keeping Up with Ch-Ch-Ch-Changes

One thing is certain about networks: They keep changing. Your map is only as good as the information that it contains, and it's only useful if the information accurately reflects what's out there in the real world.

Allocate time to stay up-to-date and make updating the map and its database a priority whenever things change. Because others may have to use the map, you must include anything you do to the network; because you also need to use the map, anything anyone else does to the network must be in there, too.

Look at the need for a current network map this way: Looking at a map is less work than walking around and looking at things. If the map is correct, you don't have to go anywhere to look things up. If it's out-of-date, you better start walking — and recording what you see.

Get Ready for the Real Thing

If you have money to spend, you can find software products that help maintain your map for you. Many *management consoles* — special purpose programs used to manage entire networks — include the capability to merge a logical, electronic map of your network that it finds for itself with a set of scanned in-site plans. Some also include electronic links to just the kind of database described earlier in this chapter. This database can accommodate the information about your network, its machines, and its software that we have recommended that you collect. Unfortunately, you still have to collect the data that goes in the database, but all the infrastructure you ever want comes predefined. Novell/Intel's LANDesk network management suite is certainly worth investigating, as is Novell's LANalyzer for Windows package.

Other alternatives for network inventory are available from third parties. These alternatives are not always network management products per se, but they cost much less — typically, from $300 to $500 per file server. We recommend looking at LAN Directory from Frye Computer Systems, BindView from BindView Technologies, or LAN Auditor from Horizons Technology. All these products offer great database support for doing network inventories. If you have a network of any size, they are well worth the investment.

Stay Current, or Get Lost

After you have made the investment in building a network map and the database that goes with it, you have to make an ongoing commitment to keep things up-to-date. After all, you don't have just a one-night stand going here — it's a real relationship, and any good relationship requires maintenance.

The moral of the story is to stay current, or you will wind up getting lost following a map that leads to where things used to be. This is today, so make sure that your map and your database reflect what's out there now. Don't just sit there — check it out!

Chapter 7

Beyond Installation: Living Off Your LAN

· ·

In This Chapter

▶ Maintenance: Paying now versus praying later

▶ Upping the ante: Upgrades, uprevs, and one-upmanship

▶ Getting help when you need it

▶ Building a routine

▶ Noticing the obvious

▶ Keeping it clean

▶ Looking beyond the network

· ·

*Y*ou may be inclined to think that all the fun has ended when you finally get your network installed and working. In truth, the fun is really just beginning. The fun will continue to grow for quite some time as more and more users become familiar with the network and as your users begin to appreciate what the network can do for them.

Getting a network up and running is a significant accomplishment and a noticeable milestone. Keeping it running is no less of a challenge, but that job doesn't seem to have the glamour — or to deliver the recognition — that making something out of nothing can confer.

Be that as it may, keeping your network running is probably one of the most important jobs you will ever do. The trick is to plan on regularly spending time on that task and to anticipate your users' needs rather than react to them. A proactive approach is always better than a reactive approach. This chapter gives you some useful tips and advice about how to get into a proactive mode with your network. More important, you get the information you need in order to stay proactive, even as things change.

Maintenance: Paying Now versus Praying Later

Look at your network from a new perspective — one of keeping up with its pieces and keeping things working — and what do you see? We can't be 100 percent sure about what you *do* see, but we can be confident about what you *should* see:

- A collection of user machines that belong to the folks who use the network
- A collection of servers and related paraphernalia that provide the services to those users
- An agglomeration of cables and possibly some hubs, routers, or other gear that helps to glue together the users and the services

Somebody uses each one of these collections some of the time. The servers and the glue, however, are collections that everybody uses all the time but that nobody — except the person or group responsible for the network — wants to acknowledge, let alone manage.

The sad truth is that when networks work properly, no one really notices them. The only time networks get the attention they deserve is when they're not working; when that happens, however, the people who receive the attention seldom appreciate it. Your job, as you may have already guessed, is to maintain that state of cheerful oblivion that is the hallmark of any well-run network.

What does it take to get them to leave you alone?

Given that you would rather get no attention than have to face the ire of your collective user base, what does it take to achieve such ignorant bliss? The one-word answer to your question is *maintenance*.

If you keep things running smoothly and shield your users from changes and other sources of discomfort, you can achieve the sought-after status of being left alone. If you don't keep things running smoothly, you will be the scourge of your peers and the envy of no one. It's not really much of a choice, but it's clear which is the lesser of the two evils.

Contented users are quiet users

Keeping your network running smoothly and efficiently keeps those pesky users out of your hair and lets you concentrate on doing your real job without lots of testy interruptions. What are the secrets, you may ask, to keeping them quiet? Here are a few worth minding:

Keep the network running at all costs

Because interruptions of network service rile users, the safest course is to make sure that the network stays up during prime working hours, no matter what contortions that requires you to make. Believe us — even if you have to jump through some amazing hoops to make this happen, the result is worth your trouble.

Schedule downtime and spread the word

Every network has to go down occasionally, even if only for a few minutes. Backing up the server can slow things down to the point where the network might as well be turned off, and most equipment or cabling changes take the network out of service altogether.

Schedule these events at least a week in advance, preferably outside the main workday hours. Let your users know so that the folks who have to be there outside normal working hours aren't unpleasantly surprised to find themselves at work without a system to use. You would be amazed at how vociferous some people can get when they find that their plans to catch up on some last-minute changes or to meet an impossible deadline have been eighty-sixed by an unavailable system.

Keep an eye out for trouble

Half the problems on networks come as no surprise to anybody — or at least, anybody who's been paying attention. If you keep yourself on the right side of that equation, you can stay ahead of the users who otherwise would be breathing down your neck. If you think that the dragons are bad, wait till the users come after you.

Educate users

Although time to hold hands with your users is always in short supply, answering a question once is still easier than having to answer it repeatedly. Whenever upgrades or additions force changes on your network, let your users know ahead of time that things are going to change and what impact these changes may have. When things do change, tell 'em again. Then give them more details about exactly what has changed and how they will have to deal with the brave new world the changes have wrought.

When changes involve upgrading software or changing applications completely, a little anticipatory training does wonders to alleviate anxiety and prepare your users to handle what's new in a more cheerful frame of mind.

Keep an eagle eye on growth needs

Nothing succeeds like success, and networks are particularly prone to this phenomenon. After your users get a taste for networks, they may begin to bang on them beyond your wildest dreams. Be ready to grow, because that's where success will lead you.

Get your report card on a regular basis

Take the time, or make the time, to check with your users regularly. Don't just ask them how you're doing or what they think of the network. Ask them what they want to be able to do or what they want to be able to do more easily. The whole idea is to provide value to your users and to make them better able to do their jobs. Sometimes giving them what they want isn't enough. Sometimes you also have to prod them to want more than they think they need.

If you can stay in touch with your users and keep them informed, you build a loyal base of advocates. If you can empower them to do their jobs better, you build a reputation for getting things done. Staying ahead is hard work, but it does have its rewards.

Upping the Ante: Upgrades, Uprevs, and One-Upmanship

Part of living with networks means dealing with a continually changing landscape. The technology keeps changing as it gets cheaper and faster. The software keeps changing as it gets more powerful and feature-laden. And users keep changing as they discover new and more innovative ways to use the services a network can bring them.

Maintaining a network means anticipating regular changes and planning to deal with them. In addition to scheduling changes, we strongly recommend scheduling regular network maintenance. Because change is inevitable, why not plan for maintenance and allocate specific times to deal with it? The worst thing that can happen is to get to your maintenance period and not have to do anything special to fill the time. If our experience is any indicator, that normally isn't a problem.

So, what if the XYZ MegaSpreadsheet comes in on Tuesday and your next scheduled maintenance isn't until the following Monday? This occurrence not only lets you free up some time to do maintenance but also provides a way to build in a cushion for change — for informing your users, figuring out whether training will be needed, and getting ready to make whatever changes are necessary.

When you add software upgrades or new releases, you may want to consider adding to that cushion and take some extra time to test new releases before inflicting them on your users. At the very least, you should keep old versions around and available on the network. If the new stuff doesn't work out, you can easily roll your users back to the previous version.

Generally, you control the pace of change and take advantage of new releases and new software in a way that best fits your schedule and your users' needs. Random change is the most difficult to tolerate. After you get your users trained, the rest should be easy.

Getting Help When You Need It

Networks are like most other systems — most of the time they just chug along in a steady state of equilibrium, shifting only with user demand. But when things change, the system gets stressed, and that's when networks are most likely to break down. If you plan to make changes, you should also plan for the possibility that those changes may cause some unforeseen side effects. That way, if things break, you are ready with Plan B.

Before you move on to Plan B, here's what you can do to avoid having to use it:

- ✔ Schedule major changes over three-day weekends. This practice can give you an extra day to get things working should you need it.

- ✔ Find out how to contact technical support before you roll up your sleeves and start changing things. If you plan to work over a three-day weekend, make sure that tech support also plans to work.

- ✔ See whether your reseller (the folks who took your money for the original product) or your vendor (the folks who built the system or software or whatever and who probably took your money for the upgrade) can arrange to have someone on tap to help in case things get weird. As journalist Hunter S. Thompson says, "When the going gets weird, the weird turn pro." Find out who the pros are at your reseller or vendor and figure out a way to get to them when you need them. Bribery is okay, as long as you can get help when you need it.

You need Plan B only if things get so messed up that you cannot get back to where you started (with no changes) by the time your users show up at work on Monday morning. For Plan B, you should arrange to beg, borrow, or steal (just kidding!) a replacement unit for your server or whatever unit is being mucked around. That way, if worse comes to worst, you can replace your hopelessly screwed-up system with a reasonable facsimile. If your users never figure it out, you can heave a big sigh of relief.

The moral of the story is, plan for disaster but hope for a miracle. If the former happens, you are ready to deal with it. If the latter occurs, you can revel in having a free weekend, just like everybody else.

Building a Routine

The key to successful network maintenance is to build a routine that everybody gets used to. You probably will wind up being on first-name terms with the janitorial staff and the rent-a-cop in the lobby, but notoriety isn't what it's cracked up to be.

By scheduling regular maintenance, you train your users and your management to expect and accommodate change. You also make it possible to control how and when things change, and you can plan to deal with problems if they occur.

The best thing about a routine is that you know when things will change and what has to be done to make that happen. The worst thing that can happen is that you get stuck in the middle, unable to go forward or backward. If you're ready for this contingency, you can fire up Plan B and keep right on going.

Maybe consistency really *is* the last refuge of the unimaginative. But because imagination is a dicey quality for a network, that's probably not such a bad thing.

Noticing the Obvious

Paying attention is a key ingredient in dealing with users. It's also a crucial element in maintenance of any kind. When the painters or the air conditioning guys or the plumbers come calling, you should keep an eye on them, especially if they're going spelunking in the ceiling where your network lives. When the electricians come around, you should make sure that they know which conduit is for electricity and which one is for network cables. You'll hate it if they get it wrong. Another worry — and the bane of many campus networks — is to watch out for the guys with the backhoe. More innocent networks have died from an errant backhoe than anyone ever wants to pay for.

Keep your eyes peeled for what's going on around you and your ears tuned in to what users are saying. If you can keep up with the latest gossip, you can often stay ahead of the well-intentioned but often malign influences that otherwise can put a hex on your network.

Keeping It Clean

When dealing with resources that everybody shares, keeping things clean is an important chore. If this concept doesn't make sense, think of the company refrigerator down in the lunch room. If someone didn't post a sign that says "Anything left in here over the weekend will get tossed on Monday morning," what kinds of science experiments would you find growing in there after a few months?

Guess what? Your network server is the electronic equivalent of the company refrigerator. Everybody uses it, but nobody wants to keep it clean. And most users, sooner or later, forget that they left the electronic equivalent of a tuna casserole sitting in there since last Christmas.

If you want to keep your network running smoothly, you're going to have to sweep away the unsanitary buildup that always develops. Fortunately, NetWare helps you: You can set up the file system on a server so that it limits the amount of disk space users get. By keeping this number on the low side, you can make your users clean up after themselves. For the truly lackadaisical, you can purge files that users haven't accessed for a number of days (you get to pick the number). Or, on NetWare 4.*x*, you can use storage migration to copy unused files from the disk drive and to a magneto-optical disk or even to tape.

From a system perspective, you should keep old versions of software around for a while after adding new ones. But when the new stuff becomes old hat — typically, after one or two months — you have to remember to ditch the old stuff. If you're truly conservative, you can let the arrival of the next new version seal the fate of the version that's one generation back from the one you're using. That way, you have only two copies of stuff around all the time.

Even though disk space keeps getting cheaper, and the *disk farms* attached to servers keep getting bigger, keeping the files pruned and shipshape is still worth your while. Besides, you have to make room for all those Windows applications.

Looking Beyond the Network

Our last maintenance tip is to consider the world beyond the network from time to time. Hey — look — we know that your network is the most absorbing thing there is, but get a life! Actually, what we really mean is that the network is usually just a piece of your business and that you should consider the impact of losing other parts of your company's systems.

What happens if the mainframe goes south permanently? What about the phone system? Or, even worse, what happens if the whole place goes up in flames and nothing remains but a charred skeleton?

Generally, this stuff falls under the heading of disaster recovery. If your company entrusts just a part of its business to the network, somebody should have a plan for recovering from its complete and utter destruction. If the network is all that your company uses, that plan becomes essential.

Many consultants can help you devise a disaster recovery plan for your network (and other key ingredients of your business environment), but all such plans boil down to a few essentials:

- ✔ Always have multiple system backups (for a more thorough discussion of backups, please see Chapter 16).

- ✔ Store at least one backup set off-site (preferably in a fireproof vault).

- ✔ Make arrangements to gain emergency access to systems similar to yours for fallback use. These arrangements are expensive, but at least you can get back to work without losing everything.

To take advantage of these services, of course, you have to build a detailed plan, and you have to go through the motions needed to put it into action.

Don't worry — this kind of thing always seems like total overkill until the unthinkable happens. When it does, you will thank your lucky stars that you planned ahead. If you decide not to build a disaster recovery plan after what you have learned here, at least it will be an informed decision.

Part II

Organizing and Managing Your NetWare Network

Nobody knows how it happened! We were running peripherals into the network about the same time Sally was braiding her corn-rows, and, well, just don't turn anything on!

In this part . . .

The marketplace has selected NetWare as the champion of the commercially available network operating systems (NOSs). Because it's not a popularity contest, there must be some good reasons why this is so. NetWare comes in multiple flavors, with different capabilities. Despite these differences, any flavor of NetWare offers more horsepower and better network access than any of its competitors. Check the accolades from the trade press: NetWare still wins more awards for its networking abilities than all its competitors combined!

Here's why: NetWare makes it possible for PCs, Macintoshes, UNIX machines, and other computers to work together and to share files, printers, and all kinds of other services. The big attraction is that NetWare works to bring business people close together and make them more productive.

This part of the book explains how to design a NetWare network and how to manage one after it's up and running. We talk about the full range of NetWare's capabilities so that you can understand what this baby can do. You begin with a road map of NetWare's many versions and implementations. Starting with the NetWare file system, you get a guided tour of NetWare's built-in services and networking abilities.

To keep things safe, sound, and secure, you explore NetWare's access controls, as you deal with your server's security capabilities, and you discover the steps that are prudent for maintaining a well-protected network. Part II also helps you investigate NetWare's print services: the in and outs of installing printers, establishing print queues, and dealing with the many kinds of output your users come to expect from their networked printers.

Chapter 8

A Road Map to NetWare

. . . .

In This Chapter

▶ Beginnings: The early versions

▶ Introducing NetWare 2.*x*

▶ Welcoming NetWare 3.*x*

▶ Climbing to NetWare 4.*x*

▶ Figuring out what you have

▶ Choosing what you really need

▶ Getting more information when you need it

. . . .

*N*etWare celebrated its twelfth birthday in February 1996. Curiously, NetWare has also been through 12 major versions in those 12 years. In this chapter, you find out just enough about ancient NetWare to know where today's products are coming from. You also get a quick overview of each new, fresh version so that you can understand what NetWare is about and so that you can tell the differences between the two currently available flavors.

In the Beginning . . .

Today, Novell is a colossus of the networking world. Its 1995 annual revenues broke the $2 billion mark. It employs more than 4,000 people worldwide, with offices in 30-plus domestic locations and another 28 locations outside the United States. During the past 12 years, Novell has built an empire from networking software.

From the ashes rises the Phoenix!

The birth of NetWare began as a part-time project for developing a disk server operating system by a bunch of graduate students at Brigham Young University, next door to Provo, in Orem, Utah. This group called itself Superset, and its members, especially Drew Major, remain a key technology asset within the company. Major surely qualifies as "the father of NetWare," if any single individual can be said to wear this mantle.

X marks the spot!

One thing you notice in this book, and particularly in this section, is that versions of NetWare get lumped together with an *x*, like this:

✔ v2.*x* is used to refer to all versions of NetWare that begin with a 2 (v2.0, v2.11, v2.12, v2.15, and v2.2).

✔ v3.*x* is used to refer to all versions of NetWare that begin with a 3 (v3.0, v3.1, v3.11, and v3.12). New versions of 3.*x* are less frequent now than they have been in the past, because Novell is concentrating its development efforts on 4.*x*. Today, NetWare 3.*x* might be considered obsolete by some

(translation: it's still supported by tech support, but no new development is underway).

✔ 4.*x* is used to refer to all versions of NetWare that begin with a 4 (4.0, 4.01, 4.02, 4.1, and 4.11). New versions of 4.*x* are also usually under development at Novell; by the time you read this, you should be able to find out whether there's a new 4.*x* in town.

Note: In an effort to save ink, Novell has dropped the *v* in front of its NetWare version numbers, beginning with NetWare 4.0. That is why we refer to v2.*x* and v3.*x*, but use 4.*x* rather than v4.*x*. Who says that product names are arbitrary and capricious, anyway?

Because NetWare's origins precede those of DOS, Superset's original effort was to build server software that could service CP/M and UNIX workstations. That six-week contract was renewed several times as the project grew in size and expanded in scope. Today Superset has been fully absorbed into Novell proper, but its members are still the second-largest Novell stockholder, collectively speaking. In any case, after 12 years, the relationship between Superset and Novell is obviously not short-term. Many people believe this group is a major force inside Novell.

ShareNet becomes NetWare/S-Net

The original version of NetWare was called ShareNet, also known as S-Net, and was based on proprietary servers built around Motorola's 68000 processors (the same family, incidentally, around which the Macintosh is built). This version of NetWare, which became known as NetWare 68 or NetWare/S, represents the first version of the product family.

Shortly after ShareNet was born, IBM introduced the DOS operating system for PCs. Ray Noorda, Novell's president and CEO until 1994, deserves credit for realizing that DOS was an important phenomenon. He encouraged attention toward this fledgling new operating system, in addition to the focus on UNIX and CP/M. By the end of 1983, up to 24 PCs could be attached to the ShareNet server by using serial RS-422 connections running at a whopping 232 Kbps.

In the following year, NetWare became a real network operating system. Support for ARCnet boards in the NetWare 68 server was added, connecting the server to a real network for the first time. This support also multiplied the speed by an order of magnitude, to 2.5 Mbps.

When IBM released its second-generation PC, the PC XT, ShareNet was renamed to NetWare/S-Net and Novell began to move the server software from its original 68000 server platform to run on this new platform. The first PC-based version of NetWare, known as NetWare/86, required a gargantuan 640K of RAM and a 10MB hard disk.

Even then, Novell supported multiple kinds of workstations. It kept up support for CP/M machines, even after adding support for DOS, and also offered S-Net NICs for some other microcomputers that today sound like sideshow attractions: the Victor 9000 and the ill-fated TI Professional.

Counting bits and bytes in computer-ese

Speed and capacity are measured in bits and bytes in the language that computer geeks like to speak (it has only a superficial resemblance to English). For the record, here's how this stuff works.

A *bit* is the most basic unit of information for a computer. It's a location in memory, on disk, or anywhere else computers can get to that's set to either 1 or 0 in value. Because 1 and 0 comprise two distinct states, this is called a *binary system*. Everything else that computers do comes from ones and zeroes (which is pretty amazing, we think).

A *byte* is eight bits of information treated as a single chunk. Most alphabetic characters can be represented by a single byte, which is why bytes are used to state the size of most computer-storage stuff, from memory to disk storage to tape cartridges, and so on.

Computer sizes, capacities, and speeds are often stated in terms of either bits or bytes. We cover others as they come along, but the speed stuff covered in the section "ShareNet becomes NetWare/S-Net" works like this:

- *Kbps,* which stands for *kilobits per second,* is a rating of volume over time, otherwise known as speed. A kilobit equals 2^{10} or 1024 bits, which is pretty close to 1,000 in base 10 (humans count in base 10, and computers count in binary, or base 2), which is why they call it a kilobit. For the record, 232 Kbps is pretty slow for network stuff.

- *Mbps* stands for *megabits per second.* One megabit is 2^{20}, or 1,048,580 bits. Because this number is pretty close to a million in base 10, it gets the prefix *mega.* When we say ARCnet runs at 2.5 Mbps, this number is significantly faster than S-Net, but it's still pretty slow by network standards.

At the time, no one knew that the PC would become the dominant desktop machine, and Novell embarked on the strategy of supporting all desktops with a sufficiently large market share to command attention, if not respect. Support for CP/M continued until 1986, when DOS emerged victorious in the battle for PC operating system supremacy. While in its NetWare/86 phase, NetWare went through three revisions — a 1.0 version and 2.0 and 2.1 versions.

Say "Hello" to Advanced NetWare

When IBM introduced its 80286-based PC AT in 1985, Novell followed suit with a new version of NetWare to exploit that powerful new platform's capabilities. This new version, which became known as Advanced NetWare, was released as v1.0 in 1985 and quickly was followed by v2.0 in 1986. Advanced NetWare ran on both PC XTs and PC ATs, but it was designed to take advantage of the AT and performed much better on that more capable platform.

Keeping up with Intel

By 1986, a NetWare trend was emerging, one in which Novell would push to develop NetWare for the most powerful Intel platform available and exploit that platform's advanced hardware and instruction set capabilities. This support also has continued to this day, with versions of NetWare available that require a minimum of an 80386-equipped PC and that can take advantage of 80486-, Pentium- or PentiumPro-specific capabilities, if they are present. (Today, we don't recommend anything less than a Pentium CPU.)

Advanced NetWare supported as many as 100 simultaneous users, a capability that was unmatched when it was introduced. The server could be configured to act solely as a server, called a *dedicated server,* or it could act as a workstation and a server, called a *nondedicated server*, to help purchasers get double-duty from one of their machines. Advanced NetWare also witnessed the introduction of read-after-write media checks, called *hot fix,* and included built-in router support for as many as four NICs in a single server. Built-in routing was required because of Advanced NetWare's support for 100 simultaneous users. Many networking technologies don't allow 100 devices to be attached to a single cable (and, therefore, to a single NIC). Advanced NetWare also added support for as much as 16MB of RAM (the maximum allowable amount on an 80286 processor) and for as much as 2 gigabytes (GB) of disk storage.

Today, using a much more powerful machine on your desktop is not unthinkable, but at the time this network's storage capabilities made for a raging monster of a PC. This level of capability began to command respect from the business community and represented Novell's first widely accepted network operating system. At the same time, Novell began to get a reputation for building reliable, high-performance software, reflecting its broader use in the marketplace.

SFT NetWare

SFT NetWare was released in 1987, as the first in a series of System Fault Tolerant (SFT) NetWare products. The idea was to stress the software's reliability and capability, helping Novell continue to expand its increasing business market share. NetWare was beginning to step into the big time, and MIS managers accustomed to built-in integrity mechanisms and reliable software systems were making it clear that NetWare had better be capable of playing.

At this point, Novell began touting its hot fix media checks at its first level of SFT capability and started talking about its second and third levels. SFT Level II includes the hot fix feature from SFT I and provides support for duplicating data on a hard disk, either by duplicating drives through a single disk controller (called *disk mirroring*) or by duplicating drives and controllers (called *disk duplexing*) for even more reliability. These two approaches, depicted in Figure 8-1, illustrate that doubling hardware expense for disk drives can greatly improve reliability.

SFT Level II also includes transaction tracking capabilities, referred to as the Transaction Tracking System (TTS). TTS lets database and file system operations be logged as they occur and can then re-create them if the server crashes. This capability virtually guarantees that only transactions in process (and not yet complete) will be lost if a system fails. In plain English, TTS made a NetWare server very reliable. That's why NetWare continues to support SFT Level II in new NetWare versions to this day.

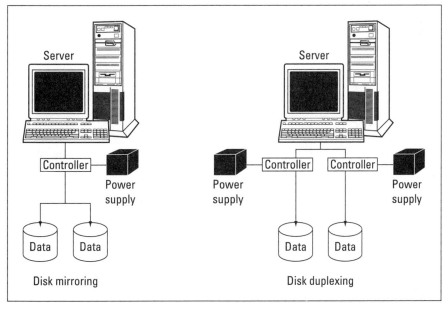

Figure 8-1:
NetWare
SFT III
supports
two
methods for
duplicating
data stored
on disk, for
improved
reliability.

At the same time it introduced SFT Level II, Novell introduced the concept of SFT Level III, in which entire servers were duplexed and appeared to the network as a single server, for the ultimate in server reliability. Unfortunately, building the technology to support this level of system fault-tolerance proved more difficult than originally thought. Though Level III initially was promised for delivery in 1989, a limited release version did not make its way into customers' hands until late 1992, and a commercial version of NetWare SFT Level III based on NetWare 4.1 shipped at the end of 1994. Figure 8-2 shows how SFT III turns two servers into one and illustrates its use of a special link between the two machines to keep them tightly synchronized. SFT III capabilities are available for NetWare 4.11 or IntranetWare as a cost-plus option.

Introducing NetWare v2.2

Today, Novell no longer sells NetWare v2.2, but it represents about 20 percent of Novell's current installed base of nearly 3 million copies of NetWare of all kinds. Because this translates into 600,000 copies still in use, we bet that at least a few of our readers are running this version today.

As far as logical progressions go, v2.2 should be considered the next NetWare version, immediately following SFT NetWare 286. NetWare v2.2 offered all the features of SFT NetWare 286 and shipped with a large collection of hardware drivers — for NICs, disk drives, tape drives, and the like — right in the box. Best of all, v2.2 was much easier to install than its immediate predecessor.

Figure 8-2:
NetWare SFT III makes two servers act as one to provide more reliable service; if the primary server fails, the secondary takes over automatically.

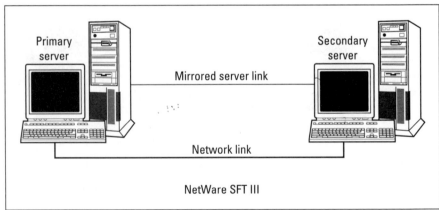

Primary server

Secondary server

Mirrored server link

Network link

NetWare SFT III

This list shows some of NetWare v2.2's distinguishing features:

- ✔ Sixteen-bit operating system

- ✔ Supported DOS, OS/2, Macintosh, and Windows workstations

- ✔ Aimed at small businesses, professional offices, and departmental workgroups

- ✔ Offered support for resource sharing, workgroup productivity applications, and simple administration

- ✔ Permitted addition of a limited number of add-on software modules, called *value-added processes* (*VAPs*) per server (most commonly used for record management and printing)

Who's using v2.2?

As late as 1992, more copies of NetWare v2.x were in use than any other kind of NetWare. Most of NetWare's users belong to its original constituency — smaller networks of 15 or fewer users who tend to control their own environments and who typically do not have access to centralized support from MIS. Somebody, therefore, gets elected to take care of most of these networks part-time, instead of managing the network as a full-time job. Today, NetWare 2.2 is no longer available as a new product, but a market still exists for used copies, especially in the Third World.

Should I consider building a new network around v2.2?

Even though first-time network buyers may be asked to consider purchasing a used copy of NetWare v2.2 (or some other 2.x version), we cannot, in good conscience, recommend it. The main reason is that NetWare v2.2 is no longer part of the Novell development cycle. Because it is a mature product, which means that v2.2 is being maintained and supported, it no longer receives the benefits of much attention or the incorporation of much new technology. Put a different way, v2.2 is not getting much time anymore from the Superset gang.

We can list only two valid reasons for purchasing a used copy of v2.2 today. This is iron-clad, inflexible, and nonnegotiable, so don't ask us for any exceptions:

- ✔ A special-purpose application that doesn't run on anything other than v2.2

- ✔ The need for a nondedicated server (you *must* be able to use the server as a workstation)

Welcoming NetWare v3.x

Because NetWare v3.0 was introduced slightly ahead of the consolidation of the v2.x family, you can argue that the introduction of a next generation of NetWare is what made the consolidation of the 16-bit versions a reality. When it shipped in the fall of 1989, NetWare v3.0 represented a major step forward from v2.x capability, but not until Novell shipped v3.11 almost 18 months later were all the promised capabilities delivered.

So what made NetWare v3.11 special? Why was it such a significant advancement over the v2.x NetWare family? NetWare v3.11 was special for many reasons, but the following ones were some of the most significant:

- ✔ A full 32-bit operating system.

- ✔ Supported add-in software modules, called *NetWare Loadable Modules (NLMs),* to extend NetWare's basic functionality (see Chapter 12 for details). Third parties offered add-in products for NetWare 3.11 — and still do for NetWare 3.12 today — that span everything from automatic uninterruptible power supply (UPS) support, to high-performance data-base management systems, such as Oracle, Sybase, and Informix.

- ✔ Built-in routing and support for IPX, TCP/IP, and a subset of SNA; add-in support is also available for AppleTalk, OSI, and others.

- ✔ Support for DOS and OS/2 file systems; built-in, add-in support available for AFP, NFS, and OSI FTAM (File Transfer, Access, and Manipulation), with a single underlying file system, enabled users on all platforms to share common files.

- ✔ Server-based backup architecture, with built-in SBACKUP.NLM and numerous third-party enhancements available.

- ✔ Enhanced server and network management, using SNMP, IBM NetView, and third-party NLMs, and support for remote management over the network.

Whereas NetWare 2.x garnered accolades and recognition for the Novell file and print services, NetWare 3.x opened the door for an entire market of network-based services and capabilities. In addition, NetWare 3.x's support for multiple protocols, multiple desktops, and built-in routing helped boost its usage. It became the integration platform of choice in businesses that had to create order from chaotic, scattered communities of some or all of these: DOS and Windows PCs, Macintoshes, UNIX machines, and IBM mainframes and look-alikes.

With NetWare 3.11, Novell delivered a networking platform that could meet the needs of most business networks and did not require its purchasers to swear allegiance to one particular platform or operating system. Because this plat-form fostered the mentality of continuing to use existing systems, instead of throwing them away or trading them in for new ones, this open-minded attitude has earned Novell its customers' appreciation and respect. Many people (including us) also believe this approach forced Microsoft to do likewise with later implementations of its network servers (most notably Windows NT Server 3. 5 and new versions).

Still using NetWare v3.x? Time to consider an upgrade!

Today, about one-third of Novell's installed base is using v3.12, including many of the Fortune 1000 companies. NetWare v3.12 was Novell's most popular platform until 1995 and has only been supplanted since then by 4.x versions of NetWare. The latest 4.x versions — NetWare 4.11 and IntranetWare — include so much additional capability and functionality that most experts (including us, if we can aspire to such a lofty designation) believe that Novell has come up with a killer upgrade for NetWare 3.x holdouts.

Should I consider building a new network around v3.12?

NetWare 4.11 and IntranetWare have been introduced just as we are writing the third edition of this book. NetWare 3.12 still represents about 25 percent of Novell's current sales levels, but this proportion of 3.x to 4.x sales is declining rapidly. Because NetWare 4.11 and IntranetWare deliver so much capability and functionality, we don't think you should build a new network around v3.x unless you need some features and add-ons that just aren't available for NetWare 4.11. We don't even recommend extending an existing v3.x network with additional v3.x servers. We think that you should buy 4.x NetWare for all new server purchases and think very seriously about upgrading all v3.x (and older) NetWare versions to NetWare 4.11, if not IntranetWare.

Climbing to NetWare 4.x

In March 1993, Novell introduced NetWare 4.0 at the InterOp trade show in Washington, D.C. The accompanying fanfare and a whiz-bang, high-tech demonstration showed a live network of 1,000 workstations being handled by a single server, which was automatically reconfigured to 1,000 servers being managed by a single workstation. This display was intended to prove to the skeptics that 4.0 indeed could handle 1,000 users on a single server and that large-scale integrated networks could be built on the 4.0 platform, which is where the reconfiguration to 1,000 servers came in. The demonstration was a raging success, and even skeptics were wowed. In early fall 1993, Novell shipped a multilingual version of 4.0, number 4.01, that was code-named FIGS, for its capability to support French, Italian, German, and Spanish, in addition to English support in the original 4.0 version.

But NetWare 4.x offers more than just increased capacity and the capability to accommodate large collections of servers. In addition to doing everything that v3.12 can do, 4.x also offers a whole slew of enhancements and new capabilities. Read on for a list of new and interesting NetWare 4.x features:

- ✔ **Any-size system support.** Shipping versions can support 5, 10, 25, 50, 100, 250, 500, and 1,000 users per server; this capability really covers systems from the smallest to the largest. With the introduction of 4.1, licenses become additive: that is, you can install two 10-user licenses on a single server to create a 20-user license, or a 5- and a 50-user license to create a 55-user license, and so on. This additive license feature makes NetWare much more affordable, especially for organizations trying to grow servers over the 50-user mark.

- ✔ **Built-in directory services.** Users can ask for things by name rather than by address, and the network appears as a logical whole rather than as a collection of individual, isolated servers. NetWare 4.11 and IntranetWare introduce significant improvements to NetWare Directory Services, along with helpful planning, migration, and configuration utilities.

- ✔ **Built-in TCP/IP support.** NetWare 4.11 ships with all the client and server software necessary to run NetWare using IP transports instead of IPX, if that's what you want to do. It also includes built-in IP routing capability. IntranetWare adds support for significant additional IP-based services, including a Web server, an FTP server, an IPX-to-IP gateway, and more. What's more, Novell has already announced that its next major revision of NetWare (scheduled for release late in 1997) will support completely native TCP/IP transports for all clients.

- ✔ **Built-in Macintosh support.** Since the introduction of 4.1, NetWare has included all the software necessary to support Macintosh clients, either over AppleTalk or IPX.

- ✔ **Improved IPX routing.** Since the introduction of 4.1, NetWare includes software for the IPX-based NetWare Link-State Protocol (NLSP) for routing, which supports larger networks and imposes less overhead and activity than the older IPX-based RIP routing protocol that it supersedes.

- ✔ **Graphical utilities.** Users and administrators can interact with the network by pointing to objects on the screen, rather than by entering arcane NetWare commands at the keyboard.

- ✔ **Common file system.** Such a file system supports shared access to native DOS, Windows NT and 95 (NTFS, LFN), Macintosh, NFS, and OS/2 files.

- ✔ **Built-in disk compression.** Typically, disk compression can almost double the storage capacity of most hard disks (available as a configuration option when adding disk drives to the server).

✔ **Foreign language support.** Users can run NetWare in Chinese, English, French, German, Italian, Japanese, Korean, Russian, and Spanish. This includes all user interface text, both for client and server utilities, and online documentation.

✔ **Enhanced network security and audit capabilities.** These features include single login to the network, background security checks, and support for standard digital signatures.

✔ **Vastly improved network monitoring and management facilities.**

✔ **Storage migration facility.** Seldom used files can be aged onto secondary or tertiary storage systems (typically read-write optical media, and tape).

✔ **Improved wide-area network capabilities.**

✔ **Improved system performance, memory allocation, and memory protection.** NetWare 4.11 also includes support for multiprocessor server hardware at no additional cost.

✔ **Automatic update/migration tools.** These tools can help automate the process of upgrading from 2.x or 3.x to 4.x.

✔ **CD-ROM based installation.** One disc means that no floppy shuffling is required in order to install 4.x, plus you get auto-sensing of server NICs, hard disk drives, and CD-ROM drives (thereby completely automating the configuration of the most standard NetWare server components).

✔ **Built-in support for CD-ROM and other optical disk formats.**

✔ **Support for application developers.** Such support helps to build imaging, multimedia, and telephony-based applications. Today all these kinds of applications are available for NetWare 4.x.

✔ **Online, electronic documentation.** A powerful search engine makes technical data much easier to find than scanning the foot-high pile of manuals that has characterized previous versions of NetWare. If you want paper manuals for NetWare 4.11 or IntranetWare, though, you have to pay extra.

This is a great deal of information to absorb, so I give you an abridged version. NetWare 4.x's most significant new capability is a directory service that makes interacting with the network much easier and more intuitive. NetWare 4.x does a great deal to enhance performance and extend storage capabilities. NetWare 4.x also comes in multiple languages and is easier to install and maintain than are previous versions.

NetWare 4.x has much more to offer than just improved large-scale behavior and better wide-area networking support. We think that just the performance improvements, doubling of disk space, and improved installation and online documentation are worth the upgrade price. But only you can decide whether these new bells and whistles are enough to get you to switch in the near future.

What's the deal with IntranetWare?

In October 1996, Novell released a new brand name for NetWare, *IntranetWare*, to indicate this version's strong support for in-house networks (called *intra*networks for that reason) based around the same industry-standard protocols and services that have made the Internet such a howling success in the past couple of years. To indicate Novell's commitment to this burgeoning technology and to entice its installed base to try this version, the company is pricing IntranetWare upgrades more cheaply than standard NetWare 4.11 upgrades. In other words, Novell is giving customers more capability and functionality for a lower cost to try to shift their installed base to what everyone — including Novell — perceives as the wave of the future: TCP/IP-based networks and services. To answer the question that names this section of our chapter: The deal is a good one and was deliberately designed that way.

Here's what the IntranetWare bundle includes, along with a brief explanation of each element:

✔ **NetWare Web Server 2.5:** A set of NetWare NLMs that enable your NetWare server to act as a Web server, this feature also includes a browser-based interface to NetWare Directory Services. Web Server 2.5 includes support for common log formats, Perl and BASIC script interpreters, and a Java runtime system and is bundled with client license for Netscape Navigator as well. Taken together, these components deliver a complete and highly functional Web services environment for NetWare.

✔ **FTP Services for NetWare:** Enables NetWare servers to provide file sharing for intranet and Internet users with FTP client capability.

Moving up to 32-bit software

From a CPU power standpoint, NetWare 4.*x* takes full advantage of the Intel 80x86 platform (NetWare v3.0 was originally known, in fact, as NetWare 386 v3.0). NetWare 4.*x* is a completely 32-bit operating system, with the capability to address much more memory than its predecessors. More important, it takes advantage of the multiprocessing capabilities of 80486, Pentium, and PentiumPro processors (and some RISC machines as well) to offer fast, elegant support for multitasking environments.

In plain English, NetWare 4.*x* can keep multiple tasks around and switch among them very quickly, providing the illusion that it can do several things at a time. This capability makes NLMs possible and gives NetWare its extensible, flexible capabilities. Because the 80486, Pentium, and PentiumPro processor are more alike than different, Novell didn't find building new versions of NetWare necessary for each new processor. Instead, NetWare 4.*x* can sense whether it's running on an 80486 or some kind of Pentium and, if it is, take advantage of the advanced features that more modern chips can offer.

✔ **NetWare MultiProtocol Router with WAN Extensions:** A software router that works over wide and local area networks. This feature provides concurrent routing of IPX, TCP/IP, and AppleTalk with optional support for SNA, NetBIOS source-route bridging, and LLC2 applications. WAN Extensions allow a NetWare server to connect to the Internet or other online services over ISDN, leased lines, frame relay, or ATM without requiring an external router (the correct interface must, however, be installed into the NetWare server itself).

✔ **IPX/IP Gateway:** Allows network users access to IP-based intranet and Internet resources without requiring TCP/IP software for each client machine. The gateway translates between NetWare's native IPX protocol and TCP/IP, using IPX to communicate with local servers and clients and IP to communicate with remote hosts. Because the gateway handles WinSock clients seamlessly, users need only launch Netscape Navigator (or any other WinSock 1.1-compatible application) at their desktops, and the gateway handles the connection from there.

✔ **Integrated IP support:** Delivered through a set of server and client modules, this support is designed to simplify network and systems management and to make accessing TCP/IP-based resources, including the Internet, easier for users. It also provides a built-in migration path to native TCP/IP support within NetWare, planned for 1997.

✔ **NetWare Application Launder:** Provides an easy way to let users access applications from within this utility, without requiring definition of icons or shortcuts for each one. Applications shown are associated with the user's login ID, so that applications are available wherever the user chooses to log in (and may be controlled by the network administrator).

IntranetWare includes a few other odds and ends, but we cover the most important aspects here. By and large, we think IntranetWare is a pretty good deal, indeed.

Who's using NetWare 4.x (and IntranetWare)?

As we're writing this book, Novell is planning to ship more than 300,000 upgrades from earlier versions of NetWare 4.x to 4.11. We bet that these folks will use 4.x. This group of Novell customers has multiple servers (often hundreds or thousands of them), multiple locations with wide area links, or special application needs that cry out for NetWare 4.x. Today, though, Novell is positioning NetWare 4.11 and IntranetWare as the best network operating system for environments of all sizes, from large organizations to small ones. Novell's fifth iteration of this 4.x product has garnered accolades from early adopters and the trade press, and 4.11 looks like it will enjoy the same level of popularity as NetWare v3.11.

Should I consider building a new network around NetWare 4.x?

If you're trying to put in place a large-scale, full-featured network, 4.11 and IntranetWare have been completely outfitted with all the options that made v3.12 so attractive. Today, more than 50 percent of the NLMs and other add-ons that work with NetWare are directory-enabled and plug right into NDS, for easy installation, configuration, and management.

Simply put, directory-enabling an application means that the application can talk to NetWare Directory Services on your behalf to find out what printers you use, what file systems you can access, what your e-mail address is, and so on. This means that directory-enabled applications are smarter and can do more things for you. Novell expects this directory-enabling feature to propel NetWare 4.11 into the forefront of networking technology, and so far, the reports coming in are quite positive. We think this capability makes NetWare 4.11 and IntranetWare your best choices for future NetWare networks.

Figuring Out What You Have

Now that you know what kinds of NetWare are available, how can you tell which kind you have (assuming that you already have some)? The answer's easy — all you have to do is look.

Let the server tell you

If you can get to your server and watch it boot up, it will tell you which version of NetWare it's running. The server shows you a message that looks something like this (the details vary depending on which version you're running):

```
Novell NetWare v4.11 (100 user) 10/02/96
```

What could be easier? Well, the VERSION command tells you exactly what version of NetWare is running, in case you miss the start-up message!

Let your workstation tell you

If you're running a DOS or Windows PC, NetWare can tell you about itself, if you know how to ask. By typing **WHOAMI** at the DOS command prompt, after you log in, or by checking the About . . . entry under the Help menu for the NetWare Client, you see the details about which version of NetWare you're connected to:

```
You are connected to Server AUS-NIX running NetWare v4.11
(250 user)
```

What does it mean?

If you're already running one of the current versions — NetWare v3.12, or NetWare 4.11 or IntranetWare — the message means that now you know you're okay. If you're running something else, the first thing to consider is whether you can get an upgrade to bring yourself into synch with Novell.

You may be wondering, if the NetWare version that you have is working, why should you bother? The two primary reasons that you want to stay caught up are:

- ✓ If anything breaks, getting technical support for a shipping version of software is easier than getting support for an outmoded version. This statement is as true for Starfish Software's SideKick as it is for NetWare.

- ✓ Eventually, you have to add a new user or some additional elements to your server. Finding drivers, shells, redirectors, or whatever for outmoded versions of software can be a form of torture so horrible that we can't even conceive of such suffering, let alone describe it.

We urge you to price out right away the cost of an upgrade to NetWare 4.11 or IntranetWare (which will probably be the better deal of the two) from whatever version you're currently using. Novell has restructured its pricing and is offering special deals on upgrades to coincide with the introduction of a new version of NetWare 4.*x*. Even if you don't actually upgrade, you should still look into the cost.

Picking What You Really Need

Let your budget and your needs dictate which version of NetWare you use. Because the newer versions typically do more and cost more, wanting more means paying more for what you get. If you can live with a less capable version, you may elect to do so, but please consider our earlier argument about what's getting the attention and where the technology is going. Also consider that Novell restructured its pricing at the end of 1996 and has made owning NetWare "more attractive than ever before," as the automotive companies like to say.

What works today may not continue to work as your needs expand and change. Planning far enough ahead to be able to anticipate changes means not getting surprised by the changes. This planning requires frequent reassessments of the trade-offs between capability and cost, and between the time spent changing things versus the time you spend explaining why your users can't do the things they want. Try to build a system that you and your users can live with for a while. Then everyone can concentrate on doing their real jobs.

Covering the Waterfront

This book is not the be-all and end-all of NetWare information. We deliberately try, in fact, to keep the book simple and lighthearted and stress concepts and overview over details. If you get in a situation in which you need details, we want to recommend some places to find them:

- ✔ Novell ships a boatload of documentation with its products. Hard-copy manuals are available for NetWare 3.12, 4.11, and IntranetWare for an additional fee, but all ship with CD-ROM based documentation. Although NetWare's documentation can sometimes be difficult to follow, it's an excellent source of hard-boiled technical information.

- ✔ NetWare is a popular computer-book category. You can find several yards of books about NetWare that range from introductory texts to detailed discussions of system management, troubleshooting, electronic mail, and much more. If you need more information, spend an afternoon plowing through these resources with some specific questions in mind.

- ✔ The people who sold you NetWare generally have some expertise with the product. Some resellers charge you for their time, and others help for free; don't overlook this resource, because it can save you time, aggravation, and money.

- ✔ Novell offers a yearly subscription to a CD-ROM database of technical support and other NetWare-related information, called the *NetWare Support Encyclopedia (NSE)*. It costs $495 for a year's subscription. Because the NSE contains regular updates of all current technical support issues and copies of all current drivers, patches, fixes, and so on, it's an invaluable source of NetWare information.

- ✔ The Novell Web site (`http://www.novell.com`), the CompuServe NetWire forums, Internet USENET newsgroups, and the America Online networking forums are great places to go for help. Because Novell people and other experts support users there equally, you can get the benefit of both the party line and outside opinions in the same place. The Web site or NetWire are two of the best places to go with questions or problems, and they are often the best source of answers. For more information about using the Internet, NetWire, and other online resources, check out Appendix C.

- ✔ Novell doesn't do much direct customer support, and none of it is free. You can call in if you have already paid for service, or you can charge support calls to a credit card through 1-800-NETWARE or 801-861-7000. When you have exhausted other means of support, try this one.

Because so much NetWare is out there, many sources of information about NetWare are available. When you need details or just need help, you can get what you need if you know where to go and what to ask.

Chapter 9

SCSI-Wuzzy Wasn't Fuzzy, Was He?

· ·

· ·

SCSI is pronounced *scuzzy,* but it doesn't live up to the way it sounds: SCSI stands for *Small Computer System Interface.* Once upon a time, SCSI was the only way to attach disk drives that were bigger than 528MB (or 1024 cylinders, whichever came first) to PCs. If you've got a NetWare server of any age — more than a year or two old — chances are the server is already using SCSI for the server drives. Today, most servers have drives of 1GB capacity or larger, and finding servers offering a total of 10GB or more of total disk space is not unusual.

SCSI lets a PC communicate with and control up to seven devices for each SCSI controller card installed. SCSI can even support multiple controllers in a single machine. We haven't seen any PCs with more than two SCSI controllers installed ourselves, but having up to seven SCSI controllers on a single computer is possible. Theoretically, this capability means a total of 49 possible SCSI devices.

SCSI is still a controller technology of choice for NetWare servers — which is why we talk about it here. SCSI is also the controller that most CD-ROM players use nowadays. And because NetWare v3.12 and all the 4.*x* flavors ship only on CD-ROM today, we think you'll find that feature a compelling reason to add a SCSI controller to your NetWare server, if it doesn't already have one.

The really neat things about SCSI are:

✔ The broad range of devices that it supports, including hard disks, optical disks, tape drives, printers, scanners, CD-ROM players, and more.

✔ Its ability to handle multiple devices without siphoning power away from the computer's main processor.

✔ Its speed. SCSI comes in several flavors: SCSI-1, SCSI-2, Fast SCSI, Wide SCSI, and SCSI-3. Each flavor has a different top speed, respectively, of 5 Mbps, 10 Mbps, and 20 Mbps for the last three. All these transfer rates are pretty fast, but the fastest is about the best a PC can do when moving data to and from an external device these days.

SCSI is a standard controlled by the American National Standards Institute (ANSI), with specifications for the various flavors available from ANSI, 1430 Broadway, New York, NY 10018; phone 212-642-4900.

To add SCSI devices to a PC, you first have to insert a SCSI *controller* (sometimes called a SCSI *adapter*) into the PC's bus and connect the devices to the card. After that, you have to install the various SCSI devices that you want the computer to talk to.

In addition, each SCSI device has to have a unique SCSI identifier, or SCSI ID, so that it can be identified and addressed on the chain of up to seven such devices that can be attached to any SCSI controller. (In fact, some top-end SCSI adapters can handle two such chains, for a total of 14 devices.) Finally, the system must have access to special pieces of software, called *drivers,* to teach the PC how to communicate with the SCSI controller and any devices that may be attached to it. This is as true for NetWare as it is for DOS, OS/2, UNIX, or any of the other operating systems that can run on today's PCs. Because NetWare is all we care about here, you get all the details in the section "Configuring NetWare for SCSI Devices" later in this chapter.

SCSI Configuration Tools and Techniques

When you are working with SCSI devices and drivers, some tools can be quite helpful. Andy Rathbone's *Multimedia & CD-ROMs For Dummies,* 2nd Edition, (IDG Books Worldwide, Inc.) provides lots of useful details on SCSI, CD-ROM installation and troubleshooting, and CD-ROM drives (especially Chapters 2 and 6). In addition, most of the adapter manufacturers include SCSI installation, management, and diagnostic software along with their hardware these days, making mastering the fuzzier aspects of SCSI technology easier than ever.

Adaptec's EZ-SCSI

Adaptec, Inc. (based in Milpitas, California), is a large manufacturer of disk controllers and sound cards. It is also the company that helped to develop the Advanced SCSI Programming Interface (ASPI) so commonly used for SCSI drivers and related software. Adaptec offers a broad range of SCSI controllers, all the way from 8-bit SCSI-1 1520-class adapters to the 3940-class Wide SCSI controllers to the state-of-the-art AHA-3985 Multi-channel PCI RAID Adapter for the Peripheral Component Interconnect (PCI) buses in today's leading-edge PCs.

RAIDers of the Lost Ark

RAID stands for Redundant Array of Inexpensive (or Independent, depending on who you ask) Disks. That's a fancy way of saying a big box of SCSI hard drives hooked together to provide a high-capacity, redundant expanse of disk space. RAID comes in different two flavors: hardware-based and software-based. RAID is also offered in levels numbered from 0 to 7.

Hardware-based RAID offers a higher degree of protection, typically including the ability to "hot-swap" a malfunctioning drive without bringing the server down. Software-based RAID is typically cheaper than hardware-based RAID and is usually limited to drive mirroring or duplexing. Mirroring is the practice of using two identical drives on the same controller with all data written to both drives simultaneously. If the primary drive fails, the mirrored drive automagically becomes the primary drive and no data is lost. As a matter of fact, we know network administrators with mirrored server hard drives who were not even aware that a server drive had failed. Duplexing is the same concept as mirroring except that the two drives are on separate controllers, thus expanding the redundancy to the controller hardware.

One benefit of having a collection of hard drives connected via a RAID controller is that read and write operations can occur simultaneously across multiple drives. Thus data can be spread across multiple drives to provide both data resilience and increased data access speed. The spreading of a string of data across multiple drives is called striping. Parity is a way of making sure that the data stored on the drive is an accurate representation of the original data.

Here is a quick overview of the different levels of RAID technology:

✔ **RAID Level 0:** Stripes data without any redundancy. Technically, RAID Level 0 is not really RAID at all, but RAID 0 is frequently mentioned as a desirable feature by RAID vendors.

✔ **RAID Level 1:** Offers data redundancy on mirrored drives.

✔ **RAID Level 2:** Superseded by Level 3.

✔ **RAID Level 3:** Stripes data in bytes across multiple drives with a separate drive dedicated to parity data.

✔ **RAID Level 4:** Stripes data in blocks across multiple drives with a separate drive dedicated to parity data.

✔ **RAID Level 5:** Stripes data in blocks across multiple drives with one set of parity information distributed across the data drives.

✔ **RAID Level 6:** Stripes data in blocks across multiple drives with two sets of the parity information distributed across the data drives.

✔ **RAID Level 7:** Stripes data across multiple drives with distributed parity information and each drive on its own SCSI controller. Level 7 is the ultimate in hardware redundancy: very expensive to implement and is currently supported by only a few high-end vendors.

✔ **Various combinations of levels such as RAID Level 0+1 and RAID Level 35 (a.k.a. Level 3+5):** Combinations of different levels offered by some vendors mostly as a marketing gimmick rather than true RAID innovation.

Whatever your server's bus type or performance requirements, chances are Adaptec's got a SCSI controller worth considering for your machine. Adaptec gets around the 1024 cylinder limitation of DOS by offering BIOS software, which replaces the portion of the PC BIOS that addresses the hard drive. Be sure to follow the Adaptec SCSI adapter instructions closely regarding this BIOS substitution. In certain circumstances this BIOS software must *not* be installed for the drives to operate correctly. Visit the Adaptec Web site (www.adaptec.com) or the Adaptec Bulletin Board System (BBS), 408-945-7727, for more information.

In addition to offering Novell-certified SCSI adapters, Adaptec also includes a handy set of utilities and software called EZ-SCSI with its products. It also licenses this software to vendors like Hornet Technologies, who include Adaptec SCSI controller chipsets (for example, AIC-6260 or AIC-6360 based SCSI controllers) in its products.

EZ-SCSI is worth getting to know because it includes a full set of drivers, several excellent SCSI diagnostic and status-checking utilities, and one of the best on-line SCSI tutorials we've ever seen anywhere. If you're using an Adaptec product, or one built around an Adaptec chipset, be sure to install and use EZ-SCSI: It's one of the few products that calls itself *easy* that actually lives up to the name. If you have a chance to use it to help with SCSI installation for DOS, we think you'll see what we mean.

If your Adaptec adapter did not ship with a copy of EZ-SCSI, you can inquire with the company about purchasing one. Contact Adaptec at 800-959-7274 from inside the United States or at 408-945-8600 from elsewhere. You can also download a copy of EZ-SCSI and the latest Adaptec SCSI drivers for NetWare from the Adaptec Web site at http://www.adaptec.com or the Adaptec BBS at 408-945-7727.

Corel SCSI Network Manager and Corel SCSI version 2

Unlike Adaptec, Corel Corporation's SCSI products are not hardware specific. Both products fill some particular niches in the quest to install SCSI-based devices and to make CD-ROMs available to network users. If you try to install a CD-ROM player on a PC and want a simplified installation utility, along with some useful documentation, a broad collection of up-to-date drivers, and a collection of CD-ROM and SCSI applications, Corel SCSI version 2 is worth considering. It offers most of the same capabilities as Adaptec's EZ-SCSI but supports more than 150 named SCSI adapters. From our viewpoint, Corel SCSI version 2 is only helpful in getting your CD-ROM player installed, so you probably want to use it on a workstation after getting through the installation process to make its $195 list price worthwhile.

After you install your CD-ROM player and decide to use it as a NetWare device, Corel SCSI Network Manager, NetWare version, comes into play. It allows end-users to access individual CD-ROMs as if they were NetWare volumes, while speeding up access and improving file-sharing and security. Network Manager requires workstations to load the MSCDEX.EXE driver (which consumes about 39K of RAM) to take advantage of its increased speed and security. You may want to experiment with built-in CD-ROM support for NetWare v3.12 or 4.1 before opting to purchase Network Manager ($595 list price). Network Manager, however, improves access to CD-ROMs over the network and lowers the load that such access imposes on the server where the CD-ROM is installed.

Other sources of inspiration, perspiration, and information

Lots of on-line information about SCSI and CD-ROM technology is available from the vendors mentioned in preceding sections and from other vendors of Novell-certified adapter, device, and driver technology as well. If you read through the certification bulletins for disk controllers, you find other names like DPT, Future Domain, BusLogic, Inc., and many more offering certified components for use in NetWare servers.

Consult one of the two standard product references for networking products — the *LAN Times Buyer's Directory* or the *LAN Magazine Annual Buyer's Guide* — for information about vendors and how to contact them. Many of them run forums on CompuServe, have Web pages, Internet e-mail addresses, or their own BBSs. Talk to them; find out what they know, and how they can help you. Above all, make sure that you use a Novell-certified SCSI adapter for your server and that you get the latest drivers for it from the manufacturer; these are the two best preconditions that we know of for a successful installation!

Configuring NetWare for SCSI Devices

Guess what? We lied about NetWare being all that you have to care about when it comes to SCSI. Because a NetWare server actually boots DOS first so that it can load and run NetWare — and associated device drivers and support files — you actually have to install a SCSI driver and CD-related software for DOS before you can switch over to NetWare.

After you configure your server for CD-ROM for DOS, you can either load the NetWare files from DOS and blow off using the CD-ROM player as a NetWare device, or you can take advantage of NetWare's CD-ROM support to make the player available as another drive to all your network users. Personally, we think the latter option is so attractive that we have kept one of our CD-ROM drives on the network so that any PC on the network can read from the CD-ROM installed in the player.

You can also buy CD-ROM drives today that attach to the new *Extended IDE* (Integrated Drive Electronics) disk controller interface. These drives work fine when your PC is running DOS and/or Windows, but you must load special NetWare drivers for such CD-ROM players to use them when NetWare is running. If you want to use an IDE CD-ROM player as a NetWare device, the system *must* load the NetWare Peripheral Architecture NLM (NWPA.NLM), its device loader partner (NWPALOAD.NLM), and the IDEATA.HAM module. Then, the system loads an IDECD.CDM driver for your chosen IDE CD-ROM player so that it can work. (CDM stands for *custom device module* not *CD-player module;* you use a file with the same extension for a SCSI-based device as well). Unless you're using an exotic IDE or SCSI controller, or a no-name CD-ROM player, NetWare 4.11 installs all this stuff for you. But first, your server has to be able to read the CD from DOS. Read on to learn what's involved.

Doing the DOS thing with CD-ROM

CD-ROM setup differs from model to model, and from brand to brand. But all setups require a SCSI driver with the necessary configuration information to be installed in the DOS CONFIG.SYS file. After the driver is loaded, you then load the Microsoft CD Extensions file (MSCDEX.EXE) to make the CD-ROM format intelligible to DOS.

To install a SCSI controller, consult the manual that comes with the adapter for configuration instructions for the adapter itself, and for any SCSI devices you plan on attaching to the controller. We, for instance, happily use one controller on our NetWare 4.1 server to support two disk drives, a CD-ROM player, and a Digital Audio Tape (DAT) tape drive for backup purposes.

Although the method for setting SCSI IDs for devices attached to a single controller varies — some do it with DIP switches, others with pinwheel switches, still others in software — every device attached to the same controller must have a different SCSI ID. The controller itself is usually set to ID 7, so make sure that each of the other devices is assigned a unique ID from 0 (zero) to 6. If you happen to screw up and assign duplicate IDs, you soon notice that some of the devices sharing the same ID may be invisible to your PC. So do the DOS thing by following these steps:

1. **Start by installing a general SCSI driver.**

   This driver will usually be some flavor of *ASPI* driver or an equivalent. ASPI stands for Advanced SCSI Programming Interface and provides a common layer of code for the drivers for SCSI devices to talk to.

2. If you use SCSI hard drives, install a device-specific driver.

The second step in getting any SCSI device to talk to your PC is to install a device-specific driver so it can talk to ASPI or its equivalent. For hard disks and DOS, this driver is usually named something like ASPI2DOS.SYS or ASPI4DOS.SYS. It's the file you include in your CONFIG.SYS file (and it actually loads both a hard disk driver and the ASPI code, all in one lump). Some adapters require a separate ASPIDISK.SYS driver to be loaded as well, so be sure to RTFM (Read The Fabulous Manual).

3. Load a specific driver for the CD-ROM player.

This player, which is named something like ASPICD.SYS, is also in your CONFIG.SYS file. In addition to supporting the drive as a DOS device, you also identify the CD player with its own ID number. If you have multiple CD-ROM drives installed, you need to reload this driver for each drive, each with its own unique ID.

4. Load the Microsoft CD-ROM extensions that let DOS read the information included on CD-ROM discs inserted into the CD-ROM player.

This file is named MSCDEX.EXE and is loaded in the AUTOEXEC.BAT file. Today, we're also starting to see some replacements for MSCDEX.EXE from other vendors — like Stac Electronics — that require less RAM and provide extra features. These should also work fine for your NetWare installation.

Doing the NetWare thing with CD-ROM

All the work you did in the prior section was just to let your PC access the CD-ROM discs that NetWare 3.12 and 4.11 ship on. This action lets your server read the files that make up NetWare and copy them onto the hard disk.

After that, you can load NetWare and blow all that old-fashioned DOS stuff away. Think of it as a form of bootstrapping that's necessary to get NetWare running, and you just may find it a little less aggravating. Those of you who've installed earlier, diskette-based versions of NetWare will appreciate the convenience of working with one or two CDs instead of 30-plus diskettes. Those of you who've never had to suffer that way should be glad not to know what you're missing!

If you want to install NetWare from a CD-ROM drive configured as a NetWare device, you'll really want to upgrade to NetWare 4.11. It's the first-ever version of NetWare to include automatic configuration and device-sensing. In English, this means NetWare 4.11 (and IntranetWare, of course) looks at your server to see what kind of disk controller(s), hard disk(s), CD-ROM player(s), and NIC(s) you have installed. The software includes drivers for all the common brands and devices. In most cases, this means NetWare configures itself, and you won't have to worry about any of the folderol that was required in earlier versions.

NETWARE

4.x

NETWARE

3.x

Dealing with CD-ROMs on NetWare 4.1 (and earlier versions)

To begin with, you have to do yourself with these older versions what 4.11 does for you. First, you have to load the NetWare disk drivers to access SCSI devices and then you can deal with the CD-ROM player.

For NetWare v3.12, the SCSI disk drivers enable NetWare to access the SCSI adapter. You also must load an additional NetWare program called CDROM.NLM to provide NetWare 3.12 the same function that MSCDEX.EXE provides for DOS — namely, the ability to access CD-ROM files as if they were part of a disk drive-based file system. After these drivers are loaded, working with the CD-ROM player is just like using any other NetWare volume.

Happily, NetWare 4.x includes built-in CD-ROM support, so you can use the same controller for disk drives and CD-ROM players without missing a beat.

Here's the step-by-step process to follow for loading NetWare files from a CD-ROM player acting as a NetWare volume:

1. **Start with a SCSI CD-ROM that's been correctly installed for DOS.**

   Note: If you're running NetWare v3.12, the CD-ROM device must be attached to its own SCSI adapter (this means you need a second SCSI adapter for your server, if you're already using SCSI drives). You cannot use a single SCSI adapter to service both a CD-ROM and one or more hard disks that you intend to use as NetWare volumes. This situation is true only during the installation process, however.

2. **Start up the CD-ROM player and begin the installation process.**

   Set your drive to the letter assigned to the CD-ROM device and change directories to

the NETWARE.312\ENGLISH or NETWARE.411\ ENGLISH directory (or whatever language you want to use). Execute the INSTALL batch file and follow its instructions.

3. **To copy the NetWare files to your \SYSTEM and \PUBLIC directories, switch to the NetWare Console screen.**

   The shortcut way to do this is to hold down the Alt key while simultaneously striking the Esc key.

4. **Use the LOAD command to load the disk driver (usually called CDNASPI or ASPICD).**

5. **Load CDROM.NLM.**

   NetWare 4.x includes built-in CD-ROM support and automates this step completely.

6. **Type MOUNT SYS: to mount the system volume for NetWare.**

7. **Mount the CD-ROM volume next.**

   If you type **CD DEVICE LIST**, the name of the CD-ROM volume appears. Use that name in the MOUNT command, for example MOUNT NETWARE_41.

8. **Switch back to the Install utility (ALT+ESC).**

   Continue the installation by copying System and Public files to their appropriate destinations (SYS:SYSTEM and SYS:PUBLIC, that is).

   That's all there is to it. Now, you can DISMOUNT the NetWare CD-ROM and load another CD. Use the CD DEVICE LIST command to get its name, and MOUNT that volume.

At this point, we recommend loading the on-line documentation CD for NetWare 4.11 and browsing through it to get acquainted with a great new search engine and a fine way to find your way around your newly-minted 4.11 server.

Curing the Pre-Installation Jitters

If you've got any doubts about your ability to complete a CD-ROM based NetWare installation, we'd like to suggest a few stress-reducing techniques to help you over this sometimes tricky hump. Take a few deep breaths, pat yourself on the back, and say to yourself, "Anyone can do it!" Then walk yourself through the checklist below, and you'll be ready to rock and roll.

✔ The most important step to a successful NetWare device installation — and this is as true for other adapters like NICs as it is for SCSI controllers — is to make sure that a driver exists for the adapter that you want to use for the version of NetWare you plan to install.

Novell Labs tests and certifies devices and drivers for vendors who are willing to pay for the privilege. Although not every vendor participates in this process, we strongly recommend that you use only certified adapters and drivers. You won't have to worry about whether the combination works with NetWare if you use only certified adapters and drivers.

Each certified device and driver combination becomes the subject of a certification bulletin that is prepared by Novell labs and includes the information you want regarding driver file names, sizes, and dates. You can obtain certification bulletins by calling one of the Novell Labs FaxBack numbers at 800-429-2776 inside the United States or 801-414-5227 anywhere else in the world. For a detailed description of the certification bulletin format, request FaxBack DOC# 10097.

✔ Make sure that you have the latest DOS drivers for the SCSI adapter to which you plan to attach the CD-ROM player. If you're not sure, you can find out by talking to the board's manufacturer and asking, or by checking on CompuServe or another on-line service and asking for help. Be sure to specify the make and model of the adapter and give the file names, sizes, and dates for the driver files that you already have. Also tell what version of DOS you're using.

✔ Try a test installation of the DOS SCSI and CD-ROM drivers before you schedule a NetWare installation. If you can't get the DOS install to work, you can't install NetWare from the CD-ROM that's not working, either. Once you've successfully read files from a CD-ROM in the drive, you can move on to the NetWare phase.

✔ If you can find a person or group of people who've already completed an installation of the NetWare version that you're planning to install, talk it through with the group and plan your moves step-by-step. By forestalling potential problems with your plans, the person or group may be able to tell you how to *actually* perform the installation and save you lots of time and worry. Contact your local reseller (the company that sold you the NetWare you want to install), local NetWare user groups (see Appendix B for more information), or folks you may know at other companies or organizations that are also using NetWare.

The old adage about prevention and cure applies to installing NetWare and CD-ROMs, so try to get ready to have your most successful installation experience ever. If you do, you probably won't be disappointed.

Chapter 10

Concrete Ideas for Laying the Foundation

· ·

In This Chapter

▶ Booting a server the proper way

▶ Logging in and out

▶ Crafting a well-designed login script

▶ Shutting down a server properly

▶ Recovering from some common network emergencies

▶ Maintaining your network

▶ Backing up your files

· ·

S ome of your questions about NetWare have to be "Why did Novell design NetWare the way they did — what difference does it make whether NetWare is a 32-bit, cooperative, multitasking operating system or not? Who cares?" The short answer to these questions is that Novell built NetWare that way because it works!

It's true that NetWare has lots of ugly details under the covers. It's also true that Novell and hundreds of thousands of NetWare users discover and report lots of bugs every year. This adds up to numerous patches and fixes and to many warts and blemishes if you look at NetWare up close and personal. Doesn't sound very appealing, does it?

Given all these shortcomings, why does NetWare make up 60-plus percent of the network operating system market? Because NetWare demonstrates that, if you build a network around NetWare, it will work. And NetWare works with many different networking topologies, networking technologies, and other kinds of software, networked or otherwise:

> ✔ NetWare servers do their jobs by using any of thousands of combinations of different manufacturers' PCs, network interface cards, printers, hard drives, coprocessors, and food processors. Oops! Ignore that last one — we slipped!

✔ NetWare client PCs can be any of thousands of PC models built since 1982.

✔ NetWare can connect you to a multitude of other systems over its network, such as DEC VAXes, IBM mainframes, and UNIX workstations.

And everything about the network *all* works in concert. What does the NetWare 32-bit, preemptive, multitasking operating system do? *It works!*

Will Bootups Walk All over You?

You cannot have a network until you have a server that's operating, and you cannot have a server that's operating until you are able to boot it up. The exact procedure for booting your NetWare server varies according to which version you install. The basic procedure for NetWare 3.*x* and 4.*x* is to simply boot the server PC with DOS and run the SERVER.EXE file from the NetWare CD-ROM or diskettes.

The end result of the bootup process is that you have a server that is up and running, until you decide to take it down (hopefully until then, anyway). The difference between booting a server and bringing a server down is that you can always choose when to bring it up, but you cannot always choose when the server comes down. Occasionally, despite your best efforts, a server comes down on its own, in what is accurately called a *crash*.

Getting the boot

The first step toward getting your server ready to boot up is to install and configure the operating system software.

The 4.11 non-shuffle

Installing NetWare 4.11 is even easier than installing its predecessors. Although NetWare 4.11 works in pretty much the same way as 3.12 (except for a detour to set up NetWare directory services), it all comes loaded on one CD-ROM, with a second for online documentation. The biggest advantage for both 3.12 and 4.11 is that no disk shuffling is involved in the installation — mostly because (other than the single floppy that contains the license information) you don't have any disks to shuffle!

During the installation process, you see numerous options to perform comprehensive analysis and testing of the server hard drive. These disk analyses aren't quite as critical as they used to be, because Novell-certified hard drives now ship with any bad sectors already marked. *Novell-certified* means that the hard drive manufacturer has submitted to and passed an extensive suite of Novell tests to ensure complete compatibility with all versions of NetWare.

In general, the process for installing NetWare 4.11 is very similar to that for installing CD-ROM based versions of 3.12, except for the detour while running INSTALL.NLM to perform initial NDS (NetWare Directory Service) setup and configuration.

The 3.12 waltz

Meet NetWare 3.12. Novell listened to all its customers' complaints about server installation and decided to fix this awkward process with NetWare 3.0 (which was quickly upgraded to 3.1, and even more quickly to version 3.11, and followed in late 1993 with the current version 3.12). NetWare 3.12 now ships on CD-ROM, so all it takes is getting past the CD-ROM installation (which Chapter 9 covers), and you're ready to go. The following list shows all the steps required to get the server up using NetWare 3.12:

1. **Insert the one and only CD labeled NETWARE 3.12.**

2. **Type** D: **(or whatever drive letter you've assigned to the CD-ROM player) and press Enter.**

3. **Run INSTALL.BAT from the \NetWare.312\ENGLISH directory.**

4. **Execute SERVER.EXE. (That is, type** SERVER.EXE **and press Enter at the server's keyboard.)**

5. **Load INSTALL.NLM (type** INSTALL **and press Enter) and follow the instructions from there.**

   (Don't forget to check out the display information that's available from the main INSTALL menu; don't forget the license diskette, either.)

Your server is now up and running. It's that easy. Granted, you cannot do much with your server yet, but this method is much quicker and simpler than ever.

NetWare 3.12 employs the concept of dynamic loading and unloading of server drivers and programs called *NetWare Loadable Modules,* or *NLMs*. The server install program is an NLM. The server console monitor program is an NLM. The network interface card driver is a type of NLM. The hard drive driver is also a kind of NLM. You get the idea.

To get your server *configured* — the process of installing all the drivers and definitions you need in order for NetWare to work with your other hardware and software — follow these steps:

1. **Type** SERVER.

2. **Load the disk driver for the type of hard drive installed in the server PC.**

3. **Load the driver for the type of NIC you have installed.**

Your server is now up and running. If you add a new NIC, you just have to change the driver you load rather than regenerate a whole new operating system program.

Prepping your hard disks for NetWare

A bad sector is an area on a hard disk that, for some reason or another, doesn't play back what's recorded. A bad sector may be the result of a manufacturing defect, damage to the drive's platters during shipment, or the wrong phase of the moon. The fact is, that area cannot be used. By marking bad sectors in the drive's manufacturing process, manufacturers now save you the time of having to find them and mark them for

yourself. It may not sound like much, but Novell's Install NLM includes a surface scan option to test server hard drives for an anomalies. The surface scan process has been known to take hours on a large hard drive to complete its analysis job. So having somebody else take care of this process for you is better, unless you have way too much time on your hands!

T-I-I-M-M-B-B-E-E-R-R: Graceful Logins and Logouts

Logins and logouts are very similar to booting up and bringing a server down. Logging in, like booting up a server, is an action required in order to gain access to the shared network resources. Logging out, like shutting down a server, is strongly recommended although not absolutely required. This section provides more information about each kind of network action.

Logins

The login process occurs when NetWare verifies that you are who you say you are — by asking for a password — and when NetWare grants you access to the shared programs and printers on your server. The server checks your login name and password against the database of network definitions. If you are in the database and you have typed the correct password, the server knows which files and printers you can access.

During the login process, a NetWare server can run a list of commands called login scripts. A login script is just like the AUTOEXEC.BAT file that your computer executes every time you boot up your PC, except that the login script executes only when you successfully log in to a NetWare server. Your AUTOEXEC.BAT batch file executes DOS and batch commands when it runs. The network login scripts can also execute DOS commands, NetWare commands, and a wide selection of batch-type commands that are available only to login scripts.

The comings and goings of NLMs

Note that NetWare's 4.11 and 3.12 device drivers and NLMs are dynamically loadable. If you want to unload a database NLM to conserve memory, you can unload the NLM without bringing the server down. If you have a server utilization NLM that you use to monitor server performance, you can run your test and then unload the NLM from memory. This single achievement from Novell did more to ease the administration of network servers than any other event in the ten-year history of PCs.

Your network probably has a system login script that runs for all users and a personal login script specific to each user. The system login script runs commands that are common to every user and executes first. Typically, the system login script maps users to directories needed by all network users, like PUBLIC and DOS. The user login script executes immediately following the system login script, but only if that user has a personal script defined. The user login script contains commands specific to that particular user, such as capturing to the nearest network printer and mapping to an application directory. Users can add commands to their own scripts or the administrator can place commands there for them.

The login script-definition process is identical for each version of NetWare, although a few minor variations exist between versions in the kind of login script commands available. Listing 10-1 shows the system login script for the 3.11 network at our company. Listing 10-2 shows the user login script for user MARY_JO. These listings have been created to help you get an idea of how flexible and useful these types of scripts can be.

Listing 10-1   A Sample System Login Script

```
REM - System login script created on 1-10-93 by ETF
REM - Script last updated on 4-22-93 by KKF
REM - Don't show login script commands during execution
MAP DISPLAY OFF
REM - Say hello to each user by name
WRITE "GOOD %GREETING_TIME, %FULL_NAME!"
REM - MAP to public directories used by all users
MAP INS S1=SYS:PUBLIC
MAP INS S2=SYS:DOS_V60
MAP INS S3=SYS:UTILS
REM - MAP to each user's "home" directory
```

(continued)

Listing 10-1 *(continued)*

```
MAP ROOT H:=SYS:USERS\HOME\%LOGIN_NAME
REM - CAPTURE a default printer for all users
CAPTURE L=2 Q=5TH_FLOOR_LASER
REM - IF statements choose mappings and captures
REM - for members of groups
IF MEMBER OF "FINANCE" THEN
   MAP INS S4=SYS:APPS\FINANCE
   CAPTURE L=3 Q=FINANCE_LASER
END
REM - COMSPEC tells your PC where to find the DOS
REM - command interpreter
COMSPEC = C:\DOS\COMMAND.COM
REM - Use the DOS SET command to set DOS environment
REM - variables
DOS SET=PROMPT $P$G
REM - The # sign runs a DOS command or .EXE file
REM - This one runs a virus-scanning program
#VIR_SCAN.EXE
REM - Use EXIT to leave the login script
EXIT
```

If you use the EXIT command in a login script file, it bypasses other logins that may follow that command later in the script. It's OK to use EXIT after the last script to be run from a login script file, but otherwise, you can end up missing something!

Listing 10-2   A Sample User Login Script

```
REM - Login script for user MARY_JO created on 1-15-96 by
       ETF
REM - This Login script was last updated on 9-13-96 by MKF
REM - PHASERS let the user know his login script is run-
       ning FIRE PHASERS 10
REM - MAP to a shared directory used by MARY_JO
MAP ROOT I:=SYS:APPS\PAYROLL
REM - CAPTURE to a network printer in MARY_JO's area
CAPTURE L=3 Q=PAYROLL_LASER
REM - MAP shows the user all defined drive mappings
MAP
REM - EXIT quits the login script and runs a batch file
EXIT "WIN31.BAT"
```

You probably notice in these login scripts some commands that don't look familiar, such as `FIRE PHASERS 10` and `WRITE "GOOD %GREETING_TIME, %FULL_NAME!"`. These commands are part of some versions of the NetWare login script language. This script language gives you extensive control over tasks that NetWare performs when users log in. You can learn more than you ever want to know about the login script language by studying the supervisor guides for each version of NetWare.

Logouts

As mentioned, logging out is not an absolute requirement for NetWare users. NetWare automatically logs you out if you just turn off your PC. If you don't log out, however, you can make your local network administrator mad at you in a hurry.

The most obvious reason to log out is to prevent anyone else from accessing the network on your account. While you're out to lunch, your workplace rivals can send prank e-mail messages to the boss and sign your name to them. This situation may seem like a minor joke, but it can become a serious breach of network security if you have access to sensitive information on the server.

We cannot tell you how secure you want your network to be. We can point out, however, that the majority of unauthorized uses of corporate networks are from people who leave themselves logged in while they are away from their desks or from users who set their password to an obvious word or number — such as their spouse's name or their own birthday.

Although we suggest that you always require passwords on all your servers, we know of many networks that don't use passwords. A network that has no required passwords is safer than a network that requires passwords but has no password policing. A network without passwords has no illusion of security, and a network with poorly protected passwords may lull users into a false sense of security.

Logging out is also very important for each user because of limitations in some network tape-backup programs. A user who remains logged in overnight has files open on the server. Open files prevent some tape-backup programs from backing up properly. One file that is sure to be open when users are logged in is the network database of user and resource definitions. This file is one that is crucial to network operation and critical for inclusion in system backups.

Don't Bring Me Down, Dude

Shutting down (with the DOWN command) a NetWare server is important because it provides for an orderly shutdown of all server files and resources. File corruption is a real possibility if you simply turn off a server PC. You can end up with the PC equivalent of scrambled eggs when someone turns your server off rather than shuts it down.

In fact, you usually see some error messages during the next bootup following an improper shutdown. Also, NetWare may take a few minutes to resynchronize those system files that it keeps duplicated in memory following an improper shutdown. (Improper shutdowns are one of the reasons it keeps those duplicates!) Although the NetWare operating system is pretty good at recovering from such unexpected interruptions, the best way to ensure a smooth bootup of a NetWare server is to always bring it down correctly.

Always try to notify your users before shutting down your server. An error saying that the server is not responding can be quite a shock to someone who is about to save a ten-page document. Both versions of NetWare include the capability to broadcast a message to all users from the server console. Use this broadcast capability to warn your users that the server will shut down in a certain number of minutes. They will thank you.

To shut down a NetWare 4.11 or 3.12 server, go to the server console and type **DOWN** at the : (colon) prompt. When the DOWN command completes, you can type **EXIT** to return to the DOS prompt.

We say that computers are either booting, up, or down. When a computer starts up, it begins by reading a small program that tells it where to go to find the information it needs to get itself started. It then uses that short program to read the programs it really needs, and starts itself up by beginning with a small, dumb program and winding up ready to rock 'n' roll. Because it's similar to the phrase "pulling yourself up by your own bootstraps," this program became known as a bootstrap loader. What does a bootstrap loader do? It boots up the computer. End of story.

As long as a computer is running properly, it is said to be *up*. A server that stops working abruptly because of software or hardware failure is said to *crash*. A server that has just crashed or is turned off is said to be *down*. A server in an airplane performing a loop that hits a tree is said to be in an *upside-down crash*. A server wearing a pair of boots would just look plain silly.

Double your hardware to double your life expectancy

The NetWare operating system has the capability to perform disk mirroring and disk duplexing on server-attached hard drives. *Disk mirroring* means that you can install duplicate hard drives, one active and one backup, that NetWare writes to simultaneously. If a crash or other problem occurs with the active drive, NetWare automatically begins to use the backup drive and notifies you of the switch.

Disk duplexing not only mirrors the drives but also provides the capability to use totally backed-up and redundant disk controllers. *Disk controllers* are the adapter cards that make the drive go round. With disk duplexing, you have redundancy of most of the critical moving parts inside your server. We always use disk duplexing and strongly suggest that you do, too, whenever your budget permits. Duplexing beats just having spare controllers and hard drives in stock

because it doesn't require you to bring the server down immediately to make repairs. You have the luxury of postponing repairs until a more convenient time for both you and your users.

Novell's latest development in server redundancy, what Novell calls *System Fault Tolerance* (SFT), is a product called SFT III. SFT III is a copy of version 4.11 that mirrors the entire server PC to another PC. Server Fault Tolerance gives you the ultimate backup plan if any hardware component in the active server fails. A dedicated network connects the two servers, usually over fiber optics and keeps both servers in synch. Granted, this solution can be expensive, but it is well worth it in truly mission-critical environments. Another consideration for protecting your server's data is the technology known as RAID. You can find a complete discussion of RAID in Chapter 9.

Lightning Can Be a Real Charge!

You cannot keep emergencies from striking your network, but a contingency plan for each of several common problems is absolutely essential. The collective experience of a generation of computer-keepers says that it's not a matter of whether emergencies hit, but rather when and how often. Boy Scouts make great network administrators because their motto is "Be prepared."

Frequent server backups are *de rigueur* for the successful network administrator. Find a good, automated, tape-backup unit with twice the capacity you can ever imagine needing in your wildest server dreams (or nightmares). This item on your contingency plan is so versatile that it can be used in almost every imaginable emergency recovery situation. As Karl Malden says: "Don't leave home without it!"

A philosophical question: If a server crashes in the middle of a forest, is there any sound? Of course! It's the sound of a forest of network users feverishly dialing the phone number of their network administrator (who is at home, sleeping — it's the middle of the night on a weekend). Then there's the sound of users calling the network administrator's boss to complain that the server still isn't up. Then there's the sound of the network administrator's boss calling the network administrator demanding to know why the server isn't back up already. You think we're kidding, don't you? *Not!*

Look, Ma — It Eats Out of My Hand!

The proper care and feeding of a new network guarantees that you don't grow any new gray hairs as your network matures. Proper care and feeding also means that any balding you experience as a network administrator is the result of your genes, not the result of tearing clumps out as you recover from your own mistakes. Neglect or mistreat a network, though, and it's not just your hand that it bites. The rest of this section covers the list of some of the most important things you should remember regarding maintaining your network.

Backups, Backups, and More Backups

You absolutely must develop an effective server backup strategy now or pay dearly for the lack of one later.

Your first line of defense for any network problem, emergency, or anomaly is a current set of server backups. One of your first decisions as a network administrator is to decide how important the server data is to your organization. You may talk to your boss and other managers to get a good feel for this issue. We suggest full server backups — that means every single file on your server — at least once a month, and incremental file backups — a backup of all files that have changed since the last backup — at least once a week, if not every day. This rule of thumb is for noncritical server data. You should back up mission-critical data every night, if possible. If only we can find a way to back up data before we even know what it is. . . .

We completely devote Chapter 16 of this book to backing up — and restoring — your network servers. If you're responsible for a network — any network — you should read this chapter, hopefully before you have had cause to weep!

Documentation, documentation, documentation

The one thing every administrator despises is documenting the network. No substitute exists for a paper backup of your server directory structure and user accounts. Many network performance-monitoring programs include sophisticated options for documenting your server hardware and software. The goal of this paper trail is to retain the ability to accurately rebuild the server if your tape backups fail to restore properly following a catastrophic server failure.

Get a big binder and print every login script and server configuration file you can get your hands on. Find a good network configuration report utility and run it weekly. You save hours or days of downtime later with good server documentation because you don't have to scramble to find the information you need. Who needs to poke around a scrambled hard disk with a sector editor in the middle of the night, anyway? You shouldn't have to if you compile this information. Figure 10-1 shows a sample server documentation sheet. You should fill out one page like this for every server on your network. You can also purchase software utilities to automate the server documentation task.

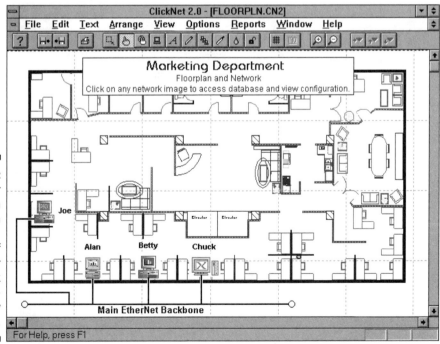

Figure 10-1:
A server configuration documentation sheet is a vital part of your network disaster-recovery plan.

You also need good documentation of the network cable installation for trouble-shooting purposes. We have seen one loose network connection in an office blow another user down the hall completely off the network, while the user directly hooked to the bad connection remained unaffected. This kind of troubleshooting is impossible without at least an idea of which cable connects to which PC and how it gets there. If you have a cable-installation company install your cabling, be sure to get several copies of their cabling diagram before you pay them. Again, a little work now can save hours of agony later, not to mention the recrimina-tions. Figure 10-2 shows a sample network cabling documentation layout.

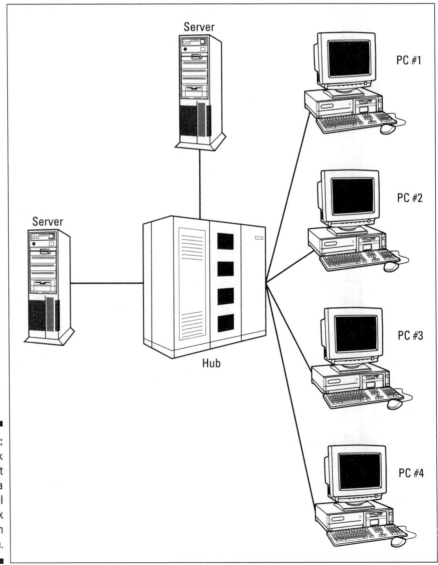

Figure 10-2:
A network layout from a commercial network documentation program.

You can place a number of excellent PC client inventory programs in the system login script and get an accurate hardware and software snapshot of each of your user's PCs. Figure 10-3 shows a printout from a typical client PC inventory program.

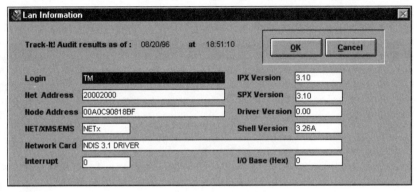

Figure 10-3:
A client PC inventory program is useful both for disaster-recovery and for tracking software licenses.

Did we mention . . . backups?

Don't forget that the long-term success of your network is tied directly to the quality of your server backups.

We cannot emphasize this point enough: *Back up your server often!*

Uninterruptible power supplies

The savior of many a server is the *uninterruptible power supply,* or *UPS.* UPSs contain a rechargeable battery that provides your server with a backup power source if its A/C power fails. The UPS senses that A/C power has gone away and automatically kicks in to supply power to your server on a few milliseconds' notice. If your server contains critical data, you shouldn't go without one; even if it doesn't, a UPS is still a good idea.

Spare parts

Purchasing spare replacement parts for critical server components is not only great insurance, it's now cheaper than ever. PC prices have dropped dramatically in the past few years and your spare parts inventory plan is a primary beneficiary. Critical items such as hard drives and network cards can be purchased for less now than at any time in recent memory.

Clean power is good power

Modern UPSs frequently also have line conditioning and filtering built in. Although a power outage can certainly be a critical occurrence for a server, your server is more likely to suffer hardware damage from normal fluctuations in line voltage, called *sags* and *spikes*. A good UPS smooths out the drops and surges in the power going to your server. We consider a line conditioning UPS to be a no-brainer requirement for all servers.

Recent advances in technology have endowed UPSs with brains: UPS manufacturers are including a microprocessor in the electronics of the UPS. This feature lets the UPS talk intelligently to the server. A UPS can tell the server about the quality of the incoming electrical power, notify you when the battery backup is supplying power, and even perform an orderly shutdown of the server when the battery nears exhaustion. Many UPSs also have a NetWare NLM included to give you sophisticated control of the system. Some UPSs can even dial your pager or home phone number through a modem hooked to the server to let you know when the power is out.

Now, if we can just teach our UPS how to make us fresh coffee in the morning. . . .

Having these common parts on hand can mean the difference between one hour of server downtime and one or two days of server downtime. The price reductions should also benefit your users' efforts to upgrade their local PCs. You can purchase a Pentium PC for less than what a 386-based PC cost in 1990. Take advantage of the buyer's PC market to purchase spare server components and upgrade equipment for user PCs.

We recommend a 90 MHz (megahertz) Pentium PC with a super VGA monitor, 16MB of RAM, and a 540MB hard drive as the minimum PC purchase for new network users. It's not that existing users can't get by on much less, but a PC configured as recommended should be ready for any new PC and networking developments in the next few years. For your new server purchases, we recommend a 166 MHz Pentium PC with as much RAM and hard drive space as you can afford (at least 64MB of RAM and 4GB (gigabyte) of disk space, at a minimum). We also feel that, at the very least, you should make use of the inherent NetWare disk mirroring or duplexing capabilities as a first line of defense against data loss.

Last but not Least — Backups

Did we mention the importance of server backups yet? Just in case — don't forget a good backup and restore strategy!

Chapter 11

NDS: The Brains Behind NetWare 4.11

· ·

In This Chapter

▶ What's so keen about NDS?

▶ How the Directory works

▶ Dos and don'ts for Directory design

▶ Why you should upgrade to NetWare 4.11

▶ Partitions, replicas, and containers: More than kitchen concepts

▶ An overview of NDS Utilities

· ·

*F*irst things first: In order to get you to understand what NetWare Directory Services (NDS) is all about, we're going to have to ask you to pay attention. When we talk about a directory, that's not the same thing as a Directory. A *directory* (no initial capital) is a file system data structure that organizes files into named groups called directories. A *Directory* (initial capital) is a special kind of database that contains and organizes information about a computing environment and the users and resources that make it up. In the context of this chapter, the word *Directory* refers to the database that underlies NDS. We do our best to keep this subtle distinction from getting confusing, but you still have to mind your ds and Ds to stay with us!

If the Directory is the database that underlies NDS, what are Directory services? By extension, *Directory services* are the facilities for creating, storing, accessing, organizing, managing, and using the diverse kinds of information about users and resources that are stored in a Directory database. Simply put, the Directory lets you build a model of your network, your users, your machines, and your organization in a database; and Directory services lets you use this database to find your way around the network — and to keep the model in synch with reality. NDS is a way of letting you and your users see the way the world works (at least, your part of it) as reflected by your network, the equipment, and the people who use it.

To fully and properly cover the NetWare 4.11 NDS, we'd have to write another whole book on the subject. Instead, we just want to get you two acquainted, and get you interested enough to pursue a further relationship on your own! By the time you finish this chapter, you should know where to look in order to find what you need.

What's So Keen About NDS?

Let's face it: Networking is here to stay. And, as networks have gotten bigger and more capable, more and more users have been confronted with their complexity. Finding what you need or want on a network and then getting from here to there after you've found it can be hard work. The need for a Directory service springs from the frustration that network users necessarily experience as they try to wend their way through a tortuous labyrinth of software, naming conventions, and *laissez-faire* information sharing policies.

"Wouldn't it be great," you're tempted to say, "if everybody shared a common view of the network and you could just find the things you need by asking for them?" In a nutshell, this kind of capability is what Directory services are all about. The idea is to provide a common, distributed facility that can supply services — not just information about them — to all network applications and users, no matter what computer they're using, or what service they need.

NDS is an object-oriented implementation of Directory services that lets you build a model of your world, using sophisticated naming schemes and a powerful distributed database to build that model. NDS provides access to all network resources to everybody on the network, regardless of where the users or the resources are located. NDS may be divided into multiple, cooperating pieces, but it acts like one big, happy, coherent information system.

Novell is pretty proud of NDS. In fact, Novell has a right to be — NDS compares favorably with any other Directory service on the market today and beats the pants off many of them. Table 11-1 shows you why, as it outlines some of the features and benefits of NDS.

Table 11-1	NDS Features and Benefits
Feature	*Benefit*
Simple administration	Every supervisor uses the same management facilities and shares a common view of the network. All resources maintain a single identity throughout the entire network.

Feature	Benefit
Advanced security	NDS incorporates state-of-the-art security features to provide a single login for all network resources. Access is handled through hierarchical access control lists that are comprehensive but easy to manage.
Usability	NDS database structure makes retrieving Directory objects easy and efficient, and reduces network traffic. Powerful searching tools allow objects to be located in lots of ways, including wild card and exact-match lookups.
Reliability	NDS includes a built-in replication mechanism so that the danger of losing access to the Directory, through system failure or regular maintenance downtime, is minimized.
Flexibility	NDS is designed to accommodate change easily; components of the Directory can be split or merged, and objects moved around as needed.
Scaleability	NDS can handle the needs of large and small organizations, because it can model simple, flat structures as well as large, complex ones.
Compatibility	NDS provides bindery services, to let 2.*x* and 3.*x* servers (and older NetWare clients) access NDS information. NDS also includes utilities to exchange data with other databases and Directory services.
Open-ended	NDS lets you redefine Directory objects and structures, or create new ones as needed.

All in all, NDS offers considerable power, both to model the organization that it must serve, and to let members of that organization use that model to readily access information and resources anywhere on the network.

How the Directory REALLY Works

NDS was developed as a tool for modeling information hierarchies to accommodate the levels of companies, operating or business units, departments, teams, work groups, and so on, of which most organizations are composed. In other words, the NetWare 4.11 Directory was designed to be an easily understood model of the network it represents. NDS uses an underlying database to store descriptions of the elements, called *objects,* that make up the world it models. As such, NDS is consistent with the ISO/OSI standard known as X.500, which was developed to provide a standard way to organize information that needs to be broadly accessed and shared. Today, you can already buy products that make things like telephone directories, corporate organization structures, and service directories available using X.500-derived technologies. Some day, as the standard matures, all of these systems, including NDS, will be able to freely exchange information.

What's in the schema things?

As a database, the Directory is governed by a set of rules that define how the Directory is structured. This set of rules is called a *schema*, which defines how objects are related, how they are named, and what kind of information they can contain (and how information is stored in the database). The foundation for all items in any NDS database is a set of object classes, which defines the kinds of things that the database can accommodate, called the *base schema*. Unless you change these definitions, this foundation defines the terms you can use to describe your organization within an NDS database.

An object lesson

By now, you're probably wondering why we keep calling the contents of the NDS database *objects*. The reason is simple: This term is a standard way of describing how things in the world (real stuff, in other words) get represented by computer programs. Objects have names, which is how you identify them. Objects belong to object classes, which is how they get related to each other, and how their basic representational capabilities get defined. Objects have associated properties, which are names for categories of related information, and include values for properties (which is how objects represent the things they're supposed to model).

Try thinking of it this way: An object class defines what makes up any object that belongs to that class. For the object class *book,* we may have to define properties like *title, author, publication date,* and *publisher.* For one book, *title* may be *Networking with NetWare For Dummies,* 3rd Edition, *author(s)* Ed Tittel, Deni Connor, and Earl Follis, *publication date* 1996, and *publisher* IDG Books Worldwide, Inc. Other books still belong to the same object class, *book,* but have different properties for title, author, and so on.

NDS distinguishes among three kinds of objects:

- ✔ [Root] object, which defines the name of the Directory database
- ✔ Container objects, which organize parts of the database into named containers
- ✔ Leaf objects, which model actual stuff out there on the network like users, printers, servers, and so on

The NDS Directory is called a Directory tree because it is represented as a root with branches that make their way out to support leaves. Trees are a nice way to represent hierarchies and, because that's what NDS is designed to do, it's only natural that Novell should ask us to return to our arboreal ancestry.

Rooting around the Directory

Every Directory tree, like every real tree, has only one root. For NDS, the [Root] object provides a convenient way to name a distinct NDS database (of which there can be many, on any single network). The [Root] object can contain any of the other container objects, but it must occur at the top of the tree (for display reasons, computers draw trees upside-down).

Handling containers

Container objects come in a variety of flavors, based on the ISO X.500 model. The valid containers for NDS include the following:

✔ **Country** (C): The Country object designates the countries where your network lives and organizes other objects within each country. The Country objects must appear beneath the [Root] but before other container objects, if present in a Directory tree. {optional}

Root object

Container objects

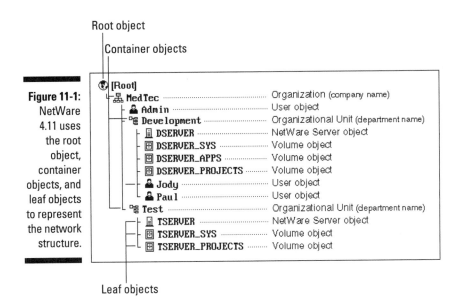

Figure 11-1:
NetWare
4.11 uses
the root
object,
container
objects, and
leaf objects
to represent
the network
structure.

Leaf objects

✔ **Organization** (O): The Organization object helps to organize other objects in a Directory tree and allows defaults for User objects within that container to be set. An Organization can be a company, a division, a research or academic institution, a department, and so on, but it's customarily used as an intermediate level of hierarchy — that is, between one container above it in the tree and others below it in the tree. An Organization object can contain Organizational Unit, Locality, and Leaf objects, and may be contained by a [Root], Country, or Locality object. {Required}

✔ **Organizational Unit** (OU): The Organizational Unit object provides a way to break an Organization into suborganizations and provides a way to organize leaf objects in the Directory tree. Large complex organizations may have several OU levels, whereas simple, smaller ones typically have only one. The OU object lets you set defaults for NetWare login scripts and to create user templates for User objects in that container. OU objects can contain Locality, other OU or Leaf objects, and must be contained by Organization, other OU, or Locality objects. {optional}

✔ **Locality** (L): The Locality object designates physical location for the portion of the Directory tree it contains. Locality objects can contain Organization or OU objects and may be contained by Country, Organization, or OU objects. {optional}

Note: If the object is labeled {Required}, at least one must appear in every Directory tree; if it's labeled {optional}, its presence is permitted, but not required.

Raking the leaves

Directory leaf objects are where the action is: By definition, they don't contain other objects, but simply represent something on the network like a user, server, printer, computer, or whatever. Leaf objects must be created within a container object, to situate them within the model of your organization. The kinds of leaf objects NDS supports by default are depicted in Figure 11-2. These are the elements from which you build your network within NDS, after you've built their container structures.

Each class of leaf object has associated properties that describe the object to be modeled. A User object, for example, contains a login name, e-mail address, password restrictions, groups memberships, and more. Some properties are required and must be supplied before the object is complete; others are optional and can be added if and when they're needed.

Standardizing on property values in your database is important to make searching the Directory tree easier (and more predictable). You can't easily find all the printers in Building 2 if you sometimes enter "Bldg2," sometimes "Building 2," and sometimes "B2" in the Location property of multiple objects. Picking a single, standard name like "B2" ensures that a search on that value will return the desired results. *Remember:* Confusion is its own reward!

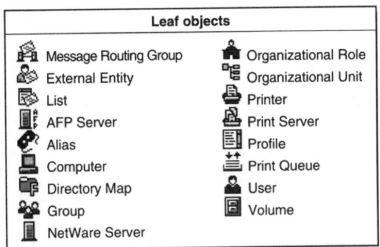

Figure 11-2:
NDS Leaf
Object
Classes.

Access to the Directory tree is controlled by a set of access rights to objects in the tree. Users may only be able to read (Browse) the contents of most of the tree to keep them from making unwanted changes. Supervisors usually have one or more of the following rights to objects in the tree:

Object Rights (apply to entire objects):

✓ **Supervisor:** Grants all rights to the object and its properties.

✓ **Create:** Grants the right to create new objects within a specified container in the tree.

✓ **Delete:** Grants the right to delete objects within a specified container in the tree; container objects cannot be deleted unless all contained objects are deleted first.

✓ **Rename:** Grants the right to change the object's assigned name, which changes its reference in the Directory tree.

Property Rights (apply to object properties, as constrained by Object rights):

✓ **Add/delete self:** Lets you add or remove yourself as a value for a property, but no other value changes are allowed.

✓ **Compare:** Lets you compare a supplied value to an actual property value; returns only True or False, does not supply actual value.

✓ **Read:** Grants the rights to view the property value(s).

✓ **Supervisor:** Grants all rights to the property.

✓ **Write:** Allows you to add, change, or remove any values of the property.

Container assignments typically restrict what ordinary users can see at all; within containers, ordinary users have very few rights other than Browse and Read, except for Add/delete self.

Dos and Don'ts for Directory Design

In this section, we suggest a few approaches that you may find worth considering when designing your Directory, along with a few no-nos you definitely want to avoid. Unfortunately, this list is not exhaustive — we shy away from trying to anticipate all the ingenious ways that people can find to do things.

Do:

- ✔ Try to get your hands on some current organizational charts for your company, department, or whatever group(s) of people you'll be building a Directory for. Check the chart out with some local managers just to make sure that things haven't changed since it came off the printer! Try to keep up with the changes as you're implementing the org chart's NDS equivalent. Your network directory design goal should be to match the physical organization as closely as possible with the org chart's NDS counterpart.

- ✔ Make sure that you build a prototype directory and get management approval before exposing your creation to the whole company. You don't want to have to learn what *recanting* means from personal experience.

- ✔ Take geography into account when building a Directory, as well as organization affiliation. Take note of where your servers are and who's using them as a strong indicator of how location affects the resources and equipment that people use.

Don't:

- ✔ Try to get things right the first time out or bite off more than you can chew. Starting small is best, perhaps with a subset of the organization, before laying out a grandiose Directory structure that nobody can understand (or use). Don't go wild with partitions and replicas at first, either.

- ✔ Assume that you know anything about your organization's structure without checking with somebody else. This is as true for models and prototypes as it is for the real thing. What you think of the Directory isn't what counts, what management and the users think is what matters. Ask them for feedback (you'll get plenty, anyway).

- ✔ Be discouraged when things keep changing or when important parties to the discussion can't agree. Change, disagreement, and chaos are also part of organizational life. Just be glad those processes haven't been automated in NDS, too!

Lots of times, building a Directory forces an organization to confront its structure (or lack thereof) for the very first time. This can be an unsettling experience for everyone involved, so don't feel singled out for cruel and unusual punishment. Besides, isn't driving some really critical issues and decisions for a change nice?

Directory Assistance Help Is at Hand

Novell's decision to include bindery emulation in NetWare 4.0 (called bindery services starting in 4.1) means that you don't have to rush out and upgrade all your servers right away. You can keep existing servers running as-is, while slowly phasing in Directory services as your budget and resources allow. If you start small and learn how to work with NDS, you'll be better-equipped to handle a large-scale migration with the benefit of increased familiarity. You'll also be able to puzzle your way through a workable model for your organization and maybe even secure the sign-offs from management that are so often necessary for a successful deployment of a Directory service. Time can be your best friend, simply by providing the opportunity to fully understand NDS for yourself and to explain its features, benefits, and implications for the other people in your organization.

Don't forget to check all possible avenues for information about Directory design in your quest to build your organization's version. Keep your eye on the computer trade press for stories on this subject. Check the online services (the Internet, CompuServe, and so on) for tips and information. Read the Novell publications (like *AppNotes*) for an insider's view (the references included at the beginning of the "Introduction to NDS" manual are all worth reading). There's no dearth of information, to be sure — you just have to work a bit to find the pieces you need!

But there's another form of NDS help available for those who already have NetWare servers. Preferred Systems, Inc. (West Haven, Connecticut) offers a product called DS Standard (a reduced functionality version is included with NetWare 4.11) that captures bindery-based information from servers around the network and automates the analysis and migration work needed to create an NDS equivalent. By itself, this service can be a valuable method for making the switch, especially if your organization wants to take advantage of the cost-saving features of NetWare 4.11 — you don't have to let a large or complex NDS implementation stop you in your tracks.

In addition, DS Standard offers the ability to create Directory models without making a change to your real networking environment and to play what-if games with those models' layout, naming, and organization. This capability lets you work your way through multiple alternatives, while seeing the resulting Directory trees in the form they would take under NDS. Finally, DS Standard includes a collection of online documentation, tutorial, and technical information called "The Assistant" that by itself is worth the price of entry for the wealth of useful NDS design and implementation data it contains.

Why YOU Should Upgrade to NetWare 4.11

We hope it's obvious to you by now that NDS makes living and working with a NetWare network easier for everybody, including users and administrators — especially after they've climbed the learning curve. As the fifth release in the NetWare 4.*x* family, NetWare 4.11 represents a major step forward from the previous versions, primarily because the NDS utilities now permit users and administrators to interact with the Directory easily and effectively.

But there's more to this directory stuff than meets the eye: Over the next year or so, you'll begin to see more network applications that have been what Novell calls *Directory-enabled.* In English, this means that applications will also be able to communicate with NDS, to locate and report on printers in your neighborhood, to find the right volumes where the data files live, or to automatically supply the correct e-mail address right when you type in a user's name. Once applications can locate resources and request access to network services on your behalf, your life will get a lot easier, whether you're an administrator or a user.

If you like the idea of smart applications and the concept of interacting with your network and its resources through a single, coherent graphical presentation, you'll probably be impressed with NetWare 4.11. If you don't like these ideas, hang back from the stampede of other users who do! How else could Windows be where it is today?

Partitions, Replicas, and Containers Are More Than Kitchen Concepts

By now, you've probably figured out that you can slice and dice an NDS environment in several ways. In this section, we explore the key concepts for how the Directory is organized *(containers)* and how the database is distributed *(partitions)* and copied between servers *(replicas).* Each of these concepts helps make the Directory a useful tool for governing your network, but each one plays a different and equally important role.

Contain this!

As we mention in "An object lesson" earlier in this chapter, a container is a special kind of Directory object; it's made specifically to contain other objects and to give the collection of objects it contains a name. That's why the [Root], the Organization, Location, and Organizational Unit objects are all containers — because they provide a way to model how a real organization is structured and located. This concept provides a useful on-screen abstraction for users looking at a Directory tree and helps them locate themselves and the resources that they're after.

At the root and on the trunk of a well-designed Directory tree, you typically find a hierarchy of container objects with leaf objects more or less restricted to the ends of the branches (usually beneath Organization Unit or Location objects). The way a tree is organized is important, because physical divisions of the underlying database should parallel its layout, and you want to keep the root and trunk available to everybody, while only distributing the branch areas where they're needed. This strategy comes in handy when you start partitioning your Directory, as you see in the next section "Power partitions."

Power partitions

A partition actually consists of a piece of the Directory database, usually cut out along container lines. The idea is to situate the partition that people use most nearby, on a server in their immediate neighborhood. Making the trunk and the root easily accessible without creating too many copies (we get into that in the next section) is a good idea. Repeated use creates network traffic, so you don't want people who don't benefit from the traffic — local users — to be subjected to it unnecessarily.

In general, try to keep the number of partitions as small as possible without lumping too many dissimilar users or departments together. Following this reasoning, keeping the Accounts Receivable and Accounts Payable users in a single partition probably makes sense, but keeping the manufacturing and shipping users together may not make sense. Let physical and political proximity be guides rather than absolute rules.

Revealing replicas

Replicas exist for one primary reason — to provide a backup for the Directory database for any partition you may create. The idea behind the replica is that it provides a mirror of a primary (or original) partition to which users can turn should the server that runs that primary partition fail for any reason. If you make the Directory the key to the network, and the door is kept locked to those without keys, keeping a spare key around is a good idea!

Novell recommends that every partition have at least one replica for every partition you create (unless you only have one server — in that case, replication isn't an option; a replica will be automatically created for the second and third server brought up in every NDS partition). The more a partition is used, or the closer it is to the root and trunk of your Directory tree, the more replicas there should be. For large organizations (with hundreds of servers), Novell recommends as many as four replicas for heavily used partitions. Replicas can even be stored outside the boundaries of a partition for additional safety. As a nice side effect, such replicas will be referenced by users local to a particular network outside the partition, cutting down on the amount of network traffic that such access can potentially generate.

However, you should also be aware that keeping multiple replicas synchronized can cause some network overhead and can even cause problems on large WANs. The ideal course is to strike a balance between the number of copies and the overhead that they can incur.

Tool Time: An Overview of NDS Utilities

As befits the nerve center for NetWare 4.11, NDS includes a number of related utilities to help manage the Directory environment. The tools can help you create and maintain directories, fix 'em when they're broken, glue 'em together (and take 'em apart), and all kinds of other neat stuff.

Because the Directory is such an important part of your NetWare 4.11 environment, we wouldn't recommend playing with these tools just to see what they can do. If you want to play, set up a separate Directory for that purpose (an unwritten rule for Directory management is "NEVER mess around with a production directory unless you absolutely have to!"). If you must play — and we think it's an excellent way to learn — create a nonproduction Directory that nobody but you can see and fool around with it. Even if you screw things up completely, you won't have your users forming a lynch mob, because they can't use the network anymore.

To get familiar with these utilities (especially the ones you won't encounter in a normal installation and Directory setup), we recommend that you start with a little light reading: Consult the "Introduction to NetWare Directory Services" online manual that ships with NetWare 4.11.

For the time being, Table 11-2 gives a condensed tour of the tools and utilities that you can use when working with NDS. Have a nice trip!

Table 11-2	NDS Utilities
Name	**Description**
DSMERGE	Use as a server console utility to merge the roots of two separate Directory trees, allowing all the parts to communicate and share data. Also use DSMERGE to rename a Directory tree and to review name and time synchronization information in the Directory.
DSREPAIR	Use as a server console utility to check and repair problems with the Directory database regarding records, schema, bindery objects, and external references. Also reports on time and replica synchronization status.
DSTRACE	Use as a server console utility to check time and replica synchronization status and to diagnose NDS errors.
INSTALL	Use as server console utility to install or upgrade the server's NetWare version, to modify its configuration, and to perform server maintenance. When all else fails, you can even use INSTALL to blow NDS away, prior to re-installing a new Directory.
NETADMIN	Use this to manage NDS database objects and properties; this DOS utility lets you view, create, move, delete, and assign rights to NDS objects and manage access to your network.
NWADMIN	A Windows utility that lets you manage NDS database objects and properties, just like NETADMIN, but easier to use. Commonly accessed through an icon named NWADMIN, this utility also provides tools to create users and groups, set up printing services, and set up and manage Directory partitions and replicas.
PARTMGR	Use at a client workstation to carve up and distribute your Directory database, and to manage partitions and replicas.
SET (NDS Parameters)	This command is used to configure many aspects of NetWare's operation. For NDS, the relevant parameters include controls for an NDS trace file, time intervals for Directory maintenance processes and synchronization tasks, to mark NDS server status, and to specify bindery services contexts for 2.x and 3.x servers and users.
TIMESYNC	Use at the server console to check time synchronization on servers around the network and to select your synchronization method and related time servers.
UIMPORT	Use at a client workstation to import user objects and their properties from an existing database into NDS.

Working with NDS is like learning a new language or another way of thinking about networking. If you take your time and try to absorb the technologies it uses while learning the ways it works, you'll find it to be an invaluable tool. We also recommend that you read everything you can find about NDS and try to learn as much about it as you can. The online documentation and the documentation for DS Standard (included with NetWare 4.11) are great places to start! After that, we recommend any of the following resources:

- ✔ Gamal B. Herbon, *Designing NetWare Directory Services*, M&T Books/Henry Holt & Co., New York, NY, 1994.

- ✔ Jeffrey F. Hughes and Blair W. Thomas, *Novell's Four Principles of NDS Design*, Novell Press/IDG Books Worldwide, Indianapolis, IN, 1996.

- ✔ Peter Kuo and Jim Henderson, *NDS Troubleshooting*, New Riders Publishing/Macmillan, Indianapolis, IN, 1995.

Of the three books, the Hughes and Thomas team effort is the most current and benefits from its authors "real" jobs in the Novell internal Consulting Group, where they function as a high-level system resource for customers and colleagues.

Chapter 12

The File System: Center of the NetWare Universe

. . . .

In This Chapter

▶ The NetWare File System (simplified)

▶ Common server file-system layouts

▶ Finding your way around the file system

▶ Setting up utilities, applications, and more

▶ File system access

▶ NetWare 4.*x* and 3.*x* file system specifics

▶ Inoculate your server from nasty viruses

▶ Taking care of business

. . . .

*I*n Chapter 10, we discuss the key to the Novell NetWare success — namely, that it works as advertised. This chapter gets down to the nitty-gritty on how the NetWare file system works and why it works the way it does.

We discuss the general principles behind the NetWare network operating system philosophy and how the Novell design decisions can affect your fledgling network. We also talk about the specific differences between the version 4.*x* and 3.*x* file systems.

No matter how hard we try to make this material light and entertaining, things still get pretty technical every now and then. So put on your thinking cap and dive right in. Just don't file it under *F,* for forget.

Just What Exactly Is a File System?

A *file system* is the way the network operating system handles and stores files. NetWare fools your PC's DOS operating system into thinking that the server hard drives are local hard drives. This sleight of hand is called *redirection.*

On the server side, the NetWare file system is a total replacement for the functions of DOS. In fact, you cannot run normal DOS commands directly on a server after the server is "up." Only special NetWare commands, called *console commands,* are run from the server keyboard. Of course, workstation users can use most DOS commands on the server network drives that they access.

DOS stands for disk operating system. The first-ever DOS was written for mainframe computer systems many years ago, but it's been through some changes over the years. The NetWare file system completely replaces DOS on the server with an optimized, 32-bit, cooperative, multitasking, multi-user, file server network operating system. The phrase *32-bit* means that NetWare can handle data in bigger chunks than 16-bit DOS can. *Multitasking* means that the file server processor doesn't have to wait for the completion of one task to begin another task. If the processor has to wait for a hard drive to retrieve data, the server can process the next request in line until the hard drive finishes fetching the original request. Each of these steps takes place in a matter of milliseconds. That's pretty fast!

NetWare divides the file server disks into areas called volumes. A *volume* is a logical, or nonphysical, division of hard disk space. You can define multiple volumes for a single disk, though we don't recommend doing this. We think that some network folks are a little too picky, and they sometimes define multiple volumes on one hard drive as a way to organize their data. With NetWare 4.*x* and 3.*x,* you have no reason to impose such stringent structure to your NetWare volumes. We can accomplish the same goal with a well thought-out server directory layout. We show you how in this chapter.

NetWare versions 4.*x* and 3.*x* support a total disk space of 32 terabytes, and volumes can span or be spread across multiple hard drives. Once again, though a single server hard drive may contain multiple volumes for both versions of NetWare, we recommend against it.

The NetWare Prairie Schooner: Navigating the Server Plains

Think of the NetWare volume as analogous to the root directory on a DOS-based PC. In other words, the volume is the top of the NetWare directory structure. Underneath the volume in hierarchical fashion, you can have lots of directories and subdirectories and even sub-sub-sub-subdirectories. The root directory of the volume is like that of a tree; directories branch from the root; subdirectories branch from directories, and so on.

When you install NetWare on a file server, the INSTALL program creates the default volume named SYS and five default directories on volume SYS called LOGIN, PUBLIC, MAIL, SYSTEM, and ETC. The first four directories are fairly self-explanatory. The last directory, ETC, is used by NetWare 4.x and 3.x to store some stuff that doesn't really fit anywhere else. Here's the NetWare directory deal:

- ✔ LOGIN is where the server stores programs necessary for users to log in.

- ✔ PUBLIC is the directory in which the server stores general server and workstation utilities for use by all users.

- ✔ MAIL contains unique directories for each user in which the server stores all individual login script and printer configurations. In earlier versions of NetWare, Novell shipped an electronic mail package called MAIL. This directory stored the individual mail messages for users. As NetWare changed, MAIL didn't. (Go figure!)

- ✔ SYSTEM is the directory in which the server stores files necessary for the network operating system, server upkeep and administration, as well as some utilities intended for use by only the network supervisor and supervisor equivalents.

- ✔ ETC holds files that lets user workstations connect to TCP/IP host computers. (For more information on TCP/IP, please consult Chapter 4.)

You should plan carefully how you organize your file server directories before you install the NetWare software. We suggest that you keep all individual files out of the server root directory. Create directories in the root directory called DOSAPPS, for your DOS applications, and WINAPPS, for your Windows applications. Each application should have its own subdirectory under the appropriate directory, as shown in these examples where the application files are located:

```
SYS:DOSAPPS\WORDPERF
```

and

```
SYS:WINAPPS\WINWORD
```

With this kind of organization, controlling access to each application is easy because these directories can be *flagged* as *read only* so that none of the users can accidentally erase your applications files. You can also give users a *home directory* in which they can store anything they want (anything you have the server disk capacity to store).

You can limit a user's storage capacity on each server volume by using SYSCON for versions 2.2x and 3.x and by using NETADMIN for version 4.x. Define a directory in the root called USERS, as shown in this example:

```
SYS:USERS
```

And then create home subdirectories using each user's login name:

```
SYS:USERS\EDDIE
```

Generally, you should give each user full rights to only his or her home directory. Users should not be allowed to browse through another user's home directory. What if your users want to share files with each other? Create a directory in the SYSTEM root called SHARED with subdirectories for each department or group of users that wants to share files, as shown in these examples:

```
SYS:SHARED
```

and

```
SYS:SHARED\MARKETNG
SYS:SHARED\ACCNTING
SYS:SHARED\ADVRTSNG
```

This system makes it easy for you to grant rights to shared directories by using the NetWare group feature. Create a group called MARKETNG, made up of all the members of the marketing department, and give the group all rights to the SYS:SHARED\MARKETNG subdirectory. Other departments cannot see the group's shared data, but users can copy files to the server and notify other group members to retrieve the file from the shared directory.

If you want a common area in which the entire company can share files, grant all users full rights to the SYS:SHARED directory but restrict each department's subdirectory access to group members only.

Hopping, Skipping, and Jumping Around the Server

Now that your directory definition is complete, how do you get around in this monstrosity of a file server? Finding your way around does get tricky when your server directory tree has more branches than an anthill has ants. This is one reason that the server directory structure is so important.

Name every directory with a meaningful name so that even a stranger can understand which programs are located where on your server. Organize similar programs under a general directory, such as DOSAPPS, and then let each succeeding subdirectory get more specific. Remember that many programs require subdirectories under the application directory for system files and accessories.

You should handle server security with NetWare's trustee rights and directory flag capabilities. Trying to hide programs and data on your server eventually grows frustrating and tiresome for both you and your users. Even a medium-size server can have so many different directories that you can get lost in your own network. Our server directory motto is "A subdirectory for everything and everything in its (well-labeled) subdirectory."

The good ol' DOS CD, or Change Directory, command is one way to get around in your file server. Be careful, however, when you are changing the directory if you have mapped a search drive to a particular directory (you can find more information about MAPping drives later in this chapter). Some of your applications may not run if you change a mapped directory to another directory.

Suppose that you have set up MegaWord to run from the G drive. If you go to the G drive and change the directory to another directory, when you type **MW** to start MegaWord, the program will not load. We suggest that you map an unused drive letter to the subdirectory you want to explore and leave any predefined or application drives alone. If you do get lost, logging out and then logging in again is a good way to restore the mappings that you originally had.

Another way to navigate around your file server's directory tree is to use the built-in NWUSER utility or to employ a menuing package like Saber's LAN Workstation or even the Windows File Manager application from Microsoft. These utilities give you a graphical overview of the server disk so that you can point and click to determine which directories and files you can see and manipulate. These graphical directory interfaces typically make moving, copying, and even deleting files simple with the click of a mouse or keyboard key. Of course, you can only delete files that you have the NetWare rights to delete; if you are logged in as supervisor or an equivalent, however, you can accidentally do lots of damage.

Operator? Get Me Directory Information: The Impact of 4.x on the File System

When Novell designed NetWare 4.x, it left the basic directory structure unchanged. NetWare still creates five directories in the SYS volume (SYSTEM, LOGIN, MAIL, PUBLIC, and ETC), and it changes the method with which the user views them. Because NetWare 4.x can handle oodles of servers, navigating the directory structure can sometimes be confusing.

In NetWare 4.x, you can locate files by either their NetWare Directory Services (NDS) names or by their physical names. NDS names are designated by container objects such as organizational units, which designate the department the user works in. Containers branch off from other containers, and at the boundaries of the Directory tree, leaf objects that represent users and other network resources such as printers are grouped. For example, containers may have names such as MARKETNG, ACCOUNTG, ADMIN, and SALES. John in accounting at ABC Corp. would locate a file called MYSTUFF.DOC, in the container ACCOUNTG on volume SYS.

With older versions of NetWare like version 3.*x* and 2.*x,* you have to "attach" to each and every server that stores files or applications that you need to access. The NetWare 4.*x* file system organization makes accessing network resources really easy for users because they can login to the network only once and receive access to as many file servers and other resources as they have rights to. NetWare 4.*x* provides this network-centric method of network access by distributing a copy of the entire NDS database to each server on the network. Under NetWare 4.*x* and NDS, *any* server can authenticate your log in and provide you with the rights and drive mappings you need, not just the one or two servers where the files reside.

Set Up for a Smash: Utilities, Applications, and More

Most network-aware applications that you install have sophisticated installation programs that do all the dirty work for you. You usually only have to pick a suitable spot in the server directory structure, press the Enter key or click on OK, and insert the disks on demand in order to install a modern network application.

The tricky part is making those applications and utilities available to your users. Many good DOS and Windows menuing programs are designed specifically to run on a NetWare file server. The network administrator must set up each application only once on the menu, including any required MAP commands or printer CAPTURE statements, and all network users can highlight the program they want from a menu list forever afterwards.

Some DOS and most Windows menu programs include sophisticated filtering, application metering, and security features. *Application metering* keeps track of the number of users concurrently running a particular application. If you have purchased only five licenses for MegaWord, your DOS or Windows menu can ensure that you stay legal by limiting access to five users at a time.

Some menuing programs also enable you to control which users can execute or even see specified selections on the network menu. If you have sensitive data in a particular application, you can easily limit access to a NetWare group, called MANAGERS, for example. Users who try to execute sensitive applications and are not a member of the MANAGERS group receive a message that unauthorized access is not allowed. This feature gives you an easy way to dynamically control who can and cannot execute certain programs on your menuing system.

You can allow your users to run network applications in several other ways. One simple way is to create batch files that execute any required MAPpings or CAPTURE commands and then start the desired application.

Create a subdirectory on the server just for network batch files. We call the batch directory on our server SYS:PUBLIC\NETBATS. Every user that has a search drive to the PUBLIC directory will be able to execute batch files in the NETBATS subdirectory from the system login script. (Read more about system login scripts later in this chapter and about the relevant commands for login scripts in Chapter 17.) All a user has to know to run a network application is the name of the appropriate batch file. The rest of the commands are issued automatically.

For users with Windows on their workstations, a number of menuing packages can replace the Windows Program Manager, thereby eliminating any fears about altering the Windows WIN.INI file. With remote access software, you can make this task easy — you can vicariously visit each workstation to make the changes, or you can use one of the software distribution packages available to do it for you automatically.

You can avoid a little of this misery by defining program icons that point to the network batch file on the server for each program. Most setup changes need to occur only once in the batch file itself without disturbing each user's Windows setup.

Unfortunately, more bad news comes when you are using Windows to run network programs. Because Windows gives you the "opportunity" to start multiple programs at the same time, you must be sure that your batch files don't map to the same drive letters. If your MegaWord batch file performs the following map statement:

```
MAP G:=SYS:DOSAPPS\MEGAWORD
```

and your MegaDraw batch file performs the following mapping:

```
MAP G:=SYS:DOSAPPS\MEGADRAW
```

Windows gets *very* confused. Windows accesses the MegaWord directory okay, until you execute the MegaDraw batch file with MegaWord still running. Windows then changes to the MegaDraw subdirectory on the G drive to run MegaDraw.

The next time MegaWord scans the G drive for a file it needs in order to operate correctly, the file will not be found because Windows is still sitting in the MegaDraw directory. Strange, but true. If you decide to give your users access to network programs in Windows, be very careful that none of your batch files maps different directories to the same drive letter. You can also look into third-party Windows utilities, such as Saber LAN Workstation or Norton Desktop for Windows that remove this restriction from Windows use on a network.

How to Use the File System

Users gain access to the file system primarily through the MAP command. MAPping a drive letter to a directory on the file server lets your users directly access that directory like any other DOS drive. The following line shows the syntax of the MAP command:

```
MAP [option] [drive letter:=volume name:path]
```

In the `MAP` command, `option` is one of the following (for each of these options, the characters in bold are the acceptable abbreviations; if you don't want to key in the entire word, you can get by with just the bold parts):

- ✔ **INS**ert: Inserts the search drive mapping without deleting other mappings
- ✔ **ROOT**: Maps a drive to a fake root
- ✔ **DEL**ete: Deletes a currently assigned drive mapping
- ✔ **REM**ove: Same as DELete
- ✔ **N**ext: Assigns the next available drive letter to the drive mapping

   Note that the options shown here are optional components of the MAP command.

Drive mappings can be a regular mapping or a search mapping. A *regular mapping* gives the user access to a specific volume, directory, and path on the server only when the drive letter is the current directory. The user can access the directory and path by referencing only the assigned drive letter rather than the entire server path.

You add a *search mapping* to your PC's path for locating commands not in the current directory. You do not have to be at the drive letter prompt of a search mapping in order to find and execute the program. You can create search mappings by using the combination of S and a number, as shown in this example:

```
MAP S1:=SYS:DOSAPPS\MEGAWORD
```

You can issue drive mappings in the system login script, in individual user login scripts, in batch files, or manually at the DOS prompt. The operating system executes MAP commands in the system and user login scripts every time the user logs in to the file server. The process of logging out of the server deletes all drive mappings automatically. NetWare allows a total of 16 search mappings to a server or a total of 26 drives, including local DOS drive letters.

NetWare 4.*x* also introduces the concept of *Directory map objects*. A Directory map object enables the network administrator to define map commands that point to an object rather than to a specific volume and Directory on the server. If the path to that object ever changes, you have to update only the object definition, not all of your user's MAP commands. This new feature gives the administrator the flexibility to change object features and locations and not worry about breaking previous commands set up for each user. To assign a Directory map, you use the NWADMIN utility and select the container for the Directory map object.

To make NDS setup easier, NetWare 4.11 includes a greatly simplified installation that includes an auto-detect routine that recognizes and configures drivers for most common hardware adapters and server peripherals. Under the NetWare 4.11 Simple Installation, most hardware and software configuration questions are answered for you. All you must provide is the organization name, a password for the administrator, and the time zone where the server resides. Now that's one simple server installation!

NetWare 4.11: Now for Something Completely Different

All bets are off with NetWare version 4.11. The radical new design of almost every aspect of the file server operating system throws even the most experienced LAN administrator for a loop. The old-fashioned 3.*x* bindery services are no more (although 4.11 includes bindery emulation — called bindery services in 4.11 — to retain compatibility with NetWare 2.*x* and 3.*x*). Gone is the administrator's familiar menu interface, SYSCON. You must now come to grips with a redefinition of the way networks are structured and maintained. Version 4.*x* introduces the concept of NetWare Directory Services and network objects.

An *object* can represent real-world objects such as users, printers, countries, and groups. Basically, we stop defining application directories and server paths and instead define objects with certain characteristics. After an object is defined, you can refer to anywhere else you want in the directory by defining an alias. If the original object changes, you don't have to go back and change the setup of every alias of that object in the file system.

By changing the object itself, the other references to it are not affected, but the changes are made through the directory structure. For example, if you define a printer object as an HP LaserJet Series II, you then can copy references to that object wherever a printer object is needed in your organization. If you upgrade that printer to an HP IIIsi, you have to update only the original object definition. All other references to the printer remain unchanged. Make sense?

NetWare 4.01 and below allow an administrator to assign only 500 objects in each container. NetWare 4.1 goes for broke by increasing the number to 40,000 objects per container. Imagine administering that!

NetWare 4.x also includes new features to help network administrators deal with enterprise-wide computing needs. Automatic file compression is one such feature. The new 4.x built-in file-compression capabilities enable you to set a threshold number of days before a file is automatically compressed. When a user accesses the compressed file, NetWare 4.x automatically uncompresses the file on the fly. The compression and decompression process is totally transparent to the user.

NetWare 4.x also introduces the concept of the *High-Capacity Storage System* (HCSS). HCSS uses rewritable optical disks, similar to audio CDs, to "migrate" less frequently accessed data from the server hard drive to the optical disk jukebox subsystem, called near-line file storage. The server hard drives contain online files that are available almost instantly.

If files have migrated to the jukebox, the server must copy them back to the hard disk before they can be used. Just like file compression, where "stale" files get compressed in the background, the least active server files are migrated automatically to optical disk according to a predetermined threshold. By using both file compression and HCSS in NetWare 4.x, your server can store and access larger file capacities than a similar server can with NetWare 3.x.

Turn Your Head and Cough: Your Server versus Computer Viruses

You spend a great deal of time and effort in the modern network environment fighting the infection and spread of computer viruses. Computer viruses are malicious or prank programs that can do everything from displaying a humorous message on your monitor to deleting every file from your hard drive.

The server file system is an ideal breeding ground and point of infection for computer viruses. Users can unknowingly store rogue programs on the server, and every other PC on the network can be infected. We strongly recommend that you purchase a virus-scanning program for both local PCs and the server itself.

NetWare 3.x: File system specifics

NetWare 3.x supports as many as 250 users and massive amounts of RAM and disk space. As much as 4GB of memory and 32 terabytes of disk space is pretty impressive stuff. Version 3.x also supports as many as 64 volumes with as many as eight volumes or volume segments supported on each hard drive, and each volume can consist of as many as 32 segments. Clearly, NetWare 3.x is a huge step up in complexity and performance from the days of NetWare 2.x. Version 3.x enables you to configure and tune the server while the server is up and running. Much of the memory management required for version 2.x is now dynamically allocated by the file server operating system in version 3.x.

NetWare 3.x uses the concept of NetWare Loadable Modules, or NLMs. NLMs provide low-level operating system access for programs designed to run directly on the server. Novell-certified NLMs meet design guidelines for memory usage and are tested extensively by Novell. Obviously, a privileged program running on the server has the potential for crashing the server if everything is not running properly, and we have certainly seen it happen. So far, third-party companies have released everything from database engines to virus scanning programs in NLM form. The NLM concept is a great way to encourage developers to write extensions to the operating system without sacrificing NetWare's famous compatibility.

To a network user, virus scanning resembles backing up vital files: Even if virus scanning is available and convenient, some users simply don't see the importance of it. On our network, the Windows menuing program our users employ to access network resources includes a selection to scan the user's local hard drive for viruses.

We recommend that users perform the virus scan at least once a week (once a day is the policy on many corporate networks) or before they copy a file from diskette to the network. We also have a dedicated virus-scanning NLM that we run on the server to watch for virus infections. Your best defense, however, against a virus wiping out large amounts of data is to have regular and up-to-date backups. That way, if a virus does infect a disk, either network or local, you can restore your most recent virus-free backup and get back to business.

With this technique in mind, think about the importance of timely backups. If you have to go back a month or even several weeks to get a clean backup to recover from a virus attack, you will have lost *a great deal* of work. Don't forget that viruses may have been around for a while, so please check before you assume your backup is clean. In case you still haven't gotten the message . . . BACK UP, BACK UP, BACK UP!

NetWare 4.x: More files, but the same system!

NetWare 4.x supports the same file system features as 3.x, except that it also offers file-by-file disk compression and disk block suballocation. Both of these features let you fit more files on your disk drives than you can with 3.x — up to twice as many, in fact. For some users this savings on disk space (and associated costs for additional drives) was enough to justify the costs of an upgrade. Otherwise, in terms of number of files, drives, volumes, and so on, the NetWare 4.x file system is identical to NetWare 3.x's.

No Rest for the Weary: Taking Care of Business

A network administrator's job is never done — or so it seems to network administrators. Even when things are running smoothly, you have your hands full doing all matter of upkeep and housecleaning. We consider everything from network backups to sweeping the server room floor to be part of your job description, no matter what your job description says.

By now, you should be acutely aware that server backups are an integral part of any LAN administrator's daily routine. Prompting your users to back up their local hard drives is also time very well spent. Pick one of the many tape-rotation schemes and stick to the schedule.

Be sure to store regularly at least one full, current copy of your backups off-site, to protect yourself from fire, theft, or other catastrophe. One company we know of simply mails a complete set of backup tapes to a division in another city once a week. The contact in the other division mails back the "old" tapes every time a new backup is received. The tapes then can be reused in the normal backup scheme. This company is comfortable that at least two complete copies of the server backups are off-site (either stored or in transit) at all times.

Other companies spend much more time and money having tape backups professionally stored by disaster-recovery specialists in climate-controlled caves deep underground. Some administrators we know simply keep a set of backups at home as a form of off-site storage. Other companies do nothing at all. Determine what kind of backup strategy you can afford and are comfortable with and stick to a regular schedule.

Another regular duty of a NetWare 3.*x* or 4.*x* LAN administrator is to monitor server disk usage and deleted files. Particularly if you choose not to limit each user's storage space on the server, you have to monitor how much disk space is being used by each user.

There is no faster way to crash a server than to allow the server hard drives to become full. Users neither know nor understand that server disk storage is a finite resource. We have had users back up their entire 500MB local hard drive to the network server so that they can reformat. It doesn't take many users to store that much data at one time before your server runs out of disk space.

Again, users consider the files they store in their home directory on the server to be personal property. The average user typically stores lots of games, résumés, and recipes in a home directory. Though your company may have a clearly stated policy forbidding such personal use of network resources, don't just begin erasing files at will. Explain to users that these types of items are against company rules; then give them a reasonable amount of time to copy the files to disk and let *them* erase the server copies.

Only when users repeatedly refuse to delete personal material from their home directory do we advocate that the administrator delete those files. Many users keep complete copies of applications stored in their home directory. This practice can be a massive waste of space because you may have 10 or 20 copies of the same program being stored in different places on the server.

A gentle reminder that the application is either already available elsewhere on the network or is known to be an illegal copy usually prods the user into deleting the files.

One final bit of housekeeping with versions 3.*x* and 4.*x* is to keep track of the number of deleted files retained on the server. The server erases all visible signs of a deleted file yet retains the file for salvaging as long as disk space remains. When the server runs out of disk space, deleted files are purged on a first deleted, first purged basis.

As a conscientious network administrator, you should occasionally browse through the list of deleted files, using the SALVAGE utility in version 3.*x* or the FILER utility in version 4.*x,* for any files deemed important enough to be salvaged right away or trivial enough to be purged right away.

Chapter 13

Network Security: It's Not Just for Cops and Robbers

● ●

In This Chapter

▶ Working with NetWare security and why you *do* care

▶ Assigning trustee assignments

▶ Assigning directory rights

▶ Working with application and data rights

▶ Setting up application security

▶ Setting file attributes to control file access

● ●

*N*etWare's security isn't a laughing matter, unless you *want* to be the butt of the joke. You should expect to be vulnerable if you haven't done everything you can to secure your LAN rights. Security means keeping the good guys in and the bad guys (the ones who want to destroy your data — or just steal it) out. You don't want the bad guys to wreak havoc on an otherwise stable LAN.

The way NetWare creates security, by limiting access to directories and the precious files within them, makes sense — if you know how to deal with it. Having a twisted mind helps you deal with network security, too. You don't have to be the type of paranoid person who reads the obituaries in the newspaper to see whether you're in them, but it can help. Security *can* be completely under your control. Controlling network security gives you a chance to play cops against the robbers trying to get in.

Unless you give NetWare security some passing thought, the security on your LAN is about as effective as having a toy poodle guard your home. Users who aren't allowed on the LAN can get on; users who are allowed on the LAN may sneak into areas they shouldn't. At best, chaos can ensue; at worst, your company's competitors may be better informed about your secrets than are most of your own insiders.

With some thought to how security will run on your LAN, you can make it as impenetrable as Alcatraz, without having to buy a private island for your network.

Keeping Watch: Setting Up the Right Controls

After you let users on your LAN, you can set access controls on the network to keep them from running amok and destroying files and data in their wake. The controls make security as tight or as loose as you want. If you know that Joe cannot be trusted with Sally's files, you can keep his prying little fingers out and limit him to playing with his own stuff. Or you can give groups of users access to common files so that those who work together, stay together. These rights and attributes tell you what you can do with a file or directory; they can also control who has access to the network, which files and directories they can access, and how they can use these resources. Pretty heady stuff.

You have to ask these types of questions: What's the right level of security for my network? Do I need to act like the warden at Alcatraz, or can I be entirely trusting of my LAN users? If you don't know the answers, begin by locking things up tight and shutting all gates to intruders. Then you can relax your security procedures as you find that you can trust the people working on your LAN. You don't want to let everyone in on the company's salary records and then find that the lone gossip in the crowd tells everyone else. Think about it.

This chapter covers the byzantine, confusing, and thoroughly abstruse topic of NetWare security, with a heavy dose of general-purpose LAN security thrown in. The danger is that the level of detail, stupefying as it is, may put you to sleep. Don't be lulled. This stuff, as tricky and odd as it is, is really important. Stay awake! Pay attention! Your LAN, your company — and, ultimately, your job — are at stake here.

It ain't easy being a NetWare supervisor

Security starts before you begin to think about configuring the network that you have just installed. During installation, NetWare automatically creates two accounts: the one called SUPERVISOR has unlimited privileges, and the one called GUEST has — you guessed it — much fewer privileges. More about that later.

The user of the SUPERVISOR account controls the network (for NetWare 4.*x*, two key accounts offer total control: ADMIN and SUPERVISOR). The supervisor can create and delete users and change those users' access to files and directories. The supervisor creates the initial directory structure for the specific file server and has access to the entire system — quite a formidable responsibility. The responsibility for a badly built file system or for loosely administered security can be pinned directly on the supervisor. Everyone looks for the supervisor when something goes wrong.

Because the supervisor has access to the soft underbelly of the network, he or she is one of the only people who can control whether NetWare security works.

If a LAN is big enough, NetWare 3.x supervisors can grow their empires and create other managers, called *workgroup managers,* who have limited capability to grant access to files or directories for workgroups under their control. In the 4.x realm, they can actually control who gets to mess with what parts of NDS, for even finer control over network resources. Supervisors can also create *operators,* who can perform certain operations from the file server console or print server.

The supervisor's rights don't end with the creation of users and the administration of the NetWare file system. The supervisor can modify the system login script, which is the part of NetWare that controls the drives a user automatically maps to and that defines the printers users print to. The supervisor also can decide whether users see those cute "Time to get to work" messages when they log in.

Finally, the supervisor gets to be head inquisitor and prosecutor. The supervisor can run programs that detect intruders trying to break into the LAN. Because the supervisor is so powerful, no one, including the supervisor, can delete the SUPERVISOR account on NetWare 3.x. For NetWare 4.x, this applies to ADMIN only, but the key difference is that you can delete ADMIN if you try. Because this completely disables administrative access to the network, we don't suggest you try this. In fact, we're sorry we mentioned it at all!

Visiting hours

The other account automatically created in v3.x is GUEST. Network administrators usually have two views of GUEST. One is that guests shouldn't be allowed on the LAN. Because GUEST is automatically a member of group EVERYONE (the group that contains everyone else on the LAN), visitors using the GUEST account can get into anything a member of EVERYONE can see. And because guests are simply that — guests on the LAN — you cannot expect them to know what they are doing.

Many supervisors delete GUEST immediately with the SYSCON utility in NetWare v3.x or with the NetWare Administrator (NWADMIN) or NETADMIN in NetWare 4.x. The capability to delete GUEST brings out the downside of security, which, as everyone knows, is called *paranoia!* (If someone is really out to get you — and they may be — you're not being paranoid, you're being realistic.)

The other view of GUEST is more magnanimous and much less paranoid. Many administrators keep the GUEST account to help their regular users with printing. If you create GUEST as a queue user with PCONSOLE on each file server, when users choose CAPTURE or NPRINT to print to that file server, the print job logs in as GUEST. If you do this, users can CAPTURE to file servers that they wouldn't otherwise be able to use. In addition, because you can use this technique to make all your printers generally available, your users won't complain that they can't get to the 17-page-per-minute printer in the marketing department. If you decide to keep the GUEST account, you should grant GUEST exclusive rights to PUBLIC only for printing and limit that account's access to other parts of the file server.

For more information about printing, see Chapter 15.

If you don't want help, don't do this

Supervisors can also create superusers just like themselves. Called *supervisor-equivalents,* these users have the same rights and privileges as the supervisor. If you're the system administrator, you don't want to create superusers often. Too many superusers can result in an out of control situation, just like too many cooks in the kitchen can. You may want to create a back door to the system for yourself because the SUPERVISOR account can be susceptible to virus attacks and other devious measures. This account can be a secret supervisor-equivalent that nobody else knows about, for example.

If you're the supervisor, the best approach to working on your network is to create an account without supervisor equivalence (like everyone else), where you do your day-to-day work, and reserve SUPERVISOR logins for strictly supervisory duties (for NetWare 4.*x* this means ADMIN and SUPERVISOR). Believe it or not, this technique can prevent problems that might otherwise spoil your day. Having two accounts also keeps you from forgetting that you can trash the whole file system and then doing just that accidentally.

Supervisors and users can also set user accounts to be security-equivalent to each other or to group accounts. You can set security equivalence through SYSCON in v3.*x* and by way of NWADMIN or NETADMIN in 4.*x*.

Using other empowered entities

Supervisors aren't the only ones who have power over the LAN, but control starts with them and trickles down to others on the LAN. If day-to-day responsibilities get to be too much to handle, you can create workgroup managers in v3.*x* who manage subsets of users to help you. In NetWare 4.*x,* NDS managers take care of their own fiefdoms, which are the individual partitions of the NetWare Directory Services (NDS) database.

Suppose that Jenny in the accounting department can create users when new people are hired. She can delete those users when they are fired. Jenny has a fiefdom in accounting — she controls the disk directories and files that her users can access, when they can work on the LAN, and when their passwords change. She can assign to the network any access that she herself possesses. If Jenny decides to be generous, she can create an account manager to help her out. The account manager can do everything that Jenny can do, except create and delete users.

The primary determinant of who manages a network, or a portion of a network, is who's knowledgeable, available, and nearby — in that order. This approach doesn't always produce the best results, but it's better than nothing. If you want to take security (or other convoluted networking topics) seriously, ask for some training.

NetWare 4.x Security Specialties: Single Login, Digital Signature, and More

Novell's newest network operating system, 4.x, has lots of ways to catch network crooks. It offers more protection at individual workstations and at the file server. The biggest difference between NetWare versions, though, is 4.x's ability to let users log in one time only, whether to one file server or many. NetWare 4.x also adds a complicated, but very secure, login procedure based on digital signatures, protection of the network operating system kernel against errant programs, increased security for its directory system, expanded intruder detection, and government C2 security-equivalence. If NetWare 4.x leaves any security tweaks out, you need a military arsenal of snooping devices to find them (for really security-conscious users, a similar software retrofit is available for v3.1x).

Technical stuff you want to read for NetWare 4.x

Doesn't it bug you when everything is going along fine and then someone changes the rules? That's just what Novell did. NetWare 4.x gets rid of the SUPERVISOR account in favor of specialized users who have supervisory rights for different parts of the LAN and tasks. Because NetWare 4.x views the network not as a single file server or even as a collection of file servers but as a single entity (the network taken as a whole), no sole person has, or needs to have, control over the entire network. Individuals exist who may be responsible, for example, for the directory partition that marketing uses or for the sales partition.

Or a specialized user may exist who has the ability to audit the network.

ADMIN itself has access to the *root* of the directory tree. ADMIN therefore can create the network's initial directory structure, and it can create administrators to manage segments of the directory tree, called *partitions*. Or ADMIN can create a portion of the initial structure and let partition managers create the rest. The result is a more flexible and capable administrative environment, but one that you must think through and match to your organization's structure and needs.

NetWare 4.x starts its security regimen when a user logs in to the network. In previous versions, the password was sent in encrypted form across the network from the workstation to the file server. NetWare 4.x dispenses with traveling passwords — it uses a digital authentication feature that builds a password for each login to prevent sophisticated users with protocol analyzers or other snooping devices from catching passwords as they traverse the network. NetWare 4.x foils password thieves like this:

1. The user runs LOGIN.EXE from his or her workstation.

2. Two programs on the workstation request the server to authenticate the login.

3. The server issues a private key, which is encrypted. The user then enters his or her password.

4. Programs on the workstation decrypt the key, build a digital *signature,* perform authentication, and send the proof of the signature and authentication to the server. The signature consists of a combination of the user's name, his or her workstation's node address, and the day and time of login. The workstation continues to request to log in to the network.

5. The server checks the credentials, and if they match what the server expects, the server lets the workstation log in.

Programs running on the file server also aren't any longer a threat to network security, as they were in NetWare 3.x. NetWare 3.x can only run NetWare Loadable Modules within the core (which is called the *kernel,* just like popcorn) of the network operating system. In NetWare 4.11, however, Novell has enabled special recovery techniques to allow your server to *abend* (short for *Ab*normal *End*) and gracefully recover without bringing the entire server down. Now you can test suspect or new NLMs without quite as much risk of crashing the server.

Let us warn you that although the new abend recovery features of NetWare 4.11 are a welcome relief in the battle against buggy NLMs, a rogue NLM can still bring the server crashing down to its PC knees. A server crash, however, is just not as likely to happen as it once was. NetWare 4.11 also has the good manners to write the abend messages to a log file on the DOS partition and append that information to the server error log on the SYS volume when and if the SYS volume is available again. Let's be careful out there.

Security has been augmented in 4.x to make room for NetWare Directory Services (NDS), which we discuss more in Chapter 11. While NetWare 3.x has only file system and login security, NetWare 4.x adds NDS security, which lets the network manager control access to the network resources.

NDS security permits access to be assigned to network objects such as printers or other resources. For users to use that object, they must have access to it. In NDS security, rights are assigned that flow down the directory tree, just like in 3.x. Objects may have BROWSE, CREATE, DELETE, RENAME, or SUPERVISOR rights. BROWSE lets users see objects but not view its properties. CREATE lets users define new container objects. DELETE lets you delete empty containers and leaf objects. RENAME lets you change a leaf object's name. Finally, SUPERVISOR gives you rights to every object.

Each object also has property rights that specify the actions users can take. These rights are COMPARE, READ, ADD or DELETE SELF, WRITE, and SUPERVISOR. If you have the READ right, you can view a properties value; if you have WRITE rights, you can change property values. NetWare 4.x also maintains an *Access Control List,* which is assigned for each object. This list contains the access rights of the object.

Last, 4.x also has added traps for intruders, including those required by the government classification called C2 security, which are established in NETADMIN. Whereas 3.x allowed intruder detection only at the file server level, 4.x lets you nab intruders within containers. That means NetWare 4.x is good at keeping tabs of the smallest details and those minuscule intrusions on someone else's stuff.

Ack! A Bad Hair Day: NetWare Attributes Need Managing, Too

Just like hair, NetWare files and directories have attributes that determine what you can or cannot do with them. Mismanaged attributes are similar to out-of-control, flyaway hair; when they are managed correctly, however, attributes permit you to style your LAN any way you want. The NetWare file and disk directory attributes differ, based on the version of NetWare you are using, but certain attributes are common to all versions to date.

Table 13-1 shows the attributes that apply equally to NetWare v3.x and 4.x. These attributes are the ones that you use most commonly — the tools that you need in order to manage your file system and control access to your server. Don't memorize them unless you're a compulsive control freak, but do find out how to use them. Over time, they will become your best friends. For now, though, they probably seem a little confusing.

Beginning with NetWare v3.0, Novell added other attributes that are specific only to that version. Because file and directory attributes didn't change between 3.x and 4.x, these attributes work with NetWare version 4.x, too.

Table 13-1	Common NetWare Attributes
Name	*Description*
ARCHIVE NEEDED (files only)	If you back up your system, you use this attribute. The operating system changes it when the file is modified — you don't have to worry about setting it yourself.
EXECUTE ONLY (files only)	.COM and .EXE files are the only files that have this attribute, which keeps these files from being copied or changed. Use this attribute with caution: After you have assigned it, you cannot remove it. The only thing that you can do to override this setting is to copy the files again from their original disks. Some .EXE programs will not work when set to EXECUTE ONLY. This happens in packages that call other programs — almost like an overlay. Remember to have a backup somewhere of these programs, because tape backups won't usually be able to copy (or restore) them either.
HIDDEN (files and directories)	This attribute lets you hide files and directories so that they cannot be found with the DIR command. If you know how to use NetWare, you still can see files and directories with NDIR, the NetWare command-line utility, but only if your rights include FILE SCAN. If you don't know how to see hidden files, you're probably not a real NetWare aficionado.
\SHARABLE (files only)	In NetWare, this attribute lets two or more users access the same file simultaneously. When files are created or copied to a file server, they are nonsharable. Before making files sharable, be sure that the application that uses these types of files can handle multiple simultaneous users. (Sharable rights are required for programs such as those used by database management systems, whose files must be shared in order to do what they're supposed to.)
SYSTEM (files only)	This attribute hides the file from the DIR command. This attribute is another one that lets you see files with NDIR. (The same rules apply: You must have the FILE SCAN right.) This attribute is intended to keep NetWare's own system files from being snooped — or worse.
TRANSACTIONAL (files only)	NetWare's transaction tracking system uses this attribute, which keeps database files from being deleted.
READ ONLY (files only)	The look-but-don't-touch attribute lets a user read or execute a file but not write to, erase, or rename it. RENAME INHIBIT and DELETE INHIBIT are assigned as part of READ ONLY.

Name	Description
READ/WRITE (files only)	This attribute is similar to having free rein in a candy store — it lets users read and write to files and overrides the READ ONLY attribute. All files are set to READ/WRITE as a default.
COPY INHIBIT	This attribute sounds like what it means. It doesn't allow copying of files having this attribute, and it applies only to Macintosh files.
DELETE INHIBIT	This attribute is the same as COPY INHIBIT. You cannot delete or erase these files or directories. It applies to both DOS and Macintosh files, however.
PURGE	The bulimic security option is an irreversible attribute. After you have assigned PURGE to a file and it is deleted, you cannot do anything to salvage it. Don't mess with PURGE, unless you're feeling suicidal. If you do, you had better have a backup handy just in case. Once you set a file's attribute to PURGE, it's gone for good.
RENAME INHIBIT	This attribute doesn't let you rename files or directories, so don't change your mind. If your current rights include MODIFY, though, this attribute has no effect. It is as obscure as it sounds and seldom used.

Auditing 4.x Style: The Whole Shebang

NetWare 4.x creates a paper trail that exceeds what most companies want. It allows network auditors to be created in the NDS database. The primary responsibility of network auditors is auditing the collection of 4.x servers on the network and the users of those servers.

A 4.x-specific utility, AUDITCON is the key tool in the auditor's toolkit. We talk more about AUDITCON in Chapter 14.

The Easy Way Out: Tips for Setting Attributes

Now that you know which attributes files and directories can have, you're curious about how you can change them. Aren't you? *Not!*

You can set file attributes in several ways. With NetWare 4.x, you can use the NWADMIN utility to assign and manage users, directory, and object rights. The DOS-based version of NWADMIN is called NETADMIN. You can also use NETADMIN to manage rights under NetWare 4.x. NetWare 4.11 also has a new 32-bit administration utility called NWADMN95.EXE for you Windows 95 and Windows NT users.

With NetWare 3.x, you can still use the venerable FILER utility and the FLAG or FLAGDIR commands. If this concept sounds confusing — it is. If you're not sure about what to use, try these utilities one at a time. If one of them works, use it and stick with it.

The following list gives some tips for learning what you need to know about attributes:

- ✔ Flag EXEs and COMs as SHARABLE, READ ONLY, and EXECUTE ONLY. If a file modifies itself, don't set it to READ ONLY (or it will not work properly).

- ✔ Flag OVL and DAT as SHARABLE and READ ONLY.

- ✔ Set files such as database files that use the Transaction Tracking System (TTS) to TRANSACTIONAL. This action helps to ensure proper handling from NetWare for transaction-oriented files.

Stand Up for Your Rights: Directory, File, and Trustee Rights

Before users log in to the LAN, the only disk directory they're permitted to access is SYS:LOGIN. From that directory, they can log in to the LAN or run SLIST to see which servers exist on the LAN. As users log in, their usernames (also called login names) are verified by the system. If the users are known to the system, they may be asked to enter a password. If they aren't known, their login attempt is rejected. After users enter the correct password, they are admitted to the system. Incorrect passwords lead to rejection, just like invalid usernames do.

Users' access to the system depends on the rights they have to files and directories on the file server and the attributes assigned to those files and directories. These rights are stored in a database called the *bindery* in NetWare v3.x. The NetWare directory replaces the bindery in 4.x, but the schemes remain pretty similar. When you assign to a user access rights to a particular directory or file, the user becomes a *trustee* of that directory or file. The rights the user possesses are called *trustee rights*.

All versions of NetWare share common rights to disk directories, files, and trustees. Table 13-2 presents a comprehensive list of NetWare rights that apply to security concerns (it doesn't cover storage-specific rights added with NetWare 4.*x*, however). These rights are worth getting to know because you use them to determine who gets to do what to your file system. It's just like the law: With security rights, ignorance is no excuse!

Table 13-2	NetWare Security Rights
Name	*Definition*
ACCESS CONTROL	Gives the user who possesses it ultimate control. It lets you control all other users' rights. You can change the inherited rights mask and trustee assignments for directories or files.
CREATE	Lets you make directories and create files.
ERASE	Lets you erase files if their attributes are not set to READ ONLY or some other attribute that prohibits deletion.
FILE SCAN	When you use DIR, you do not see files unless you have the FILE SCAN right.
MODIFY	You should treat this right carefully and give it only to users who need it. MODIFY lets you change or rename files or directories and their names and attributes.
READ	Lets you open files that another person isn't using or as long as they have not been set with the EXECUTE ONLY attribute. READ also lets you run executable programs.
SUPERVISORY	The ultimate right; it grants access to everything. The inherited rights mask cannot touch this right.
WRITE	Like READ, WRITE lets you open files. It also lets you write to them as long as they aren't in use by another person or set to READ ONLY.

Two approaches to network security

In NetWare 3.*x*, you log in to a single server with LOGIN, and use ATTACH to attach to the other servers that you want to access. Novell calls this approach *server-centric*. NDS uses a network-centric approach instead, which makes life much easier. With NetWare 4.*x*, when users log in to the network, their rights may include access to other servers without those users knowing anything about it. In other words, NDS removes the behind-the-scenes details from the user's view. The user simply logs in to the NDS tree, and the NDS database automagically gives the user the correct rights to every network resource to which they have access. How's that for progress?

The right way to assign rights

Just as with most things in life, a recommended way exists to assign rights to users and groups for NetWare. Rather than have to learn from the school of hard knocks, follow these steps to avoid the bumps and bruises that this type of a diploma can cause:

1. Assign users to groups and assign rights to the group. It's easier than assigning the same rights to a bunch of people who use the same applications.

2. Don't give users rights to the SYS:SYSTEM directory. This directory contains the bindery. Access to the bindery invites trouble on your LAN.

3. The SUPERVISOR should not have a home directory or mailbox. Both are encouragements to do day-to-day work in the SUPERVISOR account, which is exactly what you should avoid.

4. Never give users SUPERVISOR or ACCESS CONTROL rights to their own directories.

5. Users should have CREATE, MODIFY, FILE SCAN, and WRITE rights to the files to which they need to write.

6. Some applications use temporary files, which they store in a data directory. If you are using one of these directories, give users WRITE, ERASE, MODIFY, FILE SCAN, CREATE, and READ rights to those directories.

7. Don't assign CREATE and MODIFY rights to executable files.

8. Don't give users READ or FILE SCAN rights to other users' personal directories.

9. Give users all rights except ACCESS CONTROL in their mail directories.

10. Don't give users WRITE rights in the SYS:\PUBLIC directory.

11. Don't give users access to the root directory of the volume. Rights flow down the directory structure. If you give users access to the root directory, you have a system in which anyone can go anywhere and do anything.

12. Set the four main NetWare system directories (SYSTEM, PUBLIC, MAIL, and LOGIN) off the root to DELETE INHIBIT and RENAME INHIBIT.

Protecting Your Inheritance

In this section, you find out how rights pass down through directory structures in the NetWare file system, whether you assign them explicitly or not. Understanding how inheritance works can keep you from inheriting unnecessary headaches.

Trickling down the directory tree: Trustee or inherited rights

Sharing work on a network means sharing files with colleagues and coworkers. Whenever you're using files that belong to someone else, some of your rights to those files or directories will be those that their owner has explicitly assigned to you (as a trustee); the remainder of those rights, however, are inherited from those of their real owners. Knowing the difference between trustee rights and inherited rights can sometimes be important, so understanding the distinction is important.

Sound confusing? For a better understanding, suppose that you use these directory paths:

```
SYS:\APPS\DOSAPPS\WP\DATA
SYS:\APPS\DOSAPPS\WP\DATA
SYS:\APPS\WINAPPS\WORD
SYS:\APPS\WINAPPS\SPREAD\EXCEL
SYS:\APPS\WINAPPS\SPREAD\PARADOX
```

If a user on a DOS-based machine has rights to the directory DOSAPPS, he has the same rights to the subdirectories WP and DATA unless other rights have been imposed for those subdirectories that limit rights. The user is called a *trustee* of the subdirectory DOSAPPS. A Windows-based user may have rights beginning at the directory APPS because he needs access to both DOS and Windows applications. A Paradox user who doesn't do any word processing may need to be granted rights only to the PARADOX subdirectory and not have rights any higher on the directory tree.

Phantom of the NetWare opera: Using the inherited rights mask

The notion of an inherited rights mask (a *mask* is a quick way of blocking things off, or limiting options in computer-speak) in NetWare 4.x and 3.x limits the rights a user has in any given directory. Suppose that Bob has rights to CREATE, MODIFY, READ, WRITE, and FILE SCAN for a particular directory, but his *inherited rights mask* allows him only to READ, ERASE, and FILE SCAN. You could then say that Bob has *effective rights* only to READ and FILE SCAN.

You could change the *inherited rights mask* with the FILER utility in v3.x or change the equivalent capability, known as an *inherited rights filter*, with NWADMIN in 4.x and extend or curtail Bob's capabilities. Think of using the mask or filter as a way of reducing the fullest possible set of rights — the maximum rights — to the set of rights that can be used — the effective rights.

NetWare v3.*x* and 4.*x* use the inherited rights feature (mask or filter) as a tool to ease security administration for network managers. The inherited rights feature shows which rights a user can inherit from the parent directory. This feature can further limit the rights a user has. By default, a user inherits from the parent directory all rights to the system. You can revoke these rights and limit them by using FILER, SYSCON, GRANT, REMOVE, ALLOW, and REVOKE in v3.*x* or using NWADMIN in 4.*x*. After you assign an inherited rights feature to a directory, the resulting rights for any particular user in that directory are called the *effective rights*.

Examining and Changing Your Rights and Attributes

A number of utilities exist to let NetWare users look at or change their rights and attributes. These utilities work for both supervisors and regular users (but of course, supervisors inevitably get to see more than normal users do).

NetWare 4.*x* uses the following utilities to set and adjust user, directory, and object rights (but other utilities are available for 4.*x* that are worth exploring):

- ✔ **NWADMIN** — The NetWare Administrator
- ✔ **NETADMIN**
- ✔ **NETUSER**
- ✔ **RIGHTS:** Replaces ALLOW, REMOVE, REVOKE, and GRANT in v3.*x*.
- ✔ **FLAG:** Incorporates same functionality as FLAGDIR in v3.*x*.

NetWare v3.*x* uses a different set of utilities to set and maintain rights:

- ✔ **RIGHTS:** Lets you view trustee and effective rights.
- ✔ **ALLOW:** Lets you view and modify the inherited rights mask for files or directories.
- ✔ **REMOVE:** Lets you control and remove effective rights for users or groups.
- ✔ **REVOKE:** Lets you control and remove trustee rights.
- ✔ **FILER:** Lets you view and set file and directory attributes and control rights. Shows the inherited rights mask for v3.*x*. Shows trustees to users with PARENTAL rights.
- ✔ **FLAGDIR:** Lets you view and set directory attributes.
- ✔ **SYSCON:** Lets you view and control trustee rights.
- ✔ **GRANT:** Lets users or groups assign rights, remove rights, and control rights.
- ✔ **TLIST:** Lets you view trustees of a directory.

Chapter 14

Keeper of the Keys: Managing LAN Security

. . . .

. . . .

*N*ow that you have the rights and attributes you can use to control your LAN under lock and key, so to speak, you need some really important information about keeping your LAN secure. This is the fun stuff — you get to show your true colors and keep tabs on what's going on out there on the desktops of America.

By way of NWADMIN, NWADMN32, NETADMIN, or SYSCON, you can put additional limits on a user's access to the system. You can limit the number of workstations that a user can work from at a time (typically one) and control which particular workstation that a user can work from (his or her own).

If you have users who are always greedy about getting more disk space, the NetWare management utilities let you limit the amount of space that they can use. You can require that all users enter passwords to log in to the file server and that the passwords have a certain minimum length, be changed periodically, and remain unique. Doing these things keeps users on their toes and keeps any would-be intruders guessing.

Eighty-Sixed from Working on the LAN

If you really want to get strict about security and don't think that keys to the building do the job, you can restrict user access. You can restrict access by limiting the period when a user can log in to the system by time of day or day of the week or by setting a date after which logins are no longer permitted. You can also corral your users into a defined space and define the *home directory* to which they must first log in. This directory typically is \USERS*xxxx,* where *xxxx* is the name of whatever user you want it to be.

The Ins and Outs of Logging In and Out

Most intruders are easy to catch. They casually stroll up to a workstation when someone isn't looking and try to read the rightful owner's e-mail while the owner is away. Logging in to the network when you start and logging out when you finish working or leave your desk is one of the easiest ways to protect your data on the LAN and keep your mail about the boss private.

Every night before going home, log out. Some companies may even require you to log out every time you leave your workstation. If you don't, some companies are mean and take your login rights away. Don't tempt fate. Use this mantra whenever you are around a LAN: "Log out, log out, log out!" Do it. It's a cheap form of protection. Think of it as "safe computing."

The new-fangled v4.x login

With NetWare 4.11's NDS, you log in to the network rather than in to a particular server. The 4.11 client installation program creates a bigger, better NET.CFG than you've ever seen. Several of the parameters in the NET.CFG file specify the context and other login details in place of the old practice of specifying the server name as part of the LOGIN command. Figure 14-1 shows a sample NET.CFG file created by the NetWare 4.11 client installation program. Note the NDS context information.

With these new additions to the NET.CFG file, all you have to do to log in to the NetWare 4.11 network is type in your user name like this:

```
LOGIN FRED_GARVIN
```

Figure 14-1:
NetWare
4.11's client
installation
inserts login
information
into the
NET.CFG.

```
PREFERRED SERVER = earlvis
LINK DRIVER EPROODI
      PORT 220
      FRAME ETHERNET_802.2

NetWare DOS Requester
      FIRST NETWORK DRIVE = F
      NETWARE PROTOCOL = NDS BIND
```

Log in the old-fashioned way

You have two ways to log in to a NetWare v3.*x* network: You can put the login commands and your password in your workstation's AUTOEXEC.BAT file. But that's kind of a dumb thing to do because anybody who takes the time to peek at your AUTOEXEC.BAT will know what your password is. Duh! Or you can do it the way we like to set up logins for users on our networks: you can put only the LOGIN statement in your AUTOEXEC.BAT. The user then only has to enter his or her password each time the machine boots up. The only time this arrangement doesn't work well is if two or more users share the PC on a regular basis.

The following code shows an example of an AUTOEXEC.BAT file with the LOGIN command inserted for the convenience of the user.

```
@ECHO OFF
PROMPT $p$g
PATH C:\WINDOWS;C:\DOS;
SET TEMP=C:\TEMP
SET MOUSE=C:\MOUSE
CALL C:\NWCLIENT\STARTNET.BAT
F:\LOGIN LOGIN BIGSERVER/FRED_GARVIN
```

Or as a last, low-tech method for your network users, you can simply teach your users to enter the commands manually.

To log in, you have to enter the file server name, followed by your username, like this:

```
LOGIN BIGSERVER/FRED_GARVIN
```

Notice that the server name BIGSERVER is separated from the username by a forward slash mark (/). If BIGSERVER is the only server on your network, you can dispense with its name and simply enter your username, like this:

```
LOGIN FRED_GARVIN
```

If your network has more than one server, supplying the right server name is vital when you are logging in, especially if it's the only server that you can use.

Next, you are asked to supply your own unique password, as discussed in the following section.

Passwords: How to Build 'Em, Use 'Em, and Keep 'Em Fresh

As though all the other forms of security weren't enough (and they aren't), NetWare also lets you protect your files and directories from prying eyes. You can assign a unique password for yourself and for each user on the LAN.

Simon says this about passwords

Several dos and don'ts about passwords are worth remembering. These guidelines are especially helpful when you are trying to keep your users able to use the network without opening the door to any one who happens to cruise by. The following list specifies things you definitely should do and some things you assuredly should avoid:

Do:

✔ Change your password periodically. A network manager can set an expiration period for passwords in NWADMIN, NWADMN32, NETADMIN, or SYSCON; a good network manager uses this capability. Requiring changes once a month is a good interval.

✔ Require passwords to be at least five characters long. Shorter passwords are easier to guess.

✔ Use a password that you will remember. Asking for help when you forget something important is embarrassing. (Remember that guy in *Annie Hall* who couldn't remember his mantra?)

Don't:

- ✔ Use the name of your dog, cat, wife, or husband as your password.

- ✔ Tape your password to your desk.

- ✔ Give your password to anyone else.

- ✔ Use a password less than five characters long.

- ✔ Make your password too long, either. NetWare lets you create passwords of as many as 127 characters. Only a fool would create a password that long. *Don't* be a fool.

If you forget your password, the network manager can easily change it with NWADMIN, NWADMN32, NETADMIN, or SYSCON. As a user, you can't. Nor can you save the old password. That's the penalty you pay for forgetting: a new opportunity to forget again.

Security begins (but doesn't end) at home...

As you get used to dealing with NetWare security, you notice that some situations tend to recur. Some things can go wrong or get weird because of inadequate security planning. Table 14-1 documents some typical security problems — some of which can have extreme consequences — that are totally avoidable.

Table 14-1	Avoidable Security Problems
Problem	*Prevention or Solution*
Password problems	Password problems of all types exist. You have less-than-savvy network managers who never require users to have a password, who never change their own passwords, or who allow passwords that are short and easy to guess. Be proactive and set up password security in NWADMIN, NWADMN32, NETADMIN, or SYSCON.
Supervisor equivalence	Make as few users as possible supervisor-equivalents.
Access to root directory	The first rule of security in NetWare is "Don't let users get to the root directory." When they have access there, they have access everywhere. Enough said.
Login script (or lack thereof)	Login scripts both permit and prohibit access. Each user on the network can have his own login script that extends, or overrides, the system login script.

(continued)

Table 14-1 *(continued)*

Problem	Prevention or Solution
More than enough rights	Give users the rights to only those directories and files that they need to use. Don't be lazy. If you can't trust certain members of a group, restrict their rights.
Workgroup managers	If your organization is large enough, set up workgroup managers so that they can manage the users in their departments. This process frees you to do something really important on your LAN, like your work.
Lost users	Users disappear, they get fired, they leave the company. Don't leave them on your system — you leave gaping holes in your security when you do. Whenever a user should no longer have rights on the LAN, delete the account or have the workgroup manager, account manager, or partition manager do it.

. . . And at your neighbor's, too!

Many network managers use diskless workstations to better control what goes on, or what comes off, their LAN. If users cannot copy stuff to or from floppies, users are severely limited as to what kind of work they can do. Also, if you want your LAN to be really secure and you have users who work from home, don't let them transfer files to the office. Make them bring in any new or changed files on a disk so that you can scan them for viruses. Or install virus-scanning software in NetWare's system login — which always runs when a user logs in and precedes individual login scripts — that automatically scans any floppies before anyone can assess them.

Stuff only code-breakers need to know

Before the introduction of NetWare v2.15x, passwords were sent across the wire in clear text, which made them susceptible to password snooping. Now, all subsequent versions of NetWare can send encrypted passwords across the wire. NetWare even stores the passwords in encrypted form in the bindery (version 3.x) or in the NetWare Directory (version 4.x and higher), whichever applies to the version you're running. The algorithm is so complicated that supposedly even Einstein would have a tough time breaking it. Our advice: Don't bother trying!

Now for Some Audit Checks

NetWare 4.*x* includes a new utility called AUDITCON. Users defined as *auditors* for segments of the network can monitor specific events on the network. They can see when users log in and log out; when any rights or attributes change; and when users create, modify, or delete files. This utility offers a great deal more information and provides considerably better accountability than the previous audit capabilities built in to NetWare. It also takes up space and adds overhead to your system; only you and your company can decide whether AUDITCON is worth the space and overhead. Because the auditing stuff was designed for banking and securities trading audits, if what you're doing resembles those industries, you probably will find it interesting. It's also a great source of info for the insatiably curious or persistently snoopy.

NetWare v3.*x* has rudimentary auditing features. You can run the SECURITY utility to show the holes in your file server's security. You can even view a log that lists possible intrusions as unauthorized users try to log in to the network. But you can't do any full-scale auditing (not from a utility designed for that purpose) of the network without buying special-purpose, add-on software from Novell — and that is for NetWare v3.12 only.

Intruders aren't welcome here

NetWare lets you protect your LAN from unwelcome guests with the NWADMIN, NWADMN32, NETADMIN, or SYSCON utilities. You can record invalid login attempts. You can even lock out users after a specified number of incorrect logins and keep them off the network for a specified time. If you have intruder-detection turned on, you can record the workstation address that the intruder is using to try to get into the system — if you keep a list of the locations that correspond to workstation addresses. (And you wonder why we think creating and maintaining a map of your LAN is a good idea!)

Keep servers under lock and key

The truism that a determined miscreant can always find a way to subvert security is as true for LANs as it is for your home or office. If the bad guys want in, they find a way. The best approach is to advertise that you're hip to security and to let them know that other places may offer easier pickings.

If you don't want the bad guys testing your network security, put servers in locked rooms to which only authorized individuals have keys. Novell has always recommended that servers be stored in physically secure locations for the very good reason that anyone who knows what he is doing can bring down an accessible server and bring it up under DOS. If the bad guy *really* knows his stuff, he can use a low-level disk editor to change some key values and set himself up as the SUPERVISOR.

For the truly paranoid, a simple lock isn't sufficient. If your application is sensitive enough to create concern, you should consider using an entry-control system that tracks who's coming and going, or you should install a camera to monitor entries and exits. These security measures may be a little extreme for most companies, but controlling who accesses your servers is the best way to keep out of harm's way.

Troubleshooting the Security Gotchas

In administering a network, garden-variety network mistakes can be as common as fleas on a dog and as uncomfortable as flea bites. Fortunately, the network mistakes are easier to get rid of than fleas; but if mistakes aren't caught in time, they can be even more devastating than fleas.

Table 14-2 includes most of the common security mishaps that you're likely to encounter. You will get to know them anyway, so why not check them out? After all, you'd probably prefer to find out how to prevent network security mistakes by reading about them instead of making the mistakes yourself.

NetWare's minimum password length defaults to five characters, and most supervisors we know stick by this rule.

Table 14-2	Common Security *Gotchas*
Gotcha	*Prevention or Cure*
Front door is missing; no back door	Not having a back-door account to the network if you are the supervisor is a common and costly mistake. This mishap is similar to forgetting your password, a costly and all-too-common mistake. Several utilities exist that enable you to change the SUPERVISOR password; if you have forgotten it, however, you probably don't deserve to use those utilities.
I forgot my password.	If you're a user on the system, you're luckier than the supervisor who forgets her password. At least you have an out: You can have the supervisor change your password (if the supervisor is there and assuming that we're not talking about the forgetful dolt referred to in the preceding *gotcha*).

Gotcha	*Prevention or Cure*
GUEST accounts were left on the system.	Having a GUEST account with broad privileges on your system can be worse than having houseguests. Houseguests smell like dead fish within three days; GUEST users begin to stink even sooner! Networks that have GUEST accounts are more susceptible to unwanted visitors than are networks that don't encourage GUEST users for anything except printer access. If you have any temporary users on the LAN, set them up with an account and give them passwords.
The SUPERVISOR account was misnamed.	Watching out for dopes and dunces can be a way of life. Any supervisors who name their supervisory accounts something like SUPER or leave it at SUPERVISOR are inviting trouble. Furthermore, if your supervisor's name is Homer, that's not a good name for the account either. That account name is too easy to figure out. Call it GUS, unless someone named Gus works for your company.
You use the account that the supervisor works in.	If you have supervisor-equivalence, don't use that account for your day-to-day work. Use it only for managing the LAN. When you use a word processor or tweak a spreadsheet, use a regular user account. If you leave your desk to get water because your wastebasket's on fire, who knows what can happen? You'll probably return to find charred and discarded notes. But you may also find that someone has taken advantage of your absence to delete the entire file system or to lock everyone out of the server. Ouch!
You left your file server in an unlocked area.	Everyone knows that leaving your car unlocked at the mall is not a smart thing to do — your CDs may disappear or someone might trash your stereo — but you are the only one affected. Leaving your file server unlocked in a common area can have similar consequences, but it affects many more people than just you. Lock up your file server. Don't leave it unprotected, even from naive users who don't know what they are doing. And don't let just anybody mess with it.

(continued)

Table 14-2 *(continued)*

Gotcha	*Prevention or Cure*
The supervisor's keyboard was made accessible.	If you're the network supervisor, have supervisor-equivalence, or if you are a console operator, lock your keyboard when you leave your workstation. See "fires" and "unlocked" in the preceding two "gotchas."
I didn't lock the file server console.	NetWare v3.*x*'s MONITOR lets you lock the file server console. Do it. In 4.*x,* use MONITOR. Whatever your excuse might be, making excuses instead of locking the console just isn't worth the potential trouble that an unlocked console can cause.
Not logging off.	When you leave your workstation, log off the network. This pointer belongs in the same category as leaving your car unlocked, letting kids run around the office unsupervised, and creating conditions where people can get into places they shouldn't be. So take our advice: Log off when you leave your workstation!! Some third-party utilities automatically log you off after a specified period of inactivity; if you (or your users) can't remember to log off, get one.
Someone is trying to break into system.	Intruder detection tells you the network address, the node address, and the IPX socket that any intruder may be trying to use. If you have a list of network addresses matched to locations, you can quickly find which workstation is under attack. Or, if you have a similar list for node addresses, you can sometimes use this list to determine which workstation to look for. Don't count on the node address being helpful though. Smart hackers can change the node address for any access method that supports locally administered addresses. This statement applies to ARCnet, Ethernet, or token ring networks. If the intruders are that smart, the IPX socket address doesn't do you any good.

Gotcha	*Prevention or Cure*
I ran out of grace logins; now what do I do?	You are almost out of the luck that has kept you running until now. You cannot log in anymore, and you cannot change your password. You aren't totally out of luck, though. The supervisor can assign you more logins by using SYSCON or can change the expiration date of your password. Take advantage of the situation — change your password whenever NetWare says to change it.
I forgot my password.	Here's one good reason not to change your password too often: You will forget it. If you do, the supervisor can change it for you by way of SYSCON. But you have to create a new password. Just don't forget it again (but don't tape it to your desk either).
Help! I can't get into the network.	Several reasons can explain your being unable to log in to the LAN. They are shown in this list:
	✔ You have entered the wrong username. You are asked to enter a password, or if passwords aren't required on your LAN, you receive the error message Invalid Login. Try again.
	✔ You have entered the wrong password. You receive the error message Invalid password. Try again. If you try unsuccessfully too many times, intruder detection may lock you out.
	✔ The supervisor has disabled login. Sometimes, when maintenance is necessary or when a supervisor wants to keep a particularly misbehaving user off the LAN, the supervisor disables login from SYSCON or NETADMIN. Whatever you do, you cannot log in to the LAN until login is re-enabled. Don't worry — be happy!
	✔ The network is down. You receive the message File Server Not Found. Again, you can't do much about this.
The computer says that my password's too short.	NetWare lets the supervisor set a minimum length on passwords. Imagine if your password were a single character long. With the password limitation of 40 possible characters, someone needs only that many attempts to break in to the system. Intruder detection can lock out someone trying to break in, but break-ins still may occur. The same thing applies to two-, three-, or four-character passwords.

Chapter 15

Hard Copy: Printing in the NetWare Environment

. . . .

In This Chapter

▶ Looking at the printing basics: users, printers, and queues

▶ Using the NetWare user print utilities

▶ Setting up and configuring NetWare printers

▶ Managing print jobs

▶ Sharing workstation printers on the network

▶ NetWare Distributed Print Services

▶ Using special printer functions

. . . .

*O*ne of the biggest arguments for networking since its inception has been its capability to share expensive peripherals, particularly printers. Everyone appreciates the good looks, fast output, and fancy font-handling capabilities of today's generation of laser printers, but hardly anyone can afford to put one of these puppies on every user's desk.

You get a much bigger bang for your buck if you spend a pile on a single printer and then make it available over the network. If you have to buy printers for everyone, they would have to be slower, noisier, and of lower quality just to be affordable. For better or worse, our tastes in hard copy have become too finicky for that kind of a solution to be palatable.

Networking printers also makes providing better services, such as color or duplex (both sides of a page) printing, possible. It makes it easy to situate printers conveniently for users, and it helps consolidate expenses for electricity and consumables (paper and toner cartridges or ribbons, for example).

In short, networking's capability to deliver high-speed, high-quality printing to its users is still one of the best and most powerful reasons that people and businesses use networks. Doesn't it make you wonder why the press keeps talking about "the paperless office?"

In this chapter, you get a grip on what it takes to set up, manage, and use networked printers with NetWare. You find out how users work with printing and how to manage this service for them as a network supervisor. By the time you finish, you should be ready to deliver hard copy to everyone who needs it.

Networked Printing: Spoofing the Printer Port

When you have a single PC with its own private printer attached, printing seems like the easiest, most natural thing in the world. The trickiest part is getting Windows and your applications set up with the right printer driver, so that your PC knows how to get the most from the printer it's using. So what's the big deal about printing on a network? It should just be an extension of stand-alone printing, right?

As it turns out, when something like a printer is shared on the network, a mechanism (called a *queue*) must be put in place to handle and arbitrate among competing requests for service. The job of the queue is to accept requests for service as they arrive and to hand them off to be serviced as the printer becomes available.

In other cases, the workstation's software is built with an understanding of networked printing services, like the Macintosh, and it directly initiates moving the print job over the network to a printer or print queue for service.

In the NetWare environment, print queues are usually handled by NetWare servers, dedicated PCs, or specialized printers with built-in server capabilities, any of which can act as a print server. The print server's job is to accept incoming print jobs from workstations and to store them. In Figure 15-1, the left side is an exact illustration of how a stand-alone PC with its own private printer works. The right side is a more accurate description of how the process works on a network. It shows the print job being shipped across the network into a queue, where it waits its turn to be sent to the printer (which may or may not be across the network, too) and then to get printed.

Figure 15-1:
Two views
of printing:
what users
think (left
side) and
how print
queues
work (right
side).

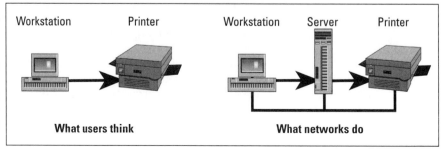

What users think   What networks do

The printing players: Users, printers, print servers, and queues

Network printing is made possible by the network access software that runs on a workstation. In most cases, network printing takes advantage of the functionality supplied by the network access software on a workstation (refer to Chapter 1). This functionality redirects print jobs from a local destination — typically, that machine's printer port — and ships them over the network to a print queue instead. In other cases, the workstation's software is built with an understanding of networked printing services, like the Macintosh, and it directly initiates moving the print job over the network to a printer or print queue for service.

In the NetWare environment, print queues are usually handled by NetWare servers or by dedicated PCs, either of which is acting as a print server. (The print server's job is to accept incoming print jobs.)

In the spirit of good printer housekeeping, NetWare print servers also offer lots of additional functionality, including these capabilities:

- ✔ Send all status messages to a queue operator and to the print server supervisor, as well as to users. (You no doubt want to use this capability, in case a user fires off a long print job and leaves for lunch, only to have the printer run out of paper ten minutes later.)
- ✔ Define and request printing on particular forms (legal- versus letter-size paper, envelopes, and letterhead, for example).
- ✔ Service multiple printers from a single queue, or multiple queues from a single printer.
- ✔ Control a printer's print modes (use regular, condensed, or expanded fonts, for example) or enable landscape printing (across the long dimension of a regular page) or portrait printing (across the short dimension of a regular page).
- ✔ Manage the contents of print queues (delete, redefine, or rearrange existing print jobs).

The two faces of NetWare's print servers, plus one!

Three kinds of print servers are available for use in the NetWare environment. First, for server-based printing, NetWare 3.*x* and 4.*x* offer a NetWare Loadable Module implementation called PSERVER.NLM. Second, NetWare v3.11 also offers an implementation that runs on a dedicated PC set up as a dedicated router. Even though both NetWare 3.*x* and 4.*x* include a DOS program called PSERVER.EXE that offers the same capability, it requires you to set up a DOS PC to act as a dedicated print server. Each of these approaches has its pros and cons, as you see in this section.

PSERVER.EXE

The PSERVER.EXE implementation runs on a dedicated workstation that can be placed anywhere on the network. Using PSERVER.EXE reduces the load on your network servers and eliminates any need to let users close to those servers (which they might need to do if printers were attached directly to those servers). Novell recommends using a 10 MHz PC AT or better for this purpose, and we concur — in fact, chances are that you use at least a 386 PC for this purpose, if not something even faster.

You can load PSERVER.EXE on as many machines as you may want to dedicate for print services. If you use PSERVER.EXE, changing print server configurations requires shutting down the print server and rebooting the workstation (or workstations) running PSERVER.EXE in order for the changes to take effect.

PSERVER.NLM

You can install your print server as a NetWare Loadable Module running on your file server. If your printing activity is minimal or your file server is not too heavily loaded, PSERVER.NLM probably makes good sense.

The PSERVER NLM is installed by default for both NetWare 3.*x* and 4.*x*. It provides server-based print queues and handling and dedicates a certain portion of the server's CPU cycles and disk space for handling print jobs. In most cases, you won't even know it's there — that is, after you set up the printer drivers, print queues, and any special form or paper handling that you and your users may need. One of the nicest improvements in NetWare 4.11 is a new shortcut method for defining printers and print queues that relieves much of the previous tedium involved in this sometimes painful task.

Just as you can do for all NLMs, you can load and unload PSERVER.NLM at will. To make configuration changes, you must unload only the PSERVER.NLM, make the necessary changes, and reload that NLM for the changes to take effect. However, you may use only one copy of PSERVER.NLM per server on NetWare v3.11 (4.*x* enables the NLM to be loaded a multiple number of times for more print connections and services).

Getting It Out: NetWare's User Print Utilities

Typically, NetWare users access printers in one of three ways:

- ✔ By using network-aware applications that know how to interface directly with NetWare print queues, or with print services through NDS

- ✔ By redirecting output away from a local printer port across the network to a NetWare print queue

> ✔ By using an explicit NetWare network print command to interface directly with NetWare print queues

Because printing is such an important need, you should explain these options to your users and make sure that they understand the basic principles of print servers, print queues, and network printing.

And-a-one, and-a-two, and an NPRINT

NPRINT is a networked version of the DOS PRINT command. Rather than send data to a local printer port, NPRINT ships its data directly to a NetWare print queue. NPRINT also has the advantage of not remaining resident after it's used: The DOS PRINT command leaves a terminate-and-stay resident portion of itself in memory to handle any future print requests, whereas NPRINT completely vacates memory as soon as it finishes its job.

NPRINT was designed to handle printing needs from programs, such as CAD packages, that cannot print to a parallel port, which are typically designed to print to serial-attached plotters. To work around this issue, you can instruct your CAD package to print to a file instead and then use NPRINT to send the print file to a network print queue.

To use NPRINT, type the command at the DOS prompt, and specify one or more filenames separated by commas. The DOS file wildcard characters (* and ?) are also supported. NPRINT recognizes a range of options, and its syntax looks like this:

```
NPRINT path\filename...[options...]
```

For NPRINT to work properly, the files specified must be formatted to work with the target printer. NPRINT default options work only if no print job configuration has been defined for the target printer; if a print job configuration has been defined for that printer, its defaults override any of the information specific to the command-line options. When in doubt, use explicit option settings.

The CAPTURE rapture revisited

The NetWare CAPTURE command redirects output intended for a PC's printer port to a NetWare queue. The NetWare shell or redirector watches for service requests that involve network activity; if it sees any, it passes them on to the network access software. CAPTURE fully earns its name because it captures output headed for the PC's printer port and passes it across the network to a NetWare print queue.

CAPTURE was designed to grab output headed for the local printer and redirect it to a network print queue. Think of CAPTURE as something that replaces built-in printer access with network printer access.

CAPTURE is typically used in a NetWare login file, either the system login shared by all users or the user's individual login file. It establishes printer redirection for as many as three LPT ports (as many as eight for NetWare 4.*x* VLM environment). Instead of being invoked as a specific one-shot command, like NPRINT, CAPTURE becomes a part of your (net)working environment. CAPTURE recognizes a broad range of options, but the basic syntax looks like this:

```
CAPTURE [options...]
```

The print job Terminator: ENDCAP

You can use the ENDCAP command at any time to end the capture of an LPT port. You use it, for example, if you have been capturing LPT1: to a network printer and want to revert to the local printer attached to your PC's LPT1: port. The syntax for ENDCAP is terse:

```
ENDCAP [options...]
```

If no options are specified for ENDCAP, it ends the capture of the LPT1: port.

The important distinction among the ENDCAP options is whether data already in the queue gets discarded; those options that have the word *cancel* in their names discard the data in the queue, and those that don't have it let whatever has already entered the queue get printed.

For NetWare 4.1 and higher-number versions, ENDCAP is not a separate command; ENDCAP is a parameter to the CAPTURE command, which looks like this:

```
CAPTURE/ENDCAP
```

Otherwise, ENDCAP works the same way.

Printing from applications

Most DOS applications print to an LPT port; they should be handled by CAPTURE. Those applications that need to print to serial or special ports probably will require manual intervention and judicious use of the NPRINT command. Some applications, especially in Windows, are network-aware and can print to NetWare print queues on their own.

Traditionally, the problem is to properly configure the application (like Word for Windows) or the environment (like Windows) with the right print drivers for the printers at the receiving end of the NetWare print queues. After this hurdle is overcome, though, network printing for these kinds of applications is quite straightforward.

With NetWare 4.x and its built-in directory services, applications can more easily find out which kinds of printers are available and configure themselves accordingly. Because directory services serve up the menu of available printer choices for selection, end users and administrators are relieved of what can only be called a tedious chore on today's older NetWare networks. Directory access does, however, require applications vendors to write their applications to take direct advantage of Novell Directory Services; consequently, we haven't seen many choices on the directory services printer menu until now.

What's in a (Utility) Name? Setting Up and Configuring NetWare Printers

Now that you have looked at NetWare printing from a user's perspective, the time has come to lift the hood a little and take advantage of the insider's view. In this section, you find out how to define printers for use on the network and how to set up queues to drive them. You also see how to configure print jobs and print forms so that you can enhance the types of services that your network printers can deliver.

NetWare has six primary print-management utilities: PCONSOLE, PRINTDEF, and PRINTCON, plus three others: PSC, NPRINT, and CAPTURE. Earlier sections in this chapter discuss NPRINT and CAPTURE, and we give PSC only short shrift here (you can read the dirty details about PSC in the online NetWare documentation if you're incurably curious). In this section, you find out how to tell the other three apart and (we hope) how to avoid what is sometimes called "P-Confusion," a state that often strikes those who fail to master the differences between these utilities.

The short version of this course tells anyone who has never grappled with the NetWare print utilities that all three utilities are kind of self-explanatory. If you know that a console is a control program for managing computer stuff, the name PCONSOLE may tell you that it's the right choice for managing printers, queues, and other related functions. You use this information to install printers on the network and to make them available to users.

Likewise, if you know that a printer definition is a database of functions that can be sent to a printer to make it perform special functions, the name PRINTDEF may indicate a utility that helps to establish and manipulate this type of definition database. You use this information to make your printer do tricks.

And if you know that print configuration jobs set up special collections of print settings that otherwise would require fiddling with arcane NPRINT or CAPTURE options, the name PRINTCON might tell you that it defines common print configurations as a labor-saving device for users. You use it to set up common print job definitions that users can ask for by name to make their printing requirements easier.

It's amazing how much sense things make, if you only know what they mean. It's even more amazing when your users begin to catch on.

PCONSOLE

PCONSOLE is the control center for NetWare print servers. If you're setting up queues, print servers, or print queues, PCONSOLE requires that you log in as a SUPERVISOR or supervisor-equivalent. If you're just changing existing definitions, a special class of user called the PRINT OPERATOR can do these things, too. PCONSOLE covers a broad range of capabilities, which the following sections explain.

Defining and managing print queues

Queues are created, named, deleted, and managed from within PCONSOLE's Print Queue Information menu. The keys to creating, deleting, and renaming queues are special function keys specific to the NetWare console menus. The Ins key inserts new entries, Del deletes highlighted entries, and F3 renames highlighted entries. Figure 15-2 shows the main menu choices for managing your print services environment.

```
Printer Definition  4.11              Thursday  September  12,  1996  12:28pm
                 User GUEST on NetWare Server RBC1 Connection 4



                          ┌──────────────────────────────┐
                          │      Available Options         │
                          ├──────────────────────────────┤
                          │ Print Devices                  │
                          │ Printer Forms                  │
                          │ Change Current Server          │
                          └──────────────────────────────┘




Press <Enter> to view print devices.

Enter=Select    Esc=Exit                                             F1=Help
```

Figure 15-2:
PCONSOLE's
Printer
Definition
Services.

When you create print queues, use short, self-descriptive names. A name like *2ndFQ* is much better than *Second_floor_queue,* even though they are similar. Shorter names mean fewer keystrokes, and because queue names get used much of the time, this technique eventually wins your users' gratitude.

Managing the print server

The Print Server Information menus are used for the following tasks:

- ✔ Creating and deleting print servers
- ✔ Managing print server passwords
- ✔ Assigning print server full names
- ✔ Defining network printer and hardware configurations
- ✔ Adding and removing print server users or operators
- ✔ Changing forms
- ✔ Problem notifications and notify lists
- ✔ Assigning and adding queues to printers
- ✔ Setting and changing queue priorities

Figure 15-3 depicts the top level menu choices for PCONSOLE, which offers considerably more functionality than we discuss here. For more information about the topics we discuss, please consult the NetWare print server manuals (or use the online help for printing-related topics if you're using NetWare 4.*x*).

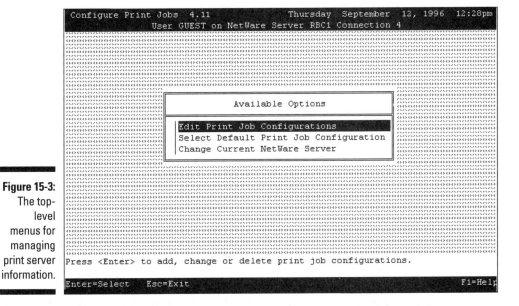

Figure 15-3: The top-level menus for managing print server information.

```
Configure Print Jobs  4.11                Thursday  September  12, 1996  12:28pm
                   User GUEST on NetWare Server RBC1 Connection 4




                        ┌─────────────────────────────────────────┐
                        │            Available Options              │
                        ├─────────────────────────────────────────┤
                        │ Edit Print Job Configurations             │
                        │ Select Default Print Job Configuration    │
                        │ Change Current NetWare Server             │
                        └─────────────────────────────────────────┘




Press <Enter> to add, change or delete print job configurations.

Enter=Select    Esc=Exit                                              F1=Help
```

PRINTDEF

After PCONSOLE, PRINTDEF is a bit of a letdown. It enables you to define forms and print devices. The forms section of PRINTDEF handles definition of form names and numbers. The print devices section lets you choose print devices and the device modes and functions to go along with them. Figure 15-4 depicts PRINTDEF's Print Server Information menu, where details about the properties of each print server are available.

PRINTCON

The last member of this triumvirate of print managers is PRINTCON. Its job is to control print configuration information that users might otherwise have to supply in lengthy option lists for NPRINT or CAPTURE.

One of the most unfortunate aspects of PRINTCON is that print configurations are defined per individual user. PRINTCON lets the network supervisor copy printer definitions from one user to another, but it's a slow and awkward process, especially for large numbers of users. The best alternatives are to use a utility to copy the same PRINTCON.DAT to all users or to share a public PRINTCON.DAT file rather than create a unique one for each individual user.

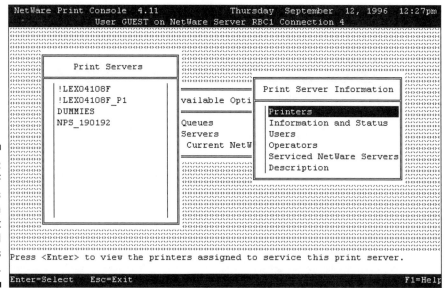

Figure 15-4:
PRINTDEF
provides
information
about print
servers and
the devices
they offer.

Print job configurations include the following information:

- ✔ Number of copies
- ✔ Type of file to be printed
- ✔ Tab size (spaces per tab for expansion)
- ✔ Form-feed handling (suppress or pass through)
- ✔ Notification (active or disabled)
- ✔ Printer ID
- ✔ ENDCAP handling
- ✔ Originating network server, print queue, print server, device type, and print mode
- ✔ The form to be selected
- ✔ Print-banner handling
- ✔ User name
- ✔ Time-out handling
- ✔ Time-out interval

Figure 15-5 shows you PRINTCON's main menu.

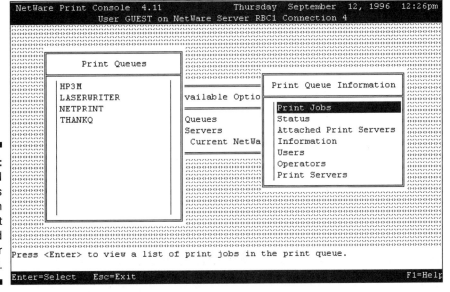

Figure 15-5:
PRINTCON
shows
information
about Print
Queues and
their
definitions.

PSC

For macho command-line users, NetWare also offers a purely command-oriented printer-control utility called Print Server Controller (PSC). PSC is cryptic and powerful — just the thing for people such as printing nerds and other power users. It's faster than starting up PCONSOLE for quick changes to print configurations, print-job setups, forms, and the like, but the consequences of even trivial typos can be, well, interesting, in the sense of the Chinese curse "May you live in interesting times."

We think that you should heed the curse and steer clear of PSC. If you can't avert your curiosity, though, you have to look this one up in your NetWare manuals.

Managing Print Jobs

PSERVER and PCONSOLE provide the best source of printer-management information. Fortunately, though, because print servers need little management, most of your activities focus on managing print jobs and the queues and printers that service them.

Checking print server operation and status

PSERVER's main menu, Current Print Server Status, provides useful information, including the following:

- ✔ Version number of the print server software
- ✔ Print server type (VAP, EXE, NLM)
- ✔ Number of printers configured
- ✔ Available queue service modes
- ✔ Current status of print server

You probably will be most interested in the last line, which tells you whether the print server is running.

Checking printer status

PCONSOLE's Print Server Information menu contains an option called Printer Server, which in turn offers an option called Print Server Status/Control.

Choosing Print Server Status calls up a list of active printers from which you can choose the printer whose status you want to know. The resulting Status menu includes information about the following:

- Printer status (paused, printing, waiting, offline, or online)
- Service mode
- Mounted form
- Server and queue information
- Current job number
- Current job filename
- Information about number of copies, size of file, percentage completed, and completion status

Again, you will be most interested in the status field or possibly in the completion information if you wonder why your job isn't finished yet.

Checking printer control

PCONSOLE or PSC lets you control most printer functions, including the following (and more):

- Start or stop printer
- Pause printer
- Abort print job
- Mount different form
- Send form feed (or feeds) to printer

You usually use these kinds of controls to handle print job changes or to kill print jobs that are running too long or have formatting or other problems.

The benefits of well-trained users

Users who understand how to get the most from the NetWare print services are better able to do what they want and less likely to bother you for help. You can choose to spend a little time in advance for training — you can get everyone together at one time or at least deal with them in groups — or fight fires on a regular basis and do for your users what they could otherwise do for themselves. Not much of a choice, eh?

Sharing Workstation Printers on the Network

NetWare also includes a DOS program that can act as a remote print server for printers attached to individual workstations. Basically, you must install a smallish piece of software that can catch output from a NetWare print queue at the workstation. When the software is installed, it can turn individual printers into network printers.

For NetWare 3.x, the name of this program is RPRINTER.EXE, short for Remote PRINTER; for NetWare 4.x, the equivalent utility is NPRINTER.EXE for Windows 3.x workstations and NPTWIN95.EXE for Windows 95 workstations. None of these programs is really a print server per se, but they provide many of the same capabilities. All three programs can be particularly useful for small, isolated groups of users who may not be close to a print server but who have at least one printer in their midst. RPRINTER, NPTWIN95, and NPRINTER provide a method for those users to use NetWare to share that printer and provide the printing services.

RPRINTER and NPRINTER are a *terminate-and-stay-resident* (TSR) DOS program. They incur some RAM overhead and impose some CPU consumption on the user's machine where they are installed. But their needs are modest: They consume between 9K and 13K of RAM for the first printer and an additional 3K to 4K for each additional printer. For best results, you should install them on a workstation that isn't heavily used; a power user is likely to feel somewhat hampered by the processor overhead these programs require. NTPWIN95.EXE is a true 32-bit Windows 95 program and uses a DLL, so that it doesn't actually consume resources except when it's running.

The programs all use a connection slot to the print server that services them, so in many ways they act just like a remotely attached printer being run by that print server. Don't forget, however, that these programs are probably running on a machine that someone else is using.

The Pros and Cons of Workstation Printing

To be most effective, the machine with the remote print utility installed should be left up and running all the time. This is the biggest drawback of all three remote print utilities: The user on whose machine one of these remote print utilities is installed can terminate print services at any time by simply crashing or turning off that machine.

RPRINTER generally does not perform as well as a printer attached directly to a print server, particularly if the workstation running the program is also running Windows. For the most reliable performance, we recommend that RPRINTER be loaded automatically in the workstation's AUTOEXEC.BAT file; then the user on that machine doesn't have to remember to load it so that others can share the printer. Fortunately for 4.x users, both NPRINTER and NPTWIN95 appear to be a great deal more stable and reliable, in addition to being somewhat less obtrusive.

RPRINTER may not load the first time you warm boot fast PCs. If this occurs, reboot the PC; it will load the second time. RPRINTER will always load from a cold boot. Also, be aware that RPRINTER sometimes does not work in high memory.

Despite these cons, RPRINTER offers terrific convenience for users who need network print services from its printer. The program has proved to be much more popular than Novell ever anticipated.

If you intend to use RPRINTER, check with CompuServe or your reseller to make sure that you have the most recent version. This program has gone through a remarkable number of revisions, and a newer version can make the difference between a working remote printer and an inert one. If you plan to use NPRINTER or NPTWIN95, the same advice holds, but it's not quite as plangent!

A Quick Guide to NetWare Printing

To quickly create printing services on your NetWare network, follow these easy steps.

1. Connect the printer to the print server or the dedicated workstation.

2. Use PCONSOLE to define the print queues that you want. Use names that mean something, such as the location of the printer or its function.

3. Use PCONSOLE to define the print server.

4. Load the PSERVER NLM on the file server. If you are using a dedicated print server, use PSERVER.EXE.

5. Load RPRINTER on any workstations with printers attached.

6. If the applications that you use are not NetWare-aware, use CAPTURE to direct print jobs to the correct printer.

Printing in the NetWare 4.x Environment

All the old, familiar utilities are still available in the 4.x environment, but a couple are easier to use than the well-worn standbys. For one thing, the Windows administration utility, NWADMIN, lets you do anything that

PCONSOLE, PRINTCON, and PRINTDEF can do and more. The benefit is that you can manage users, queues, device definitions, job configurations, and printers from a single utility rather than picking the right character-mode utility for the job that you need to do. This technique goes a long way toward eliminating P-CONFUSION (or deciding which print utility to use!).

Moving your print capabilities from NetWare 3.*x* to 4.*x* is easy. The NetWare utility NETSYNC4 does it automatically. If you have a small network consisting of less than three servers, manually migrating your printing to NetWare 4.*x* may be easier. NETSYNC4 also lets 3.*x* printing operate in a 4.*x* network. Another utility, MIGPRINT.EXE, moves 3.*x* print queues to 4.*x*.

RPRINTER has been replaced by a similar but more robust cousin, NPRINTER, that comes in both NLM and EXE flavors for use on a server or remote DOS, Windows 95, or OS/2 workstation. Like its cousin, NPRINTER.EXE, the EXE workstation version, has several command-line parameters that let you load a printer driver, view all loaded printer drivers, unload drivers, and configure as many as seven printers from a workstation. A character-mode utility, called PSETUP, can handle the management of print servers, printers, and queues if you want to work with a slightly friendlier adjunct to PCONSOLE.

As for the 4.*x* print utilities, our advice is to investigate NWADMIN's capabilities because of its friendly, easier-to-navigate Windows interface. Otherwise, stick with what you know. If you're starting fresh with 4.*x*, don't bother to learn the old stuff — focus on the current generation.

Many of the printing changes in 4.*x* are cosmetic rather than deep-seated. Because some of these improvements make print management simpler — especially NWADMIN — this is not a slam! Get to know 4.*x* printing — you won't be disappointed.

Novell's move to Intranet-based services with IntranetWare includes some changes to how you think about printing. NetWare Distributed Print Services (NDPS) looks at NetWare from a queue-based printing mode. NDPS allows users to ignore creating print queues and configuring printers. Developed with Xerox and Hewlett-Packard, NDPS enables users to simply pick a printer and print to it. NDPS-capable printers and print servers will start appearing soon. Look for the details on NDPS in Chapter 21.

Part III

Maintaining, Protecting, and Growing Your NetWare Network

"Careful, Sundance, this one's been locked up and forced to troubleshoot network problems ALLL week and he's itching for a fight".

In this part . . .

In Part III, we pick up where Part II left off and tackle NetWare's extended services and capabilities. You tackle the essential system elements required for a positive NetWare INSTALL experience and then step through basic NetWare installation and configuration topics. Beyond the robust and powerful kernel of this many-sided network operating system, you find out about its manifold functions and how to make the best of what these functions can do for you — and your network's users.

Besides getting a feel for NetWare's core capabilities, Part III arms you with the tools and techniques that you need to keep NetWare performing at its absolute peak. You grapple with backing up your server — even though it's not a universal practice, we want you to understand how dire the consequences of failing to back up can be, and how easy it is to take out insurance on your server's contents. After that, we explore the details of NetWare configuration, and recommend some basic elements to watch to keep things running smoothly and efficiently.

We close Part III with a series of chapters on user and server utilities, followed by an exploration of IntranetWare, Novell's new bundle of TCP/IP-based network services and capabilities. Recognizing that not everything works like it's supposed to all of the time, the final chapter in Part III leaves you with a pithy series of points to ponder when trouble comes your way — that is, you find out how to troubleshoot common NetWare (and network) problems.

Chapter 16

Covering Your Assets: Backing Up and Restoring Your Data

*B*acking up your hard disk or the network drives is much like buying insurance. You may never need the backup or the insurance, but they're good to have, just in case. Backing up your network servers ensures against loss of critical files and data.

As more companies use computers to store their information, the value of that data increases. If a company loses data because of a power surge or fluctuation, fire, or hardware failure, drops in revenue and customer confidence can result. If you lose data you need for a report the next day, you must pay the price of re-creating that data if you don't have a backup. If you lose your boss's data, you may wind up using a different LAN at another company, where we hope that you put your hard-earned lessons to work.

Why Back Up Your LAN? (Why Buy Insurance?)

NetWare supports a number of backup methods and technologies. NetWare itself includes built-in utilities for all versions of the product that let you simply back up the data you want and restore it when necessary. Third-party vendors also supply backup software; such products are usually more complete and more convenient to use than the NetWare built-in utilities. As with everything else, with backup software, you get what you pay for.

Currently, nearly every backup package you purchase works with only certain types of backup devices. The cost of backup hardware, whether for digital audiotape (DAT) or tape- or optical-drive-based devices, typically constitutes the major portion of any backup investment. Even though this hardware is expensive, don't skimp on the work involved in choosing the software either — ultimately, it's what you encounter most frequently, and it usually dictates hardware selection anyway.

Don't even *begin* to think that software that backs up DOS or Windows 95 can effectively back up NetWare. Although these backup packages back up files, directories, and their attributes, they can't back up the NetWare bindery or Directory, trustee assignments, user rights, print queues, or other extended attributes that NetWare requires. If you want your system to look unchanged if you ever have to restore from a backup, buy software that is NetWare-compatible. Anything less leaves you twisting in the wind.

Storage and Backup Technologies

The three kinds of storage and backup are

- *On-line,* in which data is stored to the file server's hard disk.
- *Near-line,* in which data can be retrieved for occasional use.
- *Off-line,* which means what it says — human intervention is typically required to retrieve the media when it needs to be returned to use.

On-line: On tap when you need it

On-line, which consists of a local hard disk or file server disk, is the same as primary storage. On-line storage is probably the most unusual type of backup storage and is the least commonly used, probably because it's the most expensive. If a hard disk fails, the data it contains may be lost and is difficult to recover — unless you have a backup.

Near-line: In the neighborhood but not on your disk drive

Near-line storage is quickly accessible storage like that used in read-write optical disks or CD-ROMs. It enables users to store large amounts of data on a secondary device when the file server drives fill up. It also provides a place to store static information, such as encyclopedias, dictionaries, or other documentation. Because CD-ROM is mostly read-only, it's not often used for recording, but it is a handy medium for accessing large, prerecorded collections of data.

For backup, you typically use a read-write technology, such as tape, optical, or magneto-optical drives.

Off-line: Not readily accessible but lots of it

Off-line data storage is the most common method for storing data from a file server's hard disks and from the disks of workstations attached to the network. Tape-backup devices are the most common equipment used for off-line backup. You must copy files from off-line storage to an on-line device before they're usable.

DIS, DAT, DLT, and QIC

Four common tape-based technologies exist: *digital audiotape (DAT), quarter-inch cartridge (QIC), 8-mm cassette,* and *digital linear tape (DLT).* DLT, in particular, allows storage of as much as 40 gigabytes (GB) of uncompressed data. If the tape drive supports compression, two-to-one compression is possible. The nine-track, half-inch tape you use to back up mainframes and minicomputers is seldom used in PC environments and is seldom worth adapting for use on a LAN. The tapes are big yet have a lower capacity than most other technologies, and the drives are typically big, loud, and ugly.

8-mm EXATAPE

When you think of 8-mm EXATAPE, think big. Think enterprise, but think fast, too. The helical-scan technology that 8-mm EXATAPE uses resembles what 8-mm videocassette players use. The similarities end there, however. Don't use consumer, video-grade tape for your data. You don't need data-grade tape to record *The Waltons* — nor do you want to pay that much for the tape. EXATAPE has a capacity of between 2.5GB and 5GB and represents the high end of the tape market.

Digital audiotape (DAT)

Digital audiotape is 4-mm wide (half the size of 8-mm tape) and can back up data at speeds as high as 100 megabytes (MB) per minute. It comes in one of three types: DDS-1, DDS-2, or DDS-3. All formats use helical scan technology, which writes data diagonally from edge to edge of the tape. Even though DAT tape for voice-grade applications is available, don't use it. Use data-grade tapes instead — they have a capacity of up to 12GB uncompressed space. With DAT, you get more for your money — DAT drives cost about 40 percent less than 8-mm EXATAPE.

Quarter-inch cartridge (QIC)

Quarter-inch cartridge comes in two forms: DC-600 and DC-2000, which has a lower capacity. QIC cartridges hold between 40MB and 2.1GB of uncompressed, standard format data. QIC drives write data on the tape with back-and-forth movements along the length of the tape. If you choose QIC, you're in good company — about 14 million QIC drivers are in use today.

Digital linear tape

Digital Equipment Corporation (DEC) introduced DLT. DLT holds more data than other technologies, as much as 40GB per cartridge of compressed information. It's fairly expensive and probably won't meet your needs unless you have lots of data to back up on a regular basis.

Nearly There: Near-Line Storage

Think of near-line storage as data that NetWare can retrieve easily when the data is needed but that is not stored on the file server's disk drives. As the amount of data typically stored on a LAN grows, the use of near-line storage increases. Typically, near-line storage is used for information, such as encyclopedias, that is supplied on CD-ROM or for data that needs to be used less frequently than primary storage. Most near-line storage used for backup falls in a class called *read-write optical*. Here are some of the most common examples:

- **Optical:** Optical drives are much more expensive than traditional tape media, but they hold larger volumes of information — typically from 250MB to more than 1GB. Data on optical drives is faster to access than is data on tape, and the shelf life of optical disks is long.

- **WORM:** *Write-once, read-many* devices do what their name implies — you can write data once, primarily for archiving, but you can reread that data repeatedly.

- **MO:** Magneto-optical drives, with capacities of between 128MB to over 2GB, combine laser technology with magnetics to read and write data stored on a magnetized surface. (This kind of drive is sometimes called *electro-optical*, or *EO*.)

- **CD-ROM:** You have had CD-ROM in your home and in your car for years, so you know how inexpensive CDs can be. The same holds true for CD-ROM data discs. They can contain from 550MB to more than 650MB of data. Recordable CD drives (and media) are becoming more common; a new CD-ROM format that's in the works may raise the medium's capacity to as high as 8GB in the next year or so.

A variant of CD-ROM, called *O-ROM* (for *optical read-only memory*), works on magneto-optical drives. Several manufacturers are supplying software on these disks. *P-ROM* (for *partial read-only memory*) is also available for magneto-optical drives. What's next — Q-ROM (for *quick read-only memory*)? All those who swim in alphabet soup had better have large appetites for noodles.

Juggling Multiple Media: Changers, Stackers, and Jukeboxes

One of the best ways to automate backups is to use a *changer* or *stacker.* These devices, sometimes called *autoloaders,* look like jukeboxes. When one record (in this case, an optical disk or tape) finishes playing, the changer puts on a new one. Changers and stackers are expensive, but for users who have a great deal of data to back up or don't find baby-sitting a tape unit worthwhile, a changer is a good idea. For the enterprise LAN, on which performing even incremental daily backups means shuffling numerous tapes, a changer is essential. You can get stackers for QIC, DAT, and 8-mm drives.

Racking Up Backup Issues

When performing backups, you must consider a number of interesting technical issues. To get the best bang for your backup buck, think about how much the data you're backing up can be squeezed to get the best use from your media. You should also make sure that your backup is reliable and usable and that your system runs faster than a glacier moves. Obviously, if backing up takes all your time, your users won't be able to do anything.

Look for the window: It's the only way out!

Always plan before you buy. Decide how much time you have to back up the data on the network, and buy accordingly. If you have time to back up everything, but only half the budget, decide on a plan that will get you what you need without taking up too much of your time. Though you may have the time now, you may not have it later. Also decide the most economical time to perform a backup in order to let your users make maximum use of their work time on the network.

Compression: Putting a squeeze on

Most QIC, DAT, DLT, and 8-mm drives support some form of data compression. Although compression varies based on the type of file and how much can be compressed from it, generally a two-for-one compression can be expected. Compression makes your drive *seem* as though it operates faster, but that's not really true: Because compression reduces the amount of physical data that has to be transferred to the drive by about 50 percent, as long as decompression is quick, reading a compressed file from the drive may be faster than an equivalent uncompressed version.

Reliability: Be there or be square

The reliability of backed-up data is the primary concern in a tape-backup system. Errors can occur. To prevent soft errors, which are caused by dust or other electromagnetic interference, store tapes in a clean, protected environment. To avoid hard errors, treat your tapes or CD-ROMs at the office better than you treat your tapes and CDs at home.

You can overcome other errors, caused by writing data to tape, by error-correction software included with most QIC, DAT, and 8-mm drives and with read-after-write verification. In read-write verification, the tape unit matches the data in its write buffer with the data it wrote to tape. An additional safety measure is tape verification, which involves determining that the data on the tape is readable.

Performance: Waiting for the paint to dry

The speed at which your system can back up data has a direct correlation with the sanity of your users. Tape drives that are slow increase stress; drives that are fast lessen stress. Three factors can increase the speed of your tape backup: the speed of the drive you're using, the speed of the network media, and the degree of achievable compression.

QIC drives, which can back up data at 30 to 800 kilobytes per second (Kbps) are almost as fast as DAT, DLT, and 8-mm drives. The network access method (fast or slow Ethernet or token ring) also influences the speed of your backup. Data to be backed up that is flowing across the wire can easily be too slow but, alas, never too fast.

Facing Backup Head-On: Managing the Process

Network managers all approach the backup process differently. Some back up all their data every night; some never back up their data. Backing up data is a mundane, boring task; automating and regimenting it as much as possible is what makes it manageable, if not relatively painless. Take advantage of mechanical aids for backup — you might forget, but the computer won't.

Getting it all: A full system backup

The amount of data you have on your LAN determines how you should back up. If your data collection is small enough for you to back it all up overnight, do a *full system backup*. This process consists of backing up all files and directories on the file server, in addition to backing up the NetWare bindery or Directory, rights, attributes, and directory structure. Make sure that the system you buy does a full restoration of the data as well as a backup.

A good backup isn't any good if it can't be restored quickly, easily, and reliably. Testing is the only way to be sure, and it's the only way to be practiced at restoring when the real thing happens. Like getting to Carnegie Hall, the only way to manage a good backup is to practice, practice, practice.

Catching changes: Incremental backups

If your data collection on the LAN gets so big that you can no longer do a full backup overnight, consider incremental backups as the cornerstone of your backup routine. Incremental backups are normally organized as follows:

1. Once a week, back up all data on the file server.

2. Every day, back up all the data that has been modified since the previous backup (one day's worth, in other words).

Any good backup program should let you perform incremental backups. If your package doesn't support incremental backups, throw it out and get something else.

Use it, but don't abuse it: Rotation methods

Vendors offer a variety of methods for rotating the tapes you use for backup. Palindrome (now part of Seagate), for example, relies on the "Tower of Hanoi" method. That approach uses five sets of tapes. When you add a new tape to the backup process, you use it once every two weeks. Tapes that you previously used every two weeks now are used every four weeks, and so on. This method ensures that you introduce new tapes into the mix every so often and that you use older tapes less often (until you phase them out).

Another scheme, which is more common, is called the *grandfather, father, son (GFS)* method. GFS uses 20 tapes. Four of those tapes back up daily work (Monday through Thursday). Three tapes back up work done on the first three Fridays of the month. The fourth week, you use one of the 13 *grandfather* (monthly) tapes, one for each of the 13 four-week intervals in the year. This method keeps tapes circulating regularly and ensures that no tape gets too much wear.

Desiderata: What Should a Backup Package Bring to the Party?

You have to be a smart shopper when you buy tape-backup software and hardware, just like anything else you shop for. Here are a few tips for making this venture successful:

- ✔ **File-by-file backup and restore:** A tape backup writes files by one of two methods: image or file-by-file. In backups that save file-by-file, you should be able to restore files on an individual basis. An image makes a physical copy of a drive; you should use the image method only when a drive is nearly full. (When the drive is full, an image backup saves you valuable time; otherwise, go file-by-file — the only way to restore from an image backup is to restore the whole thing.)

- ✔ **Ample file-selection criteria:** You should be able to choose files and directories for backing up and restoring by file or directory name by using wildcards (*.* or *.TXT) or from a pick list of files and directories.

- ✔ **Back up everything:** The system you choose should back up the files, the directory attributes and rights, the NetWare bindery or NDS (NetWare Directory Services) information, and all files and directories on all drives.

- ✔ **All file types:** The backup system should back up the files created on different machine types. For each file type you want to use, you load a name space at the file server console. These name spaces include DOS, Macintosh, OS/2, NFS, Windows 96, and FTAM names and attributes (the DOS name space loads automatically). Tape-backup software that is

SMS- (Storage Management Services-) compliant supports all these options and can extend itself to support new ones as Novell adds support for them.

✔ **Quick, let's get everything:** Also look for a tape drive that supports Quick File Access (QFA), which can restore files as much as 200 times faster than other methods. That's fast — which gives you lots of time to do something else.

✔ **Information interleaving:** For some really fancy sleight-of-hand, choose tape-backup software that can interleave jobs. That means that the drive can simultaneously accept data from lots of sources.

SMS-compliant systems can continue to perform their backup functions no matter what changes Novell may make to the NetWare file system and its file formats. For that reason, SMS-compliant backup systems for NetWare are the only way to go. Fortunately, most major backup system vendors are now SMS-compliant. These backup systems have many of these features:

✔ **Open files:** Choose software that accommodates files that are open during backup. We hope that you back up the system when the LAN experiences no activity, but you cannot always expect that. You may also have to back up when applications are running that may keep some files perpetually open; a good backup program should work around that limitation.

✔ **Unattended backup:** Nothing is worse than sitting and watching the paint dry. The same idea applies to backing up: Get software that enables you to start the backup and then leave. You have better things to do with your time, right?

✔ **Sufficient storage capability:** A backup rule of thumb applies here: Buy a tape-backup system that can accommodate twice as much data as is currently on your file server. You will grow into it fast enough and still be hungry for more anyway.

✔ **Comparison of files on tape to files on disk:** Some software compares data that it has backed up to files on the server's hard disk to see whether it matches. Get that type of package if you can, because it saves you time — copying a file on top of itself is similar to watching paint dry. Got that? (Refer to the discussion in the section "Reliability: Be there or be square" earlier in this chapter.)

✔ **Nonfatal errors shouldn't kill your network:** The last thing you want is for errors that occur during the backup process to cause the backup to fail or, worse, to cause your network to fail. The software you buy should log these types of errors, tell you on which files they occur, and let you decide what to do about it later. In the meantime, the software should continue to back up whatever it can.

✔ **Span multiple tapes with a single volume:** Some disk volumes are larger than the capacity of a single tape. Make sure that the software you buy lets you span a volume across multiple tapes. This capability is almost as important as being able to leap tall buildings in a single bound.

To take it a step farther, the following list shows some features that are nice to have but not necessary:

- ✔ **Backing up individual hard disks:** So you want to be a nice guy and volunteer to back up your users' hard disks, too? Some software lets you do this. If you don't have the software, however, you can encourage your users to keep the data they want backed up on the file server instead. If you have this type of software, you can back up the users' workstations across the network (if, of course, the workstations are turned on).

- ✔ **Grooming, migrating, cataloging, and archiving:** Backing up resembles running a household. You have to do some spring-cleaning every so often. Some backup software offers you ways to rid your file server disk of files that haven't been used recently or to migrate them to near-line storage or even to store them away off-line (archiving). If your package is worth anything, it will also do the necessary record-keeping and archiving for you too. In NetWare 4.*x*, you can enable migration to high-capacity storage systems, such as WORM or OM, at the volume level in INSTALL.NLM.

Do You Want Backup Standard or with Air?

NetWare has its own backup system, but it also supports backup systems from other vendors. The most common backup software included with NetWare 3.*x* is NBACKUP. You can rely on NBACKUP in a pinch, but if it's all you have, do yourself a favor — go out and buy something else for everyday backups.

Really basic: NBACKUP

NBACKUP is a workstation-based backup utility that backs up information on directories. System administrators who have FILE SCAN and READ rights to a directory can back up any information it contains. To restore files from a backup takes CREATE, ERASE, FILE SCAN, MODIFY, and WRITE rights.

NBACKUP must run from a workstation that does nothing else on the LAN, and NBACKUP can back up data to floppies, tape drives, or optical drives. We recommend the higher-capacity media for backup, especially for some of today's mondo servers. Who wants to sit and back up data to 1,000 or more floppies? (That's not even 2GB, a modest amount of disk space by today's standards.)

You can direct NBACKUP to back up other servers you are ATTACHed to. NBACKUP, however, does not back up hidden or system directories on NetWare 2.*x* LANs, nor can you use wildcards for backing up Macintosh files. NBACKUP backs up only DOS and Macintosh files. If you have OS/2 or NFS files on your server, you have to use another utility, called SBACKUP.

Basic basic: SBACKUP

SBACKUP works with both NetWare 3.1*x* and 4.*x*. As a server-based backup system, SBACKUP can handle DOS, Macintosh, OS/2, Windows 95, and NFS files on workstations or on the server's hard disk. SBACKUP works with a *NetWare Loadable Module (NLM)* called the TSA.NLM to see that data on a *target* is backed up. The target can be another file server or workstation on the LAN. In case you haven't guessed already, SBACKUP beats the pants off NBACKUP. To run the program, the SUPERVISOR starts SBACKUP from the file server console.

A new NLM, called TSA4xx.NLM for *target server agent,* was created especially for server-to-server backup in NetWare 4.*x*. (Plug in the exact version number for NetWare 4.*x* for the *x*s here. For example, NetWare 4.02 uses TSA402.NLM.) The TSA NLM creates a connection between the client and the server called a *target server* and uses a protocol called the *Storage Management Services Protocol (SMSP)* to back up the remote server.

Third-party backups

Third-party backup systems are available with a variety of features. Because you have to pay real money for them, most of them are more complete than either NBACKUP or SBACKUP. Some popular vendors of tape-backup systems include Legato, Seagate, STAC Electronics, and Cheyenne.

Storage for the Masses

The *Storage Management Services (SMS)* is the Novell method for standardizing backup for its third-party vendors. Before the introduction of SMS, whenever NetWare changed, vendors had to change their backup software to follow suit. When OS/2 and UNIX workstations began showing up on users' desktops, the same software that backed up DOS files couldn't be used. The backup vendors got tired of rewriting their software with each major release of NetWare. (Wouldn't you?)

SMS separates the details necessary to support the network file system from the backup method used and, incidentally, from the type of machine format used for those files (DOS, Macintosh, OS/2, NFS, and so on). SMS provides standard media formats and ensures compatibility among similar backup devices. Software from third-party vendors, therefore, can back up any kind of file. Even better, vendors no longer have to rewrite their backup software to track additions or changes to the NetWare file system.

SBACKUP, which users of NetWare 3.*x* may already know about, is also based on SMS.

What's Different About Storage on NetWare 4.x?

NetWare 4.*x* enables you to add to your network high-capacity storage devices, such as tape drives, optical erasable drives, and WORM and CD-ROM drives. These devices, which can create free disk storage space on the network, use the NetWare *High-Capacity Storage System (HCSS).* HCSS assumes that data is stored on the primary storage device until a capacity threshold is reached. When the disk reaches that storage threshold, the files that have been least recently used are migrated. When files are needed again, HCSS enables them to be copied back to disk so that they can be used again.

In HCSS, files are migrated to and from primary storage on a file-by-file basis; you can view files that reside on the alternate storage device with the DOS DIR or NetWare NDIR command. Although you cannot create or delete directories on an HCSS-based device, you can assign access rights in the same way you do for any other NetWare directory. A file on an HCSS device appears to be no different from files on a local drive, even though the file may be someplace entirely different.

Another technique that NetWare 4.10 adopts is a method used on mainframe computers for aging files that are nearing or past their prime. Arcada (now part of Seagate), and then Novell, created *Hierarchical Storage Management (HSM),* which lets you age files like vintage wine. Unlike wine storage, the file storage process is different. Newly minted files are used first and stored close by, and older files migrate to an HSM server. When the files are past their prime, they move to optical storage. At the vinegar stage, which means that the files are really dead, they move to digital audiotape (DAT). After the files move to DAT, retrieving them is like getting the last drop of wine from the bottle — you really have to work at it.

NetWare 4.11 fixes a boo-boo in NetWare 4.1 by now letting you back up trustee directory assignments correctly.

Emigration or migration: It depends on your view

NetWare 4.*x* gets pretty fancy at moving data around. With its migration utility, you can plan for data to move to CD-ROM, tape subsystems, or optical jukeboxes. All this capability lets you best manage your data, farming it out to remote locations if you seldom use it. When data is migrated properly, users don't know whether data is on a local drive or a migrated drive.

Scrunching things up tight

Another feature of NetWare 4.*x* is its support for compression of files on the file server. The reason that NetWare compression is tighter and faster than Stacker or whatever DOS compression utility you favor is that it uses a *two-pass compression* method. In this method, NetWare 4.*x* reads through a file once, just to analyze and record everything it can about the data it holds. NetWare 4.*x* then uses what it learns on a second trip through the file to squeeze things down as tightly as possible without compromising expansion time.

NetWare's disk-compression routines are built to be faster overall when they are reading compressed files from disk — where decompression is required — than when they are reading equivalent uncompressed files. This capability accounts for a 10 to 15 percent performance improvement for the file system between NetWare 3.*x* and NetWare 4.*x*. (We thought that you would want to know.)

Hold Still and Back Up Those Users!

Backing up users is one of those "damned if you do, damned if you don't" issues. Many third-party backup packages let you back up the users' local disk drives as well as network drives. This list shows some things to consider before you decide what to do:

✔ Backing up local drives takes additional time and leaves any unattended workstations vulnerable to attack (because they must be logged in, in order to be backed up).

✔ If you don't back up local drives, someone will holler at you sooner or later. All you can hope is that your boss, who just lost a file, is not the one hollering. That could be career-threatening (we hate when that happens).

Farm Teams and the Big Leagues: Workstation- versus Server-Based Backups

Two backup approaches are common: workstation-based and server-based. Both have their pros and cons, as you expect.

The direct approach may be the best

At least one vendor has taken a direct approach to the backup issue: Intel, whose StorageExpress attaches directly to the network media as another network device and backs up whatever you tell it to, whether it's workstations or servers or both. StorageExpress is pretty neat, whether you call it a storage workstation or a storage server. You can't buy a direct storage solution, however, without making some compromises — such solutions are generally faster than workstation-based solutions but slower than those attached directly to the file server.

Workstation-based is strictly small-time

In *workstation-based backups,* a workstation is dedicated to the backup process. Because the backup is based on the workstation, the backup doesn't affect the file server processing. You can add to the backup system without affecting the file server. On the other hand, data needs to travel across the network from the file server to the workstation, which can be slow. Several high-speed access methods are available to alleviate that problem. Also, the workstation from which you are backing up must be logged in to the network, which may pose a security threat, especially if the workstation is unattended during the backup.

Server-based is smart, fast, and less fattening

Server-based backups are generally faster than workstation-based backups and can be left unattended without posing threats to security. The backup process can slow down file server performance, however, which is why you schedule this process during the wee hours, when your users are fast asleep. That's also why this kind of backup runs unattended, because you probably want to get your sleep, too.

Practice Makes Perfect: Knowing What to Do Before Disaster Strikes

Most network managers test fate every day that they show up at work. They hope that the backup they began the night before has worked. They have never tested their backup system to see whether it does what it says it will — restore the data they have been backing up so regularly and reliably. They have forgotten the three cardinal rules of backup safety:

✔ **Document the backup process.** You won't live to regret it. Write down whether you do a full backup or an incremental backup or whether you use some other scheme. Indicate where you store the tapes so that they won't burn if the building goes up in flames. Relay everything you know about backing up the system in case you're not available after the fire is out.

✔ **Test your backup system.** Back up the LAN and then restore it. Try to retrieve files. See whether the restored bindery is as it should be. The backup system doesn't work until you can prove that it works.

✔ **Cross-train other users.** Find an assistant who's willing to learn everything you do. Make your assistant learn backup and restoration procedures cold. Getting run over by a train is a remote possibility, but it can happen. Of course, you probably wouldn't care — but someone else might.

The basic idea is to learn the mechanics so that, when the unthinkable happens, you don't have to learn or think. You can just go through the motions and reserve your cranial capacity for blind panic.

Take Care of Your Backup System, and It Will Take Care of You

Proper care and feeding of your backup system is also a terrific idea because such attention improves the odds that things will work when you need them to. And because a backup resembles a life preserver that should be used only in drills and when there's a man overboard, improving the odds is always a good thing. Follow these guidelines:

✔ Clean your tape drives often. Use a cleaning kit for tape-backup units. Cotton balls or cotton swabs don't cut it. They leave fibers on the tape and the heads.

✔ Rotate your tapes and introduce new ones on a regular basis.

✔ Watch NetWire or `www.novell.com` for the latest backup patches and fixes and for new drivers.

✔ Keep in touch with your vendor for hardware and software upgrades.

✔ Store your tapes in a dust-free, fireproof environment, preferably off-site.

✔ Before you use your tapes, re-tension them each time. Do this in the same way as you re-tension a tape cassette: Put a pencil inside one of the gears and rotate the gear until it is tight.

Tips for a Safe and Secure Backup

Practice and routine are the hallmarks of preparing for a crisis. No opportunity to restore a backup is anything less than a crisis, so we recommend the following guidelines:

- ✔ To encourage regularity, schedule your backups at the same time every day.

- ✔ Use a software package to record the users and groups on your LAN, along with their rights, attributes, and trustee rights.

- ✔ View the logs your software generates after each backup to make sure that everything happened just as it should have.

- ✔ If at all possible, back up your system when no one's using it. If you do this, you reduce the likelihood of files being open during the backup.

- ✔ Make arrangements to store a set of backup tapes off-site in case your office goes up in flames. Many data storage companies offer secure, fireproof vaults for this purpose. You can arrange for them to pick up last week's full backup when they drop off the tape from the week before (so you can recycle the tapes).

- ✔ If you can, make sure that the capacity of your tape drive is larger than the data set you want to back up. A system manager we know has to go into the office halfway through the backup to change tapes, every day of the week. Bummer!

Tangled Tapes: Troubleshooting the Top Three Problems

Although tape is a nice, reliable medium, you probably will still have problems. Again, a little practice ahead of time lets you discover what real problems you might have. For the record, this section lists some of the likely candidates you will encounter:

- ✔ **Messing with Macintosh files:** If you have Macintosh files on your LAN, make sure that the software you buy backs them up. In a Macintosh file, you have both a data and a resource fork. The software should back up both.

- ✔ **The trouble with tape:** Tape can suffer from all sorts of problems. It can break or wear out. Rotate your tapes periodically. Because tape is constantly in contact with the read-write heads of the tape unit, it may become worn in places. When this happens, *dropouts* occur, and the magnetic media can't retain data in those areas. Temperature and humidity also cause tape to wear.

✔ **Shiny shoes:** When the backup software supplies data to the tape drive at a rate slower than the unit's rated speed, it's called *underrun*. If you hear the tape unit starting and stopping repeatedly, underrun is probably occurring. The tape drive must back up the tape to read the last block it wrote, and then it must move forward to write the next block. The sound resembles that of a shoeshine — back and forth, back and forth. Although the sound may make your shoes look good, it's murder on your tape drives. If you hear this sound, you should investigate thoroughly. In most cases, a new software driver for your backup device or more server memory should help alleviate the problem.

The most important thing about backing up is making sure the deed gets done. For that reason, we favor as much automation of this task as possible. As long as they're working, computers don't forget, take sick days, or go on vacation. Just the kind of help you need to make sure that backups get done right and on time.

Chapter 17

Mysteries of the Organism: System Installation Configuration

. . . .

In This Chapter

▶ Installation overview overload

▶ The book on bindery basics and Directory dogma

▶ Why your configuration changes whether you want it to or not

▶ When to leave well enough alone

▶ The configuration utilities: NWADMIN, NWADMN95, NETADMIN, MONITOR, INSTALL, and SYSCON

▶ Setting up groups, users, and groups of users

. . . .

*H*ow do you make your new network work for you? Nothing substitutes for rolling up your sleeves and diving right in. This chapter discusses the big picture of how and why you install the NetWare network operating system. Where it is appropriate, we discuss the specifics of the installation process for versions 4.*x* and 3.*x*. So off we go, into the wild blue yonder.

Installation Basics: An Overview

Beginning with the new NetWare version 4.11 software, the differences between installing NetWare 3.*x* and 4.*x* are now significantly different. As a result, we discuss a few of the basic principles and procedures that you should follow in an installation of either version. Then we go into the in-depth installation information for each version separately.

Before you find out how to run the server, you first must walk through the server installation. The basic installation process for both versions of NetWare goes like this:

1. Gather the necessary hardware and software for server installation.

2. Run the installation program.

3. Prepare the server hard disk for the NetWare file system: Partition and format the drive from the installation program.

4. Create volumes and load the NetWare SYSTEM and PUBLIC files on the hard drive.

5. Fire up that server.

The NetWare installation manuals generally do a great job of explaining the installation process step-by-step. You have many decisions to make along the way, so be sure to keep good records. Write down the jumper settings for each adapter board that you install in your server. Learn from our mistakes — we've wasted a full third of our adult lives by failing to record every jumper setting while installing a new server. Also, note the total amount of RAM installed, the type and capacity of each hard drive, tape drives, CD-ROM drives, and any other options that may be installed in your server.

You *must* have a clear picture of what kind of hardware resides in your server and how that hardware is configured. You'll be frustrated if you have to stop in the middle of an installation to pry open the PC case so that you can check some bit of hardware minutiae. A little work up front can save mountains of work later on.

To Grow or Not to Grow

Start thinking about the future of your network and particularly the possibilities for your server. Don't buy a PC with just two drive bays because you don't think that you'll ever need more than two hard drives. Likewise, don't buy a PC with room for only 64MB of RAM on the motherboard just because you think that's all you'll ever need.

Networks and their servers tend to be wildly successful, even among people who say, before networks are installed, that they don't have any use for them. After people see how easy networks are to use and how much networks can improve their productivity, you'll have more than enough enthusiasm for continued network expansion. So please plan ahead. You'll thank us later.

Considering the drastic price cuts in PC hardware during the past few years, we suggest that you avoid cutting corners on your server PC just to save a few bucks. Buy the biggest, fastest, most expandable, and most upgradable PC that you can afford. Avoid the minority of PC manufacturers that still engineer proprietary hardware in their products in an attempt to lock you in to their architectures. You'll save money in the short run — and in the long run — if you have an industry standard PC with interchangeable parts.

With the possibility of later network expansion in mind, you have to consider that changes in network hardware can mean changes for the network software.

NetWare 3.*x* and 4.*x* are relatively easy to upgrade because their hardware drivers and configurations are *loadable.* In fact, their drivers can also be unloaded at will so that you can swap out system software components on the fly. This feature gives you the ability to easily change software settings or configurations to match hardware changes or additions without jumping through lots of hoops. Some servers support a hard drive enclosure called *RAID*, or Redundant Array of Independent (or some say Inexpensive) Drives. Some RAID devices actually allow you to remove and replace malfunctioning hard drives *while the server is still running!* We love this capability, and if you can afford a RAID setup, you can learn to love it, too.

Dial 4.11 for Installation: The New Easy NetWare Plan

NetWare has finally addressed one of the most persistent complaints about its installation: In 4.11, Novell has automated almost the entire process. That is, the biggest change in the NetWare 4.11 installation process is an auto-detect routine that has been refined and expanded. This auto-detect program attempts to recognize and automatically configure all adapters and peripheral devices attached to or installed in your server. And the good news is that *it actually works!*

Remember, NetWare 4.11 comes only on CD-ROM — so you must have a CD-ROM installed in your server. The good news is that, unlike previous versions of NetWare, the NetWare 4.11 installation can use an IDE or a SCSI CD-ROM. IDE and SCSI represent the two types of controllers that are most likely to drive your CD-ROM player. If you have any doubts about which type of controller that your server uses, consult the server documentation. You also have the option of installing your server from an existing NetWare 4.11 server on your network. We cover the CD-ROM installation because it's the most common way to install a NetWare 4.11 server:

1. **If your server did not arrive with a bootable DOS partition, create a DOS partition on your server hard drive that is at least 20MB (plus the amount of RAM on your server) in size.**

   For example, if your server has 48MB of RAM, make the DOS partition at least 68MB.

Bindery basics and Directory dogma

For pre-4.*x* versions, the NetWare *bindery* is the backbone of the network operating system. The bindery is a massive database of everything defined on the server: users, groups, workgroups, and printers. The bindery also keeps track of all information related to each bindery object, such as who has rights to a particular printer, the trustee directory rights for a particular group, or the member list for a particular group.

The bindery knows what is located where on the file server, who can access it, and when someone can access it. The bindery keeps track of which groups you belong to and which rights you have in every directory on the server. The bindery even stores your password and knows when it expires. The bindery is really the brains of the server because without it you wouldn't have a server.

NetWare Directory Services (NDS), built around the Directory database, plays a similar role in NetWare 4.*x* networks, as does the bindery for 2.*x* and 3.*x* networks. NDS goes way beyond what the bindery can do, however. For one thing, each bindery is server-centric: It sees only what's in, on, and around any single given server; NDS creates a global view of an entire network and exposes resources, services, and users to a shared view of a single, coherent network rather than of a bunch of individual binderies. NDS can even talk to 2.*x* and 3.*x* servers' binderies, to maintain compatibility and provide some management for older servers in a hybrid network.

Whereas the bindery knows what's what for any given server, NDS knows what's what for the entire network. That's why Chapter 11, which is entirely devoted to NDS, refers to NDS as the brains behind NetWare. NDS makes NetWare networks much easier to understand and use, especially as applications get plugged into the Directory, and can ask for services and resources on behalf of its users.

2. **Format the drive with the FORMAT C: /S command.**

   The /S parameter means to format and transfer all necessary system files so that the server can boot DOS when it first starts up.

3. **Insert the NetWare 4.11 CD-ROM and change to the CD-ROM drive, probably D: in most cases.**

4. **At the D: prompt, type** INSTALL **and press Enter.**

5. **Choose a language.**

   We always choose English. You should choose the language with which you feel most comfortable. See Figure 17-1 for the Language Menu.

6. **Choose to install a NetWare server, install client software, make a copy of the installation diskettes, or read the README file.**

   We suggest that you choose the NetWare Server install option. Figure 17-2 shows the choices on this screen.

7. **Choose between a NetWare 4.11 server and a NetWare SFT III server.**

   SFT stands for *system fault tolerance*. Using NetWare SFT III means that you can have a complete redundant server in total synch with your production server. In case of any problems with the main server, the redundant server takes over almost immediately. In this example, choose NetWare 4.11 server.

   Lights will flash and drives will whirrrrr! The installation main menu pops up and you're ready to make your first and probably only contribution to the process.

8. **Choose a SIMPLE or CUSTOM installation from the installation main menu.**

   If you choose CUSTOM, you have the opportunity to select every possible option and answer each installation question personally. For most small networks, we suggest that you choose SIMPLE. If you know ahead of time

Figure 17-1:
Choose the line with the language that you want to use.

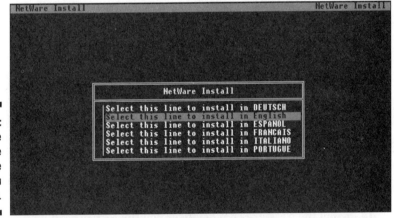

Figure 17-2:
You can choose to install a server, install a client, create diskettes, or read the README files.

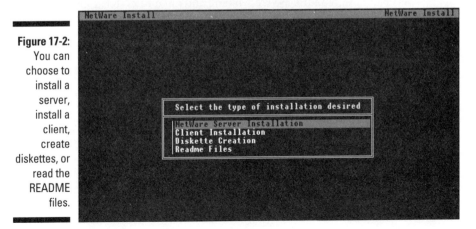

that you want to configure complex protocols like TCP/IP or that you want to span a NetWare volume across multiple hard drives, choose CUSTOM.

9. **Type in your server name and IPX internal network number when asked.**

We assume that you choose the SIMPLE installation because it should be sufficient for most users. Select a server name less than six characters long. You may be typing this server name often in the future, so the shorter the better.

The installation program copies files necessary for the installation process to your hard drive. Then the auto-detect looks for hard drives, CD-ROM drives, and network adapters.

10. **Your next choice will be to load the LAN drivers, assuming that every device was found successfully.**

If any of your installed devices are not recognized, or if install finds more than one driver for a device, you can load the device drivers manually or skip loading some drivers altogether.

11. **Select Continue Installation.**

The installation continues to configure each of your device drivers.

12. **Select Install NetWare Directory Services.**

Pick the correct time zone for your office and enter the name of your organization for the creation of the NDS tree structure. We suggest that you use your company name as the organization name.

13. **Select an ADMINISTRATOR password when asked.**

The installation program copies your server files from the CD-ROM to the server hard drive.

14. **Install the NetWare client software on the server hard drive.**

This is an option on the INSTALL menu, and once selected, it prompts you for the necessary placement information.

15. **Exit the installation program.**

That's it! You're done with the server installation!

After you complete the NetWare 4.11 installation, boot your server and load the MONITOR utility by typing **LOAD MONITOR** at the server prompt so that you can monitor your server. You are all set to network 'til the cows come home!

NetWare 3.12: Install It All

The installation for NetWare 3.12 is almost as easy as the NetWare 4.11 installation we describe above. You still need all the server hardware information that we mention in the "Installation Basics: An Overview" section. Follow these installation steps to get your new NetWare 3.12 server up and running:

1. **Format a DOS partition of at least 20MB.**

2. **Insert the NetWare 3.12 CD-ROM in your CD-ROM drive.**

3. **Load the necessary DOS device drivers to recognize the CD-ROM drive under DOS.**

   Check your CD-ROM documentation if you are unsure how to load the DOS drivers for your CD-ROM drive.

4. **At the D: prompt (or appropriate prompt for you CD-ROM drive), type** SERVER **and press Enter.**

5. **Type in a server name and an internal network number when asked.**

   Keep the server name as short and meaningful as possible; use six characters or less. The Internal IPX network number can be any unique (on your network) number.

6. **Load the installation program by typing** LOAD INSTALL **at the server prompt.**

   Figure 17-3 shows the NetWare 3.12 Install screen.

7. **Load the disk driver for your server's hard drive(s).**

   Consult your hard drive documentation for specific information on how to load the correct drivers for your server hard drive.

8. **Load the LAN driver(s) for your network adapter(s).**

   Again, consult the documentation for your network adapter for the specific driver needed.

9. **On the Installation screen, select NetWare Partitions to partition and format your hard drives.**

10. **Select Copy System and Public files to copy the necessary files from the CD-ROM to the server hard drive.**

11. **Edit the STARTUP.NCF and AUTOEXEC.NCF files under SYSTEM OPTIONS to make sure that all of your device drivers will be loaded every time the server boots.**

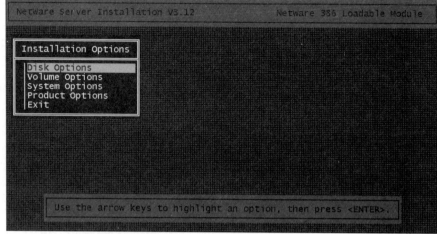

Figure 17-3:
The
Netware
3.12
Installation
main menu.

If It Ain't Broke, Don't Fix It

Even though you may know how easy it is install your server with NetWare versions 3.*x* and 4.*x,* we encourage you to make *changes* to your server with extreme caution. Think long and hard before making even minor changes.

Of course, the amount of caution should be directly proportional to the importance of the server. In environments in which the network is considered a mission-critical resource, you should thoroughly research and plan any changes. You should also carry out any changes after-hours, when an unexpected server crash may have slightly less catastrophic results.

If your company uses its network server to store games for employees to use on their breaks, you can probably make server changes with little or no warning at any point in the work day. The primary reason for caution when making server configuration changes is that things don't always go according to plan. The more critical the server, the more time you want to allow yourself to recover from any unforeseen problems after your server changes are implemented. Network administrators usually work a lot at nights and on weekends when server changes are scheduled. Making changes? We hope you don't have any important plans this weekend.

But What If It Is Broke?

If things go awry, then what do you do? Fortunately, many good sources of help are available should you need it. The online documentation is a great source of configuration and troubleshooting information. You can also check with a number of online sources to learn more about the problems you are having and possible solutions (see Appendix C). CompuServe's NetWire and the Novell's World Wide Web home page (`http://www.novell.com`) are great places to turn for help because you can search Novell's Technical Solutions Database for the solution to thousands of common and uncommon problems. You can also contact Novell directly for fee-based phone support by dialing 800-NETWARE or 800-638-9273 (outside the US, please call 801-861-7000).

For Serious Changes, Use INSTALL

Not only is the INSTALL NLM the ticket for installing your NetWare 4.x and 3.x server, it is also a crucial maintenance tool for keeping everything running smoothly on your server. If you need to work with memory statistics for NetWare, run the most current version of MONITOR for your version of NetWare.

Whenever serious server configuration changes get under way, you sometimes find yourself changing fundamental aspects of the server setup or changing out old hardware (such as NICs, SCSI adapters, and so on) for newer, improved versions. When that happens, call INSTALL (`LOAD INSTALL`, actually). This tool lets you change fundamental aspects of your server's configuration with aplomb and ease.

Because INSTALL can also do fundamental damage, we strongly advise making a complete system backup before you begin ripping the guts out of your server and changing its very soul. We hope that you don't remember this advice too late. With a backup, you can always get back to where you started; without one, all you can do sometimes is cry.

Setting Up Groups and Users

Defining your groups and users is a breeze in a small network, and a small nightmare in a large network. If you have a NetWare 4.11 server, use NWADMIN, NWADMN95, NETADMIN, or UIMPORT to create new users. Figure 17-4 shows the Create User dialog box. For NetWare 3.x, use SYSCON for adding a few users at a time. Use one of the command-line utilities, such as USERDEF or MAKEUSER, for NetWare 3.x if you create more than ten users at a time.

Creating groups is the perfect way to ease the administration burden on you, the network administrator extraordinaire. In NetWare 4.11, you can easily create a Group object using NWADMN95, NWADMIN or NETADMIN. To create groups in NetWare 3.12, use the SYSCON Group Information on the main menu.

Create groups for each network resource, such as a printer or a particular application. Grant the appropriate trustee rights to the resource. Then just add the required group members, and those users who belong to the group automatically have the rights they need to access the resource.

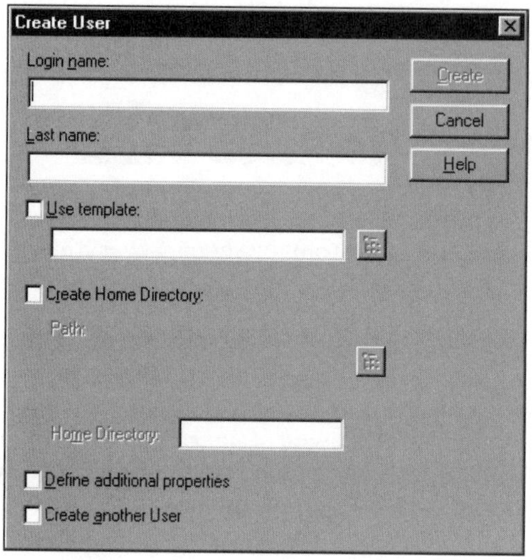

Figure 17-4:
The Create
User dialog
box.

Usable user definitions

For NetWare 4.11, log in as administrator or admin-equivalent before attempting to define new users. In NWADMIN, NWADMN95, or NETADMIN, choose Create Objects in the Directory tree, and begin creating User objects at the right location in the tree for that user. Keep user names short and self-descriptive; remember, though, that 4.x's alias facility can let users work with short names while administrators work with long ones. Here is a step-by-step plan for creating a new user using the NWADMN95 or NWADMIN utility:

1. **Click on the context in the directory tree where you want to create the user.**

   For example, if you are creating a new user in the Accounting section of the NDS tree, click once on the ACCOUNTING object.

2. **Click on the Object menu, then Create.**

3. **Click on the class of the new object.**

   In this example, click on the USER class.

4. **When the Create User dialog box appears, enter a login name for the user, the user's last name, the template name, if applicable, and the home directory.**

Please note that only the login name and user's last name are required fields, but we recommend that you fill in the other fields, too. If you want to complete the advanced object options now, also click on Define additional properties. Click on OK when finished. You can also display the Additional Properties dialog box by double-clicking on the user object in the main tree view of NWADMN95 or NWADMIN.

The additional properties dialog box is shown in Figure 17-5.

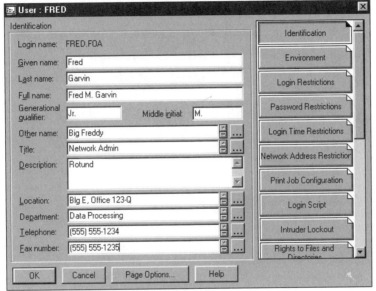

Figure 17-5:
You can define options for a user by selecting the settings pages at the right side of the screen.

In the Additional Properties dialog box, you can assign everything from a physical mail address to login restrictions to trustee rights to user login scripts.

5. Click on OK when you finish defining the new user.

After you practice defining a few users, you know the required and various optional settings and can whiz through the steps like a pro.

SYSCON: The NetWare 3.x user schmoozer

Creating a user in NetWare 3.x is just as simple as the NetWare 4.x method, just different. Here's a quick run-down of the necessary steps to define a new user in NetWare 3.x:

1. Log in as SUPERVISOR or SUPERVISOR-equivalent.

2. **Start the SYSCON utility.**

3. **Select User Information.**

4. **Press the Insert key to add a new user.**

5. **Type the new user login name and press Enter.**

   A login name can be as long as 48 characters, but we suggest that you keep it to eight or fewer characters.

6. **Set the various account restrictions through the Account Restrictions menu.**

7. **Select Change Password to set a password for the new user.**

8. **Assign trustee rights in the Trustee Rights menu.**

9. **Limit the user's available server hard drive space through the Volume settings.**

10. **Add this user to existing groups by selecting Groups Belong To.**

    You can also set this user to have the same rights as another user through Security Equivalences.

Producing users in bulk

For NetWare 4.*x*, you can use NWADMIN, NWADMN95, NETADMIN, or UIMPORT to create users in bulk. The best way to proceed is to define a user template for your chosen container and then to use that template to accommodate information about your users. UIMPORT is particularly attractive because it can be configured to accept data imported from other databases, with a minimum amount of programming effort and little or no reformatting of the imported data.

For NetWare 3.*x*, the USERDEF and MAKEUSER utilities are preferred over SYSCON for defining a large number of new users. MAKEUSER uses a batch technique and a sophisticated script language to automate user account creation. By using MAKEUSER, you can specify all the same options available in the SYSCON user-creation menus, including Account Expiration, Groups Belonged To, Concurrent Connections, and Home Directory.

USERDEF serves as both a front-end, data-entry utility for the MAKEUSER text files and as an independent user-creation tool. USERDEF lets you define a default *template* that can be used to create a large number of users with identical setups. Both utilities can save you hours of repetitive, tedious work if you need to define lots of new users.

Chapter 18

Empowering Your Users: Utilities They Can Use

. . . .

In This Chapter

▶ How to find which directories are yours and get to them fast

▶ How to find out how to change your password

▶ How to find that file you think you lost

▶ How to look at all the stuff you own and get rid of what you don't need

▶ What to do when you delete files and then wish that you hadn't

▶ How to copy files from one place on the network to another

▶ How to find out who you are, what everyone else is doing, and how LAN life is in general

▶ How to control your destiny on the LAN

▶ How to change your NetWare perspective by changing the colors you look at every day

. . . .

*N*etWare has more user utilities than you probably ever need. Some utilities are useful, and you use them every day. Others aren't much good for anything, so you never need to touch them. And then some utilities you *won't* touch — if you know what's good for you. We tell you only about the good ones and leave it to you adventurous types to test the rest.

NetWare utilities come in multiple forms but most are based on the command line or around menus. That means, with a few exceptions, that they are still DOS-based; you need to shell out to the MS-DOS prompt to use many of them. With some utilities, you type the utility's name at the command line (which looks like this: F:>). Other utilities have menus from which you choose selections that you start from the command line. Just as in DOS, everything starts somewhere; in NetWare, everything starts at the command line. For the fortunate few, some Windows-based utilities like NETUSER do almost anything you need.

The DOS and NetWare command lines don't differ much in appearance, except for the drive letters you see. In DOS, you don't ever get much beyond a C> prompt; in NetWare, you see anything ranging from drive F to drive Z.

Command-line utilities take a little more practice to get used to, although the menu utilities are pretty easy to learn with a little less practice.

Utilities generally are divided by who can use them — the garden-variety user, a privileged network administrator, or someone called a *console operator.* If you read on, we tell you which utilities users can use. First, however, we tell you about some keyboard *gotchas* that we urge you to become familiar with if you plan to tinker around with commands.

Common Keyboard Gotchas

When you are dealing with command-line utilities, a fair amount of background information scattered around the NetWare manuals could turn you into a power user, if you had time to read your way through the whole set. On the other hand, you can rely on the advice of a grizzled veteran and learn from her experience. If you are feeling bold, the following few rules may turn you into a master commander:

- ✔ If you're using a command-line utility, you can get help by typing the name alone or by adding /H, /?, or /HELP after the utility's name, like this: SLIST /H.

- ✔ When you see *path,* it means that you have to tell the network where to look for what you want.

- ✔ If you see square brackets, you can enter information or not — it's optional.

- ✔ The brackets (< >) you see instruct you to hit a certain key. This key most likely is <Enter>. Do what it says or else your command won't work. The term *hit* is used casually here. Hit is used for certain circumstances, and depress or press for others. Both work.

- ✔ The wildcard characters are the same in NetWare as they are in DOS. They mean that you can substitute something wherever the * or ? appears.

- ✔ The | character tells you to enter what is before the | or what is after it, but not both (or all).

- ✔ The ellipsis (. . .) tells you that whatever precedes the ellipsis can be repeated. For example, /option . . . means that entering multiple options at this point in the command is valid.

NetWare also uses keys that mean the same thing in any menu utility. These keys, shown in the following list, are the universal commands of choice for those in the NetWare know:

- ✔ **<F1>:** Means help in almost any language. It does in NetWare, too.

- ✔ **<F3>:** Allows you to edit an entry.

- ✔ **<F5>:** Lets you mark items you want to modify, add, or delete.

- ✔ **<Esc>:** As we all know, takes you back to the preceding menu or lets you exit from the program. Depending on the utility, the use of <Esc> differs. If <Esc> doesn't work, try <F10> or <Enter>.

- ✔ **Arrow keys:** As in many other programs, let you get where you want to go. The up arrow takes you to the preceding line; the down arrow takes you to the next line. Obvious stuff, but essential.

- ✔ **First letter:** The first-letter rule, which applies to NetWare, states, "If users enter the first letter of the menu option, they will be taken to that menu option." This rule makes sense, and it's also a great way to motor around a large selection list.

General Command-Line Utilities

Three utilities, LOGIN.EXE, LOGOUT, and HELP, are important if you meet one of four criteria:

- ✔ You want to be able to access the network.

- ✔ You want to be able to close things down and go home at night.

- ✔ You have more than one file server on your network.

- ✔ You are hopelessly lost and don't know what to do next.

You use LOGIN to log into the network. In NetWare v3.x, you log in to the server that you always log in to. In NetWare 4.x, you don't worry about logging into a specific server; you log into the network whether it consists of one file server or many. After you log in, you are connected to the directories, printers, and other resources that you need to use.

LOGIN is also used in NetWare 4.x to log into specific servers without logging out from the server you're already using. Use LOGIN servername /NS to do that. LOGIN servername /TREE lets you log in to tree.

HELP is another utility that may come in handy if you're hopelessly lost or don't know what utility to use next. Personally, we don't use it because typing the command name followed by /? (LOGIN /?) is an easier way to get help.

LOGOUT is the opposite of LOGIN — it detaches you from the server. After using LOGOUT, the only files and applications that you see are those on your hard drive.

Getting Your Bearings: The File and Directory Utilities

Novell has a bunch of built-in utilities that give you information about the files that you own on the LAN and the directories they are in. Just like DOS, these utilities let you snoop around and find out just how much information you know. You can sneak down back roads and into subdirectories that you haven't been in, or you can look for all the files that you created yesterday (in case your short-term memory resembles ours).

This section discusses some of the more common utilities that you use, including the *syntax* (the special commands you have to enter from the keyboard) for correct operation. Many times, if you need help in figuring out the syntax, you can simply type the command and see the options that you have. We split the information about utility use into four parts that tell you the utility name and its purpose, the syntax for using the command, who should use the utility, and any options you need to know to use it. Some utilities, such as NDIR (the *Net*Ware *dir*ectory command), have a language unto themselves. We explain most of the more important ones. You can dig in to the NetWare manuals (and we mean *dig*) to unearth the rest of them. Happy keyboarding — now NetWare really gets fun!

ATTACH (Only in NetWare v3.x)

You use ATTACH to connect to other file servers after you have logged in. In NetWare 4.*x,* ATTACH is replaced by the LOGIN servername /NS command.

Syntax: ATTACH [fileservername/username]

For use by: Anyone

Options: If you have an account on that file server, you may be asked for a password before you're let in. If you don't have an account, you're out of luck.

CD

The Novell CD command moves you around the directory structure just as it does in DOS or in Windows 3.1 File Manager.

Syntax: CD [\path]

For use by: Anyone who wants to get around in NetWare 3.*x* or 4.*x*.

Options: Some. Refer to the NetWare *Utilities Reference* manual for details.

CX

The Novell CX command replaces the CD command, which took you around the Directory tree. CX shows you where you are in the 4.*x* Directory tree. Your current location is called the *context,* and if you want to move somewhere else, you change the context. Just remember that CD = CX in 4.*x*.

Syntax: CX [context] *[/option ...]* | [new context] | *[/option ...]*

For use by: Anyone who wants to get around in 4.*x*

Options: You probably want to use CX before logging in to see your Directory context. That directory context must be the same as the context established in your NET.CFG file. To learn the intricate details of using CX, refer to the DynaText online documentation or type **CX/?,** Novell's universal help option.

FLAG

The FLAG command displays and lets you change file or directory attributes.

Syntax: FLAG *path* [[+ | -] *attribute...*] [*/option...*] [/? | VER]

For use by: Anyone

Options: See Table 18-1 for FLAG options.

Table 18-1	FLAG Options
Option	*What It Does*
/NAME	GROUP = *name*	This option tells you who owns the file or directory.
/D	Gives you all the details.
/FO	Lets you modify or view files.
/OWNER=*name*	Tells you which files the user owns.
/M=*media*	Lets you know how a file is searched for.
/S	Lets you search the subdirectory and any subdirectories below it.
/c	Stops the scrolling so you can get through the options fast.

MAP

The MAP command is a command that you cannot live without. You should find out everything you can about this command. It lets you assign network drives to different directories and subdirectories so that you can access them quickly when you need to get at the files within them.

MAPs can be of two kinds — search mappings or simple drive mappings. As many as 16 search mappings can exist. They automatically take you to a program located in the directory from any other directory.

Imagine that your default NetWare directory is F:\USERS\DENI and that you want to bring up WordPerfect for Windows, located in Z:WINAPPS\WPWIN. From your default directory, you can simply type **WPWIN** and rely on the search mapping defined for Z:\WINAPPS\WPWIN to locate and start up the WordPerfect application. This step sounds easier than it is, but it saves you unnecessary footwork in the NetWare directories.

Drive and search mappings that you make on-the-fly when you are logged in to the network are lost when you log out. To prevent this loss, you should define search mappings (or drive mappings, if you prefer) for your most frequently used directories in your NetWare login script. If you don't know how to do this, ask the supervisor.

Syntax: MAP F:=\USERS\DENI <Enter>

MAP S1: =servername\volume:directory\filename <Enter>

For use by: Anyone with a need for organization

Options: See the DynaText online documentation or the NetWare *Utilities Reference* manual for details.

NCOPY versus COPY

NCOPY, for — you guessed it — Network COPY, is faster than the DOS COPY command. You should use it, therefore, whenever you copy files across the network.

Syntax: NCOPY [drive: | directory\]filename [drive: | directory\]filename NCOPY F:*.* G: <Enter>

For use by: Any network speed demon

Options: See the DynaText online documentation or the NetWare *Utilities Reference* manual.

NDIR versus DIR

NDIR is another utility that bears a remarkable similarity to a DOS command. Short for *N*etwork *Dir*ectory (get it?), NDIR has some additional options. It shows you the size of files, when they last were changed, when they were created, their attributes, and who owns the file. It shows you more than you ever wanted to know about directories, too — the inherited rights mask, the user's effective rights, the owner of the directory, and the creation dates for the directory and subdirectory names.

Just like DOS's DIR, you can get carried away with all the options for NDIR, but remember them. They're invaluable for finding that file you just know you created two weeks ago Thursday.

NDIR also lets you check out the directories on your system. If you simply type NDIR, you see a list of the maximum amount of space in your current directory, the amount in use, and the amount available. It replaces CHKDIR in NetWare v3.*x.*

Syntax: NDIR [path] [/option ...]

For use by: Anyone

Options: See the DynaText online documentation or the NetWare *Utilities Reference* manual for details.

Use the /HELP format option to let you know what arcane parameters NDIR uses.

NDIR can also sort files in many different and less common ways. It can sort by file and directory attributes. It can also search for files by owner or size, or for files that were created, deleted, or modified before or after a certain date. The possibilities are endless and far too numerous to mention here. Refer to the NetWare *Utilities Reference* manual for details.

If you want to cause your administrator fits, slow your LAN down to a crawl, and generally irritate many other users, type NDIR *.*/SUB and watch the LAN creep. You will wish that you hadn't, because you won't get any work done until the LAN stops searching.

NETUSER — Don't leave home without it

NETUSER is 4.*x*'s all-purpose user tool, which replaces a number of utilities in earlier versions of NetWare. If you're aching to start using 4.*x,* NETUSER is a good place to begin. It really is one of those commands you can't live without. For NetWare 4.*x* and higher users, NETUSER replaces SESSION, parts of SYSCON and FILER, and parts of the printing utilities. It lets you print, send messages to other users, move around on the network, change your password, and change your context (see Figure 18-1). Learn to use NETUSER and then don't leave home without it.

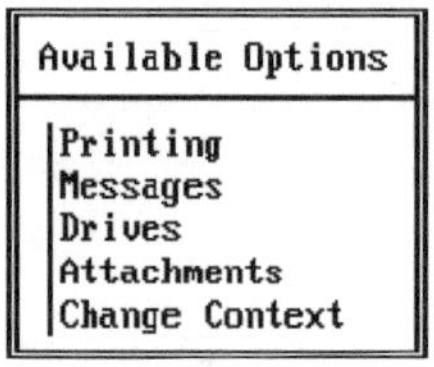

Figure 18-1:
NETUSER's
available
options.

```
┌─────────────────────┐
│ Available Options   │
├─────────────────────┤
│ Printing            │
│ Messages            │
│ Drives              │
│ Attachments         │
│ Change Context      │
└─────────────────────┘
```

Syntax: NETUSER <Enter>

For use by: Anyone who thinks that he or she knows how to use 4.x and anyone who wants to learn

Options: NETUSER is a 4.x menu utility; see the DynaText online documentation for all the things you can do.

NLIST

NLIST is 4.x's be-all and end-all utility for 4.x geeks. It lets you see objects (such as users, groups, and printers), search for objects, and find out whatever you need to know about them (their rights or whether they are logged in, for example). If you want to be a serious 4.x user, NLIST should be in your repertoire. NLIST also is the utility that draws you a map of your file and directory system. It replaces LISTDIRE in v3.x.

Syntax: NLIST [object] [=object name] [/option ...]

For use by: Anyone who is anyone

Options: The options that NLIST uses are too numerous to talk about here; refer to 4.x's online documentation for the lowdown.

NPATH

This workstation utility helps you find files and find out why NetWare is in Spanish instead of English. It shows the search path for a file.

Syntax: NPATH [utility][filename[, filename...]] [option] [/? | VER]

For use by: Everyone

Options: Lots. See the DynaText online documentation for all of them.

PURGE

PURGE does just what it says: It permanently erases files that you have erased before.

Syntax: PURGE <Enter>

For use by: Anyone with a strong stomach

Options: Nada — not one

Use PURGE only if you don't ever, ever, ever want to get the file back. If you use the /all statement, you purge anything that you have already erased.

RENDIR

For neat-freak LAN keepers, RENDIR lets you rename directories when you find that you don't like their names anymore.

Syntax: RENDIR [drive:] oldname to newname <Enter>

For use by: Users who can't make up their minds

Options: None here

RIGHTS

Rights is a utility that you can use to give other users access to the things that you own such as files, directories, and volumes. Rather than learn how to use this utility from the command line, use NetWare Administrator.

Syntax: RIGHTS path [[+ | -] rights] [/option . . .] [;? | /VER]

For use by: Everyone, but especially NetWare administrators

Options: Lots. See the DynaText online documentation or the NetWare *Utilities Reference* manual for the options.

SEND

SEND is a command that you should use only in emergencies. It allows a user to send a message from a workstation or the file server console. SEND messages are annoying to get because they stop applications from working until the person who receives the message clears it. You can also use the BROADCAST command and the SEND function in the MONITOR utility.

Syntax: SEND "message" [[TO] username|connection number]. Here's an actual message that could be sent to everyone: SEND "LOG OUT NOW, OR DIE." TO ALL. Only those wanting to tempt fate will ignore it.

For use by: Anyone with an important message to tell that can't wait for e-mail to do it

Options: Some. See the DynaText online documentation or the NetWare *Utilities Reference* manual for details.

SETPASS

This is our favorite utility for people who can't make up their minds. NetWare requires users to change their passwords every so often. For those who want control of their lives or aren't content for long with things the way they are, SETPASS lets them change their passwords.

Syntax: SETPASS <Enter>

For use by: Anyone. Suggested use: No more than once a day unless prescribed

Options: Nada — not one

Information, Please

Some utilities give you information only. They show you a plethora of information — some useful, some not. If you're a trivia freak, these utilities are for you.

CHKVOL (NetWare v3.x Only)

If you want to see how much of everything you have out there on the LAN, use the CHKVOL command. It's not much good for anything other than documenting what you already have, but when you're deciding what to name something, this information can be very useful.

Syntax: CHKVOL <Enter>
              CHKVOL VOL1: <Enter>

For use by: Anyone

Options: Zip

SLIST (NetWare v3.x Only)

SLIST is the NetWare utility for calling all servers. File servers that respond to NetWare's roll call are listed here. If your LAN has only one file server, it is the only one listed. If you have one down the hall in accounting, however, DADDY_WARBUCKS may be listed.

Syntax:	SLIST <Enter>
	SLIST DAD*.* <Enter>
	SLIST LAMBIE_PIE <Enter>

For use by: Any curious user

Options: ALL (Lists all the file servers it finds)

USERLIST (NLIST in 4.x)

Do you sometimes wonder whether you're the only one working at 10 p.m.? If you do, USERLIST helps you to find out.

Do you wonder whether your boss is in yet? Type **USERLIST BIG CHEESE** to check.

Syntax:	USERLIST ALL <Enter>
	USERLIST BIG*.* <Enter>

For use by: Anyone

Options: See the NetWare *Utilities Reference* manual for details, as well as Table 18-2, which follows.

Table 18-2	USERLIST Options
Option	*What It Does*
/A	Shows everything, including network and node addresses.
/C	Use this option if you need to read fast. It doesn't stop at the end of the display.
/H	Help!
/O	This option tells you whether listed items are users, print servers, and so on.

VOLINFO (For NetWare v3.x Only)

Lets you look at the amount of space left on a volume and the volumes you can access.

Syntax: FILER <Enter>

For use by: Anyone

Options: Nada

WHOAMI

WHOAMI is the ultimate utility if you forget who you are. If short-term memory loss strikes late Friday afternoon, type **WHOAMI** at the command line and you will instantly remember. WHOAMI shows you other stuff, too, that's not as important as your username. It tells you which workstation you're logged in from (as though you care) and also the rights and attributes you have in the directory in which you're working.

Syntax: WHOAMI <Enter>

For use by: Anyone in need of self-identification!

Options: Whoops! — before we forget — Table 18-3 shows the options that you can use with WHOAMI.

Table 18-3	WHOAMI Options
Option	*What It Does*
/A	Lists your effective rights, the groups you're in, your security equivalences, the people you manage, whether you're a workgroup manager, and other information
/G	Lists the groups you're in
/O	Shows the names of the users and groups you manage
/R	Lists your effective rights
/S	Shows your security equivalences
/SY	Shows other system information
/W	Shows whom you manage

Order from the Menu — No Substitutions Allowed

Menu utilities offer lots of support in that they present each choice that you can make at any given point in the menu tree. They also offer context-sensitive help, which means that all you have to do is press F1 at any point on a menu and the Help system explains what is highlighted. Even though it sounds easy, climbing around in menu trees all day can make you slightly daffy! This section covers the main NetWare menu utilities.

COLORPAL

You should avoid the COLORPAL utility unless you have a bachelor's degree in fine arts. This utility lets you change the colors of your soothing NetWare menus to colors that you might see on a psychedelic acid trip. Even though COLORPAL is fun to use, NetWare's menus look pretty good, considering what was available to work with when the menus were created.

FILER

FILER does lots of stuff that you can do from the command line. It shows you current directory information and displays the contents of the directory. You can choose a directory and change directories that you are using. You can view information about volumes, attributes, and effective rights. FILER lets you copy files or move them around and set the attributes of a file. Its options are too numerous to cover here (see Figure 18-2). Refer to the NetWare *Utilities Reference* manual for a blow-by-blow description.

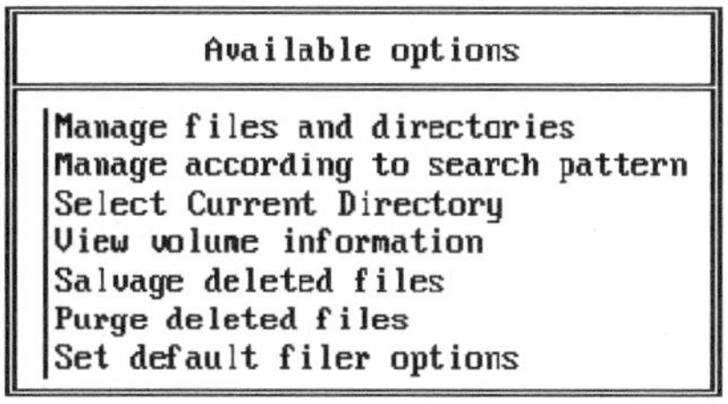

Figure 18-2:
FILER's
available
options.

```
             Available options
┌─────────────────────────────────────┐
│ Manage files and directories         │
│ Manage according to search pattern   │
│ Select Current Directory             │
│ View volume information              │
│ Salvage deleted files                │
│ Purge deleted files                  │
│ Set default filer options            │
└─────────────────────────────────────┘
```

Syntax: FILER <Enter>

For use by: Everyone (or anyone who needs some menu-by-menu file help)

SALVAGE (for those in the v3.x know)

SALVAGE has much to do with salvation. It's the catchall command that you need to use whenever you erase a file on a NetWare server that you really don't want to erase. SALVAGE gives you several options: You can look at all the files you have deleted, recover files that have been deleted, or put files back in the directories they occupied before they were erased.

Syntax: SALVAGE <Enter>

For use by: Anyone who goofed

Options: None

Because files aren't biodegradable, you can get them back with the SALVAGE utility.

SESSION (NetWare v3.x only)

SESSION lets users move around from directory to directory without requiring explicit DOS commands for manual directory changes. If you have to jump around directories often, SESSION might be just the thing for you.

Syntax: SESSION <Enter>

For use by: Anyone with couch potato(e) tendencies

Options: If you really believe that you have to use SESSION, refer to the NetWare *Utilities Reference* manual for all the boring details.

SYSCON

For NetWare v3.*x*, SYSCON is the NetWare control center. If you're a user, you can see all the information about yourself, which groups you are in, and your effective rights. If you don't have supervisor rights, you see only information about yourself.

Syntax: SYSCON <Enter>

For use by: Everyone

Options: Refer to Chapter 17 for more information on SYSCON.

Chapter 19

Master of the Console System Utilities

*W*e divide this chapter into several parts: some general, unrelated but very important utilities; some utilities you need to know if you end up managing the LAN; and some utilities you can use only from the file server console. You can get keyboard practice here; for the most part, these utilities don't come in Windows versions.

Console Management Utilities

Much of NetWare management begins at what people in the know call the *file server console,* which is the monitor attached to the file server. From the file server console, you can control normal life on the LAN. You can decide whether the network is working, get it into working condition, configure it to do different things, or disable it so that users cannot work on it. That's why, if you're a network administrator, you have to limit access to the file server console. Administering it can be a life-or-death responsibility.

In the lingo of the networking business, *bringing up* the file server means that you do two things:

▸ Boot the file server, just as you would do with a DOS machine.

▸ Enter the command SERVER from the DOS prompt.

Taking the file server down and bringing it up again is not something you do casually. It disturbs users because they no longer have a connection to the network, and it can disturb your boss because he or she no longer has a connection either. Bring the file server down in only the most extreme cases.

If you take the server down, do it after normal business hours. Spend a night or part of it away from home to do it. You may think that you deserve comp time the next day, or you may just take off the following afternoon. Believe us — you won't get that time off. When you're married to the network, your wedding to anyone else may as well be postponed.

When you're at the file server console by way of either a local monitor or remotely from a monitor on your desk or halfway across town at home (we tell you briefly how to do that later), you should know about a number of important commands. We tick off the list in alphabetical order so that you can find items quickly.

CDROM

This utility (also in v3.12) lets you use a CD-ROM as a NetWare volume. It is a utility that you have to be familiar with for most software that comes on CD-ROM discs.

Syntax: LOAD [path] CDROM

Options: CDROM works with several options including DISMOUNT, DIR, MOUNT, and CHANGE, to name a few.

Welcome to the Electronic Library!

One of NetWare's best features is its comprehensive online documentation. Whereas earlier versions of NetWare came with a foot of manuals — or more! — both NetWare 3.12 and 4.11 (and IntranetWare, of course) ship with only a slender set of paper manuals. The real information is available through Electronic Book Technologies' DynaText hypertext engine. DynaText provides a powerful search engine, includes the ability for you to create your own bookmarks and make annotations, and provides a well-organized overview of materials and information about every aspect of NetWare worth mentioning (no matter what flavor you have).

Most NetWare administrators *in the know* install the entire document set on a server so that everyone can easily access its contents. On our system, the online documentation set lives in `SYS:PUBLIC:\DOCVIEW\`, with a series of subdirectories for DOS, Windows, and Macintosh users. When we refer to DynaText references in this chapter (and in others), this is the stuff we're talking about!

CLEAR STATION

The CLEAR STATION utility lets you clear the connection between the server and a client. It's a great utility to use for those users who refuse to log out when you need to do maintenance on the network. You can also use CLS from the MONITOR utility.

Syntax: CLEAR STATION [station_number]

Options: CLEAR STATION has only two options: *n* to specify the number of the workstation and *all,* which does just that, clears out everyone.

CLS

CLS works just like DOS. It clears the screen on the file server console.

Syntax: CLS

Options: None. Nothing could be easier. But since your file server room is locked, why do you need this utility anyway?

CONFIG

The CONFIG utility does what it says, almost. Actually, it just shows you information. You can't use it to configure your system.

CONFIG shows you the LAN drivers that are loaded in your file server, the file server's network number and name, the protocols that are bound to each network adapter, and the type of packet (frame type) being sent across the network. In addition, CONFIG tells you the node addresses of the network adapters in the server and all their hardware settings. If you ever have a question about your server's configuration, CONFIG is there to answer it. And you can bet your bottom dollar that the technical support people will ask you to use it to tell them about your server profile.

Syntax: CONFIG <Enter>

Options: None

CONLOG

This is one of those cool utilities that you may never need but is great to have if you are troubleshooting for someone that is helping you remotely. It lets you capture all the messages generated at the file server console and write them to a file. The file CONSOLE.LOG is stored in the SYS:\ETC directory.

Syntax: LOAD CONLOG

Options: If for some reason, you don't want to use the filename CONSOLE.LOG, you can specify another name on the command line. The DynaText *Utilities Reference* includes a couple of other useful options.

DHCPCFG

If you're using TCP/IP services on your network, this utility lets you configure and manage the NetWare Dynamic Host Configuration Protocol. See Chapter 21 for more information on this utility.

Syntax: LOAD DHCPCFG

Options: Luckily, there aren't any.

DISABLE LOGIN

This command is the ultimate meanie. Ever wonder why you couldn't log in when you did just minutes ago? DISABLE LOGIN probably happened. See your network manager, who is probably tinkering with the system. You will be told to stay out. Go back to your desk. Do not pass go. Do not collect $200.

If you're the network administrator, you should use this command before you back up or make any repairs to the system.

If users are already logged in to the file server, DISABLE LOGIN doesn't affect them. You have to kick them off in the conventional way or send them a message with the SEND command, "LOG OUT NOW OR LOSE IT!"

Syntax: DISABLE LOGIN <Enter>

Options: It's such a simple command that it doesn't have any options.

DISMOUNT

Having nothing to do with equestrian interests, this utility lets you dismount a volume so users can't use it. It's a particularly useful command when you need to repair the volume, upgrade disk drivers, or change out a drive.

Syntax: DISMOUNT volume name

Options: Even though it doesn't have any options, you should know what you're doing before issuing this command. See the DynaText Chapter 7, "Supervising the Network."

DISPLAY NETWORKS

This utility lets you view network numbers — the number of hops from one network to another — and the number of networks that the server's router recognizes. When you're in trouble on your network, DISPLAY NETWORKS is a good utility to have.

Syntax: DISPLAY NETWORKS

Options: Doesn't it seem like the most useful utilities have no options? This one doesn't.

DISPLAY SERVERS

This utility, like DISPLAY NETWORKS, shows you the servers of which the internal router is aware.

Syntax: DISPLAY NETWORKS

Options: Nope, nada, none

DOSGEN

If you have a network that contains a diskless workstation, you want to get to know this utility. It lets you create the files needed for setting up a diskless workstation.

Syntax: DOSGEN [/? | /VER]

Options: Very few. Read the online documentation before using this utility, and then cross your heart and hope that someone gives you some money to replace those diskless dinosaurs.

DOMAIN

This utility — an option of LOAD — lets you run NetWare Loadable Modules (NLMs) in a protected area during testing.

Syntax: LOAD [path] DOMAIN [ring number]

Options: DOMAIN has just a couple of options: HELP and RING. In NetWare 4.*x*, you can use ring number 1, 2, or 3. Ring 3 is the default ring.

DOWN

Entering DOWN is similar to turning off the lights. Don't do it unless you really want to leave users in the dark. DOWN takes the file server down so that users cannot use it. This utility also makes sure that the data on your file server is safe by closing files, writing information in cache to disk, and updating all the tables it can.

Syntax: DOWN <Enter>

Options: None

Before you down the file server, use the BROADCAST command to send to all users a message that you plan to take the file server down in *x* minutes. It's just a courteous thing to do.

DSMERGE

DSMERGE lets you join two separate NetWare Directory Services (NDS) objects into a single tree.

Syntax: LOAD DSMERGE <Enter>

Options: None

DSREPAIR

Use this utility if you have problems with the NDS database.

Syntax: LOAD [path] DSREPAIR [=U] [-L logfilename]

Options: Only two. =U runs DSREPAIR automatically without disturbing you. -L keeps a log file to tell you what DSREPAIR found.

DSTRACE

DSTRACE is a diagnostic utility that lets you view NDS messages to see whether the directory is synchronized.

Syntax: SET DSTRACE = ON

Options: Just ON or OFF.

DSUTILS

DSUTILS is a menu utility that lets you perform directory services operations from DOS.

Syntax: DSUTILS

Options: None

EDIT

This handy-dandy utility lets you edit NCF or ASCII files from the file server console.

Syntax: LOAD [path] EDIT filename

Options: Nope. Nada. Zip.

ENABLE LOGIN

This command is the opposite of DISABLE LOGIN, and you should use it when you want users to be able to log in to the network again.

Syntax: ENABLE LOGIN <Enter>

Options: None. Don't you wish that there were some? Imagine the statement ENABLE LOGIN EXCEPT FOR BERT AND ERNIE. Gosh, the power of the SUPER-VISOR account (it went to our heads temporarily).

EXIT

If you want to return to DOS before shutting off the file server for maintenance, you enter EXIT after DOWN. You can then rerun SERVER.EXE to operate with new parameters.

Syntax: EXIT <Enter>

Options: This command has no options, except that you have to press the Enter key to exit. Shouldn't keyboards have Exit keys, too?

FIRE

This command tells you if your file server is on fire. Only people who have fewer brains than a three-toed paramecium should use this command.

Just kidding! No such command is available, but at least we know that you are reading this book. The closest thing NetWare offers is FIRE PHASERS. It makes keen noises when you log in!

HALT

The HALT command is used in SFT III servers to bring down an IOEngine. It works only on mirrored servers.

Syntax: HALT

Options: None

HCSS

You use this utility to view the settings and commands used in the NetWare High Capacity Storage System. If you're wise, you'll change these settings from the NetWare Administrator.

Syntax: HCSS [parameter] = [setting]

Options: Lots of parameters and settings are available. Look at the DynaText Chapter 6, "Migrating Data Using the High Capacity Storage System."

HELP

Wow! A utility that displays the help information for file server console commands.

Syntax: HELP commandname

Options: Heaven help us, none!

INETCFG

Use this utility to make configuring routing and network protocols easier. After loading INETCFG, a menu appears that lets you configure your internetwork.

Syntax: LOAD INETCFG

Options: Too many options exist to explain here. Refer to the DynaText references for IPX, TCP/IP, and AppleTalk.

INSTALL

INSTALL lets you mirror or duplex drives, format your hard disk, load NetWare floppy disks during installation, configure devices that you are adding to the file server, change or create volumes, and do other things too numerous to mention. See Figure 19-1 for installation options.

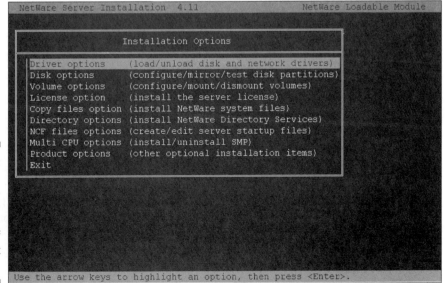

Figure 19-1: The Install utility allows you to perform a variety of management functions.

Syntax: LOAD INSTALL <Enter>

Options: Some

If you load INSTALL with the NH option, you save about 16K of RAM but sacrifice any online help.

INSTALL tells you whether INSTALL itself is already loaded (so you don't need to worry about loading it multiple times). See the online documentation or the *File Server Utilities* manual for the skinny on INSTALL.

IPXCON

This utility lets you configure, monitor, and troubleshoot routers and network segments. It can show you the status and path of IPX routers and packets and let you view all the active IPX routers on your network.

Syntax: LOAD IPXCON [/P]

Options: IPXCON has only one parameter, /P. After loading IPXCON, a menu appears that shows you router statistics and so on.

IPXPING

With IPXPING, you can PING a server or workstation to check its connection.

Syntax: LOAD IPXPING

Options: These options are easy. "Whoa" and "Giddyup." To stop sending packets, press the Esc key.

KEYB

This command lets you change the language that your keyboard uses.

Syntax: LOAD [path]KEYB [keyboard_type]

Options: If you type on a keyboard in one of the following countries, this command's for you: Belgium, Canada, Denmark, France, Germany, Italy, Netherlands, Norway, Portugal, Russia, Spain, Sweden, United Kingdom, or United States. Multinationals do not need to apply.

LANGUAGE

This utility goes hand-in-hand with the KEYD utility — use it to set the language used by system modules.

Syntax: LANGUAGE [language_name | number]

Options: Use the LIST parameter to show a list of the language names and number you may want to use.

LIST DEVICES

If you want to see what's attached to your file server, type this command. It lets you see CD-ROM drives, disk drives, or any device with a driver.

Syntax: LIST DEVICES

Options: Mercifully, none.

LOAD

This all-purpose command lets you do many essential things. LOAD lets you run the INSTALL program, which lets you diddle with LAN drivers and the STARTUP.NCF and AUTOEXEC.NCF files and install all sorts of equipment on your file server. It lets you load MONITOR, which we talk about later, and lets you run VREPAIR, which you use if, for some reason, your volumes freak out.

Syntax: LOAD's Syntax is easy. Just follow LOAD with a space and whatever program you need to run and then press the Enter key.

Options: LOAD has numerous options.

MEMORY

Sometimes we wish this utility didn't exist to remind us how little RAM we have in our file servers. The one with the most RAM wins.

Syntax: MEMORY

Options: None. If you don't have enough RAM, buy more.

MEMORY MAP

This utility tells you how much memory DOS and the server take.

Syntax: MEMORY MAP

Options: None.

MIGRATE

This DOS utility lets you migrate NetWare v2.x or v3.x binderies to Novell Directory Services.

Syntax: MIGRATE

Options: Lots. Be prepared for a long spell at the keyboard when you use this utility.

MIRROR STATUS

MIRROR STATUS shows you all the disk's partitions that are mirrored and their status.

Syntax: MIRROR STATUS <Enter>

Options: None

MODULES

This utility lets you look at the NetWare Loadable Modules loaded on the server.

Syntax: MODULES [string]

Options: MODULES supports several strings. For example, to see all the modules starting with *N*, type **MODULES N**.

MONITOR

MONITOR shows you file server utilization and what is happening on the file server. It's a command you should have loaded most of the time. Three Options are available with MONITOR: /P, which gives you information about processor utilization; NS, which turns off the screen saver that MONITOR uses; and NH, which turns off any help that you may receive with MONITOR and saves memory.

With MONITOR, you can find out who is connected to your network, get information about a server's disks and the utilization of its resources, and get information about the LAN adapters and drivers loaded on that server. Besides providing information, MONITOR lets you lock the file server console from MONITOR, unlock it when you want back in, and clear workstation connections to the LAN if, for some reason, a workstation hangs and its files are left open.

You can mount or dismount storage devices, activate or deactivate a file server's hard disk, or cause the hard disk light on the front of the file server to flash. We know that you are aching to make this light flash (we think that it's weird).

For a detailed, play-by-play analysis of MONITOR, refer to the online documentation or the NetWare _System Administration_ manual.

If file server RAM is at a premium, load MONITOR with the NH option. It saves you about 25K of memory.

MONITOR is your principal diagnostic tool for NetWare. Figure 19-2 shows the information and options available in the MONITOR utility. It is a collection of utilities typically run from the server console, to check on your server's health and well-being.

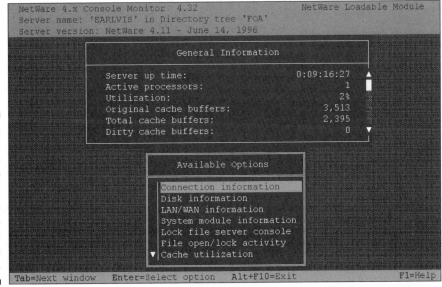

Figure 19-2:
Use the
Monitor
utility for
trouble-
shooting, as
well as to
keep an eye
on the
system.

Syntax: MONITOR <Enter>

For use by: Supervisors or console operators

Options: Refer to Chapter 17 for more details.

MOUNT

This utility lets you *mount* volumes on the file server so that users can see and use them.

Syntax: MOUNT *volumename* <Enter>

MOUNT ALL

You may want to mount volumes that you don't use often, such as historical data or last year's financial records. Remember to use the DISMOUNT utility when you finish.

Options: ALL

NAME

NAME is one of those useful commands for finding out the name of a server in room with a slew of servers. Of course, putting a sign on each of them helps, too.

Syntax: NAME

Options: None

NCUPDATE

After you've renamed or moved a container, you can use NCUPDATE to update the users' NET.CFG files so they contain the new name context.

Syntax: NCUPDATE [/? | /VER] [/NP]

Options: Use the /NP switch to automatically update NET.CFG files.

NETADMIN, NWADMIN, UUIMPORT (MAKEUSER in v3.x)

In NetWare 4.x, you can use NETADMIN, NWADMIN, or UUIMPORT to create bulk users. (MAKEUSER is the alternative to SYSCON in NetWare v3.x). Figure 19-3 shows the NetWare Administrator interface. Chapter 17 and Chapter 20 tell you how to use NETADMIN and NWADMIN. If you still have NetWare v3.x, stick with MAKEUSER; it saves you time if your users are breeding faster than rabbits. As a bonus for v3.x users, some of MAKEUSER's Options make creating users easier than it is with SYSCON.

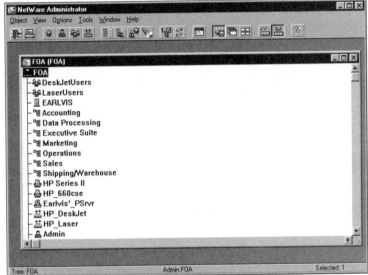

Figure 19-3:
NWADMIN
simplifies a
number of
administrative
functions.

Syntax: MAKEUSER <Enter>

For use by: Supervisors

Options: See the NetWare *Utilities Reference* manual or the DynaText online documentation for more information.

NetWare Directory Browser

A Macintosh utility, finally. Use this utility to choose from the NetWare Directory tree.

Syntax: A double-click is all it takes.

Options: Scroll, point, click.

NMENU (MENU in v3.x)

The NMENU utility lets you create menus for your users to work from. A DOS-based interface, NMENU helps you keep users where they should be in the NetWare file system. Given some time and effort, NMENU can help with other tasks, too. MENU is NMENU's v3.x equivalent. Both are a licensed subset of McAfee's menu utilities, which are much more powerful and easier to use than their NMENU predecessor.

Syntax: <NMENU>

For use by: Anyone

Options: See the NetWare online documentation or the NetWare *Utilities Reference* manual for more information.

NVER

The NVER utility lets you see information on the server such as the version of DOS, version of NetWare, and LAN driver information.

Syntax: NVER [/c][/? | /ver]

Options: Use /c if you want to scroll the information on the screen.

NWXTRACT

This handy utility lets you recover NetWare files and utilities if you blow something away. It lets you expand files from the CD-ROM or diskettes to the network.

Syntax: NWXTRACT path filename | groupname [destination] [option].

Options: See the DynaText information for groupname and options.

OFF

See CLS. This utility is the same. If you forget one, remember the other. Better yet, lock the file server room door.

Syntax: OFF

Options: None

PARTMGR

This utility lets you manage Directory partitions and replicas. You can also do this from NDS Manager.

Syntax: Point and click.

Options: Many

PING

From the console, you use PING to send an IP packet to an IP workstation on your internetwork.

Syntax: LOAD PING

Options: PONG is not among them. Like IPXPING, LOAD and ESC are the only commands you need to know.

PROTOCOL

PROTOCOL lets you view the protocols that are registered on the server or register additional protocols or frame types.

Syntax: PROTOCOL [REGISTER protocol frame id#]

Options: If you're ready to do this, checking the online documentation is better than doing it here. Search for PROTOCOL in the Utilities Reference.

RCONSOLE

RCONSOLE is one of those truly marvelous utilities that gives you calluses on your behind. It lets you look at the file server console without ever leaving your desk. Imagine, being the master of the console without ever having to see it.

Syntax: RCONSOLE [server name] [server name*]

Options: When you type RCONSOLE, you see a menu that asks you to pick a file server. Then you need to enter the RCONSOLE password for that server. From there, you can toggle between the screens on the file server console. Here are some keys that will help:

- ✔ <Alt>+F1: Displays the RCONSOLE Available Options Menu, which lets you cycle through the console screens.
- ✔ <Alt>+F2: Exit RCONSOLE and get back to work.
- ✔ <Alt>+F3 or <Alt>+F4: Toggle between RCONSOLE screens.

REGISTER MEMORY

This utility lets your NetWare v3.x and 4.x server recognize more than 16MB of memory.

Syntax: REGISTER MEMORY start_address amount

Options: REGISTER MEMORY is tricky, so fortunately you only have to do it once. Unfortunately, explaining it here takes too long, so once again refer to the online documentation.

REMIRROR PARTITION

REMIRROR PARTITION is pretty obvious: It lets you remirror partitions that have been unmirrored. You don't have to do this often, because the server automatically does it for you. If something hiccups and the server doesn't do its job, however, you can take over and force the remirroring operation to occur. Another utility lets you stop the remirroring process. It's called, appropriately, ABORT REMIRROR.

Syntax: REMIRROR PARTITION number <Enter>

Options: None — just the number of the partition.

RESET ROUTER

If you have more than one file server, you may need this command. RESET ROUTER lets you reset and update information about routers or bridges after the file server, router, or bridge crashes.

Syntax: RESET ROUTER

Options: None

RESTART SERVER

RESTART SERVER saves you a single step — exiting to DOS after you DOWN the server. Use it when you are troubleshooting the server.

Syntax: RESTART SERVER [— parameter]

Options: This is a utility that has two simple parameters: NS lets you restart the server without running the STARTUP.NCF file, and it lets you do the same thing but not run the AUTOEXEC.NCF file.

SECURE CONSOLE

The SECURE CONSOLE command is the electronic lock and key for NetWare — SECURE CONSOLE lets you lock the console and then unlock it when you're ready. If someone tries to break in to the system with a debugger, SECURE CONSOLE prevents him or her from loading NetWare Loadable Modules and from changing the date and time. It's an eminently useful utility.

Syntax: SECURE CONSOLE <Enter>

Options: None of any intruder's business

SERVER

The big mama of utilities. This is the origin, the beginning, how you bring your server up.

Syntax: SERVER [parameter]

Options: This command has the same parameters as RESTART SERVER.

SERVMAN

SERVMAN, short for *Server Manager*, lets you look at the operating system parameters and change them if you want. It also lets you view lots of stuff, such as the configuration of IPX and any devices in the server. And it lets you edit the AUTOEXEC.NCF and STARTUP.NCF files. Like the INSTALL NLM, you must LOAD SERVMAN before you can use it.

Syntax: LOAD [path] SERVMAN <Enter>

Options: None

SET

SET is a common function that is far too complicated to explain in this book. It lets you see the parameters of the operating system and change them if you want. SET commands are placed in the STARTUP.NCF file and can improve file server performance. See the *File Server Utilities* manual or the online documentation for an extensive explanation.

Syntax: SET [parameter]

Options: Lots and lots

SET TIME

SET TIME lets you set the date and time of the file server. You should reset the time the first thing when you wake up at daylight savings time, or someone surely will remind you about it. (And they think that we aren't smart enough to figure it out.) As for the date, who can be trusted to always know what day it is?

Syntax: SET TIME hh:mm:ss <Enter>
       SET TIME mm/dd/yy hh:mm:ss <Enter>
       SET TIME mm/dd/yy

Options: None

SETUPDOC

We talk about the online documentation in the sidebar "Welcome to the Electronic Library!" in this chapter. This utility lets you set up the online documentation from a Windows 3.1 workstation.

Syntax: Click on the SETUPDOC icon in the Novell Online Documentation program group.

Options: Not a lot of clicking going on. You just Install or Delete.

SPEED

This utility lets you display the relative speed of the server's processor. For example, a Pentium 66MHz machine will have a rating of approximately 3660.

Syntax: SPEED

Options: For a juiced-up utility, none exist.

TIME

See the SET TIME entry and then try to figure this one out.

Syntax: TIME <Enter>

Options: None

TRACK OFF

TRACK OFF is the opposite of TRACK ON — it turns off the router tracking screen. What's a router tracking screen? See TRACK ON for all the details.

Syntax: TRACK OFF <Enter>

Options: None

TRACK ON

TRACK ON is a useful troubleshooting utility. If you are installing a workstation and are having trouble getting a connection, use TRACK ON. It displays the Router Tracking Screen, which tells you all the data being transmitted or received at a workstation and file server. TRACK ON has lots of useful parameters. See the online documentation or the *File Server Utilities* manual for details.

Syntax: TRACK ON <Enter>

Options: Lots

UNLOAD

UNLOAD does the opposite of LOAD. It unloads NetWare Loadable Modules and the MONITOR program.

Syntax: UNLOAD NLMname

Options: None

VERSION

VERSION tells you (if you or a tech support person want to know) the version of the network operating system that you are running and its copyright notice.

Syntax: VERSION <Enter>

Options: None — just the different versions of NetWare displayed: v2.15, v2.15C, v3.11, and 4.*x*

VIEW

VIEW lets you look at files from the server console. For example, use it to take a look at your STARTUP.NCF or AUTOEXEC.NCF files.

Syntax: VIEW [filename]

Options: None. You can't even edit or modify the file.

VOLUMES

This command tells you how much bookshelf space you need for the NetWare manuals. It automatically calculates, based on the version number you are running, whether you need a full shelf or just a portion of it. If you're using 4.*x*, you don't need any shelf space — you need a CD-ROM.

An old joke in the networking industry asks, "What weighs more than your file server?" The answer is "The NetWare manuals." Seriously now, VOLUMES tells you the names of the volumes mounted on the file server.

Syntax: VOLUMES <Enter>

Options: None. Did you want some?

VREPAIR

VREPAIR can fix problems with volumes. Use it to fix damaged files or screwed-up directories. It's also recommended whenever an abnormal shutdown happens, on the off-chance that open files have been damaged.

Syntax: LOAD [path] VREPAIR

VREPAIR is on the System-2 disk (for 3.11 and earlier versions; it's on the CD-ROM for later ones). Because you may want to run VREPAIR on a damaged SYS: volume and cannot get to it if SYS: is damaged, make sure that you put VREPAIR in the DOS boot partition so that you have it if you need it.

NetWare 4.*x* will detect serious file system problems and run VREPAIR for you.

A tip about running VREPAIR: "Run it until no errors exist, and then run it one time more."

Why you may need VREPAIR

VREPAIR comes in handy in these situations:

✔ If you cannot mount a volume or if you receive a disk read error

✔ If the power goes out and corrupts the volume or if you get an error on the file server console when it tries to mirror a volume

✔ If you get other miscellaneous memory errors

NetWare's Windows and Windows 95 Utilities

Management can also take place from the comfort of your workstation. If a utility doesn't have to run from the console, Novell has a Windows utility for it.

DS Migrate

This Windows 3.x or Windows 95 utility lets you upgrade v2.x and v3.x bindery information to Novell Directory Services. It runs from the NetWare Administrator.

Syntax: Choose Tools and then DS Migrate.

Options: The utility tells you the options as you go along.

NetWare Application Launcher (NAL)

NAL is the newest of NetWare's utilities. It is Windows 3.1 or Windows 95 based and lets you run applications from the desktop that are connected to application objects. Simplified, that means that you can click on an icon to start an application from a user desktop. Think of it as a menu from which you can select items. NAL is a program group in Windows 3.1 and a folder in Windows 95. See Chapter 21 to see how NAL fits in.

Syntax: A click of the mouse is all it takes.

Options: Many more than you can think of

NetWare Application Manger (NAM)

It just makes sense that if you have NAL, you need NAM. NAM manages NAL.

Syntax: Take your finger and click.

Options: See NAL.

NDS Manager

The NDS Manager utility is so important that we dedicated a chapter to it. You can see Chapter 20 for the whole story, but for a quick look at this tool, take a glance at Figure 19-4.

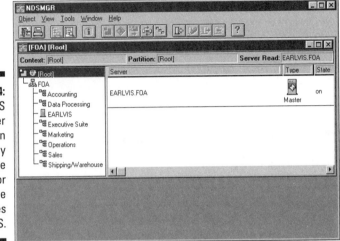

Figure 19-4: NDS Manager is an extremely valuable tool for handling the intricacies of NDS.

Syntax: Not here. See Chapter 20.

Options: Too many to detail. See Chapter 20.

NetWare File Migration

This Windows and Windows 95 utility lets you migrate NetWare v3.*x* servers to NetWare 4.*x*. Use with caution and always read the online documentation before trying.

Syntax: Point and click.

Options: Many

NLS Manager

If you care about the number of licenses you have for application software, you should care about NLS Manager. Figure 19-5 shows an NLS management window. This Windows and Windows 95 utility lets you set up metering information.

Syntax: Point and click.

Options: Too many to explain

Figure 19-5:
To protect yourself from the hefty fines of the SPA, use NLS Manager to keep track of application licenses.

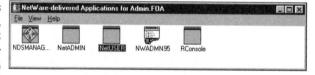

Chapter 20

NDS Tools and Utilities

● ●

In This Chapter

▶ NetWare Directory Services: an OBJECTive approach

▶ NWADMIN and NWADMN95: Doubling your NDS fun!

▶ NDS Manager: Ruling the NDS roost

▶ DSMERGE: Getting it together

▶ DSREPAIR: Using a remedy for what ails your directory

▶ Dr. DSTRACE: Meet the directory doctor

● ●

*B*eginning with NetWare 4.*x,* Novell's new file system called NetWare Directory Services is a vast departure from previous incarnations. NetWare Directory Services, or NDS, is an object-oriented, distributed naming database that greatly improves your network organization and structure while easing your administrative tasks. We discuss NDS at length in Chapter 11. For the sake of our current discussion, NDS is nothing more and nothing less than a database that contains various types of network objects, including users, printers, volumes, applications, and servers.

This NDS database is the guts of your network. The big banner feature of NetWare 4.*x* was the ability to log in to the network rather than in to individual servers in order to access resources. The NDS database is how that network login is accomplished. You can distribute copies of the NDS database to as many NetWare 4.*x* servers on your network as you wish through features called *replication* and *synchronization.* For example, if you have a remote office connected to your primary location via dial-up phone lines, configuring an NDS replica on a 4.*x* server at the remote site may be worth your time and effort. Thus, all remote user logins can be authenticated at the remote site, rather than relying on a slow and sometimes unavailable link to the central office.

If You Were a Tree, What Kind of Tree Would You Be?

Users are called *objects* in the NetWare 4.*x* NDS database (a somewhat desultory name when mere humans are reduced to objects, but that's the way it is in 4.*x*). A printer might also be an object, as might a print server or queue. A *directory map object* lets the network administrator define commands that point to an object, such as a printer or a user, rather than to a specific directory on the server. If the path to that object ever changes, you have to update only the object definition, not all your users' MAP or CAPTURE commands. This feature gives the administrator the flexibility to change the definition of objects and their locations and not worry about breaking previous commands set up for each user.

Because an object can represent such real-world objects as users, printers, countries, and groups, we can stop defining application directories and server paths and instead define objects with certain characteristics.

If you click on a volume object, you can see the profile for the volume; if you choose and then click on Statistics, you can see statistics about that volume.

After you define an object, you can refer to it anywhere else you want in the directory by defining an *alias.* (Like the alternative names criminals use to do their nefarious deeds, an alias is nothing more than another name for the same thing.) Whenever the original object changes, you don't have to go back and change the setup of every alias for that object in the file system. By changing the object itself, the other references to it are not affected, but the changes are made through the directory structure. Can ya see the beauty of this?

If you define a printer object as an HP LaserJet Series II, for example, you then can copy references to that object wherever a printer object is needed in your organization. If you later upgrade that printer to an HP IIIsi, you have to update only the original object definition. All other references to the printer remain unchanged. Make sense?

Climbing in the Directory tree

The NetWare 4.*x* Directory is shaped like a tree. It has a single root, and built on this root system are the trunk, branches, and leaves of the tree. Just like climbing a tree, you begin at the bottom and move toward the top as you navigate the Directory tree. When you traverse the Directory tree, it's called *tree-walking.* (So be it, but when we've climbed trees, we didn't do much walking. Just for kicks, humor us by imagining that you can walk in this tree.)

User Kaye requests an object but doesn't know the location of the object. Her request passes to the closest file server, which looks for the object for Kaye. The server has two ways to look for the object: It can *chain,* or it can tree-walk. In chaining, the server asks another server where the object is. If the other server doesn't know, it asks still another server. The process — servers asking other servers until one finds the object — is called chaining. In tree-walking, the server asks another server for the object. If that server cannot locate the object, it lets the first server know. The first server then asks another server, and maybe several more servers, until it finds the object. The first server has to walk all the branches itself.

Pruning, grafting, and other arboreal activities

Just like trees, networks get out of control as they grow. NetWare 4.*x* has several tools to prune, shape, or graft its Directory trees together. Using these tools ensures that your NetWare 4.*x* arbor is shapely, that tree-walking can take place effectively, and that traffic is minimized. These tools consist of DSMERGE and subtree moving. DSMERGE, the tool that performs grafting, joins two directory trees into a single tree. Moving subtrees lets the administrator, by way of NWADMIN, move the container and the objects it holds to another location, possibly another container.

The realities of replication

Because all operations in NetWare 4.*x* rely on a strong, healthy tree, a mechanism must be available for protecting that tree. The simplest way to do that is to copy the Directory tree to another location or, to be extra safe, to more than one location. Although the primary domicile of the Directory tree is called the *master replica,* giving it at least one home away from home is always smart. If one house burns down, a carbon (no pun intended) copy of it exists somewhere else. Just like reviewing your home insurance occasionally, reviewing your replicas periodically is a smart idea. NetWare Directory replicas synchronize themselves after 4.*x* installation. To modify or create new partitions, use NWADMIN or PARTMGR.

In the remainder of this chapter, we take an in-depth look at the various NetWare 4.*x* utilities dedicated to maintaining, replicating, and repairing your network's NDS database. Our first contestants in the NDS beauty pageant are the lovely and talented (nearly identical) twins: NWADMIN and NWADMN95.

Double Take: NWADMIN and NWADMN95

NetWare's primo NDS administrative utility is called the NetWare Administrator, now available in two flavors: a 16-bit version called NWADMIN that is designed for use under Windows 3.*x*, and a 32-bit version known as NWADMN95 that is designed for use under Windows 95 and Windows NT. The two versions are functionally and cosmetically identical. The remainder of this discussion refers to them collectively as NWADMIN. Just be aware that we strongly suggest you use NWADMIN only under Windows 3.*x* and NWADMN95 only under Windows 95 or Windows NT.

NWADMIN takes the place of more utilities from previous versions of NetWare than you can count on all your fingers and toes. We discuss NWADMIN in greater detail in Chapter 17. The only functions we talk about in this section are those directly related to NDS management.

NWADMIN: An administrator's best friend

In the larger sense, the ability to create, modify, and delete objects in the NDS database is the most significant capability of NWADMIN. Novell really wants NWADMIN to be your one-stop network management utility. As a result, Novell has cleverly made it possible for you to traverse all of the Windows-based NDS management utilities from the NWADMIN Tools menu. These utilities are available on the Tools menu in the NWADMIN program. Figure 20-1 shows the Tools menu in NWADMIN.

But, you say, "I look under my Tools menu in NWADMIN and/or NWADMN95 and I don't see the NDS Manager selection as shown in Figure 20-1." Fear not! Novell took the liberty of not including NDS Manager as a standard item on the Tools list, but it is easy enough to add it.

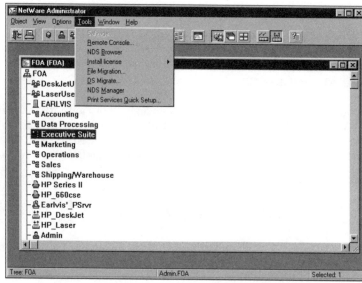

Figure 20-1:
You can run all the Windows-based NDS management utilities from the NWADMIN Tools menu.

To add NDS Manager to the 16-bit NWADMIN Tools menu, you must modify the NWADMN3X.INI file in the WINDOWS directory.

Using a DOS-based text editor like EDIT, add this line to the [Snapin Object DLLs WIN 3X] section:

```
NDSMGR = NMSNAP16.DLL
```

Then, copy the file NMSNAP16.DLL to your Windows system directory, which is usually C:\WINDOWS\SYSTEM.

The next time you start the 16-bit version of NWADMIN, you should find NDS Manager as an option under the Tools menu.

To add NDS Manager to the 32-bit NWADMN95 Tools menu, you must edit the system registry on your Windows 95 client PC. Here is a step-by-step procedure for adding NDS manager to the NWADMN95 menu:

1. **Start NWADMN95 (in SYS:PUBLIC\WIN95) and choose Save Settings on Exit from the Options menu.**

2. **Exit NWADMN95.**

3. **Click on the Start button and then select Run. Type** REGEDIT.EXE **to edit the Windows 95 system registry.**

4. **Keep double-clicking on the correct path until you are here:**

   ```
   HKEY_CURRENT_USER\Software\NetWare\Parameters\NetWare
   Administrator
   ```

5. **Choose Snapin Object DLLs WIN 95 and New from the Edit menu. Then choose String Value.**

6. **Type** NDSMGR **in the String Value dialog box and press <Enter>.**

7. **Choose NDSMGR and then choose Modify from the Edit menu.**

8. **In the Value Data field, type** NMSNAP32.DLL. **Then click on OK.**

9. **Exit the REGEDIT program.**

10. **Copy the file NMSNAP32.DLL from the SYS:PUBLIC\WIN95 directory to your Windows system directory, usually C:\WINDOWS\SYSTEM.**

    The next time you start NWADMN95, you should see NDS Manager as an option under the Tools menu.

For some strange reason, Novell ships with NWADMIN and NWADMN95 installed in the SYS:PUBLIC directory. Be sure you restrict access to these files so regular users cannot accidentally (or maliciously) wreak havoc with your NDS database.

Using the NetWare 4.x Administrator Utility

To use the NetWare Administrator called NWADMIN, you have to have an 80386 machine or higher with a minimum of 8MB of RAM (no more 4MB Windows machines). With the NetWare Administrator, in fact, a 486-class PC and a healthy 16MB of RAM is recommended. You also must have Read and File Scan rights in the SYS:PUBLIC directory (some things always stay the same). When NetWare 4.x is installed, the files for NWADMIN are automatically placed in SYS:PUBLIC, and the files for NWADMN95 are placed in SYS:PUBLIC\WIN95.

Now start Windows and create a new icon that points to NWADMN.EXE (or NWADMN95.EXE). Double-click on the NWADMIN icon located on the desktop. As the program opens, a menu bar appears that has different options for working with the objects on your LAN.

Under the top menu bar, the window in which Directory objects appear is called the Browser. This is the area in which you pick a particular object to inspect or browse. The Browser displays all the Directory Services objects defined on the network. You can choose one, such as HP LaserJet on our network. To see the details for an object, either double-click on the object or highlight the object and pull down the Object⇨Details menu. See Figure 20-2 for a view of the Browser window in NWADMIN.

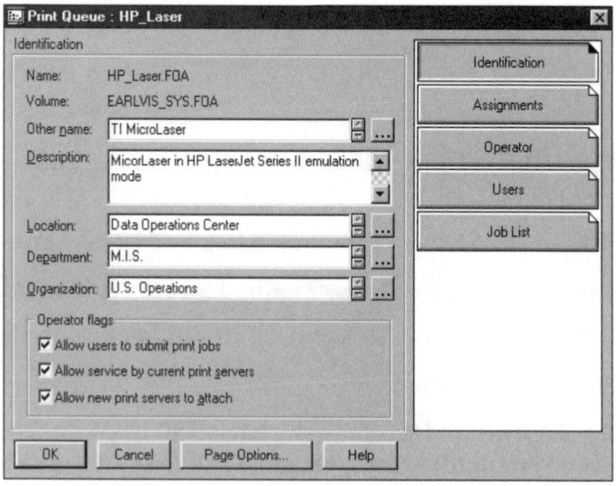

Figure 20-2: To look at properties for a printer, double-click on the printer object to see that object's details.

As you navigate through the directory via the Browser windows, you see different objects, called *container objects,* that have a plus sign (+) in front of the objects' names. These objects contain other objects. You can click the container object once to expand the tree and then click it again to compress it. Or, if you double-click on the ADMIN object, you can see the details for the ADMIN object, too. Figure 20-3 shows the details for the ADMIN object on our network.

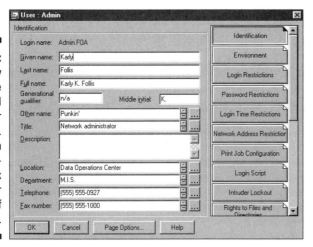

Figure 20-3:
Many
details are
associated
with user
objects.
Each button
in the right-
hand box
is another
page of
details.

You can select any of the buttons on the right side of the window or change any of the information in the main window. Whatever you do, you have to live with the changes you make. For those of you transitioning to NetWare 4.*x* from NetWare v3.*x,* you'll recognize many of the available options buttons on the right because they cover many of the main SYSCON menu choices, right down to the names that choices are called (`Login Restrictions` and `Password Restrictions`, for example). The good news is that, if you know how to use SYSCON, you already know a great deal about how to use NWADMIN.

Point to Password Restrictions and click it. You see a screen much like the one shown in Figure 20-4. The ADMIN requires a password, but so far no minimum password length has been defined. Click the box to set a minimum password length; a good rule of thumb is to set the minimum at five characters. Then point to the OK button and click on it to close the window.

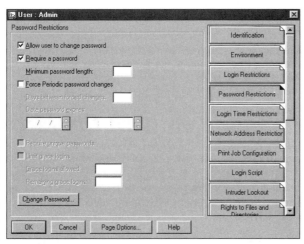

Figure 20-4:
Password
options are
easily
set for
individual
users
through the
Password
Restrictions
button.

From the details, you can also display and change login restrictions for the object, make changes to the user's login script, and show the object's rights to files and directories.

The first option on the NWADMIN menu bar is called Object. Choosing Object lets you work with the directory tree and the NetWare 4.*x* file system. From the Object menu, you can choose any particular Directory object, such as ADMIN from the Browser window. From the Object menu, you can also create a new object (a user or printer, for example), view an object's details, assign it rights and grant trustee assignments, and rename or delete an object or display. Because the Directory is made of objects, you should not be surprised that working with objects is what working with the Directory is really all about.

The other windows are View, Options, Tools, Window, and Help (we all know what that means):

- ✔ The View menu lets you work with the view currently in the Browser window. You can also set the context of a container object.

- ✔ The Options menu controls the way the NWADMIN program handles its own settings, how it confirms deletions, and how it retrieves Alias Trustees.

- ✔ On the Tools menu, you find on option for the Browser, the heart of the NetWare Administrator. This menu item is handy if you ever inadvertently (or advertently, is that a real word?) close the Browser window that opens by default each time you start the NWADMIN utility. From the Browser, you can do all sorts of tasks, including changing the context of an object. You can also see what is in the different containers, view bindery objects and queues, and perform printing administration operations. As shown in Figure 20-1, the Tools menu also lets you start numerous other NDS utilities.

- ✔ The Window menu does just what you expect if you're a Windows fanatic. If you're not but want to be, the Window menu is a standard Windows feature that lets you arrange the different windows on your desktop and switch between windows as you want.

- ✔ Then there's the Help window. This is the perfect window to turn to if you ever need HHEELLPP!

NDS Manager: Guide on with the Light On

NDS Manager is your one-stop shop for creating and managing NDS *partitions*. So what's a partition? NDS partitions are portions of the complete network directory database. A partition contains one or more containers and the leaf objects belonging to those containers. NDS Manager allows you to create copies, or *replicas,* of NDS partitions that you can distribute to other servers on your network.

Be creative: Creating new partitions

To create a new partition, start NDS Manager by running NDSMGR16 from SYS:PUBLIC or NDSMGR32 from SYS:PUBLIC\WIN95, or run NDS Manager from the Tools menu in NWADMIN. Once again, NWMGR16 is designed for Windows 3.x users, and NDSMGR32 is intended for Windows 95 and Windows NT users. Both utilities are functionally identical, so we use the term NDSMGR when referring to both utilities, unless otherwise noted.

Click once on the organization unit in the NDS directory where you want to add the new partition and go to the Object➪Create Partition menu option. You're asked to confirm that you want to create a new partition under the selected organization name. Click on OK, and NDS Manager runs through a series of checks to verify that the partition can continue successfully. Then your new partition should appear on the right side of the NDS Manager window, similar to the two partitions in Figure 20-5.

When you create a new partition as shown in Figure 20-5, the new partition is referred to as a *child partition,* and the original partition is called the *parent partition.* You may want to create a new partition to better organize your NDS structure. The process of creating a new partition is basically a split of the original partition. The organizational unit that you selected when you created the partition is now the root of the new partition.

Be aware that the partition process can be relatively slow if you already have replicas of the parent partition distributed around your network. A complete resynchronization must occur as part of the partition process. The utility may even tell you that the partition creation is complete before it actually completes synching all of the replicas. Be patient if it appears that you cannot make any partitions for a while.

Figure 20-5: The newly created FOA partition appears in NDS Manager along with the original Root partition created automagic- ally during the server installation.

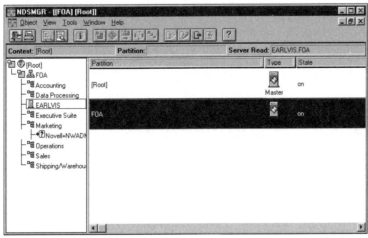

Come together: Merging NDS partitions

If you have two or more branches of your NDS tree that are closely related, you may want to merge two separate partitions into a single partition. Click on the partition that you want NDS Manager to merge. You will be asked to choose which two partitions to merge. Select the correct partitions and click on OK. This merging process may also take a few minutes to complete depending on the complexity of your network and the number of existing NDS replicas. All replicas will have to be resynched as part of the merging process.

Load 'em up and move 'em out: Moving partitions

Moving partitions is actually moving containers because you can move only containers with no subordinate containers. Be aware that moving a container also changes any and all references to the container. Creating an alias to the container that reflects the new container location is a good idea. Simply select the container that you want to move and click on the Move Partition icon. You will be asked where you want to move the partition. Enter the destination for the partition, and you're almost done. Be sure to create an alias to the original partition location because all references to the old location are NOT automatically updated.

Copy cats: Replicas and their uses

Replicas are an attractive feature of NDS for several reasons. First, replicas provide a measure of network fault tolerance because the directory is located on more than one server. If you implement replicas correctly, a single server crashing never brings your entire network down. Plus, you can always use a replica to rebuild a corrupt or malfunctioning replica.

The second benefit of replicas is to speed network operations while reducing the amount of network traffic. Thus, your network users can be authenticated by the server physically located the nearest to their PC. This greatly speeds up the login process while reducing traffic between your network segments.

To create a replica of a partition, select the partition in the NDS Manager and go to the Object⇨Add Replica menu item. Figure 20-6 shows the ensuing dialog box for creating a partition replica.

Synchronized swimming in the NDS pool

NetWare NDS automatically synchronizes replicas with their masters on a regular schedule. However, you can also instigate a manual resynch if you discover that your replicas are out of synch. You can use DSREPAIR to check whether your partitions are in synch. To manually resynch your partitions, select the partition in NDS Manager and go to the Object⇨Replica⇨Send Updates menu selection. Verify the partition that you want to resynch and click on OK.

Figure 20-6:
Choose the
server
where you
want to
copy the
replica and
indicate
whether you
want the
replica to be
read-only or
read/write.

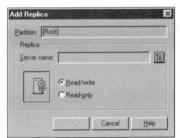

Figure 20-6:
Choose the
server
where you
want to
copy the
replica and
indicate
whether you
want the
replica to be
read-only or
read/write.

Repairman blues: the DSREPAIR utility

Even the best-designed products need a tune-up now and then. That's exactly why Novell includes DSREPAIR with NetWare 4.11. To start DSREPAIR, go to the server console or start an RCONSOLE session (you have to load RSPX on the server console first), and type **LOAD DSREPAIR**. DSREPAIR will diagnose and repair the local directory database as well as all local replica copies. DSREPAIR is an NLM that also verifies replica synchronization, logs detailed information about local replicas, and allows you to dump damaged replicas to disk for review. Figure 20-7 shows the DSREPAIR main menu; Figure 20-8 shows its many advanced maintenance and repair capabilities.

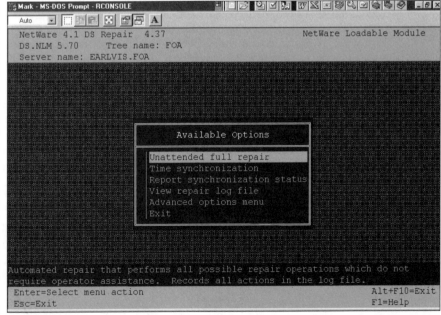

Figure 20-7:
You can
perform an
unattended
full repair,
synchronize
the time,
report on
replica
synchroniza-
tion status,
view the
repair log
file, or go
to the
advanced
options
menu from
DS Repair.

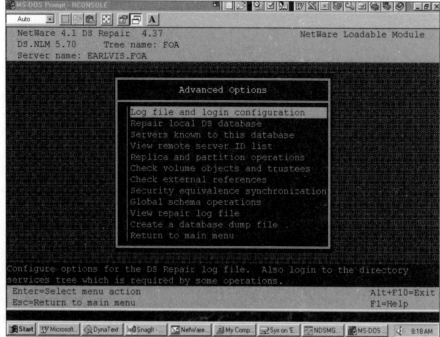

Figure 20-8:
The
Advanced
Options
menu of DS
Repair gives
you many
maintenance
and repair
options.

Out of step: Time-synching your servers

To ensure that replicas are updated properly, you have to synchronize the clocks on the servers in the network. Server clocks are just like digital watches. Over time, they slow down. When this slowdown occurs, replicas may be updated out of order and cause havoc in a large Directory tree. A master timekeeper, called the *reference time server,* maintains the network clock and provides the time to which all other servers and workstations synchronize. You can access the time synchronization program through the DSREPAIR utility.

DSMERGE into the Fast Lane

DSMERGE assists you in merging two complete trees as opposed to merging partitions within a tree. DSMERGE, like DSREPAIR, is an NLM that can be loaded from the server RCONSOLE or from the server console itself. Figure 20-9 shows the DSMERGE main menu.

Always be sure to run the time synchronization routine prior to merging or making any other tree changes.

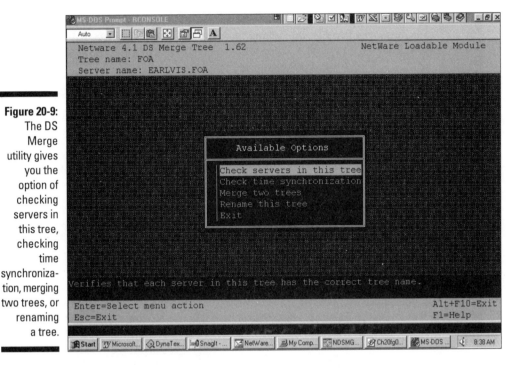

Your Utility of Last Resort: NDS TRACE

You do have one last weapon in your troubleshooting arsenal: NDS Trace. NDS Trace is a console setting that logs all directory-related errors and information messages to a console screen or to a log file. To turn on the NDS Trace function and send all messages to a dedicated server console screen, type the following:

```
SET NDS TRACE TO SCREEN = ON
```

at either the server console or in an RCONSOLE session. After you enter this command correctly, press CTRL+ESC to see a list of server screens. Pick the one titled Directory Services to view the NDS Trace screen. To disable the NDS Trace screen, type the following:

```
SET NDS TRACE TO SCREEN = OFF
```

at the server console or in an RCONSOLE session.

To send all NDS trace information to a file, type

```
SET NDS TRACE TO FILE = ON
```

at the server console or in an RCONSOLE session. If you choose to send NDS Trace messages to a file, the default filename is SYS:SYSTEM\DSTRACE.DBG. If you want to save your NDS Trace information to another filename, type

```
SET NDS TRACE FILENAME = volume:path\filename
```

Frequently, NetWare asks you to save your NDS Trace information to a file for diagnostic purposes. To disable the NDS Trace to a file option, type

```
SET NDS TRACE TO FILE = OFF
```

at the server console or in an RCONSOLE session.

In your review and monitoring of NDS Trace information, you should watch out for two categories of NDS error messages:

1. `All processed = YES` tells you that all pending replica synchronization has been successfully completed.

2. Messages numbered -601 through -699 and `F966` through `F9FE` which tell you the NDS status or errors. For NDS troubleshooting information, see the "System Messages" book in the NetWare 4.*x* online documentation.

Chapter 21

Introducing IntranetWare!

● ●

In This Chapter

▶ Defining IntranetWare

▶ Forming an Internet relationship

▶ Tackling TCP/IP networking

▶ Understanding addressing

▶ Making an Internet connection

▶ Working with the NetWare Web Server

▶ Transferring files with FTP

▶ Exploiting XCONSOLE

▶ Using the IPX-to-IP Gateway

▶ Mastering IntranetWare's marvelous miscellany

● ●

*W*ith the release of NetWare 4.11, Novell also launched a new product family called IntranetWare. This product name is meant to suggest the addition of intra- and Internet capabilities to the core NetWare network operating system.

In fact, IntranetWare marks a terrific step forward in Novell's understanding of the marketplace. In particular, IntranetWare underscores Novell's long-overdue recognition of the centrality of TCP/IP-based networking for most organizations. But probably the easiest way to understand IntranetWare is as a bundle that contains NetWare 4.11, plus a number of other already-established NetWare add-ons, and a few new elements, just to round out the product's functionality.

In the section that follows, we unpack the bundle to introduce what's inside IntranetWare; next, we discuss the pros and cons of connecting your network to the Internet or building your own intranet. Then, we take you through each of IntranetWare's major components and describe what they can do, why you may want to use them, and what you must do to install them for yourself. And we suggest reasonable alternatives and useful resources wherever they're appropriate. Because IntranetWare covers so much ground, we can't do complete justice to these add-on products (that would be the topic for another entire book), but we can help you understand them better — so that's just what we'll do!

Unbundling IntranetWare

Unbundling IntranetWare is heady stuff, indeed. The bottom line is that IntranetWare includes nearly everything you need to run a NetWare network that can accommodate TCP/IP services with the same aplomb as the native file, print, directory, and other services that you've come to expect from NetWare.

Getting the real story about IntranetWare

If you take a look at the press releases and news stories surrounding the release of IntranetWare, several things are clear:

- ✔ The difference between IntranetWare and NetWare 4.11 is primarily a matter of name and how things are packaged inside the box, rather than any real difference in functionality. In other words, IntranetWare is another name for a packaging of NetWare 4.11 that stresses NetWare's repositioning into the burgeoning Internet and intranet networking markets.

- ✔ The introduction of IntranetWare underscores Novell's appreciation of the importance of TCP/IP-based networking and gathers lots of significant functionality together for its users.

- ✔ The additional pieces that accompany the core NetWare 4.11 NOS in IntranetWare make it a potent — and useful — networking system for just about any business or organization, from small businesses that may support only a handful of computers, to the largest, most far-flung enterprises that may span the globe and support tens or even hundreds of thousands of users, machines, and oodles of other networking gear.

- ✔ The best thing about IntranetWare, to our way of thinking, is that it incorporates very little brand-new technology. It simply brings together some valuable components that are already tested and proven at customer sites. Previously sold separately, the IntranetWare bundle delivers significantly more functionality at the same prices as plain vanilla NetWare 4.1. In fact, Novell is deliberately pricing IntranetWare to make it extremely attractive to upgrade, and to purchase new copies.

Looking at IntranetWare: So what's inside?

Now that you're all excited about IntranetWare, you can look over this list of all the products that used to be sold separately but are now included with IntranetWare:

✔ **NetWare Multi-Protocol Router (MPR) 3.1:** Allows your NetWare server to attach directly to a communications provider, for TCP/IP-based access to the Internet (probably through an Internet Service Provider) or to other in-house networks, for intranet use. NetWare MPR lets you use a modem, an ISDN card, a fractional or full T-1 link, frame relay, or even ATM to make this connection. MPR acts like a network traffic cop, directing traffic through the external link when necessary, and making sure that inbound traffic passes security and access checks before permitting it to enter your network.

✔ **NetWare/IP:** Permits NetWare clients to use TCP/IP to communicate with the NetWare server, instead of native IPX. At present, Novell makes this work by grafting IPX atop the IP stack, but they're working on a *native IP* NetWare for delivery in late 1997. Even so, NetWare/IP helps organizations seeking to reduce the number of protocols on their networks or those wishing to eliminate IPX transports.

✔ **NetWare FleX/IP:** Provides IP-based file transfer services, in the form of a NetWare-resident File Transfer Protocol (FTP) server. FleX/IP also includes bidirectional print services — in plain English, this means that NetWare clients can print to UNIX and other IP-based printers, and that UNIX and other native IP clients can print to NetWare-based printers.

✔ **NetWare Web Server 2.5:** Provides a full featured implementation of an NCSA-derived HyperText Transfer Protocol (HTTP) server, including support for CGI programs, a Perl interpreter, and support for NetBasic and Java-based Web extensions. Because all these components are necessary to create an effective, interactive, and extensible Web site, they're abso-lutely essential ingredients for this NetWare-base implementation.

Atop this powerful Web platform, IntranetWare even includes Web-based server access and management utilities as well. In competitive testing, the NetWare Web Server was recognized as a bona fide screamer (it's fast) and offers top-notch security and document access controls.

✔ **NetWare IPX-to-IP Gateway:** Lets Windows clients access WinSock-compatible TCP/IP applications using only IPX transports, through a special set of NLMs on the server. In plain English, this means users can run standard TCP/IP services — like Netscape Navigator — without installing TCP/IP protocols on their machines. This gateway also supports Internet access for users without requiring each one to have a unique TCP/IP address.

✔ **TCP/IP address management services:** Includes Dynamic Host Configura-tion Protocol (DHCP) and *bootp* servers, so that network administrators can manage a pool of TCP/IP addresses for their users, without requiring static assignment of addresses for each user. In environments where people come and go, offices move, and organizations change shape, such flexibility can be a real godsend!

> ✔ **Netscape Navigator:** Is included with IntranetWare so that each licensed NetWare client (be it Macintosh, several flavors of UNIX, or Windows) obtains a legal license to run Netscape Navigator, the most popular Web browser in use today. The Web browser is more than just an Internet access tool, it can be used as a powerful, friendly interface to much of IntranetWare's functionality as well.

Great sources of IntranetWare information

Since IntranetWare takes an already rich and interesting product — NetWare 4.11 — and triples its functionality, we can't do justice to all its many pieces and parts in a single chapter. That's why we want to point out some of the best places to look for more information on IntranetWare and its many constituent products:

✔ First and foremost, read the online documentation that comes with IntranetWare. Novell is using Electronic Book Technologies' DynaText hypertext environment. This environment is strongly related to HTML and uses a Web-like interface. You can find much of what you need within the thousands of screens of online documentation included with the product.

✔ Surf to the Novell Site Map at `http://support.novell.com/sitemap/`; we find that this Web site is the best place to start prospecting for technical stuff. For more information on Novell's Internet offerings, consult Appendix C.

✔ Check out the Novell NetWare Support Encyclopedia (NSE), which is available (for a price) as a monthly CD-ROM-based publication from Novell. If you can't afford a copy, check with your reseller or local NetWare user's group; what you can't buy, you can often borrow. You can also access a lot of this information on the `http://support.novell.com/` Web site, as well.

✔ Look at Novell's home page at `http://www.novell.com/` for recent (favorable) press coverage. As we're writing this, the home page is full of pointers to recent stories on IntranetWare in *Information Week*, *PC Week*, *Infoworld*, *Computerworld*, and *LAN Times*. Those trade rags are pretty good sources of information, too.

✔ Check out the NetWare related newsgroups on Usenet. Look in the `comp.os.netware.*` groups, or in the various NetWire forums on CompuServe (check Appendix C for the details).

✔ Scope out a bookstore. In addition to the *...For Dummies* series, IDG Books Worldwide, Inc., also publishes the *Novell Press* books, which are a gold mine of NetWare (and soon, IntranetWare) information. For example, we found over 100 related titles at the Computer Literacy bookstore (`http://www.clbooks.com`) online.

One thing's for sure — a shortage of information won't be a problem. As we gathered information for this chapter, even before the product was officially released, we already found hundreds of pages of information online at the Novell Web site. By the time you read this, the amount of information will probably be much greater!

In the spirit of those timeless RonCo ads, we're tempted to say, "But wait! There's more!!" And in fact, there's more to IntranetWare than we mentioned in this book, but the rest is esoteric enough that we can let you discover it yourself without doing you a major disservice. If you're dying to satisfy your curiousity, check out the sidebar entitled "Great sources of IntranetWare information" — otherwise, skip it!

Forming an Internet Relationship?

If you want to use the TCP/IP-oriented capabilities included with IntranetWare and you're not already familiar with this world, you've got some catching up to do. In a nutshell, you need to deal with the following:

✔ You must have a basic understanding of IP addressing.

✔ You must obtain a domain name and a set of IP addresses for your network (but first, check with your IS department to make sure that you're not duplicating somebody else's effort and expense).

✔ If you want to connect your network to the Internet, you need to obtain a communications link to carry the traffic, and you need to establish an account with an Internet Service Provider (ISP) to establish an Internet connection.

TCP/IP networking is an area that has been the subject of many books. We describe some of these tomes later; first, we'll tell you a little bit about each of the things we just mentioned.

Proper IP address

Typically, IP addresses appear in one of two forms:

✔ A numeric form, consisting of four numbers, separated by periods. For example, `190.170.88.6` is the address for one of our ISP's servers.

✔ A symbolic name, called a domain name, which in the United States usually ends with either `.com` (for a commercial business), `.gov` (for a government address), `.edu` (for an educational institution), `.org` (for a non-profit organization), or `.net` (for a network service provider). Outside the U.S., domain names end in two-letter country codes, of which over 140 are currently defined. The domain name that corresponds to the preceding numeric address is `io.com`.

The really interesting thing about IP addresses and domain names on the Internet is that they must be unique. On a single network, this restriction is no big problem because ensuring that no duplicate addresses are issued simply requires a bit of care on the network administrator's part. But on the global Internet, with millions of users and domain names, an agency must be responsible for tracking address and name assignments. The group responsible for the way IP numbers are laid out in a general way is the Internet Assigned Numbers Authority (IANA); the group responsible for domain names and overall address assignments is the Internet Network Information Center (usually called the InterNIC).

IP addresses carry a certain amount of baggage with them. In addition to being unique, they also contain two parts: a network ID, and a node ID, where the number of bits assigned to the network and node IDs vary, depending on the type of IP address that's involved. This two-part organization results in a sharing of the address space allocated for all machines on a network between network IDs and nodes IDs. If more network IDs are present, then less space is available for node IDs, and vice-versa. Address *classes* are distinguished as A, B, and C, as shown in Table 21-1.

Table 21-1	IP Address Classes		
Network Class	*Network ID*	*Node ID*	*Totals*
A (0)	Byte1.	Byte2.Byte3.Byte4	126/16,777,214
B (10)	Byte1.Byte2.	Byte3.Byte4	16,382/65,534
C (110)	Byte1.Byte2.Byte3.	Byte4	2,097,150/254

The bits in parentheses, like (0), to the right of the three class designations are required start bits, used to identify each class. The *Totals* column indicates the maximum number of network and node IDs for each address type (the start bits, which are required, reduce the total number of networks in each class; more start bits mean less network IDs.

The important thing to notice about the IP addresses is that only a few huge Class A IP networks exist, with many node addresses, and many small Class C IP networks exist, with only a few node addresses each (relatively speaking). In fact, running out of IP addresses is a major concern in some circles. A D address class also exists, but it's seldom used and we don't cover it here.

Furthermore, many networks are subdivided into separate components, known as subnets, to create several smaller networks from one larger one. Such subnets are normally connected by network devices called routers (which is part of what a NetWare server can do, in fact). Most configuration entries for IP addresses ask for something called a *subnet mask,* in addition to requiring specification of a number of individual IP addresses. The address for a subnet uses the entire network ID part and borrows some bits from the node ID part to extend the network section. The borrowed bits create a unique, but related, network address for each subnet that can be used without obtaining permission from anybody, because it's a way of further subdividing what's already yours. Network administrators use subnets as a convenient way to partition their network addresses into smaller, more manageable chunks.

Obtaining a name and address (es)

In most cases, people don't worry about the general structure of IP names and addresses; they worry about their own. IP addresses for use on the Internet are assigned by the InterNIC through an application process. In most cases, unless you have a very large network, you can obtain your IP addresses from your ISP as part of the service that they deliver to you. In fact, many ISPs also handle domain name registration on your behalf. Your ISP can also furnish your subnet mask information for configuring the various NetWare IP utilities, as well.

If you want to obtain IP addresses or a domain name on your own, you can contact the InterNIC at the following URL:

```
http://www.internic.net/
http://www.yahoo.com/Computers_and_Internet/Internet/
            Domain_Registration/
```

The Yahoo! site provides pointers to all kinds of InterNIC-related information resources and commentary and is worth visiting, especially for those curious about the politics and experience of working with that body. These days, getting a domain name takes two to three weeks and costs $100 for the first two years. That means that planning ahead is important — without a domain name, installing your Web server, FTP server, and so on won't be as easy or convenient.

IP addresses for private networks

These days, you can never be too sure that your network won't someday end up connected to the Internet. Even if you're dead certain that your organization will never take that particular plunge, please consult the Request for Comment (rfc) that the governing body for Internet technology has compiled. This document is called "Address Allocation for Private Internets" and you can obtain it in one of the three following ways:

1. Send e-mail to `mailserv@ds.internic.net` and type `file/ftp/rfc/rfc1597.txt` in the message body.

2. Anonymous FTP to `ds.internic.net` (use your e-mail address as the password). Look in directory `rfc/` for the file named `rfc1597.txt`.

3. On the Web, you can find hypertext versions of the rfcs at Ohio State University; in this case, use the following URL:

   `http://www.cis.ohio-state.edu/htbin/rfc/rfc1597.html`

If you follow the Internet governing body's guidelines for numbering (your IP addresses), your life can be a lot easier when things change and your organization does decide to hook up to the Internet.

Obtaining Internet access

Two ingredients are essential to obtaining Internet access:

- ✔ A communications link to carry the traffic between your site and your ISP (and thence, onto and off the Internet). You have to pay the phone company or some other communications provider a set up charge and monthly service fees to use this link.

- ✔ A service account with an ISP to provide the kinds of access services and other goodies that you may need for your organization. ISPs can simply provide the connection between your network and the Internet, via your communications link, or they can provide e-mail accounts, Web site hosting, and numerous other services. Here again, expect to pay a one-time set up fee and monthly service fees to obtain access to the Internet through your ISP. The more services you get from your ISP, the more you can expect to pay them.

For both ingredients (the communications link and the service account), how much you pay depends on the kind of connection you use. By and large, more bandwidth costs more money. Also, your ISP's charges are determined in part by the kinds of services that they deliver to your organization. Although IntranetWare can provide most of the Internet services that you may want to offer to your partners and customers, you want to trade off the costs of doing it yourself plus the costs of higher bandwidth against the convenience and customer service that your ISP can provide. Be sure to consider hidden costs, like the 24/7 schedule so typical of Internet sites, and personnel costs involved in running a Web site, FTP server, news server, or whatever.

More IP and Internet access resources

For more information about IP and the other topics covered in this section, we recommend the following resources:

- ✔ Marshall Wilensky and Candace Leiden: *TCP/IP for Dummies,* 2nd Edition, IDG Books Worldwide, Inc., Indianapolis, IN, 1996.

- ✔ Craig Hunt, *TCP/IP Network Administration,* O'Reilly & Associates, Sebastopol, CA, 1992.

Whereas the first book is a good introduction to the topic, the last one is a worthwhile resource for any network administrator whose network runs TCP/IP.

Making the Intra- or Internet Connection

Whether you're connecting to the public Internet or simply linking multiple sites on a private intranet, the Multi-Protocol Router (MPR) component of IntranetWare is likely to be of interest. In a nutshell, this facility is a collection of NetWare NLMs that understand your network's layout and addressing scheme, to the point where they can distinguish local addresses from remote ones.

In essence, what the MPR does is to examine the addresses within packets of data moving across your network: It simply passes local traffic across the right local network segments (or leaves them alone if the traffic is between two nodes on a single segment). But MPR is also capable of recognizing remote traffic and passes it across whatever link is appropriate to direct that traffic on its way from your local network to its ultimate destination.

The version of MPR that ships with IntranetWare also includes support for a facility that Novell calls WAN Links. Instead of describing a peculiar brand of sausage, this facility permits the MPR to communicate with the kinds of interface cards that are necessary to direct traffic over the conventional or digital telephone lines used to exchange data with ISPs and other network service providers. For small or branch offices, this traffic direction capability is great, because it means that the NetWare server can act as a router, in addition to performing its other duties. That is, smaller operations won't need to purchase a dedicated device for routing purposes (larger operations, with more traffic on and off the remote link, probably want to dedicate a device to handle routing anyway, so this feature is probably of less interest in such circumstances).

Together, MPR and WAN Links help your users to communicate with remote networks, be it through the Internet or some other type of wide-area network. These components makes access to all kinds of data resources possible, for e-mail, hypertext, and even distributed applications of all kinds. Even better, the MPR can handle multiple protocols (as its name is meant to imply), so that you can use it to route IPX, IP, SNA, and other kinds of traffic as well.

For TCP/IP-related traffic, you need to know the following to configure the MPR for Internet or private intranet access:

- The router's own IP address
- The name and address of the Domain Name Server that provides name resolution services for your network (and a fall-back name/address, should the primary DNS server fail)
- The local network addresses in use
- The address of the router on the other end of the WAN Links connection

With the preceding information in hand (most of which you can obtain from your ISP, if you're connecting to the Internet), and a properly-configured link to a remote network, you are ready to install and use MPR.

Using the NetWare Web Server

The NetWare Web Server exploits NetWare's well-documented capabilities to provide superior performance and file-server capacity. Because most of what Web servers do is to respond to requests for individual documents and related objects — all of which are usually stored in separate files — this job is one at which NetWare excels. Of course, using a Web server requires a knowledge of the HyperText Markup Language (HTML), and an understanding of how to build and exploit documents written in that markup language.

For more information on this topic, we can think of no better place to start than another one of our books: *HTML For Dummies,* 2nd Edition, IDG Books Worldwide Inc. You may find Dave Taylor's *Creating Cool Web Pages with HTML,* also IDG Books Worldwide Inc., a useful resource, too.

To provide complete Web capabilities, the NetWare Web Server also includes support for Web extension software written to the standard Common Gateway Interface (CGI). Such software, usually called *CGI programs* or *CGI scripts,* is commonly written in a programming language called Perl (practical extraction and report language); that's why the NetWare Web Server includes NLMs that can interpret and execute Perl scripts. And because NetWare 4.11 includes a BASIC interpreter called NetBasic as well, you can also create and use Web extensions written in NetBasic. Furthermore, NetWare can run CGI programs remotely on another server, if written to a special remote CGI (R-CGI) interface, or locally, if written to the local CGI (L-CGI) interface. These CGI support features give the server a great deal of flexibility and capability.

Among the more interesting features delivered with the NetWare Web Server, in addition to its abilities to handle normal Web document access, is an HTML-based interface to the NetWare Directory Services. Administrators with appropriate rights can access the entire NDS database through any Web browser; ordinary users can perform routine NDS lookups, context changes, and other customary functions. NetWare's built-in access controls and file system security create a Web server environment that's nearly *unhackable* and make restricted access (like having passwords for certain documents while other documents are accessible to all visitors) easy to impose. For even greater security, the NetWare Web Server lets you create virtual file systems and names for exposure to outsiders, thereby completely hiding the true, underlying filenames and structures.

After you obtain your domain name and IP addresses, setting up the NetWare Web Server is incredibly easy, requiring simply that the name and address information be supplied, and a Web directory structure specified. Because IntranetWare also includes client licenses for the Netscape Navigator, after you supply the documents and graphics for your Web site, your users are ready to rock 'n' roll!

As a way of adding easy access to all kinds of information, Web servers have paved the way for the explosion in the use of private IP-based intranets. You can find the NetWare Web Server useful in discovering how to exploit the information resources that are probably already available within your own organization, or even to serve the public Internet. If you need additional document management capabilities for your Web documents or are interested in creating Web documents on the fly (from database contents or other application files), check out Novell's information about its GroupWise product family at their home page at `http://www.novell.com`.

Transferring Files with FTP

The inclusion of FleX/IP in IntranetWare supplies a set of NLMs (NetWare Loadable Modules) that support the standard IP-based File Transfer Protocol service. Although its name includes the word *protocol*, FleX/IP is actually a general-purpose file delivery service that can transfer files to and from any FTP server on an IP-based network.

The NetWare FTP Server supports all the standard scenarios for FTP use: It can be set up to accept anonymous FTP requests, which means that users don't need a password to access the files in a particular root directory established for anonymous service. But the NetWare FTP Server can be configured to provide password protection for entire servers, directories, or even individual files. Because the FTP's file access protection is based on NetWare security, files outside the purview of the FTP Server are secure from access through FTP — in fact, these files are completely invisible to unauthorized users.

Like the Web Server, this FTP Server can expose a virtual file system to outside users that presents a deliberately different public face from its physical layout and actual file and directory names. This provides an extra layer of security that can repel would-be system crackers. It's even possible to overlay certain directories for both Web-based and FTP file transfer access — that is, so both the NetWare Web and FTP Servers can access the same files — so that users can employ the file transfer mechanism that works best for them on your network.

Installing and configuring the NetWare FTP Server is a matter of supplying the root domain name and IP address, and configuring the root directory (or directories) for the files to be delivered via FTP. At the same time as you do this configuration, you specify the type of access permitted (anonymous or pass-word-controlled) and establish an access profile for authorized users, where appropriate.

FTP services can deliver a useful mechanism for providing access to a collection of shared documents and other files. Such collections can be quite useful for supplying on-demand printable forms, manuals and instructions of all kinds, organizational policies and procedures, and lots of other information. When used in combination with the World Wide Web, these shared collections (of documents and other files) can help to curtail paper consumption, and replace physical movement of documents with e-mail, file transfer, and other forms of electronic delivery.

Exploiting XCONSOLE

One of IntranetWare's more interesting capabilities is aimed at the UNIX crowd. Those organizations whose networks include large numbers of UNIX servers, or whose network management is UNIX-based can appreciate the XCONSOLE utility. Simply put, XCONSOLE supports a NetWare user interface for administration and server access through the X Windows environment, a graphical user interface supported on many UNIX workstations and other, similar computers.

Administrators still must understand the details and behavior of the NetWare Server interface, but XCONSOLE gives them additional flexibility. By using the XCONSOLE utility, network administrators can open a window on any X Windows workstation and perform activities remotely across the network. Without XCONSOLE, they need to do the administrative activities at the NetWare Server's console itself (hence, of course, the name for this utility).

Installing XCONSOLE is just a matter of adding a small number of NLMs to your NetWare (or IntranetWare) server, and defining permissions for those who will be allowed to use X Windows to access the server. Of all the utilities we've covered in this chapter, this one comes closest to being a no-brainer to install!

Using the IPX-to-IP Gateway

Most experts agree that only a few networks really have to run TCP/IP at every workstation, and then run only TCP/IP on their networks. Peaceful coexistence of TCP/IP with IPX on many NetWare networks has been a common practice for years, but another alternative is well worth considering: using an IPX-to-IP gateway that runs at the server. This Gateway permits users to gain access to

IP-based services through the server by passing data atop IPX to the gateway NLMs that run on the server; at that point, the data are reformulated for delivery to an external IP-based network. Similarly, incoming IP-based traffic is reformulated for delivery over IPX to clients.

With access to an IPX-to-IP Gateway, users need only a small and compact piece of software on their desktops, instead of a complete protocol stack, to run TCP/IP-based applications. For network users lucky enough to enjoy desktops with fast processors and plenty of RAM, gateway access may sound like a frill, but for those using older machines with slower CPUs and limited RAM, it's a necessity. Even those with faster, more commodious machines can appreciate the simplicity and ease of access in a single-protocol environment.

Novell's IPX-to-IP Gateway depends on a special software interface to TCP/IP applications, called WinSock, to do its job. Because WinSock is supported primarily on Windows clients, this special interface doesn't do much for Macintoshes or UNIX workstations (but these machines have less trouble with multiple protocol stacks or native IP operation than do PCs with Windows, anyway). But for those users with WinSock capability, the Gateway permits them to run standard IP-based applications like e-mail clients, Netscape Navigator, FTP, and other software written to the WinSock interface, across an IPX network with no apparent changes in behavior and little apparent effect on performance and reliability.

Thus, the explanation for the Gateway's popularity can be summed up in a single word — convenience. The Gateway is convenient:

- ✔ **For users,** because they have less overhead and complexity to deal with on their workstations

- ✔ **For network administrators,** because they can handle IP address management, network access, and security matters without having to involve users even one little bit

The aspect of convenience also explains what's necessary to configure this service: knowledge of IPX network addresses and usernames, plus knowledge of the available IP address pool, domain names, name services, and other IP-specific information. But because all this information should be in the hands of the network administrator, the IPX-to-IP Gateway is not that difficult to install and configure.

One of the nicest side effects of using the IPX-to-IP Gateway is that it provides increased security for your network when you attach to the Internet or to another shared IP-based network. Because the prevailing protocol outside the gateway is TCP/IP and the protocol inside the gateway is IPX, even if outsiders penetrate your network, they won't be able to access anything. Also, the Gateway can completely block external access to resources on the NetWare side, so outsider access is really not much of a concern anyway.

Novell's decision to include the IPX-to-IP Gateway in IntranetWare offers what we think is the best solution for NetWare users who wish to obtain Internet access: an easy, convenient way to mine the Internet's rich resources, with built-in security and access controls. Formerly available only to those willing to spend the extra money for this capability, inclusion of the Gateway in IntranetWare is probably one of its most valuable capabilities (and certainly puts the pressure on other companies that used to make a business from such gateways).

IP Management Miscellany

To those already familiar with IP networking, what we're about to cover — the utilities available in IntranetWare for managing IP addresses, like name to address translation and related functions — may sound like a litany of familiar tools and technologies. To those unfamiliar with this world, we point you back to the TCP/IP resources (particularly Craig Hunt's book) that we mentioned in section "More IP and Internet access resources," in this chapter. You definitely want to understand what these utilities do and how they work, before you're ready to mess with any of them. In the meantime, the following is a list of what you can choose to install and use as part of IntranetWare's TCP/IP environment:

- ✔ **ARP, RARP servers:** ARP stands for Address Resolution Protocol, and can turn an IP address into a symbolic name; RARP stands for Reverse ARP, and goes the other way.

- ✔ *bootp* **or DHCP:** In truth, the Dynamic Host Configuration Protocol is an enhanced and more generalized implementation of *bootp,* but both permit network administrators to issue IP addresses from a pool, instead of forcing them to make static assignments of such addresses. This capability makes administrators' lives considerably easier and IP network management simpler; in other words, it's a great boon to NetWare networks. If you don't know which utility to use, allow us to recommend DHCP. Because IP addresses cost money, using DHCP lets you get away with a less than one-to-one match between users and addresses and can save organizations with occasional IP users from ongoing costs.

- ✔ **Domain Name Services (DNS):** The native name services environment for TCP/IP is DNS. This collection of NLMs permits you to set up an independent NetWare-based name server, or to mirror your ISP's name server (for those who connect to the Internet), at your own site (which can help cut down on network traffic).

You run across more little goodies in the IntranetWare environment, but the ones we've covered in the previous sections are the most important. As you get to know the product better, you may find other IntranetWare utilities that come in handy from time to time.

The associated NetWare utilities

If you spend much time messing with TCP/IP on an IntranetWare server, you end up working with these console utilities:

✔ **DHCPCFG:** The DHCP control center, where IP address leases and expiration terms are determined.

✔ **INETCFG:** Used to handle NetWare server NIC configuration. Because binding TCP/IP to any NIC that carries IP traffic is an important configuration step, you'll probably get to know this utility well.

✔ **NWIPCFG:** If you elect to use NetWare/IP, NWIPCFG is its command center. It duplicates some UNICON capabilities, and is useful for configuring DNS client software if you rely on an external DNS server (typically, your ISP's).

✔ **UNICON:** The main IP utility, where DNS and NetWare/IP services, among others, are configured, monitored, and maintained. Logging services and configuration changes will occur here as well.

Mastering IntranetWare

If you've read this whole chapter, your head may be spinning from an IP-induced brain cloud. Yes, an awful lot of *extra stuff* is involved in running and using IntranetWare, but using it can be incredibly valuable to you and your organization. Remember, we've just barely scratched the surface of all the many services and utilities. Unless you're already one of the IP cognoscenti, you definitely want to bone up on TCP/IP terminology, protocols, technologies, and services before venturing into the IntranetWare realm.

But don't let our words of warning discourage you from exploring the capabilities of IntranetWare. We believe that NetWare by itself is pretty good stuff. But the added facilities in IntranetWare make the 4.11 environment even more powerful and can make your network a great deal more valuable to your organization. In particular, we think that you may find the NetWare Web Server, combined with the IPX-to-IP Gateway, incredibly useful — this combination can turn ordinary IPX network clients into raging intranet monsters with very little effort.

And because the impetus to intranetworking is largely driven by Web-based documents and applications, IntranetWare supplies a powerful and functional platform from which to explore these capabilities. But the Gateway can also guard the door: While providing your users access to the public Internet, the Gateway can also open up a whole universe of information and services that may heretofore have been unavailable to your NetWare users. Thus, the final element that makes IntranetWare so compelling is the MPR, which permits you to link your server directly to an ISP, and your users to the Internet.

By the same token, the other many capabilities in IntranetWare shouldn't be ignored. As your knowledge grows, and your users' sophistication increases, you find that some of the more esoteric components of this environment becomes less mysterious and more germane to your networking needs. That's why it's so important to dive right in and discover as much as you can about the wonderful world of IP networking in the IntranetWare environment!

Chapter 22

Troubleshooting Common Problems

· ·

In This Chapter

▶ Troubleshooting step-by-step

▶ Why network printers don't print

▶ Why some DOS commands and applications don't work with NetWare

▶ Command-line utilities for getting things done

▶ Troubleshooting user PCs

▶ Living with VLMs

▶ When volumes disappear . . .

▶ How to live through a file server crash

▶ What to do when the network goes on vacation

· ·

*N*ow that your network has been up and running for a few hours, or days, or months, your first real problem rears its ugly head. What do you do? We have good news and bad news for you. The good news is that you get to use this chapter on troubleshooting. The bad news is that you frequently *have* to use this chapter on troubleshooting.

Remember our network motto: "On all networks a little rain must fall." If the rain doesn't get you, surely the misbehaving applications, faulty wiring components, glitchy servers, and balking printers will.

The hardest part of network troubleshooting is that so many different variables and components can act up. The error messages that you see only compound the problem. A malfunctioning network interface card can cause your spiffy new word processor to get a `Network Error Reading Drive X` error message. Doesn't help you to identify the problem much, does it?

This example shows you the quirky nature of network troubleshooting: The error messages rarely coincide with or identify the root problem. Quite the opposite, the error messages frequently point you in the wrong direction. That's when you don your Double-Naught Network Spy Sleuthing Hat with matching NetWare Error-Message Decoder Ring and hit the streets.

They Shoot Troubleshooters, Don't They?

The first step in troubleshooting network problems began when you first installed your servers and network cabling. The proper documentation of the network is the most important step toward successful troubleshooting.

If you don't know how things were, how do you know when things are fixed? You did document every step of the original installation, didn't you? You certainly know the interrupt setting of the server NIC and where your network hubs are physically located — right? Right?

Trust those of us with greater experience and who have endured many more all-night server rebuilding parties: Every hour that you spend documenting your network before a big problem occurs saves you ten hours when the server croaks and you can't remember who manufactures the hard drive controller. Backups are almost as important as network documentation and crucial to network survival.

Your LAN survival kit

Before the first problem strikes, put together a LAN Bugaboo Survival Kit. Your kit should include at least the following items:

✔ Documentation of the server, cabling layout and design, user PC setups, backups, and so on.

✔ A complete and recent set of server backups.

✔ As many spares as you can afford: NICs; network cables, connectors, and terminators; hard drives and controllers for vital machines; monitors; and so on.

✔ Someone to talk to when network travails strike. Someone to bounce ideas off and milk suggestions from. We use the Internet as a great knowledge base. Be sure to check out the Novell Web Site at http://www.novell.com. Or you can ask for ideas from a friend who knows networking, the reseller who sold you your hardware or

software, the geeky PC guy with the thick glasses and bad haircut back in the corner cubicle, or one of the many books available that are dedicated to troubleshooting NetWare problems.

✔ An Internet account, so when you need to find a program update, new driver, or help configuring something, you can get it fast.

✔ Diagnostic gadgets and tools: an ohmmeter, soldering iron, wire-crimping tool, cable tester, protocol analyzer, and so on. A few tools — some very cheap, some not so cheap — can be a big help when you are looking for hardware problems and even some software problems. Just remember the First Rule of Network Troubleshooting: The more complex your network, the more expensive your diagnostic gadgets and tools tend to be.

The Trouble with Troubleshooting

The way you approach problem-solving is almost as important as fixing the problem. If you aren't careful, you might fix the problem but may not figure out how you fixed it. Here are a few tips:

- **Change only one thing at a time.** Changing more than one thing at a time may fix the problem, but you won't know exactly how you did it. Plus, you can unknowingly also cause other problems.

- **If possible, remove the misbehaving PC from the network and see whether the problem persists.** This step often tells you whether the problem is a result of network problems or stand-alone-itis.

- **Simplify things until it works.** If you have a PC with all nine expansion slots filled with everything from a fax-modem board to a two-port game card, try removing cards *one at a time* until you identify the problem.

  If you load 53 different terminate-and-stay resident programs in your AUTOEXEC.BAT file, remove them one at a time until you can identify the conflicting program (or programs).

- **Be suspicious.** You're a Double-Naught Spy, so start acting like one! Always be skeptical of error messages, particularly any message that is vague or offers no information about the cause of the error. Seemingly unrelated server and cabling problems cause a large number of simple-sounding DOS errors.

- **Learn from your experiences and the experiences of others.** Don't let your network keep shooting you in the foot. Be diligent and try to not make the same mistake more than 10 or 20 times.

- **Cabling is *always* a prime suspect.** We have said it before, and we will say it again: The network cabling is the most used, most abused, and most confused component of any network.

Now that your documents are in order (you did document everything, didn't you?), the next step for a network troublehound is to begin ruling out probable causes. After you have some idea of where to begin looking for the cause of the problem, you can look at possible solutions for a number of common troubleshooting problems.

When Wires Wreak Havoc

If it weren't for cabling, we wouldn't have networks. If it weren't for cabling, we'd have fewer problems. If it weren't for cabling, we might not have jobs. Some estimate that cabling causes 50 percent of the problems with networks. Here are some tips to follow:

✔ If you're still using thin Ethernet, make sure you have the right kind of coax (RG-58U). Anything else is for wiring cable TV or ARCnet, which isn't used much anymore.

✔ The same tip applies to terminators. Ethernet uses 50-ohm terminators. Any other kind will cause problems.

✔ While you are installing cabling, label the cable ends. Buy the best quality cable that you can and check the building and fire codes for rules that you must follow. Don't route cable over fluorescent lights, around motors, by AC power lines, or over refrigerators — you're inviting trouble if you do. Don't use cable from different manufacturers. Keep patch cables short. Don't use silver satin, untwisted telephone-type cable that you buy at your local electronics store. Meet distance requirements and hire certified cable installers. Whew!

✔ If you are using thin Ethernet, check for missing or bad terminators if you see trouble.

Balk Like a Dog: Why Network Printers Don't Print

Printers don't print for as many different reasons as there are printers. The following is a partial list of what causes printer problems:

✔ Bad printer cable

✔ Printer cable too long

✔ Printer not turned on

✔ Printer not online

✔ Print server not connected

✔ Network print queue not set up properly

✔ User hold on printer queue

✔ Printer out of paper

✔ Printer memory error

✔ Printer hardware error

✔ PC port not configured correctly

As you can see, troubleshooting a network printer can be a long and trying process. So many things can go wrong that you're probably asking, "Where do I begin?"

Start at the printer and work your way back to the user's PC. Attempt to print a test page from the printer control panel. Check the printer cable for a secure connection. Make sure that the printer is set up for the same type of connection as the cable: parallel, serial, or some type of built-in network connection. If the printer is connected to a server or attached directly to the network, use a parallel cable to connect the machine to a DOS-based PC and try the following command from the DOS prompt:

```
C:\> COPY CONFIG.SYS LPT1:
```

If this command works, you can eliminate both the printer and the cable used for the test as problem suspects. Next check the print queue setup and status in PCONSOLE and check the print job configuration in PRINTCON. If the user is running Windows, check the printer driver and Print Manager settings. Try to print to the network printer by using the following NPRINT command-line utility:

```
C:\> NPRINT C:\CONFIG.SYS Q=LASER1
```

You can also enter a CAPTURE statement to see whether the printer queue name is available on the network:

```
C:\> CAPTURE L=1 Q=LASER1
```

Send print jobs to the printer and check the print queue active job list in PCONSOLE to see whether the data gets to the queue. Make sure that there is no hold on the queue in PCONSOLE. Last, and most drastically, you can try using a protocol analyzer to decode the printer job packets bound for this printer.

Printer troubleshooting should be a systematic series of steps that begins at the network printer and ends with the user's PC. As we always say, change only one thing at a time. Examine every piece of hardware and software between the application and the printer paper output tray. Don't be afraid to call on experts and the manufacturer's technical support personnel. You can persevere over any kind of printer problem with patience, knowledge, and an occasional bit of good luck.

Friend or Foe: Why Some DOS Commands and Applications Don't Work with NetWare

DOS and many early DOS application programs were developed years before anyone had even heard the term *PC network*. Some DOS commands and programs, therefore, don't know how to react to the LAN environment. Most conflicts between DOS and the network are a result of DOS thinking that it resides on a stand-alone PC with one or two hard drives physically installed.

If you try to execute, for example, the DOS command CHKDSK on a network drive, the command fails with the error message `Cannot CHKDSK a network drive`. CHKDSK was designed to detect and correct file allocation table (FAT) problems with local hard drives. If users could CHKDSK a network drive, they could wreak havoc with all the files residing on the file server. You can see how some DOS commands would be useless or very dangerous when run in a network environment.

Many old DOS applications (and even a few new ones) aren't written to run in a network environment. Those programs expect a standard DOS-based local hard drive on which to execute their computer code.

You have seen lots of early DOS programs that could be installed and run only from the C drive. Even if you have a second hard drive or drive partition and want to install one of these old programs on the D drive, you are out of luck. Most shortsighted programming like this is long gone, but many programs still are designed to run only as stand-alone programs. To prevent copyright violations, computer programmers sometimes code their programs specifically so that they cannot be installed on a network. Other programs cannot handle concurrent access of files from different users. Sharing is not in their nature.

We have some good news among all this doom and gloom. Most current computer applications support network installation. All modern network database programs handle record locking, file sharing, and transaction tracking with ease. Because even word processors and spreadsheet programs are now "network aware," they can easily be run in a network environment. Always be careful to check for network compatibility when you purchase new software for your users.

Stop Making Nonsense: Command-line Utilities That Get Things Done

Novell does not send you unarmed into the battle of the network troubleshooters. All three versions of NetWare come with an extensive collection of command-line utilities, which are listed in the online documentation or the NetWare *Utilities Reference* manual. The reference manual is also available online for those running v3.12 or 4.*x* NetWare. These utilities are a crucial part of your network tool chest. You can save many hours of troubleshooting if you know which tools to use to get the job done. We cover some of the most important ones in Chapters 18 through 20, so you can even start there if you want.

Troubleshooting Workstations: Brain Surgery for PCs

The most frequent call that you receive as a network administrator is from a frantic user who asks, "Why can't I log in to the network?" Although the answer that we think of first is usually "Must be a nut loose behind the keyboard," we don't suggest that you use it on your users. Try to be very analytical in your approach to all network troubleshooting. Do any error messages point you in the right direction? Is the cable connection to the back of the PC secure? Has the user changed the hardware setup lately? Has the PC been moved? Is the Caps Lock or Num Lock key on when it shouldn't be, or vice versa? Can other users log in? Did someone run a cable over the coils of the refrigerator?

Most users who cannot log in have mistyped their passwords or used passwords that have expired, and they are locked out of the file server. Other users may not be able to log in because you've exceeded the number of users that your version of NetWare allows. You may come across an occasional user, however, who honestly cannot log in. Put on your Double Naught Spy hat and start sleuthing.

You may be surprised how ingenious users can be when working with their PCs. Most users will tell you that nothing has changed on their PC in the past five years. A few hours under hot interrogation lights usually gets them to admit that they recently installed a different network card, changed the interrupts on their modem, revamped their AUTOEXEC.BAT, and swapped hard drives with the guy down the hall.

If NETX or IPXODI and the VLMs (Virtual Loadable Modules) load successfully but a file server cannot be found, look at the network cabling and hubs. If NETX or IPXODI or the VLMs don't load, you probably have a software configuration problem. If your user's PC locks up at either predictable or unpredictable times, you probably have a memory conflict in their hinterlands.

After you look for cabling and connector problems, your next step is to boot the PC and check the network setup. If you don't know the memory address, I/O address, and interrupt setting of the NIC in question, pull the cover off the PC and make a note of each setting or use the diagnostic software for the LAN adapter to check its settings.

Be sure that the correct driver is configured and that the IPX settings match the settings on the user's NIC. If the settings don't match, you must either change the jumpers on the NIC or use the adapter configuration utility on the diskette to reconfigure the NIC.

If you're using NetWare 4.*x* and NDS, your approach will differ somewhat. Check the version of IPXODI that's running, examine your user's NET.CFG file (which should document for you all the detective work that you would have to do if you were using an older version), and see what happens when the VLMs that the users need try to load.

If all things load successfully, but they can't attach to any server (4.*x* or otherwise), look for a cabling problem in the immediate neighborhood. If all the VLMs or other software won't load, check the NET.CFG file for possible conflicts or outright errors (you can use Microsoft's MSD.EXE to see what it thinks the machine configuration is). Also see what's also being loaded into memory during bootup or beforehand, to make sure your users haven't been doing some "operator errors" of their own. This is where your set of boot and driver disks can come in handy — you did remember to bring them, didn't you? By looking for conflicts and eliminating them, you can usually detect and correct whatever problems are causing difficulty.

Never count out the luck factor when you are helping your users fix their network problems. Sometimes you just walk up, and everything miraculously starts working flawlessly. Just smile and tell users that that's why they pay you the big bucks. Take the credit while you can 'cause you'll have more than enough times when nothing you do seems to help. That's one of the joys of networking.

Some tips for VLM users

When you go to troubleshoot apparent VLM difficulties, be consistent, patient, and thorough in your problem diagnosis. These tips help you develop all those admirable qualities:

- Check the order that VLMs are loaded.

- Make sure that IPXNCP.VLM is loaded.

- Make sure that you are using NETX.VLM and VLM.EXE instead of NETX.COM or NETX.EXE.

- Make sure that you have enough memory.

- Once in a while, VLM.EXE will pause and display A file server could not be

found message. When this happens, check that the frame type that you specified in the requester matches the frame type that your file server uses. Then check the cabling. If the server connection from the workstation still doesn't work, try connecting a known working machine to the cable. If that machine can't log in, check the cabling. When you still don't see any results, check your configuration of the NIC again.

- When VLM.EXE freezes a workstation, most of the time your network configuration is wrong.

Do unto others

Most PC users consider their PC and everything on it to be their personal property. Always be respectful of your users' privacy and personal preferences when you are making changes to their PC. We try not to change any CONFIG.SYS or AUTOEXEC.BAT options without discussing the implications with the user. This courtesy is particularly important with the more sophisticated users in your organization: They may have spent months getting their PCs set up to their liking. Remember that you are the network administrator, not the administrator of each individual PC. That title belongs to each user.

Survival Techniques: Cannot Connect to File Server

Boom! Your file server just crashed and you don't know why. What do you do next? First, count to ten and take a deep breath (it may be the last one you get for a while). Write down any error messages from the server console screen or from any of your users' screens. The next obvious step is to turn the computer back on and see what happens. Nine times out of ten, the server comes back up successfully with no intervention from you. It's that tenth time that can be a bugger. This section provides a few suggestions about how to deal with a server that doesn't want to come right back up.

Poll your users to rebuild a portrait of what the server was doing at the time of the crash. Some crash causes are obvious: Lightning strikes your building, for example. Other crash causes can be, shall we say, more subtle. We have had crashes in which the server was operating normally at the time of the crash and no errors were observed. We still don't know what caused some of the crashes on our network. We did, however, discover the cause of some recent crashes: The building managers had been turning off the air conditioner on weekends. When the day heated up here in Texas, the server went KA-FLOO-EY.

Airplane pilots are taught to undo the last thing they did when they are confronted with mechanical problems in the air. Likewise, we suggest that you look for any recent changes to the network cabling, server, or installed applications when you are trying to pinpoint the source of problems. If the server crashed right after you loaded the new version of MegaWord on your server, try unloading the MegaWord software and see whether the server returns to normal. If you connect a new segment of cabling just before the server locks up hard and fast, try removing the new cabling and rebooting the server.

Frequently, server crashes damage the server database, called the *Directory* or the *bindery* (for pre-4.*x* servers), or other software files open at the time of the crash. The server displays messages at bootup that the Directory has been damaged, or your database may display error messages after a server crash.

Refer to your pre-4.*x* NetWare manuals regarding the BINDFIX program and when its use is warranted, or check your NDS Administration manual regarding recovery of damaged directories (this is why replicating directory servers is a good idea, by the way). Or refer to the application manuals for any specific recovery techniques for databases and other types of programs.

Consider buying Alexander LAN's Server Protection Kit. Its automated crash-handling programs will run diagnostics and restart the server when it crashes. Alexander SPK repairs damaged NetWare volumes when the server starts and helps if you can't mount your SYS volume. Also, if you have had disk crashes, add Ontrack Data Recovery's ODR for NetWare to your troubleshooting repertoire.

Gone to Jamaica, Mon: What to Do When the Network Goes on Vacation

Your phone begins to ring off the hook. Irate users want to know why the server is down in the middle of a busy day. You saunter nonchalantly over to the server console and everything appears to be running normally, although no users are attached to the server. Your network cabling, hubs, bridges, and routers just went on vacation, and you're left holding the proverbial bag. What to do, what to do?

Remember our earlier advice: You should undo the last thing you did. As you begin to look for network problems, run diagnostics on any hubs or network "black boxes" that include diagnostics routines. Check all the cable connections in your wiring closet. In particular, check all connections between your server and the rest of the PCs on your network. Without the network card and cable between the server and the rest of the network, none of your users can connect to the file server, even though the file server remains up and running. You might also try bringing your server down and then restarting it. Run the diagnostics disk that came with the NIC installed in the server. Replace the NIC, if possible, but only with an identical NIC. This is no time to be changing your basic hardware setup.

If you have access to a cable scanner, check your cable plant for any shorts or open circuits. Remember that cable scanner anomaly distance reports are frequently inaccurate, but they can still point you in the right direction. An ohmmeter can come in handy on Ethernet cabling, but only if the entire network is down — its use tends to disrupt any network activity that is still going on. A protocol analyzer can also be a good tool for tracking down the source of the problem, although most protocol analyzers cannot point you to a physical location the way that a cable scanner or TDR can.

If all these steps fail to get your network back up, begin working with a small subset of your network workstations to isolate the problem. Connect your server directly to one other PC and see whether they can talk to each other. Then insert a network hub between the two to see whether communications continue. Then add additional cable segments and machines, one at a time, until you locate the offending PC or cable. From that point on, repairs are usually easy to concentrate on. Leave as much of the network operational as possible so that your users don't grab torches and chase you into an old castle. Your network eventually will return from Jamaica, and then *you* can take that long-deserved vacation. On second thought, maybe you had better call in every few hours, just in case.

No Volume Is No Good!

Look Ma, No Volume: When you bring up the server, a volume won't mount. This is one of those problems you hope that you never see but inevitably will. It's a symptom that something's gone wrong. Try to remount the drive (MOUNT volumename). If this doesn't work, run VREPAIR. With VREPAIR, what's good once, is always good again — run VREPAIR until you have no errors, and then run it again.

Part IV
The Part of Tens

The 5th Wave   By Rich Tennant

"Just as I suspected. We've got shorts in the wiring".

In this part . . .

When Moses came down from the mount, how many commandments did he have? Ten.

Each chapter is this part is a list of commandments, guidelines, suggestions, ideas, and other stuff worth paying attention to when you're wrestling with NetWare. We'd like to claim divine inspiration, but instead, we're going to lean on brute experience and careful attention to the expertise of our betters and peers.

Maybe that's why some chapters have more than ten items, some have less, and some are right on the magic number. However many items you find, they're calculated to help you save time, skip common gotchas, and deal with everyday mayhem on your NetWare network.

The best Part of Tens that we know doesn't appear in this section — it's the part where you count to ten when you're losing it so that you don't blow your stack! And although we don't give this count-to-ten technique a chapter of its own, it's probably the most worth remembering and should get the most use. Enjoy!

Chapter 23

Ten Tons of Trouble: The Network's Broken!

● ●

In This Chapter

▶ *Dropping off* the network

▶ Slowing down isn't always good for your network

▶ Losing sight of servers or workstations

▶ What to do when the network's missing in action

▶ Running out of running room (disk space, that is)

▶ Preventing hardware damage from power failures

▶ Violating cable-length restrictions

▶ Realizing that occasional problems are the hardest ones to fix

▶ Knowing that no login means no network

● ●

*O*kay, so things aren't going like they're supposed to. In fact, they're not going well at all. Don't worry — everybody's network breaks every once in a while. Before you give way to a full-scale panic, first check out our rogues' gallery of common network *gotchas*. Chances are, one of these is the one whodunit; if not, though, you may still get inspired enough to figure things out anyway.

Is anybody out there?

The most disconcerting problem for anybody on the network is when the whole thing goes away. Nobody can even access the network, let alone log in. You *hate* when this happens, and so do your users, but what can you do?

The most common cause of *network interruptus* is a break somewhere in the cable. This problem is far more likely to happen on a bus topology than on a star topology. If it does happen on a star, go immediately to the hub that services the users affected and, most likely, you are at the source of the problem.

When a bus topology fails, the most common cause is a break or interruption in the cable. Look for someone who is changing offices or for people messing around near the cable. If you're lucky, somebody disconnected the wrong thing; if you're unlucky, you have to splice a broken cable. If you're *really* unlucky, the break is in a trench in the ground where a backhoe has used its unique ability to find and break cable on your network.

File server not found

Users who have been mucking with their machines are likely to notice the preceding NetWare error message as a symptom that something is wrong. If things were working yesterday but have mysteriously quit working today, the first thing to check is what has changed between now and then. Perhaps someone made changes to the AUTOEXEC.BAT or CONFIG.SYS files or to the Windows Registry, or maybe someone forgot to reconnect the PC to the network. Start with the wires and work your way up to the software: Check the connection to the network, the NIC, and the network software configuration, in that order. Sooner or later, the cause of the disconnection jumps out and bites you. Again, cable problems are the most likely cause.

Networking in geological time

Under some circumstances, a network begins to run really s-l-o-o-o-w-l-y. Even if you don't notice it yourself, don't worry — your users notice, and they will rush to let you know. Curiously, nothing stimulates hurry like a slow network. Can this be a case of opposites attracting?

The most common culprits for excessively slow networks are as follows:

- Cable shorts that cause the network to work only intermittently
- Server problems that constrain resources, such as running out of disk space or running low on available memory
- Excessive user demands on the server

Your best diagnostic tool is to go to the server that has slowed down and check the MONITOR or NWADMIN utilities. If you look through the various displays, especially those related to network utilization, the file system, and server memory, you typically get enlightened right away. The intermittent-short problem is much trickier to catch, but it typically shows up in the form of lots of transmit-and-receive errors in the network utilization display. An error rate that is higher than 2 percent of total traffic is abnormal and should clue you in to potential cable troubles.

Help! I can't get there from here

On networks that have more than one server, especially when long-distance connections may be involved, the day may come when you cannot get there from here. The obvious thing to check first is the link between *here* and *there*. In most cases, the link is down, or the router that ships traffic between the two locations is on the fritz. Checking the link is the first step; making sure that traffic can flow across the link is the second. A reset of the link most often does the trick — especially if a modem is involved. Checking the router may require the link to be reset, too (especially if you're using a dedicated NetWare router).

Oh, no! The network has gone away

When the network goes away, first check to see who is affected. If a single workstation is affected, proceed as directed in the "File server not found" section earlier in this chapter; if multiple workstations are affected, get out the network map and see how the workstations are related to each other. Chances are, they're all on the same cable segment or connected to the same hub. If that's the case, look for cable or hub problems in the affected neighborhood. If everybody's out of commission, proceed as directed in the first section in this chapter, "Is anybody out there?"

The server's out of disk space

Running out of disk space on your server is an unassailable argument for good housekeeping, which we advocate in Chapter 12. After you root around on the disk that's full, throw out the stale stuff, and remove the not-so-necessary files that build up over time, go back and reread Chapter 12. Then, you can practice prevention in the future instead of having to clean up full disks.

The key is to make some space. You should survey your file system, find out who the big consumers are, and tell them to clean up their acts. Another approach is to check out electronic mail files and clean them up yourself. NetWare keeps deleted files around until you PURGE them, so you should clean up right away. Look around for bogus temporary files created by applications (Microsoft Word is especially good at this). Deleting all files with a .BAK or .TMP extension is also a good idea.

By going through these motions, you make some much needed room. As a follow-up, consider tightening disk allocations for individual users or adding more disk space.

Running a NetWare server without at least 10 percent disk space free is danger-ous. Why, you ask? NetWare needs room to breathe — for such things as print queue files, temporary working files, and so on — and room in which to work. Without some empty space, things can really slow down. Double the 10 percent of free disk space if you turn on transaction tracking or auditing, because they both consume appreciable amounts of disk space.

NetWare 4.*x* includes an option to compress files stored on disk. Using this option can effectively double your file storage space and may justify the upgrade costs all by itself. If you have done everything you can to prune your file collection and still are nearly full, price the cost of adding disk space versus the 4.11 upgrade. (If you're going to move to NetWare 4.*x*, you may as well get the one that really works — NetWare 4.11.) Expanding your file storage space with software may be worthwhile.

Coming back from power outages

Okay, the power has gone away, and it has just come back. NetWare servers would rather be shut down gracefully than have their plugs unceremoniously pulled. Unfortunately, the latter is the effect of a power outage.

You have to restart the file server and perform any necessary file system repair. If you're lucky, that's all you have to do. If the server has been hosed, however, you may have to restore from a recent backup and break the news to your users that they have lost their work. Be prepared to be unpopular.

Consider getting an *Uninterruptible Power Supply (UPS)* for your servers. If a power outage occurs, a UPS gives you enough time to shut down the server gracefully and avoid file system damage (most UPSs will even perform the shutdown on your behalf). The right UPS even lets you run for a while without A/C. (If you don't have a UPS on your workstations, however, nobody will be up and running to care.) At a minimum, install a high-quality surge suppressor and spike arrester on your server; this device should protect you from outright damage if lightning gets up close and personal.

If losing a server means losing business, consider NetWare SFT III as a possible alternative. SFT III greatly improves the odds against server failure, but you must balance that benefit against increased hardware and software costs. Run the numbers for yourself. If doubling up on server hardware and using SFT III is cheaper than being down for 30 minutes to an hour, you'll know.

Breaking the rules

People find many creative ways to break the rules of networking, ranging from excessive cable lengths or connection violations, to having more users trying to log in than your NetWare license allows. Rules were made to be broken, but you have to be prepared to suffer the consequences.

The closer to the wire these violations occur, typically the more dire the consequences. For instance, what happens to the sixth user who tries to log in to a NetWare server that has a five-user limit? The sixth user receives a polite rejection — an informative error message that indicates that no additional user connections are available. On the other hand, exceeding cable limitations can cause intermittent failures if the violations aren't too extreme or outright, and total network failure if the violations are way over the line.

Again, prevention beats cure every time. If you know the rules and stay inside them, you are completely safe. If you don't follow the rules, you have to begin troubleshooting. Unless the problem is completely obvious, begin at the cable and work your way up to the software. Persistence and thought pay off, and practice helps improve your response time.

Intermittent failures

Patterns of errors that come and go are the trickiest kind to nail down. Intermittent problems are far more likely to be caused by hardware, especially cable shorts or loose connections, than by anything else. However, blaming hardware for the problem should be more of a tendency than a hard and fast rule.

The first thing to do when you face an intermittent problem is to determine its scope; figure out who's affected and where they are, and catalog the symptoms. Pay attention to everything, no matter how unrelated to the problem it may seem.

As an example, the weirdest intermittent problem we have ever encountered resulted from running an unshielded cable through an elevator shaft. Trouble occurred only when the elevator was in the immediate neighborhood (within one floor of the cable). At those times, the elevator interfered with the signals running through the cable. At all other times, everything worked fine. The solution was to reattach that section with a new, heavily shielded coaxial cable in a metal conduit.

We also hear stories about similar problems being caused by using industrial vacuum cleaners and moving servers to mop underneath them, among other strange and wonderful events. If you're lucky, you won't have such a story to tell yourself. Just keep your eyes peeled for the out-of-the-ordinary situations and, as always, round up the usual suspects.

I can't log in

Not being able to log in can result from a multitude of causes, but typically the problem is limited to a single workstation. Again, the cabling is the most common culprit, so start at the cable and work your way through the NIC to the software. Users who have made recent changes to their environments may have inadvertently redefined their DOS PATH to leave out the directory with the network drivers, or AUTOEXEC.BAT simply may not be loading the network software.

When you are troubleshooting user workstations, bring with you a set of bootup disks that include appropriate network software (IPX, NETX, ODI drivers, or VLM.EXE, and necessary VLMs). You can fire up the workstation with your own environment by booting from these disks. This process tells you immediately if something's out of whack with the workstation's software.

If you have a portable or laptop with a network connection, you can bring that with you and connect it to the network in place of the suspect machine. That, too, lets you know right away whether the network's working. The biggest difference between this strategy and the disk approach is size and weight. You decide.

When you're troubleshooting, the key ingredients are a positive attitude and persistence to see your problem-solving through to its inevitable conclusion. If things seem hopelessly screwed up, take a break: Go for a walk, call a friend, go have a cup of coffee. Often, you get so wound up in decoding the symptoms that clues right in front of your nose elude you. If you get too wound up, you miss the symptoms. A little relaxation gets your creative juices flowing and restores your deductive abilities. If Edison's best hours were spent daydreaming, why not yours?

Chapter 24

Keeping Track: Ten Things to Write Down about Your Network

. . . .

In This Chapter

▶ Labeling cables

▶ Keeping track of connections

▶ Watching for cable-length violations

▶ Mapping out equipment

▶ Keeping a list of which NICs go where

▶ Building an inventory for each machine on the network

▶ Knowing whom to call when things get out of hand

▶ Keeping good records of support calls

▶ Bringing all the elements of your network together on a to-scale map

▶ Stocking spare parts

. . . .

*T*his chapter is a checklist of what you want your network map and your database of configurations to include. Refer to Chapter 6 for an eloquent argument of the virtues of making a network map and a database of configurations to go with the map.

Where are the cables?

The most important thing to indicate is where the ends are and how they are color-coded or labeled (this is especially critical for twisted-pair wiring, in which cables run in packs and tend to look alike). For a truly complete reference, record the code from the outside of the cable (typically printed on the insulation) and the name of the vendor, if available.

Where are the connections?

For wiring schemes, such as coax, that involve taps, knowing where (and how many) connections exist is important for staying on the right side of the rules.

How long is each cable?

You can get information on the cable length in two ways — the easy way and the expensive way. By measuring as you go, you can accurately keep track of how long each cable is as you lay it out. If you're dealing with already installed cable or if you didn't keep track along the way, rent a Time-Domain Reflecto-meter (TDR) and use it to measure each cable. Especially with twisted-pair, don't be surprised when you find some scary length information: Cabling folklore is full of stories about finding a cable that has a whole spool of wiring hidden in the ceiling. Because you often cannot see the wires, the only way to tell how long they are is by measuring them electronically.

Where's the networking gear, and what kind is it?

When you keep track of the locations of any hubs, routers, concentrators, or other pure networking gear, you know where to look when you need to find it again. Keeping track of network addresses, used and unused ports, and other configuration information about these devices is also a good idea. While you're at it, record the manufacturer, model, and serial number, too. You may be able to get some of this information from the original purchase records, but you need the serial number or company equipment tag number to identify which piece of equipment is which.

Know your NICs

Make sure that you keep at least one manual from each kind of NIC you use and that you have a source for the latest and greatest drivers for each one. The manual's best feature, typically, is that it includes the number of the manufac-turer's technical support hotline. The tech support people can tell you everything you need to know about the NIC and its software.

Also, for each NIC installed, write down any and all of its current settings (IRQ, memory base, I/O port, and DMA channel, for example). If you don't mind gumming up the back of your PCs, write down this information on a small label on the outside of the case. That way, you don't have to open the case and pull out the NIC just to check its settings. Recording this information in a configuration database is an even better idea.

Know your nodes

Each machine on a network is called a *node* (borrowing from mathematical terminology), which refers to each point on a connected collection of lines as a node. For each machine, keep track of its hardware configuration and software configuration, and record an inventory of the software it contains. This information, too, has a rightful place in your configuration database.

The vendor file

Inevitably, you buy pieces and parts of your network from all kinds of sources: mail order, local computer stores, and maybe even a direct sales representative. You also buy stuff from different vendors. Building a vendor file that includes the following information for each vendor whose equipment you own is a wonderful idea:

- ✔ Name(s) and model number(s) of the item(s)
- ✔ Date(s) and price(s) of purchase(s) (for each item, a copy of the invoice or purchase order is a good idea and is often necessary to get help from tech support)
- ✔ Serial number(s) or other identification information
- ✔ Vendor's address and phone numbers for sales and technical support

By keeping all this information in one place, you are ready to call for help at a moment's notice. You also have all the information you need to convince the tech support person that you have a legitimate reason to ask for help.

The contact log

Every time you call a vendor, a reseller, a professional support organization, or anyone else of importance to your network, make a log of the call. Record the date, time, and the name of the people you speak to. If they promise you anything or advise you to do anything, write that down, too.

This log has two kinds of value: If things get really weird, you have a record to support your side of the story. On a more positive note, you can use the log to figure out who's worth talking to on the other end of the line and ask for that person by name the next time.

The plans, the layout, the map

Get a set of engineering or architect's plans for your building or office (or barn, or whatever). Use the plans to record cable placement and length and machine placement. This map becomes the key to finding things and to figuring out just how big a problem may be if you suspect that the cause is a cable or hub. Having a map is a simple thing, really, but incredibly valuable.

Don't mark up the original plans — check your local Yellow Pages for a drafting or architectural supply store. Most of them can copy blue lines or other architectural drawings for you. Then, when you have created your network map, make a few working copies of it so that you can mark up a working copy and not mess up the original. You probably want to supply a copy to your building management or facilities people — they can use it to forewarn outside contractors before such people start messing with your network. Avoiding trouble is easier than fixing it when something happens.

Spare change or spare parts?

Over time, you'll build a stockpile of spare parts and unused cable. Keep a list of what you have and where it's stored. That way, if you get hit by a beer truck, the person who replaces you can find stuff when it's needed. Consider keeping a list of spare parts an exercise in following the golden rule — if you had to take over from someone else, you would want the same thing, wouldn't you?

As the eminent cyberneticist and mathematician Alfred Korzybski so poignantly remarked, "The map is not the territory." True though that statement may be, the map is the best tool we know of for finding your way around the territory. All the best networks have one — why not yours?

Chapter 25

The Ten Things You Have to Know before Anyone Else Can Help You

Sometimes you get stuck on a networking problem and just can't get past it. A good rule of thumb is to guess how long a particular job will take before you begin. If you find that half your original estimate has expired and you're not as far along as you think you should be, maybe you should bring out the heavy artillery.

To deal effectively with another person, whether it's somebody from tech support or just plain old Fred, the NetWare guru from next door or down the hall, address the concerns in this chapter to get things moving again.

For tech support calls, assemble the facts

Technical support operations require that you identify yourself as a legitimate owner of the product or system being supported. It's much like checking into a hospital: Before a hospital admits you, you must identify yourself and provide proof of insurance (or at least an ability to pay). Building a file of contact information beforehand is also a good idea. If you have such a file when the chips are down, you can locate the appropriate vendor's Web site address, BBS, tech support hotline number, and FAXBACK information without uprooting every piece of paper in a two-block radius.

For tech support, you have to know the name of the product in question and its serial number or provide proof of purchase. If you have built the purchase-records file we suggest as a part of the network map and configuration database, you have this material right at hand. If not, start digging — some technical support operations won't talk to you until you can provide this information, so be prepared to rattle it off when you are asked. At the very least, tech support will ask you to provide proof of purchase (like an invoice or receipt) or a serial number for the product you want supported.

What's the situation?

Write down everything you can think of about the system that the problem involves.

If the system is a workstation, write down every interface with settings information for each one, the kind of CPU, the amount of memory, the type of disk drive and controller, the version of DOS, copies of the AUTOEXEC.BAT and CONFIG.SYS files, lists of INITs or System Extensions, or whatever special drivers and widgets your machine loads while it's booting up.

If the system is a server, write down everything we already mentioned plus the version of NetWare and the copies of the relevant files, if applicable.

The idea behind writing everything down is to completely document what you're dealing with.

What's the problem?

Give as accurate a description of the problem as you can, including any error messages that crop up. (Copy down the error messages verbatim, especially if they involve numeric codes or crash dumps.)

What's new or different?

If your system was running until you made a recent change or addition, describing what has changed and why you cannot get back to where you started is very important.

Which avenues have you already explored?

If you have tried to fix the problem on your own, recount whatever you tried and what the results were. By doing this, you may save the other party to your conversation some time and energy. Ask whether the troubleshooter is interested in knowing about the blind alleys that you already explored.

What happened?

If a power outage has occurred or if someone has accidentally pulled the plug on your server, please tell your support contact about it. Make sure that you test the A/C outlet to be sure that the receptacle has power, and make sure that the PC can power up. If the PC has no power or the unit is dead, the response is different than if you can at least turn it on.

Does the problem have a history?

Sometimes a badly damaged file system or a failing disk drive starts off with small, occasional faults and then gets worse and worse over time until the system fails altogether. If the problem you're having has been in the making for a while, let the other person know how long it has been happening, how it began, and how the symptoms have progressed.

Be clear, concise, and polite

Having your system or network go down in flames is upsetting, but the people trying to help you cannot deal with your emotions. They can deal only with your problem. Take a deep breath and do your best to calm down.

If you can clearly and directly describe your problem and the other information that tech support needs, things go much faster. If you have done your homework and you have built the configuration database and files we suggest, you should be able to tell the support people everything they want to know as soon as they ask.

Offer to send information by modem or fax to speed up the process

If the help you seek isn't in the neighborhood, you should tell the technical support people what information you have gathered and ask whether you can upload or fax it to them (assuming that you still have the capability). Especially when the problem involves contents of configuration files or other computer information, a copy for the person on the other end of the conversation can be a real time-saver.

Ask whether you can do anything else

Getting carried away with worry is easy to do when things are broken. If you can focus on how well you're communicating and keep checking in to see how you're doing, you can be more objective and focus on getting the information across. The more good information you can give, the better (and faster) the results should flow. A positive attitude works wonders, too.

Getting help requires going through the painstaking process of re-creating the environment and the causes of whatever problem prompted your pleas for help. The more you can do to depict the circumstances accurately and objectively, the better your support person can function. Just remember that you both share the same goal: to get things working as quickly as possible.

Chapter 26

Ten Things to Know before Making Changes to a NetWare Server

● ●

In This Chapter

▶ Making two complete backups before changing your server

▶ Getting acquainted with the server's file system layout and contents

▶ Documenting the server's hardware configuration

▶ Knowing what the server is running

▶ Documenting special network addresses

▶ Mapping out the routers and where your server fits

▶ Finding and mapping all print servers, print queues, and network printers

▶ Surveying your server's situation

▶ Getting acquainted with the server's user accounts and defined groups

▶ Documenting your server's NetWare version number and researching the current installation

● ●

*T*he power of common practice is strong, and the power of common expectations is even stronger. Although most servers tend to have similarities in their setups, each has its own unique quirks and kinks. You must thoroughly understand these differences among servers when you take over a NetWare server, especially before you bring your own individual perspective and personality to bear and begin changing things to fit your own ideas of good structure and organization. In case you miss or forget something, this chapter presents a checklist so that you can become familiar with the network that you have — and get back to where you began if you need to reverse all engines.

Make two complete backups

A complete backup means that you copy everything. Why, then, do you want two of them? For insurance — if anything is wrong with one of them, the other backup should still be okay. If you are going to make network changes, these backups are your lifeline back to a known, working system configuration.

Map out and inspect the file system

Print directory structures of the SYS: volume and other NetWare volumes. Try to understand how the pieces fit together: Does the file system follow conventional NetWare structures, or does it do its own thing completely? The answer to that question lets you find your way around this server and figure out what, if anything, must change. While you're looking around, inspect the files to see whether the system has been cleaned up. Look for lots of outdated files, unnecessary duplicates, and .TMP or .BAK files in mass profusion, and check the contents of the e-mail directories in SYS:MAIL and its user subdirectories. Avoid the temptation to clean up as you go — you're making a survey, remember?

Map out the hardware configuration

Unless you're lucky enough to inherit a server from someone who already has made a network map, with the configuration database to go with it, you have to do some sleuthing. Print copies of the AUTOEXEC.NCF and STARTUP.NCF files, and other .NCF files you can find for other NLMs (NetWare Loadable Modules) in use, and check the various LOAD statements at the operator's console as the server boots up. This information is a good start for most of what you need to know.

If you work on a NetWare 4.x server, be sure to examine its Directory setup as well as whatever configuration information is at hand. This activity can be an invaluable guide to the servers and other resources out there on the network. In addition, you can document how your organization is modeled from a NetWare perspective.

Make a list of add-ons that are in place

Regardless of the version of NetWare in use, make a list of NLMs in use. Unless you're manually loading some NLMs after startup, you should be able to get this information from the startup configuration files (STARTUP.NCF for NetWare 3.11, for example). This information tells you which services are available to users and who cannot load and unload NLMs anyway. You can also check this information in the Modules section of the NetWare MONITOR utility.

NLM is a way of adding functions and services to both NetWare 3.*x* and 4.*x* servers. Finding a 3.*x* or 4.*x* NetWare server with less than a dozen NLMs is unusual; some servers may have more than 50 running.

Map out the network addresses and configuration

You have to get the network number for the internal IPX network inside the server, plus the network numbers for any of the networks to which the server is attached (typically, one additional network address per NIC installed). You also have to get network addresses or address ranges for other protocols in use, including TCP/IP, AppleTalk, OSI, SNA, or whatever else may be installed.

Understand how routing works

If you run NetWare 3.*x* or higher, the server can act as a router. Check to see whether routing for protocols other than IPX is enabled. If a dedicated or stand-alone router is in use, map out the networks it services. Build a routing map of the network that shows the network addresses involved and the routers that link individual networks together. This map shows you how data moves around on your internetwork.

Map out the print services

Create a list of the printers, print queues, and print servers on the network. Add locations for print servers and printers to your network map so that they are easy to locate when you need to find them. Try to determine which kinds of forms or special service queues have been set up and how users are directed to use the currently available print services. If everybody's pretty happy with the way printing works, you probably should leave things alone until you fully understand them.

Check the environment

Check out the physical situation of the server. Is it in a secure area or out in the open? Does it have an Uninterruptible Power Supply (UPS) or a surge/lightning suppressor, or is it just plugged straight in to the wall? Does it have adequate cooling and ventilation? Negative answers to any of these questions should spur you to consider improving conditions, at the very least. If everything is satisfactory, you can move on to other concerns.

Learn the users and groups

Check to see who has accounts defined and what their patterns of use for those accounts may be. You should work backups and system maintenance around normal working hours, so determine what those hours are. See who the heavy users are so that you can provide the services they need. As a newcomer, you may want to talk to the heavy users and find out what they do and don't like about the network as it currently stands.

If you work on a 4.x server, familiarize yourself with the directory structure for this environment. Is the server the sole occupant of a stand-alone Directory tree, or is it a part of a larger directory services environment? What's the structure of the tree, and how are containers, users, and groups defined within it? You can use the directory services Browser to climb around the Directory tree and become familiar with it. The more you know, the better prepared you are to deal with whatever comes your way.

Check the NetWare version and inspect the patches and fixes that are in place

The final check is on the currency of your NetWare version. The first thing you have to find out is the version number (and revision, if applicable). The next thing you have to look into is which patches and fixes are being applied during the loading process.

Investigation of the startup or configuration files pays off again during this final check. These files tell you — or someone who knows more than you do — how up-to-date your server is. If you can't tell, try to find someone who can so that you both can decide whether you should install new changes and enhancements on your system.

The whole idea when you take over an existing server is to become as familiar with its design and layout as if you had built it yourself. If you're lucky, the server is laid out along familiar lines — the well-worn defaults that most folks use — and you can begin to feel at home right away. If not, you have to do a formal investigation. This procedure takes time, but the effort is always rewarded.

Chapter 27

Ten Paths to Perfect Printing

In This Chapter

▶ Keep print configurations simple

▶ Build CAPTURE into the login script to avoid user-induced printing problems

▶ Don't leave NPRINT to your users

▶ Set up separate queues for envelopes, special paper, or print forms

▶ Keep your Macintosh and UNIX print users separate from DOS and Windows users

▶ Dedicate a machine for print services

▶ Use remote printing only when nothing else will do

▶ Train your users to kill print jobs

▶ Listen closely to PCONSOLE

*D*espite NetWare's importance as a print service provider, printing is not a perfectly transparent thing in the NetWare environment. Maybe that's because thousands of different kinds of printers are out there, each with its own eccentricities. Maybe that's because print services require many more bells and whistles for occasional special use than normal, everyday printing ever requires. Maybe it's because providing perfection for print services is a difficult thing to do.

Whatever the case, printing seems about as clear as mud until you really get the hang of it — and even then, it's a dirty job. In the meantime, our ten nuggets of wisdom should keep you out of unnecessary trouble and help you stay on the beaten track to provide print services that work. Our advice: Worry about perfection later; just get your printers printing.

Don't get fancy unless you're forced into it

Basic printing requires one printer, one queue, and one print server. Why do any more, unless you have to? And, if you do, take it slow and careful.

Make sure that what you provide (whether it's special queues, print forms, or additional services) works before you give it to your users. From the users' perspective, the only thing worse than not having what they need is being told that a service that the user wants is available on the network but is not currently working.

Handle CAPTURE for users yourself

Write a good system login script that defines basic capture capability, test it thoroughly — particularly with DOS applications from inside Windows — and then put it where users cannot escape from it. If special CAPTURE definitions are needed, write batch files for each one and build them into user access to the applications that need them. If you do it yourself and test it well, you can get it right.

If special needs exist, consider spending some time with PRINTDEF to service them. Your extra work pays off by hiding some of the tricky details from your users.

Set up NPRINT batch files for applications that need them

The same thing is true for NPRINT as for CAPTURE — you should embed access to the applications that need special treatment in batch files that can deliver working NPRINT services. If you set your users loose with enough knowledge to try but perhaps not enough to succeed as do-it-themselfers, you will have only yourself to blame when they come crying for help.

What's in a name? One form per queue

If you have to set up print services to handle envelopes, letterhead, preprinted forms, labels, and more on your printers, set up special print queues for the most heavily used ones. LABELQ is a good name, for example, for label-printing jobs that can be queued up, and ENVQ is good for envelope-printing. You get the idea.

Special services for Macintosh, UNIX, and more

If you have to service AppleTalk- and/or TCP/IP-based printing on your server, set up separate queues for those special users. Having separate queues lets AppleTalk and TCP/IP users access their print jobs more directly, and it lets you more easily troubleshoot the special kinds of problems that they're prone to have. For both AppleTalk and TCP/IP based users, expect to be asked for — and to provide — PostScript printing capabilities. (Many IP-based users work happily for years without knowing that a filename that ends in *.ps* is a PostScript file; if you're lucky, you can keep things that way.)

Dedication is a wonderful thing

If you have an extra, unused PC lying around, consider setting up a dedicated print server using PSERVER.EXE. This approach has the following advantages:

✔ Lets you keep your NetWare server locked up

✔ Lets you separate print services from other services and provides better response time for all of them

✔ Lets you locate printers (and the dedicated print server) sensibly — close to their users — rather than as dictated by restrictions on the length of the printer cable or the location of your main servers.

Use RPRINTER only sparingly

RPRINTER, the remote print server DOS TSR, can be a real godsend, especially for small, isolated groups of users who otherwise must trudge halfway around the world to pick up print jobs.

If that's not the case, don't use RPRINTER just because it sounds like a neat idea. The use of RPRINTER on machines that users employ as their everyday desktops means putting print services at their mercy. If the users reboot often or turn their machines off while print jobs are in process, they can make life miserable for other users, which makes it equally miserable for you.

Another good reason to upgrade to NetWare 4.11 is that RPRINTER has been replaced/rewritten. You'll find the new print utility, called NPRINTER, to be much more reliable and usable than RPRINTER ever dreamed it could be. If you must use a remote printing utility with NetWare 4.*x,* make it NetWare 4.11 and NPRINTER. Some heavy users have told us this utility alone makes the upgrade worthwhile.

Be quick on the kill!

Teach your users how to kill their own print jobs. This job takes some time and effort, but it is well worth the time (and interruptions) it saves you. It also saves at least one tree, if not a small forest (every ton of paper consumes an average of 17 trees).

The Status apparatus

The information provided by PCONSOLE's Printer Status menu or
IntranetWare's NDS-based printer services can tell you most of what you need
to know to keep your printers up and running and to find out why they're down
or when they're not running. Use one or the other regularly, and if you have a
dedicated Print Server, keep the PCONSOLE status window for that server on
display at all times. It'll come in handy.

The secret to print services that work is not to get too fancy and not to rely too
much on the kindness or perspicacity of your users. Doing it right typically
means doing it yourself and making sure that it works before giving it to users. If
you live by these rules, you stay out of the printer problem zone.

Chapter 28

Ten Unbeatable Backup Techniques

*O*nly 40 percent of all NetWare servers are backed up regularly. That frightening but totally predictable statistic makes us wonder how the majority manages to rationalize living on the brink of unrecoverable disaster. This statistic proves what we have always believed — that there's absolutely no guarantee that the majority is always right.

If you want to risk everything against the chance of failure and loss, we can't stop you. If you're smart, however, you will get into the backup habit and be ready to fend off Murphy when he eventually does show up (Murphy's Law: What can go wrong will go wrong). If you're prepared, you can laugh him off; if you're not, you'll play the crying game. Follow the ten prescriptions in this chapter, and you'll never have to play.

Buy a big enough backup system

The biggest problem with the backup process is that it must happen regularly to be any good. The more data you have to back up, the longer it takes (and the more media is required to accommodate it).

Don't cut corners by buying a cheap, low-capacity backup system when you have an expensive, high-capacity network. If you can back up everything to a single tape or magneto-optical disk, that's good. If you can back up to that medium a multiple number of times, that's even better.

The idea behind a high-capacity backup is to fit everything you need on your backup system so that you don't have to be on hand to shuffle cartridges or disks or whatever. Because backup usually happens on weekends or in the wee hours, this approach helps you get your beauty sleep. If the network's just too big to fit on a single platter, cartridge, or whatever, consider buying a stacker, changer, or jukebox instead of a single-play unit. (For more details on all this backup stuff we talk about here, consult Chapter 16.)

Completely automate the backup

The best way to ensure that backup happens is to let the computer handle it. The only good backup is a fresh one, and you can make the computer do it every day — no excuses accepted. If you make yourself responsible, the inevitable excuse doesn't make up for the data lost as a consequence.

What you miss is what you lose

When you select backup intervals, you make a trade-off in frequency against time and expense. The key is to figure out how much data you can afford to lose before the loss really begins to hurt.

Most businesses that make this decision rationally decide that a day's work is about all that they can do without. That amount has as much to do with the fact that they can back up only at night as it does with damage control. Think long and hard before you stretch that interval. Think about what the loss of several days' or a week's worth of work can cost you and your company.

Set up off-site storage

If you go through the trouble of backing up, take the next step and arrange to store a set of backups off-site. In many areas, you can even store backups in underground bunkers that can get your data through most catastrophes. This method may be overkill, but having a backup somewhere else ensures that your backup doesn't get barbecued if your building goes up in flames.

Plan for disaster

The next step after planning off-site backup storage is arranging for a backup site on which to install your backup. If your company cannot do business without your network, arranging access to an equivalent system is worth the money if your main system ever is completely out of service. This process, called *disaster recovery,* may seem completely unreasonable, but if you need it, you have no other choice.

Practice makes perfect

The best backup system in the world, and a completely fresh backup in hand, doesn't do you any good unless you know what to do with it. And, if your backup system doesn't work, your backup is worthless.

The only way to find out whether things work is to try them and see what happens. The only way to get good at restoring from a backup is to practice, practice, practice. That's why we say here: "Practice makes perfect." Try restoring to a blank disk. Find your original NetWare CD and tape backup discs, serial numbers, unlock codes, and adapter settings. Recovering a file is different from recovering a system. Be prepared to do either!

A good approach to staying in top backup shape is to do a restoration drill once every three months or so. Then, when a real crisis happens, you can concentrate on getting back to work and dealing with the problems at hand, instead of first learning how to restore.

The pros and cons of workstation backups

After you get into the backup habit for your servers, the next hurdle to jump is deciding what to do about workstations. If your users can be trained to keep their important stuff on a server, you don't need to back up workstations. If not, you must decide whether backing up the workstations is worth the additional time, expense, and effort.

Typically, the only employees who routinely merit this kind of consideration are your bosses. Sometimes covering your assets means covering theirs, too!

Rules for rotation mean equal wear and tear

As you get your backup scheme going, remember to introduce new media from time to time. Chapter 16 discusses a variety of rotation schemes in some detail, but the important thing is to keep from completely wearing out the tapes, cartridges, or whatever. Worn media can render a backup unreadable and therefore worthless. Pick a rotation scheme and schedule, and stick with it.

How to deal with upgrades and changes

Another occasion for backing up is easy to overlook: Whenever you change a server's hardware or software, a failure may result. If you cannot time your upgrades or changes to follow your regular full-system backup, you have to time a backup to follow the upgrades or changes. Backing up first and making changes second is much safer, though.

The backup desiderata: What to look for

When you buy a backup package, you should consider many factors (refer to Chapter 16); the following list, however, shows the top three considerations:

- ✔ **File-by-file restore:** Users lose files, and sometimes the NetWare SALVAGE utility just can't get them back. A file-by-file restoration lets you restore only what you need and saves time and frustration.

- ✔ **Automatic backup scheduling:** If the package you're looking at doesn't let you automatically order up regular, full, and incremental backups, move on to the next candidate.

- ✔ **SMS compliance:** If you're backing up NetWare, pick a solution that supports the Novell Storage Management System. This step insulates you from the impact of potential file system changes and ensures that similar media can be read on backup systems from multiple vendors.

The bottom line is to get the most effective backup package you can find that meets your needs.

Backing up is the cheapest form of insurance for your company's investment in the systems it uses. Even though most companies don't take advantage of this potential lifesaver, try to stay ahead of the herd.

Chapter 29

Ten Symptoms of Growing Pains

. . . .

In This Chapter

▶ Erratic network performance

▶ Really s-l-o-o-o-o-w network response

▶ You have more users than NetWare connections

▶ You're always short on disk space

▶ The traffic is excessive because the wires are getting too crowded

▶ Your users have growing pains

▶ The network is growing by itself

▶ Servers crash or lock up regularly

▶ Your backup system is too small to accommodate all the data that you need to back up

▶ You (or your server) get burned in effigy

. . . .

So your network is up and running and things are going well. Did the Lords of Chaos ever have a more tempting invitation to come and shower trouble all over your head?

Nothing succeeds like success, the saying goes, so growing pains are the inevitable reward for doing your job well and pushing networking to boldly go where it's never gone before. Just as your pants legs got a little too short when you were outgrowing them as a youth, you can tell when the fabric of your network begins to stretch. This time, though, your ankles are showing because you're running around like crazy, putting out fires.

If you keep your eyes open for the symptoms we describe in this chapter, you can begin measuring for the next expansion before your network starts bursting out at the seams.

Erratic performance begins

If all network users get to work at about the same time and fire off their workstations right after that, immediately bringing the network to its knees, you may be nearing the limits of your server or network capacity.

If you have only one NIC in the server, you can get a boost by splitting the cable layout in two and attaching half the users to one of a pair of NICs instead. If you've already got two NICs, consider adding one or two more, and so on.

If your server's getting short on running room, the cure is a little more drastic. Maybe you need to buy a second server (and a second NetWare license, and more disk drives, NICs, and all the other stuff) and split up your user community.

Living in geological time

If the server starts out slow and then speeds up, that's one thing. If it starts out slow and stays that way, then you have another problem entirely. The most common cause of server slowdown is cramped RAM, and the first thing to try is adding some more.

As we're writing this book, 16MB of RAM costs about $125 (depending on speed). This is about as cheap a performance fix for NetWare as you're ever likely to find. In fact, you'd better act fast, because memory can't stay this cheap for much longer.

You have more users than slots

The temptation always exists to save money by scrimping on the number of users that a NetWare license provides. Even though at first all users may not want to be logged in all the time, a major consequence of a successful network is that all users want immediate network access.

If more users want to use the server than the number provided by the license, the cure is pretty easy. You can upgrade a NetWare license from a lower number to a higher number of users at any time. The cost is about 65 percent of the difference between what you paid and the cost of an entirely new license for the higher number. If you don't have to do a major hardware upgrade along with it, this approach can be downright reasonable.

One of the best changes in NetWare 4.1 is the concept of an additive license: If you've got a 25-user license for NetWare and want to add users, you can just add another 5-user license to your existing one (for a total of 30), rather than upgrading to the next level (which used to be 50 users). Careful buyers can weigh the costs of buying multiple licenses to get the best deal on the number of users that they really need to support.

Constant messages tell you that you're out of disk space

Disk capacity on a server is usually the first resource to be stretched and is one of the easiest to fix. All you need is money — to pay for more disk drives and possibly a controller to go along with them.

Because of the disk compression that NetWare 4.x provides, try pricing a 4.11 upgrade, rather than the disk purchase, and buy whichever one is cheapest. Don't worry — the time always comes when you need more disk space, but you may want to wait and buy a whole new server with newer, faster disk technology.

Excessive traffic exists on the wire

If MONITOR or NetAdmin keeps telling you about excessive transmission errors on the network, you may be overloading the carrying capacity of the network medium. This situation probably means that you're asking the wire to carry more traffic than it can really handle.

In this case, you may want to think about adding more NICs to the server and splitting the wiring into subsets, to reduce the traffic that any particular cable segment has to handle. You can tell that this technique will help if your server utilization stays below 30 or 40 percent, but the wire gets congested anyway.

You get dirty looks in the hallway

Users may not always tell you how they feel about network performance, but if you start catching lots of dirty looks, consider them a warning that things are getting out of hand. If you're smart, this situation will never happen to you.

Things you never knew existed show up on the network

When mystery printers, workstations, and more — even mystery servers — begin to show up on your network, it's a clear indication that more stuff is out there and that you need more resources. The first thing you should do is up your capacity; the second thing is to go out and resurvey your network to get a new handle on it.

Regular server crashes or lockups occur

Server failures or hangs are a clear indication that all is not well in Mudville. If this problem begins to happen regularly — like maybe at the end of the month, when the folks in accounting are running the numbers, or at other peak load times — you know that the server is being stretched beyond its capacity. Again, the rule is divide, duplicate, and conquer.

Your backup capacity is insufficient

One clear signal of growing pains is suddenly discovering that your backup system cannot accommodate all the hard disk storage on your server anymore. Think about upping your coverage — or think about the impact that staying up to hand-feed the existing system will have on your life. (You do have a life, don't you?)

A server gets burned in effigy on your desk

You must have missed those dirty looks in the hallway but — hey, now you know! Get cracking on increasing resources, or they may burn *you!*

Growing pains are good because they mean increasing demand for the services the network provides. If you can stay ahead of them and add capacity before things get out of hand, you will be a hero. Watch for the warning signs and head 'em off at the pass.

Part V
Appendixes

The 5th Wave   **By Rich Tennant**

"You know that network OS has quite a sense of humor".

In these appendixes . . .

In the appendixes, you find a glossary, tips on getting help
with your network, and a great guide to online information about networking. Carry on!

Appendix A

Glossary: Everyday Explanations of Techno-Babble Networking Terms

10BASE-2 On the Ethernet freak's sanity scale, falls somewhere between 10BASE-T and 10BASE-5. It doesn't weigh as heavily as 10BASE-T, has the same properties as 10BASE-5, and is what most Ethernet networks are composed of. Try it — if you don't mind the problems a bus topology can cause.

10BASE-5 The cabling that many old buildings have. Definitely antiquated Ethernet stuff, this type of cabling is rapidly being replaced by 10BASE-T. If you use 10BASE-5, expect derision from those in the know about LANs, unless you are using it for distance sake, but at least you will work with bulky, heavy, copper media.

10BASE-T A cabling option for the Ethernet access method that uses unshielded twisted-pair (not telephone wire) to make its connections. This stuff is cheaper than Cheapernet (10BASE-2) and more versatile. If you want to be part of the in crowd, this is the media to use. Use Category 5 if you're smart.

abend Means *ab*normal *end*. Simply, this process happens when the server crashes, and it sounds better than the unsavory term *abort*.

access method Messages are communicated across the network by rules called *protocols* and access methods that govern their access to the network cabling. When you think networking, remember that without an access method, you don't have any on-ramps to the network.

access privileges Similar to having the keys to the candy store, these privileges tell you what you can do with files or directories.

account Have you ever opened a checking account at the bank? Certain restrictions exist, and a variety of plans are available, all aimed at making you "accountable." The account that each user has on the LAN works in the same way.

account manager This guy is two rungs down the management ladder. Account managers have less authority to manage the LAN than do Supervisor or Workgroup managers, but they have definitely more authority than simple users do.

active hub The carbo-loading, low-fat device of the networking access methods. An active hub is used to congregate and distribute data to workstations on the LAN in a star or distributed-star topology.

adapter Like the ignition switch on a car, the adapter gets workstations talking on the LAN. Placed in the workstation's bus, the adapter communicates requests between the workstation and the physical media that connects the LAN.

ADMIN Like SUPERVISOR, ADMIN is the big kahuna of networking. ADMIN has access to the root of the directory tree. ADMIN can therefore create the network's initial directory structure and create administrators to manage segments of the directory tree called *partitions.* Or ADMIN can create a portion of the initial structure and let partition managers create the rest.

aliases Not everyone has an alias. However, if you've ever been on the other side of the law, you probably know someone who does. In NetWare 4.*x,* objects can have aliases that help to identify them.

AppleTalk The name of the set of protocols developed by Apple Computer, whose Macintosh was one of the first mass-market computers to offer built-in networking capabilities. In most cases, where there's a Mac, there's also AppleTalk.

applications You cannot have one application without the other. Networks need applications like you need air to breathe. Being without applications is similar to having a car with nowhere to go. Word processing programs, spreadsheets, and e-mail are examples of applications.

archiving The process of removing old files from the server so that there's room for vibrant and fresh new files. If you ever want any of the old dogs back, you unarchive them. Archive media can be CD-ROM, WORM, RAID, or — simply — tape.

attach What you do to connect to a server other than the one you are logged in to. In NetWare 4.*x,* you use LOGIN /NS.

attributes The characteristics that define what users can do to the files and directories managed by NetWare. Attributes vary by user or group and affect whether a file can be copied, deleted, executed, modified, and so on.

AUTOEXEC.BAT The file that contains the commands that enable you to start your computer in the manner you want. You load the NIC driver in this file, and you can put the LOGIN command in it.

AUTOEXEC.NCF Like the AUTOEXEC.BAT file, this file is used to boot the server. It lets you load the server drivers and any NLMs that the network operating system uses.

back door The secret entrance that network administrators use to get into the network in case something happens to the SUPERVISOR account.

backbone If your network gets a slipped disk, it's just as incapacitating as when it happens to your back. A network backbone connects file servers in a single, unified internetwork.

backup This term has nothing to do with raising your hackles, but it can cause you to do so if you don't have one. This refers to the procedure you should perform on your LAN every night: Save the files on the network to some form of off-line storage.

bad sector An area on a hard disk that for some reason doesn't play back what's recorded. The problem might result from a manufacturing defect, damage to the drive's platters during shipment, or the wrong phase of the moon. The fact is, that area cannot be used. By marking bad sectors in the drive's manufacturing process, manufacturers now save you the time spent having to find them yourself. It may not sound like much work, but the Novell disk-analysis program, called COMPSURF, has been known to take three or four days to finish.

base I/O address Many devices have an I/O address that identifies them to the system, just as your address lets you get junk mail. See also *I/O address.*

base memory Like the IRQs and DMA, the base memory setting on an NIC must be unique. You have to watch for potential address conflicts and steer around them, and you typically use jumpers to set the base memory address. Common settings for network cards include C000h, D000h, and D800h.

baseline Gives you a snapshot of the network to establish what normal activity patterns look like. It involves capturing statistics that describe how the network is being used throughout the course of a normal working day.

bindery A database that NetWare v3.*x* uses that contains information about the users, groups, and other devices on the LAN, such as printers. Like some people and their Day-Timers, if they lose them, they just cannot cope.

BNC The BNC connector, which has a great deal of weird lore behind it, is simply the type of connector that thin Ethernet networks use to attach the media to the NIC.

boot What you do to your workstation when you turn it on or to the server when you load SERVER.EXE.

buffer space NICs contain their own RAM to provide working space for information coming on and off the network. It's called buffer space because it provides room for incoming and outgoing data to be stored.

bus A network topology type in which all computers are attached to a single, shared cable. A bus topology is most commonly used for Ethernet networks or other contention-based networking schemes.

cache Squirrels cache nuts so that they can eat them in the winter. Like the expansive pouches in a squirrel's mouth, NetWare stores data in caches so that it can get to it quickly later. Ick!

CAPTURE A NetWare print utility that redirects local printer ports to network printers.

CD-ROM A device similar to the one at home that plays Allanis Morrisett, but it's less inflammatory. It just stores data that you think is important enough to save.

client A desktop machine is called a client on the network, or simply a client. Calling it a *desktop* focuses on its role in supporting an individual, who typically is working at a desk; calling it a *client* focuses on its network connection. Whatever you call it, it's still the same thing: the machine you sit in front of when you're working.

coaxial cable A two-element cable, with a center conductor wrapped by an insulator, which is wrapped by an outer conductor that is typically a wire braid covered by still more insulation. Coaxial cable (or *coax,* as it prefers to be known) is used for cable TV. Even if you don't think that you know what it is, you probably can relate to cable TV.

communications Communications establish the rules for the way computers talk to each other or what things mean.

compression A mathematical technique for analyzing computer files to squeeze them down to a smaller size. A feature of most backup systems, compression is also available in NetWare 4.*x,* which can compress files stored on the file server. According to Novell, this kind of file compression can result in an increase in storage capacity that is better than two to one.

concentrator Applies directly to Ethernet, where it concentrates a number of workstations so that they share the same path to the file server. A concentrator is typically composed of 8 or 12 ports into which workstations attach along their own media segments.

CONFIG.SYS See your DOS manual for an explanation (this is a NetWare book).

connection number When a device logs in to the file server, it is given a connection number, which then identifies that device's ongoing network session, as a way of directing replies back to satisfy its requests for network services.

connections Include the physical pieces of gear needed to hook up a computer to the network and the wires or other materials — known as the *networking medium* — used to carry messages from one computer to another or among multiple computers.

console The monitor attached to the file server. You can access the console remotely with RCONSOLE or across a modem line with ACONSOLE. Either way, you get to it, and if you're the only SUPERVISOR, no one else can. Special NetWare commands called *console commands* are run from the server keyboard.

console operator This dude has the authority to use the file server console.

containers and container objects Just like that storage area behind the stairs, similar objects are organized into containers in NetWare 4.*x* Directory Services.

contexts In NetWare 4.*x,* each object has a context that identifies its location in the directory tree. An object's context is important; taken out of context, it has no meaning.

conventional memory The memory below 640K. Normally, your LAN drivers are loaded in this space if you have room.

crash See *abend,* not the Highway Patrol.

DAT Stands for *d*igital *a*udio *t*ape; a special kind of 4mm-wide recording tape used in some computer backup systems. **Note:** Even though computer backup tape and audio recording tape are the same format and size, the two are usually quite different from each other. This means that you should not use an audio tape to back up your network. (Even though you can use a computer tape to record Pearl Jam, computer-grade tape costs so much more than audio-grade tape that you probably can't afford it.)

dedicated server A PC you cannot use to type a letter, play a computer game, or run any programs directly on the keyboard and monitor. In other words, a PC at which you cannot sit down and perform useful work directly. Most network operating systems require their servers to be dedicated PCs. NetWare v3.11 and 4.*x* require dedicated servers.

default drive The drive in which you are placed when you log in to the network. The drive letter most commonly used for the login drive is F:, it probably maps to something like SERVER\SYS:\USERS\HORACE — that is, if your name is Horace (although the server's name is probably not SERVER).

default server If the default drive is the one you log in to, what do you think the default server is? If your file server is the only file server on the LAN, it is also the default server. More tough questions to come.

digital signature NetWare 4.*x* locks up the gates tight against intruders. Users enter their passwords just like in NetWare v3.*x*, but in 4.*x*, the password is joined to a encrypted key that allows the server to decide if the workstation should have network access or not. The password is never transmitted across the network, thereby foiling thieves with snooping devices.

directory Similar to the Yellow Pages. Even though directories are not alphabetical, they organize the files on a file server volume. Not to be confused with the NetWare Directory maintained by NetWare Directory Services on 4.*x*-numbered versions of NetWare.

directory entry Every file on the system has a directory entry. If your system gets clobbered, NetWare uses the Directory Entry Table to reconstruct it.

disk duplexing Not only mirrors the drives but also provides the capability to use totally backed up and redundant disk controllers. *Disk controllers* are the adapter cards that make the drive go round. With disk duplexing, you have redundancy of most of the critical moving parts inside your server. We always use disk duplexing and strongly suggest that you do, too, whenever your budget permits. Duplexing beats having spare controllers and hard drives in stock because it doesn't require you to bring the server down immediately to make repairs. You have the luxury of postponing repairs until a more convenient time for both you and your users.

disk mirroring A process in which you can install duplicate hard drives, one active and one backup, which NetWare then writes to simultaneously. If a crash or other problem occurs on the active drive, NetWare automatically begins to use the backup drive and notifies you of the switch.

disk subsystem A fancy name for some extra storage on your file server.

DMA (*direct memory access*) DMA works by matching up two areas of memory, one on the computer and the other on the NIC. Writing to the memory area on the computer automatically causes that data to get copied to the NIC, and vice versa. To set a DMA address means to find an unoccupied DMA memory block to assign to your NIC.

drive mapping When you map a drive, you give the system instructions so that you can find it fast. Most users have mappings to their default directories, to their MAIL directories, and to the PUBLIC directory.

driver The guy behind the wheel of a LAN adapter.

EISA A type of PC bus with a 32-bit wheelbase — er, make that data path. (We're writing a car-repair manual on the side.)

Ethernet Everyone's all-time favorite network-access method.

EVERYONE A group created automatically when NetWare 3.*x* is installed. EVERYONE is a good catch-all group in which you can put everyone who should have the same access to all the same applications.

FAT An abbreviation for *file allocation table*; a list of all the pieces of disk storage space that make up a file, for each and every file on the NetWare server. DOS also uses a FAT-based file system, but it's considerably less sophisticated and powerful than NetWare's.

FDDI The Fiber Distributed Data Interface, a 100-Mbps network-access method. It's very fast, but very expensive, so you probably won't see it on your desktop any time soon.

fiber-optic cable This type of cable is built around conductive elements that move light, not electricity. For most fiber-optic cables, the conductive element is most likely a form of special glass fiber rather than copper or some other conductive metal. Even though plastic-based fiber-optic cable is available, it's not as light-conductive as glass and cannot cover the long distances that glass can. The beauty of fiber-optic cable is that it's immune to electronic and magnetic interference and has tons more bandwidth than do most electrical cable types.

file server The device on a network that services requests from the workstations.

file system The way in which the network operating system handles and stores files.

FILER NetWare's built-in file- and directory-management tool, available to both end users and administrators. You can use it to move, delete, or rename files and directories, to review attributes and rights, and to navigate around the file structures on NetWare servers.

FLAG or FLAGDIR FLAGDIR does for directories what FLAG does for files: lets their owners change access and trustee rights for particular files and directories without having to change inherited rights. You use this command to make a single file available to other users, for example, without giving access to all files or directories in any portion of your directory structure.

FTP The TCP/IP protocol suite includes a file-transfer program named FTP (for file-transfer protocol), which can copy files between any two TCP/IP-equipped computers.

gateway An electronic or software device that connects two or more dissimilar computer systems. For example, a NetWare-to-IBM-mainframe gateway takes the IPX from one side of the gateway and translates it to the SNA protocol required for some IBM mainframe communications. Gateways are becoming more common as vendors figure out how to make this computer talk to that computer.

grafting This is what occurs in NetWare 4.*x* when you run the DSMERGE utility to graft the contents of one directory tree on to another.

grandfather-father-son This term does have something to do with inheritance. GFS is a tape-rotation method for network backup in which 20 tapes are used. Four of those tapes are used to back up daily work (Monday through Thursday). Three tapes back up work done on the first three Fridays of the month. The fourth week, you use one of the 13 "grandfathers" (monthly tapes). Because a year has 13 four-week intervals, this rotation method keeps tapes circulating regularly and ensures that none of them gets too much wear.

GUEST You know what this term means — you have to be polite and follow the rules because your visit to the network is only temporary.

HCSS Stands for High-Capacity Storage System. Part of NetWare 4.*x*, HCSS lets NetWare administrators "migrate" less frequently accessed data from a server's hard drive to some kind of alternative storage medium, typically a rewritable magneto-optical drive. Because these types of media are removable and have large capacities but can retrieve data nearly as fast as conventional disk drives, we call this type of storage *near-line*. In contrast, the server hard drives contain online files that are available almost instantly. When a user requests a file that is stored on the near-line system, it first must be copied back from that system to the server's hard drive before it can be accessed (a "reverse migration" process). Like file compression, the least active server files can be migrated automatically to optical disk according to a selectable "age" threshold, based on the date of most recent access.

HELP What you call for when you cannot find the explanation in this book.

intruder Anyone trying to break in to the LAN, no matter what his or her intentions. An intruder may be your boss who's trying to break into your directories to read your latest invective against him, or someone from outside who's trying to steal company secrets. Most of the time, such people are just doltish — in NetWare, you can usually find a way to catch them.

intruder detection The series of measures that you can put in place by way of SYSCON. Lets you find the people who are trying to break into the LANs or put their paws on information to which they don't have access.

I/O address Every card in a system has its own I/O address, in which certain addresses are reserved for some interfaces, especially video cards. NICs aren't quite that picky and can typically get an I/O port address assigned from a reserved range of addresses. An I/O port gets set up to let the computer read from or write to memory that belongs to an interface. When an interrupt gets signaled, it tells the computer to read from the I/O port address, indicating incoming data. When the computer wants to send data, it signals the NIC to get ready to receive, and it writes to that address.

IP The Internet Protocol in the TCP/IP protocol suite, IP does what IPX does in NetWare — it sets up the mechanism for transferring data across the network.

IPX (Internetwork Packet eXchange) The NetWare transport protocol.

IPX.COM The file *is* IPX.

ISA A bus of the 16-bit kind used in AT-class computers.

ISO/OSI Not a cruel technician's idea of a nifty palindrome — it stands for the International Standards Organization's Open Systems Interconnect family of networking protocols. Although it was highly touted as the successor to TCP/IP and the next big "networking thing," OSI has yet to live up to its promise. Because most governments — including Uncle Sam — require systems to be OSI-compliant, a good bit of it is still out there in industry, government, business, and academia. Like TCP/IP, ISO/OSI is available for a broad range of systems, from PCs to supercomputers.

LAN A *local area network*. See also *network*.

LAN driver Like gas to a car, the LAN driver supplies the get-up-and-go and the brains for the NIC.

LARCHIVE A DOS command-line backup utility that backs up network drives to local drives or disks.

leaf object The directory in NetWare 4.*x* assumes the design of a tree. It has roots, branches, and leaf objects. Leaf objects are the end point of the tree — they can't contain any other objects and only represent themselves. Users, volumes, servers, and printers are all leaf objects.

log out What you do when you check out from the LAN.

LOGIN The LOGIN command, well, logs you in.

login script A file that can exist either individually for each user or that can serve all users. It contains commands that control the way a user views the desktop. Users can create and edit their own login scripts. Only the supervisor can create and edit the System Login script.

LOGOUT The logout command orders your breakfast and a newspaper from room service. Oops! Sorry, that's the CHECKOUT command. Actually, LOGOUT just logs you out of the network.

loopback test Often a part of a vendor's board diagnostics. Running a loopback test tells a NIC to talk to itself to see whether it's working. From an electronic standpoint, this test exercises circuitry on the card all the way up to the actual network medium interface to the login.

media filter Used with the token-ring access method to change the type of media used from Type 1 (shielded twisted-pair) to Type 3 (unshielded twisted-pair) or vice versa.

Micro Channel Another 32-bit bus used most commonly in IBM PS/2s and IBM-controlled workplaces.

name space Each time you want to add a different type of machine, such as a Macintosh, an OS/2-based machine, or a UNIX-based machine, you have to provide for file compatibility with NetWare. You do this through name spaces loaded on the file server as NLMs that regulate the cross-network conversion that has to take place.

NCP See *NetWare Core Protocol.*

NetBEUI Stands for *NetBIOS Extended User Interface* and was designed as a second-generation protocol especially to support NetBIOS-based communications. You can call NetBIOS and NetBEUI a matched set — that's what Microsoft and IBM use for their networking products.

NetBIOS Stands for *Networked Basic Input-Output System* and was designed by IBM as a networked extension to PC BIOS. NetBIOS is a higher-level protocol that runs on top of lots of lower-level protocols, including IPX and TCP/IP as well as others. Even though NetBIOS is pretty old, it's very easy to program with and consequently is used in lots of different networked applications on a broad range of computers and operating systems.

NetWare Core Protocol (NCP) An NCP is the service protocol for NetWare. Virtually every service that NetWare can provide has a NCP used to let users send requests for that service and to start the process of delivering in response to that request. The services provided by the NetWare NCPs range from file transfer to directory services lookups.

NetWare Directory Services (NDS) NDS is NetWare's entry to joining lots of LANs together without users getting lost. It consists of a database that contains all the users, equipment, storage, and other entities on the network. In NDS, users can locate network resources without knowing where they are physically at.

NetWare Loadable Module (NLM) A program loaded at the file server. NLMs can be LAN drivers, backup applications, or utilities.

NetWire Doves communicate by billing and cooing. NetWare geeks communicate with each other by way of NetWire, Novell's online service on CompuServe.

network A collection of at least two computers linked together so that they can communicate with each other. Imagine — such a simple concept.

network interface card The gear that hooks up a computer to a network and acts as an intermediary between the computer and the network is called the network interface. (For PCs, it typically comes in the form of an add-in board called a network interface card, or NIC.)

network operating system The network's main control program is called its operating system because it's the program that lets the network operate.

node Any device on the network. It can be a workstation, a printer, or the file server.

non-container objects In NetWare Directory Services, a non-container object does not include other objects. It represents real-world objects like users.

Novell-certified The Novell program that says, "Yes, it undoubtedly works with NetWare." Getting devices certified costs the vendors money, but many vendors certify their devices to keep their users happy. Neat, huh? Someone's watching out for you!

object A directory map object enables the network administrator to define map commands that point to an object rather than to a specific directory on the server. If the path to that object ever changes, you have to update only the object definition, not all of your user's MAP commands.

object classes Everyone is governed by rules. In NetWare 4.*x*, the rules for a certain type of object are called an object class.

ODI The Open Datalink Interface specification. Novell prefers that you say "oh-dee-eye," not "Odie," like the dog in the Garfield comic strip. Originally, the specification's moniker was ODLI, but it sounded strange ("odd-ly") when you said it that way. ODI is a specification for writing LAN drivers that saves vendors from work and gives users a certain comfort level that their ODI drivers will work in a predictable way.

password The LAN's equivalent to "open sesame." NetWare lets users have passwords that range in length from 1 to 127 alphanumeric characters. Passwords aren't mandatory, but you use them to log on to most networks. We don't recommend the use of overly long passwords (more than 12 to 15 characters is too difficult to remember).

peer-to-peer A method of networking that NetWare Lite and Personal NetWare use to share local resources across the network. A server-based network requires all shared resources to reside on a centralized server. A peer-to-peer network gives everyone on the network the opportunity to share the local stuff with others on the network.

print queue NetWare uses print queues to store pending print jobs, in the form of print-image files, while they wait their turn to be printed. The queue is the mechanism that handles requests for printing from users and that supplies the print-image files to the printer in the proper order. See also *queue.*

print server The device or software that controls network printing and services printing requests.

properties John has blue eyes. John works in sales. John is the sales manager. The object "John" has properties in NetWare 4.*x.*

protocol In diplomacy, refers to the rules for behavior that let representatives from sovereign governments communicate with each other in a way calculated to keep things peaceful, or at least under control. For that reason, diplomats refer to heated screaming matches as "frank and earnest discussions" or to insoluble disagreements as "exploratory dialogue." Double-talk aside, the word *protocol* captures the flavor of what these sets of rules have to do for networks. Most networking protocols consist of a named collection of specific message formats and rules for interaction rather than a single set of formats and rules. For this reason, protocols are also called *protocol suites,* not because they like to lounge around on matched collections of furniture, but because they travel in packs.

QIC Stands for Quarter-Inch Cartridge, a common format for backup tapes.

queue The British word for *line.* When several people share a printer, NetWare creates a queue to store print jobs waiting for that printer. Each printer has its own print queue. As the server sends print jobs to the printer, Lite lines them up in a manner similar to a queue forming outside a British privy. Jobs print in the order in which the queue receives them. This system means that the printer doesn't have to be available at the time that you ask to print something. The print queues accept any and all print requests as they occur and then lines up all print jobs for printing as the printer becomes available.

redirector (or **requester**) A piece of software that looks at each request for service from a user. If the request can be satisfied locally, this software passes that request on to the local PC's operating system for it to be handled. If the request cannot be handled locally, the request is assumed to be directed to the network, and the redirector then passes the request on to a service provider (also known as a *server*) on the network. Using a redirector is a pretty common way to handle network access from a desktop.

replication In NetWare 4.*x,* replication refers to portions of the server or partitions copied to other servers.

ring Token-ring uses the ring or star-wired ring topology. Real rings seldom get built because they're too sensitive to failure, but the idea of a ring often gets implemented over a bus or a star, or in the form of a redundant ring with multiple cables and pathways to improve the odds that it keeps running. Mapping a ring onto a star or a bus sounds strange, but that's how some networking technologies work.

RIP The Routing Information Protocol is a broadcast protocol (it's addressed to everyone who's listening on a network) that gets used one time per minute by every IPX router on a network to declare what it knows about how to get around on the network. (For NetWare v3.11 or higher, any server can be a router.) Routers exchange RIP packets to keep the common knowledge of how a collection of individual networks — called an *internetwork* — is laid out. This information is used to move packets around, which is why the servers that do it are called *routers.*

SAP Service Advertising Protocols advertise the services that are available on the network. SAP is a broadcast protocol, and each server sends out its collection of SAPs one time per minute in versions of NetWare before 4.*x.* In NetWare 4.*x,* the number of SAPs can be adjusted.

SBACKUP SBACKUP works with both NetWare 4.*x* and v3.11. As a server-based backup system, it can handle DOS, Macintosh, OS/2, and NFS files on workstations or on the server's hard disk. SBACKUP works with a NetWare Loadable Module (NLM) called the TSA.NLM to see that data on a "target" is backed up. The target can be another file server or workstation on the LAN. In case you haven't guessed already, SBACKUP beats the pants off NBACKUP. To run the program, the SUPERVISOR starts SBACKUP from the file server console.

schema The master set of rules that govern the type of objects in the NetWare 4.*x* directory is called the schema.

SCSI SCSI, pronounced *scuzzy,* isn't an alternative form of grunge. It's an interface in the computer to which you can attach almost anything, but mostly you attach disk drives.

search drive Not a charity drive for misplaced things, but rather a drive mapping you set so that you can find files from any drive that you are in. Typically, users have search drives mapped to the PUBLIC directory and to any other directories in which applications may be stored. That way, they're always able to run their applications and the NetWare commands and utilities, no matter what their current default drive.

security-equivalent Means that one account has the same trustee and access rights as another. Although users can confer security-equivalence on each other, this technique is most commonly used as a way for the SUPERVISOR to temporarily turn another account into a SUPERVISOR-equivalent. This capability lets other users function as SUPERVISOR without letting them learn the supervisor's password.

SEND This command sends the included text to a user or to everyone on your network. Use the ALL option with discretion because it does what it says — sends it to everyone.

server You don't leave tips for servers. They serve low-fat, no-calorie requests to clients, and the only weight they cause you to gain is the amount of information that you save in your user directory. Sometimes, when you have too much information, you must purge some of it from the server.

SERVER.EXE Everything has to start from somewhere. The SERVER.EXE file loads the network operating system software on the file server. Naturally.

SETPASS Enables you to set a new password for yourself but for no one else.

SFT III This product is Novell's latest development in server redundancy (Novell calls it system fault tolerance). SFT III is a copy of version 3.11 that mirrors the entire server PC to another PC. Server mirroring gives you the ultimate backup plan — if any hardware component in the active server fails, the other machine automatically takes over without any interruption of service. A dedicated network connects the two servers, usually over fiber-optics, and keeps both servers in sync. Granted, this solution can be expensive but is well worth the cost for truly mission-critical environments.

shell Sometimes you use this type of special program so that you can get the network going and run the programs you're really interested in using. The shell handles all service requests, and, rather than pass along things that aren't local to the network, the way a redirector does, it separates what's networked from what's not and hands things off accordingly. It, too, is a pretty common way to handle network access from a desktop (not to mention that when you put your ear up to it, you can hear the ocean).

shielded twisted-pair Not an armored couple into heavy-metal music, but rather a type of twisted-pair cable used in Ethernet networks that has a cladding around the conductive copper core.

SMS Stands for Storage Management Services, which is the Novell backup system interface. SMS automatically handles all the details that make up the NetWare file system, including name spaces, so that Novell can change its file system. SMS hides the impact, however, so that SMS-compliant backup systems can keep right on working. For this reason, we recommend that you consider purchasing only those NetWare backup systems that are SMS-compliant.

SNA Systems Network Architecture is IBM's basic protocol suite. Where you find a mainframe or an AS/400, you also typically find SNA. Because SNA was one of the pioneering protocols, companies that invested heavily in mainframe technology in the 1960s and 1970s also invested in building large-scale SNA networks.

SPX A guaranteed-delivery protocol that NetWare occasionally uses.

star A type of networking topology; consists of separate wires that run from a central point (called a *hub* 'cause it's in the middle) to devices — typically, computers — on the other end of each wire.

STARTUP.NCF This file resides on the file server and is integral to bringing up the file server.

station Short for workstation.

SUPERVISOR The big kahuna. This guy is in charge.

synchronization Each server or partition contains a replica of the directory. When something on the network changes, these replicas must get into synch. The process is called *replication*.

SYS:LOGIN The directory you use to log in to the network.

SYS:MAIL The directory that serves the same purpose as the circular file in your office. Mail is stored here after it's sent. Even though most of the stuff in this directory is ancient history, don't delete it — it's where your login script is kept.

SYS:PUBLIC The directory in NetWare Heavy that contains all the programs that are public (any user can get his hands on it).

SYS:SYSTEM The directory in which the server stores files necessary for server upkeep and administration as well as some utilities intended for use by only the network supervisor and supervisor equivalents.

sysop An abbreviation for *system op*erator, who is typically the person responsible for coordinating traffic and for answering questions on an online bulletin-board or electronic information system. The ladies and gentlemen who field NetWare questions on CompuServe's Novell-related forums — known collectively as NetWire — are the people we mean when we talk about sysops in this book.

system administrator The big kahuna in NetWare. This guy wins and controls all the marbles, but he's also responsible for keeping the servers and the network up and running.

T-connector Not a coffee-and-tea exchange — this device lets you connect a BNC connector to the media for a workstation in the middle of an Ethernet bus.

TCP/IP The real name of this protocol suite is the Transmission Control Protocol and the Internet Protocol. Because the Internet is composed of more than 9 million sites worldwide and TCP/IP claims more than 25 million users, TCP/IP is another major player in the protocol world. TCP/IP has deep roots in the UNIX community and is also widely used to link computers of different kinds.

telnet The name of a standard TCP/IP network service, which lets one computer pretend that it's a terminal attached to another computer over the network. Telnet is the way that TCP/IP users typically work on other computers over the network, when they're not working directly on their own machines.

thick Ethernet See *10BASE-5*.

thin Ethernet See *10BASE-2*.

throughput A measure of the speed of a network-access method, typically stated in bps (bits per second).

time synchronization In NetWare Directory Services, servers can't go on Daylight Saving Time. Time synchronization watches for computer time that drifts to the left or right.

token Similar to a marker on a poker table, it indicates who has the deal or which workstation can send data on a token ring, ARCnet, or FDDI network.

token ring Another one of the access methods, token ring is a networking technology that tells a workstation when it can send data over the network, by using a circulating token to grant permission. Token ring communicates at either 4 Mbps or 16 Mbps.

topology The lay of the LAN, or how workstations are laid out and connected with the file server by way of the media. See also *bus, star,* and *ring* if you want the details.

transaction tracking Databases use transaction tracking in NetWare to guarantee the integrity of the data. If someone trips over the server's power cord, transaction tracking rolls back individual transactions to the state they were in before the system crash occurred.

transceiver Using a transceiver is similar to pouring water from a pitcher into a soda bottle. It enables you to connect a network adapter for one type of media to another type of media. Commonly, you use a transceiver in Ethernet to translate from thin Ethernet to unshielded twisted-pair. In token ring, a media filter replaces the transceiver.

tree The NetWare Directory Services hierarchy is called a tree. Directory branches come off the root; leaf objects adorn the end of branches.

tree-walking In a telephone directory, you look up people by name. In NetWare 4.*x*, you do it by tree-walking, which finds the object's physical location. It seems like a perilous sport, but climbing the directory tree often is. At least it's a lofty specialization.

twisted-pair TP comes in two flavors: shielded and unshielded. It sometimes is abbreviated as STP for shielded twisted-pair and UTP for unshielded twisted-pair. The difference between the two, of course, is that one has a foil or wire braid wrap around the individual wires that are twisted around each other in pairs, and the other does not.

unshielded twisted-pair Same as twisted-pair except that it has no shielding element between the conducting strands and the outer insulator.

UPS (*U*ninterruptible *P*ower *S*upply) Contains a rechargeable battery that provides your server with a backup power source in case its A/C power fails. The UPS senses that A/C power has gone away, and it kicks in automatically to supply power to your server on a few milliseconds' notice.

user You guessed it — this is you. It could be someone else, too, but you get the idea.

user account Keeps you in control or lets you get in trouble on your LAN, depending on whether the supervisor has it in for you.

username This is you, or you, or you. It's your name on the system. Ours are DCONNOR and ETITTEL. See also *user*.

workstation Where you sit whether you're just a lowly user or the big cheese.

WORM This thing isn't segmented, long, narrow, and slimy. It stands for *w*rite *o*nce, *r*ead *m*any, and describes a type of optical-storage technology.

volume NetWare divides the file server disks into areas called volumes, which are logical, or nonphysical, divisions of hard disk space.

XNS NetWare's protocols are derived from a similar protocol set developed at Xerox, called the Xerox Networking System and abbreviated as XNS. Lots of XNS-derived protocols are out there in the networking world, but IPX/SPX is the most prevalent.

Appendix B

Screaming for Help: When and How to Get It

● ●

*W*hen you need help with the network or the software that runs on it, you can get it if you know the right steps to take. Getting the support most vendors supply shouldn't be like pulling teeth — if you know how to ask for and get the answers you need, it can be considerably more pleasant than that!

In this appendix, we focus on how best to interact with technical-support organizations. We tell you how to be effective when you work with these groups, from the standpoint of how to prepare to meet their needs and how to work with them so that they can answer your questions. And we explain what kind of help you can expect to get from these groups and how to handle the situation if your expectations aren't met.

Building a list and checking it twice

When you are organizing any network or the applications running on it, keep a list of the equipment you own (build a map and configuration database, as outlined in Chapter 6). You can do this with a variety of inventory packages, but often just plain paper and pencil are enough. Mapping your network is a boring, repetitive task, but it's critically important. It's similar to trying to collect insurance after your house burns down, without having a list of what was inside.

Record each of the network adapters on your LAN, the type of file server you use, information about each workstation, and which applications each user runs. The following list shows the kind of equipment and software you should inventory:

- ✔ Cable plant (type, length, location, end-labels)
- ✔ File server
- ✔ Workstations

> ✔ Software running on each workstation
>
> ✔ Tape-backup unit
>
> ✔ Disk storage

Know your vital stats

For your file server, you have to know its vital statistics. You have to know how much RAM it has, how much disk space, the type of network adapters it contains, which type of disk controller it uses, and which type of display. Record this information for your file server. Fill in the following blanks and save the information somewhere where you can find it when you need it.

File server

File server manufacturer: _____

File server model: _____

Processor (286, 386, 486, Pentium, PowerPC)

Processor speed (25 MHz, 33 MHz, 50 MHz, 66 MHz 100 MHz): _____

Bus type (ISA, EISA, Micro Channel, PCI,VLB): _____

Type of disk controller (SCSI, IDE, MFM): _____

Drive manufacturer: _____

Drive model: _____

Drive capacity (in megabytes): _____

Disk drives: _____

Other stuff: _____

_____

Display

Display manufacturer: _____

Display type (monochrome, CGA, VGA, SVGA): _____

Network adapter

Network adapter manufacturer: _____

Type of adapter (Ethernet, token ring, and so on): _____

Model number: _____

Interrupt set at: _____

DMA set at: _____

Speed set at (if token ring): _____

Base memory address: _____

Network adapter (for more than one)

Network adapter manufacturer: _____

Type of adapter (Ethernet, token ring, and so on): _____

Model number: _____

Interrupt set at: _____

DMA set at: _____

I/0 port address set at: _____

Speed set at (if token ring): _____

Base memory address: _____

_____

(continued)

Base memory address: _____

Display resolution: _____

Interrupt set at: _____

Storage and RAM

Base memory address: _____

Amount of RAM (in megabytes): _____

Amount of disk storage (in megabytes): _____

_____

_____

Base memory address: _____

_____

Tape backup manufacturer: _____

Tape backup model: _____

Tape drive firmware level: _____

Tape backup type (QIC, DAT, 8mm): _____

Tape backup capacity: _____

Location of off-site storage: _____

Location of on-site storage: _____

_____

Version of DOS: _____

Version of NetWare: _____

Network adapter (for more than two)

Network adapter manufacturer: _____

Type of adapter (Ethernet, token ring, and so on):

Model number: _____

Interrupt set at: _____

DMA set at: _____

Speed set at (if token ring): _____

Applications: _____

Version: _____

_____

Applications: _____

Version: _____

_____

Applications: _____

Version: _____

_____

NLMs loaded: _____

Other stuff: _____

Other stuff: _____

Now you need to make the same kind of record for each workstation on the LAN (lucky for you, most workstations have only a single NIC). While you're at it, add to the list the contents of the workstation's configuration files (for DOS/ Windows 3.*x* this would be AUTOEXEC.BAT and CONFIG.SYS files, plus WIN.INI and SYSTEM.INI). Are you getting tired yet?

After you finish these lists, you want to know more about the software configuration of the LAN. You need a listing of your server's AUTOEXEC.NCF and STARTUP.NCF files, and you have to put together lists of the following items as well:

- ✔ Usernames on the LAN and their network addresses
- ✔ Groups on the LAN
- ✔ File and directory attributes and rights for each user and group
- ✔ All loaded modules (with dates and versions) and all patches appplied
- ✔ Application structure, as managed by the NetWare Application Launcher

- ✔ Directory structure of the file server
- ✔ Drive mappings
- ✔ System login script

When you encounter a problem, document what happened before the problem occurred. List any changes you have made to files or any hardware changes you have made. Write down any error messages you have received. Know what you were doing when the problem occurred. Trust us: When you call the technical-support number, you will be asked for this information.

Talk the talk, walk the walk

Now that you have all your vital network information written down, when something goes wrong, you're ready to combat the vendor's technical-support line. When you make the call, have your ammunition ready, but be prepared for one of five things to happen:

1. You sit on *hold* trying to get through to tech support for what seems like forever, and when you do get through, it's only to leave voice mail in the hopes that they'll call back before your users lynch you.

2. You are told that it is an operator error. *Operator error* is a catchall term that technical-support people use when someone has made a mistake, but it can also come up when they don't want to deal with the question or when they don't have the answer.

3. You are told that no one in anyone's lifetime has ever done anything this stupid. Hold your ground. Even if you've pioneered new realms of the absurd, it's still the responsibility of the technical-support person to help you out of it.

4. The person you talk to doesn't have the answer to the problem but has someone else get back to you to solve the problem.

5. A nice person on the telephone helps you work through the problem.

Before you call, gather your lists together. Better yet, get close to the PC that is having problems so that you can lead the person through the problem by telling him about error messages you have received (by trying to duplicate the problem, for example).

Escalation

If you get someone on the phone who doesn't want to help, act just as you do when you have a problem with your electric bill. Ask to speak to a supervisor — in the lingo of the business, this is called escalating the call. After all, you paid good money for the product and you should get satisfaction.

The same rule applies to technical-support people who don't call you back in a timely manner — 24 hours after your call should be the absolute drop-dead time for a return call. Call again and leave a message. Record the time you first called. Record how long it took someone to call you back and keep good records. This is one time when a little documentation can come in handy.

Some vendors are starting to offer technical support 24 hours a day, seven days a week. When you buy products, find out about the technical-support line. Paying a little more initially to have good support afterward may be worth the money.

Twenty-four-hour support is critical for network hardware. No one in her right mind takes down the LAN during working hours to insert a new network adapter in the server. Think about it: If you're required to miss dinner, the person on the other end of the phone should be expected to miss it, too.

800-NETWARE and 900-SUPPORT

We hate companies with cute phone numbers, but at least we remember them — they're just a pain to dial. These two numbers are for the Novell customer service department (800-NETWARE, or 800-638-9273) and a separate for-hire technical-support company (900-SUPPORT, or 900-787-7678). Novell can help you with questions about NetWare directly, but you must be ready with a credit-card number or support-contract information; 900-SUPPORT takes questions of any kind. Both cost a pretty penny, so have your credit card handy (neither takes checks).

One-stop shopping: The TSA

In 1992, Novell organized the Technical Support Alliance (TSA) to provide better support for users. The TSA, a group of 42 vendors, cross-train each other in the use of their products. When you call a TSA member about a problem that may involve several vendors' products, you can get an answer from that vendor with just one phone call. Sounds neat, huh? Take our word for it — it is neat!

AppNotes and other goodies

The AppNotes are what everybody calls the Novell monthly publication, officially known as Novell Application Notes. This publication can provide in-depth information about a variety of topics for computer geeks who are heavily into NetWare. Call 800-NETWARE to find out more information and have your checkbook ready, too. These notes cost about $150 a year for a subscription, but they're really worth it.

For our money, another great reason to upgrade to NetWare 4.*x* is the new, improved search engine that comes with the online documentation. By using keyword searches, you can find — and get right to — help that you never dreamed existed. Now you can just enter the text for that mysterious error message and find out exactly what it means.

Lookee Louie, I'm with NUI

If you're really getting into this NetWare stuff, look into joining a NetWare user group. Organized under NetWare Users International, a group affiliated with Novell, you can find out about a group in your area by calling the universal NetWare number: 800-NETWARE.

Let your fingers do the walking

Other places exist to get help when you're really out on a limb. One of these is NetWire, Novell's online information service on CompuServe, which we cover in Appendix C along with Internet resources. Aside from the online information services, many companies also operate their own bulletin board systems, on which you can leave questions or get copies of new adapter drivers, bug fixes, and other stuff. If you have a modem, communications software, and sufficient time, you can find out more about anything that's related to networking.

Booking in the fast lane

Books that explain technical networking stuff are also available, as are classes in which you learn more about NetWare than you ever wanted to know. Look in networking magazines for NetWare training and education centers in your city. Check the computer and networking magazines, and look around in your local bookstore: You can find more information than you ever thought possible.

The masters program

Having gone through training classes, you may also decide that you want to be a certified NetWare administrator (CNA), a certified NetWare engineer (CNE), or perhaps even a Master CNE (MCNE). If you're simply a user on the LAN, none of these credentials is for you. If you're responsible for a LAN, however, you should consider one of these certifications. The CNA covers the administration of the LAN and involves taking several courses and passing tests. The CNE is for people who not only cope with the software (creating users, for example), but also work with the network hardware. The Master CNE program offers specialization in network management, infrastructure and advanced access, or groupware integration. The CNE and MCNE are for those types who consider NetWare system management a career. (Strike that thought!)

Appendix C

An Incredibly Concise Guide to Online NetWare Information

• •

*T*his appendix focuses on the voluminous amount of NetWare information and support available on the Internet and on NetWire, the collection of Novell forums on CompuServe. We show you how to find the right information and support you need to make your NetWare network a success. We also tell you the limits of what you can expect to find online and when you'd be better off getting direct phone support for your NetWare problems. The explosive growth of the Internet and World Wide Web sites has caused Novell (and almost every other major computer manufacturer) to concentrate their support efforts in the open environment of the Internet, as opposed to proprietary online systems like America Online (AOL) and CompuServe. Though there are still times when using CompuServe instead of the Internet is appropriate, this appendix definitely favors the Internet because we see it as the platform of choice for NetWare service and support.

Enter the Internet

When there's more than one of something, competition is bound to exist. NetWire forums on CompuServe used to be the only place to get timely and accurate technical support information. Not so, anymore. Though Novell still offers official service and support information in the NetWire forums on CompuServe, we see the future of Novell's online support being the Novell Web site, `http://www.novell.com`. Fortunately for those of you that only have a CompuServe account, all NetWare files, press releases, and technical documentation from Novell are now available on both the Novell Web site and the NetWire forums. CompuServe also offers a gateway to the Internet through your existing CompuServe account. We must warn you that accessing the Internet through CompuServe is both slower and more expensive than acquiring an Internet account directly with an Internet Service Provider, or ISP.

A number of Internet Web sites besides `www.novell.com` contain NetWare information and support files. Numerous discussion groups on Usenet Newsgroups, the Internet equivalent of NetWire help forums, also exist.

Through these groups, you can ask NetWare-related questions and get answers from the real NetWare support staff, other users around the world who have learned the secrets of NetWare via the school of hard knocks. We assume for the sake of this discussion that you already know the basics of Internet navigation and that you know how to configure a news reader for Usenet Newsgroups.

www.novell.com: The Novell Web Server at Your Service

World Wide Web sites tend to be dynamic by their very nature. So we can't guarantee that the Novell Web page we saw when we were writing this appendix is still intact. Rest assured that, though some of the details may change with time, you'll always be able to get product information, search the numerous Novell Web pages, and search the Novell KnowledgeBase for technical information. Here are the current choices available to you when you arrive at www.novell.com:

- ✔ **Networking Products:** The current crop of Novell product offerings

- ✔ **Solutions Showcase:** White papers and case studies of successful NetWare implementations

- ✔ **Technical Support:** Search for files updates and technical support documents, explore job opportunities in Novell Technical Support, and explore the different support options offered by Novell

- ✔ **Training and Certification:** Find out how to become a certified NetWare engineer or instructor; locate the Novell authorized education center nearest you

- ✔ **DeveloperNet Services:** Everything you ever wanted to know about developing NetWare applications

- ✔ **Other features:** Provides numerous other small links to job openings at Novell and locations for Novell's world-wide sales offices, searches the entire Novell Web site, offers Novell Press and online manuals for Novell products

Do You Know about the KnowledgeBase?

In our humble opinion, one of the most useful and used areas of the Novell Web site is the KnowledgeBase search. The Novell KnowledgeBase is where every technical detail of NetWare support is documented. If you call the NetWare phone support about a particularly pesky problem with your NetWare network, the results of that call, assuming it is a new or heretofore unreported problem, end up in a document in the Novell KnowledgeBase. Thus, this KnowledgeBase has a wealth of information regarding bugs, previously reported problems, and unique problems (and solutions) reported to Novell technical support staff. This means you can benefit from the experience of hundreds of thousands of other NetWare users without talking to each one personally.

Novell also places a document in the KnowledgeBase every time a new bug fix, file update, or new release is available to the public. So your searches in the KnowledgeBase can return both technical advice and specific filenames that can help to rectify your problem. We always use the KnowledgeBase search as our first stop when we are having unusual problems not mentioned elsewhere in the NetWare documentation. We suggest that you place the KnowledgeBase search high on your priority list for problem resolution, too.

Miles and Miles of Files and Smiles

Many of the documents in the KnowledgeBase specify that you should download an updated file or patch to resolve common NetWare problems. If you do come across such a recommendation, you can click on the name of the file directly on the KnowledgeBase document page and you will be instructed how to download the file on the spot.

But say your Uncle Vern is telling you about a new update for the NetWare CLIB NLMs, and you reckon you've just *got* to have it on your own server. The quickest way to find that new CLIB update is to go to the Novell Web page at `www.novell.com`, click on the Search icon at the top of the page, and enter in the keyword **CLIB** under "Search for Software Updates, Patches, and Drivers in Novell's File Finder." You're taken directly to the file. Click once on the filename, and it is downloaded in a matter of minutes. Uncle Vern is *so* proud that a smile will certainly cross his old and wrinkly face.

If you happen to be an old Unix guru, you may be more at home in the clutches of the Novell FTP server than the slick Novell Web pages. You're in luck! You can download bug fixes, updates, and new file releases through `ftp.novell.com`. Bring on the command line!

Other Web Resources for NetWare Information

As you can see, a plethora of information on NetWare is available from the Novell Web site. But wait, there's more! First off, the Web site offers a discussion on USENET, called `comp.os.netware`, where you can ask direct questions of the teeming masses of NetWare nerds from around the world. This is always our second line of defense if we have a really unusual situation that's not covered in any of the Novell KnowledgeBase documents. Usenet Newsgroups has more NetWare experts than you can shake a stick at. One of them will be able to offer the solution to your problem, point you in the right direction, or at least commiserate with you in your network doldrums. Don't be afraid to dive right into the discussion. The only dumb questions are the ones you don't ask!

Manufacturers' Web Pages

Another excellent route to NetWare technical support is through other manufacturers' Web sites. Nearly every major network adapter manufacturer, SCSI adapter manufacturer, hard drive manufacturer, NetWare software developer, and server manufacturer has a Web page that contains technical information and the latest drivers for their particular NetWare-related products. These manufacturers' sites can be an excellent source of hardware and software specific information. You can use an Internet search engine like Yahoo! at www.yahoo.com or AltaVista at www.altavista.digital.com to locate home pages for major hardware and software manufacturers.

They're Waiting to Serve You on CompuServe

The CompuServe Information Service (CIS) is an electronic information service that offers a selection of thousands of topics for your perusal.

CompuServe, a for-a-fee service, requires an individual account (called a membership number) with an accompanying password. Many ways exist to obtain trial access at no charge, but if you want to play on CompuServe, sooner or later you have to pay for the privilege. CompuServe charges a monthly membership fee, in addition to a fee for connection time. Some of the services available on CompuServe have additional charges as well. Be warned! It's easy to spend time — and money — on CompuServe.

Forums for conversation and investigation

When you access CompuServe, you must choose an area of interest on which to focus your exploration of the information treasures that are available. On CompuServe, information is organized in forums. A *forum* is an area dedicated to a particular subject or a collection of related subjects, and each forum contains one or more of the following:

✔ **Message board:** Features electronic conversations organized by specific subjects into sections related to particular topics (Ethernet issues, for example, are a topic, as are token ring issues; in the Ethernet section, you can expect to find discussions of frame types, drivers for particular NICs, and so on.) A given sequence of messages, chained together by a common subject or by replies to an original message, is called a *thread.* Threads may read like conversations, but messages in a thread can be separated from one another by hours or days. Following threads is a favorite pastime for those who spend time on CompuServe.

✔ **Conference room:** An electronic analog to the real thing, conference room brings together individuals to exchange ideas and information in real time. It's much like a conference telephone call except that, rather than talk to each other, the participants communicate by typing on their keyboards. Conference rooms are not for the faint of heart, and they can be frustrating for those with limited touch-typing skills.

✔ **File library:** A collection of files organized by subject that can be copied (*downloaded* is the CompuServe term) for additional perusal and use. Examples of file types found in CompuServe libraries include archived collections of interesting threads, documents of all kinds, and a variety of software ranging from patches and fixes for programs to entire programs.

Getting a CompuServe membership

You can obtain an account over the telephone or by writing to CompuServe and requesting a membership. For telephone inquiries, ask for Representative 200. Here are the numbers to use:

✔ Within the U.S. (except Ohio), including Alaska, Hawaii, Puerto Rico, and the American Virgin Islands, call toll free at 800-848-8199.

✔ Outside the U.S., in Canada, and in Ohio, call 614-457-8650.

Telephone hours are from 8 a.m. to 10 p.m. Eastern time, Monday through Friday, and from noon to 5 p.m. on Saturday. Written inquiries for a CompuServe account should be directed to:

CompuServe, Inc.
Attn: Customer Service
P.O. Box 20212
5000 Arlington Centre Boulevard
Columbus, OH 43220
U.S.A.

Accessing CompuServe

To access CompuServe, you must equip your computer with a modem and attach that modem to a telephone line. You also need some kind of communications program, to let your computer *talk* to CompuServe by using the modem and to help you find your way around its online universe. Finally, you have to obtain a telephone number for CompuServe — most of them are local numbers, especially in the United States — that's appropriate for the type and speed of modem that you're using.

Connection-time charges are based on how fast your modem is — faster modems cost more — but the higher charges are typically offset by even faster transfer speeds. If your CompuServe bill is $30 a month or more, most high-speed modems will pay for themselves in six months or less based on the reductions in fees that you realize by using one.

After you are connected to CompuServe, you enter your membership number and your password. First-time users should follow the instructions provided by your CompuServe representative or in the CompuServe Starter Kit that's available from CompuServe (for an additional fee). After you log in, getting to Novell's collection of online forums, called NetWire, is easy. When you simply type **GO NETWIRE** from the CompuServe prompt, you are presented with a menu of additional choices for Novell and NetWare information. You can even download a special augmentation to WinCIM, CompuServe's Windows CompuServe Information Manager software, that's customized with a button just for NetWire!

What Is NetWire?

NetWire is a collection of CompuServe forums, all dedicated to networking topics and all focused on Novell products or related information. NetWire is a great alternative to using Novell's telephone hotline for technical support. With more than 70,000 users, NetWire is the busiest collection of forums on CompuServe. With the wide range of Novell products and related topics, Novell uses (at the time this overview was written) 18 CompuServe forums, and they are growing all the time.

The benefits of using NetWire

The benefits of using NetWire are hard to overstate but easy to understand. First and foremost, consider the help that's available: NetWire is staffed by volunteer system operators (*sysops*), most of whom are not Novell employees but all of whom are extremely knowledgeable about Novell and NetWare topics.

The busiest sysop has set a record of nearly a thousand messages answered in one week; most sysops average at least four hours a day of connect-time, when they upload and download information to their colleagues and to you — the curious and, sometimes, the desperate.

Together with other power users, the sysops and their colleagues are an invaluable source of information, help, and advice about networking topics. As a bonus, almost all questions are answered within 24 hours of being posted. You will want to log in at least once a day, in fact, when you are waiting for replies to questions. The *scroll rate,* the speed at which messages age and get deleted from the NetWire forums, is about two days, depending on message volume.

When technical problems cannot be solved by the sysops or other power users on NetWire, sysops can escalate these thornier issues directly to the Novell engineers responsible for dealing with those topics in Novell's Services and Support. This process uses the same channels that service the Novell hotline, but you do not incur the typical fees. Calling the hotline directly can cost upward of $100 per incident, or $20 for a Novell DOS incident, unless you are covered by some other preexisting arrangement. (Get out your credit cards, please!)

NetWire is also the place to go for the latest and greatest patches and fixes for NetWare and other Novell products. The libraries that contain the files available for downloading are uploaded daily and documented extensively in catalogs of information available online. These files include the most recent patches, fixes, drivers, and tips for tuning your NetWare server for maximum effect. Lots of third-party applications and utilities are available for your perusal, in addition to a collection of *shareware* (software that you can download for free and use for a trial period, but that you must pay for in order to use legitimately).

NetWire is also the place where NetWare users of the world congregate. NetWire puts you in touch with thousands of other users, most of whom are eager to share with others what they have learned — and the mistakes they have made. Messages are posted in public forums so that all who access NetWire can see and add to the growing collection of information. As a side effect, NetWire is also the premier source of contacts for consulting, sales, and business opportunities for the NetWare community. If you need something that's NetWare-related, NetWire is the best place to begin looking.

Posting messages on NetWire

To request answers to your technical questions or get guidance about which resources are available from NetWire, simply choose the most appropriate section for the subject of your question. (To make this all-important decision, please consult the list of NetWire forums that appears later in this appendix.)

The NetWire sysops ask that you review the list of NetWire forums carefully and that you post your questions in the most appropriate area. Good manners dictate posting a question only once. Even if you are asking about a topic that may legitimately appear in two sections, posting the same message a multiple number of times wastes electronic space.

If you have a question about printing, for example, that involves a NetWare 3.12 print server, the question could appear in NETW3X Section 1 (Printing) or in NOVLIB Section 3 (Printing). The fact is, where the message appears doesn't matter — the same people end up responding to the question no matter where you post it. If you're not sure, send a message to a sysop and ask for advice. Even though this process may take time, you'll probably get an answer faster than relying on the sysops to forward messages to each other before you get to the right source of information for the answer.

The NetWire forums

As of September 14, 1996, 17 forums for NetWire were available, including at least eight that are publicly available. A special forum, called NOVDEV, is for software developers who are building applications by using Novell tools and development kits; you can access this forum only by requesting permission to join. If you're interested in joining NOVDEV, send a CompuServe e-mail message to user ID 76711,111 and state briefly why you want to get involved. (**Hint:** If you don't mention something about using Novell tools to develop code, the odds of being invited are not high!)

In the following sections, we present the current NetWire forums. The name of the subsection is the name of the forum, which is followed by a brief description of what you can find there. After that, we repeat the list of sections that are available. This setup helps you to figure out where to look for information and to get help when you need it.

NOVLIB (Forum 1)

All the Novell-related file libraries are kept in the NOVLIB forum. It offers only one section, NOVLIB, which is meant to be used solely to get library access and usage questions answered. The real action is in the libraries, each of which typically includes a detailed and abbreviated catalog of its contents.

NETW2X (Forum 2)

The NETW2X forum is dedicated to NetWare 2.x versions, typically ranging from 2.12 to 2.2, with all points in between covered daily. If you're running a 2.x network, look here first for information and for help when you need it.

NETW3X (Forum 3)

This forum is dedicated to NetWare 3.x versions, typically ranging from 3.11 to 3.12, with all points between covered daily. If you're running a 3.x network, look here first for information and for help when you need it.

NETW4X (Forum 4)

If you're a NetWare 4.x user or migrating to NetWare 4.x from another version of NetWare, this forum answers all the questions that you have. As fast as NetWare 4.x has changed in the past year, keep your eyes open for any new programs here.

NOVCLIENT (Forum 5)

The Novell Client Forum deals with workstation issues, including the NetWare shell. If you're trying to install Windows on your workstation, here's a forum that will help you out.

NCONNECT (Forum 6)

The NetWare Connectivity Forum covers all the different environment NetWare supports. Here you find information about NetWare for SAA, NetWare for Macintosh, electronic mail, fax products, communications servers, TCP/IP connectivity, and other communication issues. If you're talking from your workstation to other worlds, make yourself at home in this forum — you're going to need it.

NOVDESKTOP (Forum 7)

The NOVDESKTOP forum is dedicated to products from the Novell Desktop Systems Group, which include Novell DOS, Dataclub, NetWare Lite, Personal NetWare, and Windows NT.

NDEVINFO and NDEVSUPP (Forums 8 and 9)

If you're into client/server development, you will want to browse these two forums. One is for information about the Novell Developers Programs; the other is for supporting developers' questions.

NGENERAL (Forum 10)

The Networking General Forum groups information that doesn't fit anywhere else. Here you can find the latest information about Certified Novell Engineer programs and user groups, leave suggestions for running NetWare better, and have some serious non-networking fun in a section called The Lighter Side.

NOVHW (Forum 11)

The NetWare Hardware Forum lists the nuts and bolts of networking hardware, including LAN adapters, uninterruptible power supplies, backup hardware, and network cabling.

NOVMAN (Forum 12)

If you're managing the network, you will want to frequent the Network Management Forum. Here you can find a plethora of tips for the NetWare Management System, LANalyzer for Windows, and managing NetWare for SAA.

NOVOS2 (Forum 13)

IBM's OS/2 desktop operating system has garnered a dedicated group of NetWare users. In this forum for OS/2, you can find more information than you need about the varieties of OS/2 client software for your workstation. If you have NetWare 4.*x* for OS/2, you can also get your questions answered here. No DOS or Windows users allowed!

UNIXWARE (Forum 14)

When Novell said that one-third of its NetWare users wanted to connect to or use UNIX, NetWire took the users seriously. The UNIXWare Forum is the place to have your UNIXWare questions answered, and if you just like UNIX in general, get your fill of X Windows here.

NOVUSER (Forum 15)

The NetWare Users Forum is a good place to find help of all kinds. Here you can find companies that want to hire network administrators, classified advertisements for equipment and software, and general questions and answers.

NVENA and NVENB (Forums 16 and 17)

Novell's vendor affiliates hang out in the NOVVEN forum — typically including the folks who offer NetWare preinstalled on their hardware or systems or who offer NetWare-specific applications or services. It's a good place to get help from specific vendors. Here are a few of the present vendors: LAN Support Group, Computer Tyme, Dell Computer, AST Research, Knozall, Notework, Tricord, Bay Networks, Networth, and Blue Lance.

Surf the libraries

After familiarizing yourself with the forums, you probably will most often end up checking out the libraries (either Novell's or third-party upload libraries). The new stuff hits here first, and these areas seldom require as much reading to find what you need as the others can.

Index

IDG BOOKS WORLDWIDE REGISTRATION CARD

RETURN THIS REGISTRATION CARD FOR FREE CATALOG

Title of this book: **Networking with NetWare® For Dummies®, 3E**

My overall rating of this book: ❑ Very good [1]   ❑ Good [2]   ❑ Satisfactory [3]   ❑ Fair [4]   ❑ Poor [5]

How I first heard about this book:

❑ Found in bookstore; name: [6] _____

❑ Advertisement: [8] _____

❑ Word of mouth; heard about book from friend, co-worker, etc.: [10] _____

❑ Book review: [7] _____

❑ Catalog: [9] _____

❑ Other: [11] _____

What I liked most about this book:

_____

_____

_____

What I would change, add, delete, etc., in future editions of this book:

_____

_____

_____

Other comments:

_____

_____

Number of computer books I purchase in a year: ❑ 1 [12]   ❑ 2-5 [13]   ❑ 6-10 [14]   ❑ More than 10 [15]

I would characterize my computer skills as: ❑ Beginner [16]   ❑ Intermediate [17]   ❑ Advanced [18]   ❑ Professional [19]

I use ❑ DOS [20]   ❑ Windows [21]   ❑ OS/2 [22]   ❑ Unix [23]   ❑ Macintosh [24]   ❑ Other: [25] _____
(please specify)

I would be interested in new books on the following subjects:
(please check all that apply, and use the spaces provided to identify specific software)

❑ Word processing: [26] _____

❑ Data bases: [28] _____

❑ File Utilities: [30] _____

❑ Networking: [32] _____

❑ Other: [34] _____

❑ Spreadsheets: [27] _____

❑ Desktop publishing: [29] _____

❑ Money management: [31] _____

❑ Programming languages: [33] _____

I use a PC at (please check all that apply): ❑ home [35]   ❑ work [36]   ❑ school [37]   ❑ other: [38] _____

The disks I prefer to use are ❑ 5.25 [39]   ❑ 3.5 [40]   ❑ other: [41] _____

I have a CD ROM: ❑ yes [42]   ❑ no [43]

I plan to buy or upgrade computer hardware this year: ❑ yes [44]   ❑ no [45]

I plan to buy or upgrade computer software this year: ❑ yes [46]   ❑ no [47]

Name: _____   Business title: [48] _____   Type of Business: [49] _____

Address (❑ home [50] ❑ work [51]/Company name: _____)

Street/Suite# _____

City [52]/State [53]/Zipcode [54]: _____   Country [55] _____

❑ **I liked this book!** You may quote me by name in future
IDG Books Worldwide promotional materials.

My daytime phone number is _____

IDG BOOKS

THE WORLD OF
COMPUTER
KNOWLEDGE

❑ YES!

Please keep me informed about IDG's World of Computer Knowledge. Send me the latest IDG Books catalog.

SECRETS™

...FOR DUMMIES™ COMPUTER BOOK SERIES FROM IDG

MACWORLD MW AUTHORIZED EDITION

AUTHORIZED PC WORLD EDITION

NO POSTAGE NECESSARY IF MAILED IN THE UNITED STATES

BUSINESS REPLY MAIL

FIRST CLASS MAIL PERMIT NO. 2605 FOSTER CITY, CALIFORNIA

IDG Books Worldwide
919 E Hillsdale Blvd, STE 400
Foster City, CA 94404-9691